BodyRenewal™

Tim Firnstahl

For my mother Dorothee whose love for writing passed to me
&
For my father Jerome whose wonder of life inspired me. . .

i

ORDERING

Individual orders may be placed by calling 1-866-BODYFIX (263-9349) or by visiting our Web site http://www.bodyrenewalpast40.com to use our secure order form.

Y2K+ books may be purchased in wholesale quantities. For information please write Special Markets Department, Y2K+ Publishing, Suite 207, 419 Occidental Avenue South, Seattle, Washington 98104 or call 1-866-BODYFIX (263-9349).

THANK YOU

I am grateful to the following people without whose help this book would not have been possible. For my wife Merriann whose patience is legend. I love you. For Mary Pat Fleming and Beverly Mason who typed and corrected so many drafts we all lost count. Thank you. For my friend and superb chef Irene Mulroy who prepared and recooked my recipes until even her demanding palate was satisfied. It was a joy working with you. For Lynn Ferguson who designed this book. Your talent speaks for itself: *Res ipsa loquitur.* I fully appreciate Chuck Malody's editing efforts; he cut the text by 50%. This book is right because of Chas Ridley's meticulous final check. Well done! http://hotbooks.com   chas@hotbooks.com. I thank Rene Behnke for letting me use dozens of plates from Sur La Table. Mike Penny photographed twelve sessions, captured the food in its best repose and maintained his humor all the while: 1-206-619-2920. Q•Media printed this for me with the patience of Job: 1-800-451-5742. And last a special thanks to Louis Richmond and Hamilton McCulloh who put this book on the map: 1-206-682-6979.

LEGAL

BodyRenewal™

Fifty days that change your life. A segue into a life mode for a
flourishing physique complete with entreés, exercises, transition
facilitators and many other helping aids. BodyRenewal™ eases you into
a lifelong course for achieving and maintaining the shape and vigor of youth.

YOU CAN DO THIS

This book is about how you can recapture the essence of your youth: in your looks, in your endurance, in your attitude. You will achieve the shape and vigor of youth by stripping fat through diet and realistic exercise. Your endurance will be elevated because you will have more muscle to execute your day's activities. You will feel better and likely live longer because of improved eating habits and a beneficially conditioned body. You will have a renewed positive attitude. Your self-appreciation will rise from all the care and nurturing you shower on yourself and the impressive results you realize. No matter how many diets you have tried or failures endured, BodyRenewal™ will work for you.

Too often we place imaginary limitations on ourselves that become actual restraints. For years in track and field competition, the four-minute mile was considered beyond man's physical capabilities. Over the years thousands of athletes regularly attempted to break the four-minute barrier, but they knew it just couldn't be done. Then one day in 1954 Roger Bannister, an athlete who had refused to believe it couldn't be done, did it. But that is not the amazing thing.

Smashing the four-minute mile mental barrier set off a turn of events unprecedented in track and field history. Within five years of Bannister mastering the psychological barrier, the four-minute mile would be broken by 21 different runners 50 different times. Within 15 years, 107 runners demolished the four-minute mile 320 times. Marcus O'Sullivan has done it himself over 100 times.[1] Yet, the four-minute mile was considered beyond human capacity just a few years before.

You have demonstrated a similar psychological barrier-breaking attitude by buying this book. So let's begin.

1

WHAT CAN I EXPECT?

First, you will see pleasing body definition reminiscent of your youth. Your body will be leaner and more muscular than it has been for years.

Second, you will be more vigorous and energetic. Increased strength, added endurance and enhanced flexibility will result from the Muscle Rebuild™.

Third, you will notice a more optimistic, positive and enthusiastic attitude. You will have, after all, stripped fat, added muscle and begun a new living pattern. As a result, positive self-regard will rise, thought processes will be clearer and your well-being improved.

There is a caveat before proceeding, however. If your goal is to win the *Ironman*, there are more suitable books. If it is to enter the Miss Olympia contest, I suggest you hire a professional trainer. If it is to be a Kate-Moss-thin wisp of a girl, go to a vegetable juice spa in Mexico for six months. This book is for people with long-term, realistic goals. Having goals to be as muscled as Arnold or shapely as Cindy are silly. The bodies of professionals are their entire lives. Our lives, on the other hand, are about making a living, maintaining important relationships, having some fun and making the BodyRenewal™ youth connection.

THE BEFORE PLAN

It is simply a question of having a BEFORE strategy versus a complex AFTER catastrophe. BodyRenewal™ is about stripping fat and stopping disease before it happens. It's simple, inexpensive and emotionally rewarding. BEFORE means you boast a vigorous life, look good, have plenty of energy, and appreciate hearty self-approbation BEFORE it's too late. This approach is accomplished with little time investment, modest money and manageable emotional expenditure.

The AFTER program is a time-waster, expensive, highly invasive (think heart surgery) and emotionally devitalizing. Education may result in high income, fame may lend prestige, but what are these compared to feeling better, looking good and living long?

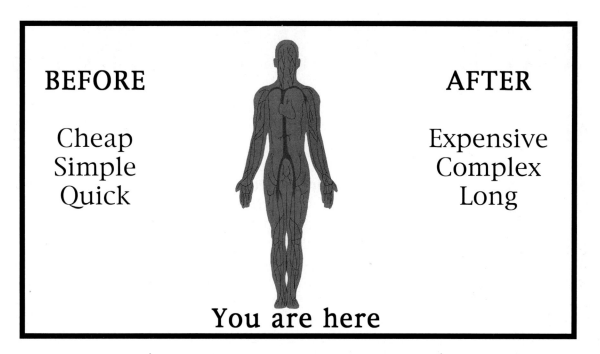

BEFORE

Cheap
Simple
Quick

AFTER

Expensive
Complex
Long

You are here

The AFTER consequences warrant reflection because the outcomes are so grim. Take a cancer like leukemia, for example. First of all, your chances of long-term survival are only 20 to 25%. Plan on spending a minimum of one month in the hospital receiving intense chemotherapy fraught with appalling side effects like overwhelming nausea, life-threatening weight loss, open mouth and throat sores, constipation, crushing fatigue, chronic insomnia, 80-year-old-skin, complete hair loss and, of course, dire anxiety.[2]

The National Cancer Institute says, however, eating right reduces all cancers by one-third.[3] Noted physiologist Jack Groppel, Ph.D., thinks we may reduce cancer by up to 80% by eating correctly.[4] We can only guess what adding exercise and positive attitude might do to increase our cancer-avoidance chances.

Of course you think, "I'm not going to get cancer." Well, OK. How about heart disease which kills 50% of us? Or strokes. The tiny, narrow, thin-wall arteries deep in the brain are very likely candidates to

burst or close off. You know the devastating potential of strokes: loss of speech, wheelchair-bound and sometimes complete incapacitation. Twenty-five percent of stroke victims simply die on the spot. On the other hand, the National Institutes of Health reports that people who lose weight and cut back on sodium reduce hypertension risk by 50%, the primary solution to avoiding strokes.[5]

YOUR BEST INVESTMENT

I f there was ever an adage deserving respect it's an ounce of prevention beats a pound of cure. You're interested in effective life approaches so let's do some quick cost-benefit analysis.

Suffering from heart disease or cancer or osteoporosis or diabetes is expensive, but who on their deathbed wouldn't give all they own for just one more year of quality life? Obviously, achieving a hale body is the cheapest and highest return-on-investment you make in life.

From a strict dollar standpoint, what does exercise cost? A few hundred dollars in equipment for proper walking shoes, several free weights and other inexpensive gear that won't exceed half of one percent of your yearly income. Dumbbells last forever and you get six months to a year out of good walking shoes. Exercise is cheap.

Switching to NeoCuisine™ is less expensive than conventional American eating. With its high percentage of whole grains, fruits and vegetables, healthful NeoCuisine™ costs a fraction of what you likely now spend. High-cost, slow-kill 21st century foods like fatty beef, artery-clogging cheeses and sodium-saturated, ready-made entreés cost plenty. Throw in America's inordinate penchant for pricey, fatty snacks like potato chips, deep-fried tortillas, Cheese Puffs® and all the rest and you have considerable expense. NeoCuisine™ cuts your grocery bill by 25%, if not more.

But when we think about investment, money isn't the only consideration. Creating and maintaining a hale, whole body entails only four or five hours a week, little more than 2% of your time. On the other hand, disease costs you 100% of your time because it is always with you. You do the math.

BodyRenewal™

BodyRenewal™ aims to build confidence and motivation. With weight loss recidivism at 80% to 90%, it makes sense to pursue youth's shape and vigor only if you have knowledge and strategies that are satisfying to you over the long run. This is not a "have to" or "should" book. Of course you should, but wouldn't it be nice if what you should do and what you want to do were the same?

The *NeoCuisine*™ approach of high complex carbohydrate with plenty of protein and low fat is safe and effective. A white paper released by Johns Hopkins Medical Institutions compares diet approaches. The report objects to prepackaged meal plans (e.g. Jenny Craig™ and NutriSystem™) because of the difficulty in switching back to regular foods. High protein diets (e.g. The Zone™, Atkins Diet™, Scarsdale Diet™) were not recommended because protein is often accompanied by saturated fat and "a high protein diet usually

cannot be continued indefinitely." As well, "there's no evidence that a diet high in carbohydrates increases appetite or causes the body to store fat."[6] A long term state of *ketosis* (characterized by bad breath) resulting from a high protein diet likely puts you at health risk. *NeoCuisine*™ is fraught with none of these negatives.

The *Muscle Rebuild*™ is designed around the reality of your limited time. You spend about 30 minutes a day exercising moderately. The Muscle Rebuild™ is specifically for Baby Boomers, not Olympians, 17-year-old football players or 25-year-old marathon champs. It was crafted with you in mind for ease of learning and execution using minimum equipment, right at home. You rebuild musculature and substantially improve cardiovascular functioning.

Surroundings Management™ deals with people, places and processes. Since environmental factors such as family,

co-workers and supermarket temptations can derail your best intentions, *Surroundings Management*™ is essential. You discover the Miracle 20™, travel tricks and how to deflect others' sabotage. *Surroundings Management*™ helps you create sufficient cues, encouragements and lean-and-fit stimuli to significantly boost your shape and vigor of youth intentions.

Control Psychology™ assists you in mastering the normal apprehensions experienced in renewing your life. In the change you are about to undertake, motivational and maintenance psychology are requisite. You learn cognitive dissonance and instant positive visualization, the power of affirmations and other worthwhile techniques.

The last chapter covers technically correct *Sustaining Forces*™ that prove invaluable in keeping fat off and motivation high. It is your plan for staying the course lifelong.

Once you understand NeoCuisine™, the Muscle Rebuild™, Surroundings Management and Control Psychology™, you are ready for your test of resolve, the decision to enter the BodyRenewal™. You judge whether or not the case for youthful shape and vigor has been made. You decide whether the strategies offered make sense. You anticipate if the shape and vigor of youth are worth the effort. The verdict is yours.

FIVE SUGGESTIONS

1 DOG-EAR AND HIGHLIGHT THIS BOOK
A quick, cursory once-over likely won't suffice. Absorb more by reading at an unhurried pace. Allow yourself to grasp the theories, tricks and techniques required for lifelong weight reduction and renewed vigor. Stripping fat, keeping it off and attaining high energy require careful study. You want a good grasp of the skill-building required for lifelong stripped fat and notable vitality. So highlight, write in the margins and dog-ear pages as testimonial to your study investment.

2 KEEP THIS BOOK HANDY AND REREAD IT
"The rapidity with which we forget is astonishing." says Dale Carnegie who admits to having regularly reviewed his own book on public speaking to refresh his memory.[7] Having marked this book, reread sections to firmly fix the information. To keep the principles of youthful shape and vigor in our conscious, we must regularly review them.

3 WRITE FIVE MINUTES DAILY IN YOUR Body-Renewal™ JOURNAL
Emerson observed that man "dismisses without notice his own thought because it is his. In every work of genius we recognize our rejected thoughts."[8] Journal writing is commonly employed in psychotherapy.

The technique is easy but powerful. Promise yourself to spend at least five minutes a day to record new shape and vigor of youth information and observations. You may have more insight on achieving the shape and vigor of youth than you might imagine. There is an added bonus. Studies show that people who customize their long-term programs are the most successful keeping weight off.[9]

4 BE PATIENT IN BUILDING SKILLS

Achieving youth's shape and vigor results from skill-building. Learning fat-stripping techniques and psychology, then recalling and practicing them, requires time. A quick read won't do. Comprehension coupled with time and practice do the trick. So be patient. Learning, at its roots, is doing it right repeatedly until the process or information is part of our being. Awareness of self for the purpose of altering behavior is a skill. It takes years to pack on the weight so pounds don't come off in a month and the expertise required to attain the shape and vigor of youth are not learned in a week. Be patient.

5 PREPARE PROPERLY

Our natural urge is to dive right in. We typically don't look at the owner's manuals for our lawn mower, VCR or car until we are stymied. Our inclination is to proceed on our own. But superior outcomes will only be achieved by carefully reading Parts II through IX. Take no steps until you're grounded in the shape and vigor of youth principles. Hey, this could affect the next 50 years of your life. Don't guffaw at the idea of "the next 50 years" because those who are lean and fit lead much longer— and productive—lives.

[1] "Elsewhere," *Seattle Post-Intelligencer,* February 14, 1998, page E7, BB403.

[2] "Praying for Deliverance Amid the Plagues of Chemo," Cathy Hainer, *USA Today*, April 15, 1998, page 9B, BB380b.

[3] "Cancer: What You Eat Can Affect Your Risk," *Mayo Clinic Health Letter*, vol. 13, no. 9, September 1995, pages 1-2, BB161.

[4] *The Anti Diet Book,* Jack L. Groppel, Ph.D., Sports Science, Inc., Orlando, Florida, 1997, page 75, BB395.

[5] "Warding off Stroke," *Tufts University Health and Nutrition Letter*, vol. 16, no. 4, page 7, BB402.

[6] "Syndrome X, The Risks of High Insulin," *Nutrition Action Health Letter,* vol. 27, no. 2, March 2000, pages 3-8, BB518.

[7] *How to Win Friends and Influence People,* Dale Carnegie, Ph.D., Pocket Books, New York, New York, 1936, page 57, #29, BB131.

[8] *Book of Virtues,* William Bennett, Simon & Schuster, 1993, New York, New York, page 522, #115.

[9] *Lose Weight Guidebook,* Mark Bricklin, editor, Rodale Press, Inc., Emmaus, Pennsylvania, 1996, page 16, BB130.

NeoCuisine™

HOW AND WHY WE GET FAT

Food is a big deal. It dictates the body's evolution, shapes world history and often rules our psyche. Hunger drives us to eat. No wonder hunger management challenges us. When the body's hungry, it wants action now. The human body is similar to a gasoline engine. When an engine's tank is empty, it must be refilled. If the tank is filled more quickly than the engine's burn rate, the tank, of course, overflows. Unfortunately, in the human body the overflow does not spill out onto the ground. It stays in the tank, our body, and turns to fat. How we get fat is one thing. Why we get fat is another matter entirely.

We get fat because the body is paranoid. Through the millennia, man has suffered enormous fluctuations in his food supply, causing the body to learn tricks to weather these fluctuations. These tricks were once assets but now, in times of plenty, they have become liabilities.

Without a regular food supply, the body had no choice but to become paranoid. It feared it wouldn't survive. These instincts weren't subtle prods but compelling urges that motivated us to eat intemperate amounts. If sometimes today we think we're pigs at the trough, it is these primordial tapes kicking in, demanding that we eat, eat, eat. The body still doesn't know when next it will have food available so it signals us to eat NOW and eat ABUNDANTLY. The body craves and covets food.[1]

Eating fatty foods is instinctive. We are inclined to eat fat because the body knows fat gives it the best survival chance. Just as we crave salt after sweating profusely and hunger for carbohydrates after we consume too much protein because serotonin is low, the body yearns for fat in an effort to save itself from the starvation that never comes.[2] The fatter we are, the more protected the body thinks it is. Fat is the body's survival insurance. Georgia psychologist Dr. John deCastro finds we feel hungrier in the fall than at any other time of year. He says, "The body's mechanism for telling your brain that you're full is suppressed."[3] The body instinctively knows to consume more food in preparation for winter, fat being its favorite.

The primordial vestige of this reality is that we prefer fatty foods over lean. In fact, the body's digestion command after satisfying its immediate nutritional needs is to EAT COPIOUSLY AND THUS STORE FAT. All those millennia of mankind going hungry gave us a body perfectly suited to defeat a diet.

So don't blame "deep-seated psychological problems" or the "fat gene" for our plump bodies. Individuals rarely lose weight with traditional psychiatric treatments despite greater insight into their problems.[4] Likewise, obesity doubled this century while our genetic make-up changed not one whit, ruling out the "fat gene" as our weight problem cause.[5]

The real reason people get fat is that through hundreds of thousands of years, light eaters died out. Only the ravenous eaters survived. Dr. Michael Hamilton, director of the Duke Diet and Fitness Center, points out, "The ability to store fat and the propensity to have a big appetite were all survival mechanisms."[6] But take heart, there is a way around this with NeoCuisine™.

THE PROBLEM WITH 21st CENTURY FOOD

Here in the United States, we have more food, more food varieties and better-tasting food than at any time in man's history. And it's cheap. Most of the stuff that tastes best is the cheapest—hamburgers, pizzas and tacos to name a few. Let's pour a little more gasoline on this fire.

During those hundreds of body-evolving millennia, man survived on calorie-sparse food of five to 30 calories per ounce. Because there wasn't much energy in the food it ingested, the body had to learn how to eat more to guarantee itself sufficient nutritional income. This taught the body to consume prodigious quantities to satisfy its caloric requirements.

But here in the 21st century foods are calorie-dense. Nestle's Crunch® bars are 120 calories per ounce. We eat bagels, pasta and pretzels which range from 80 to 110 calories an ounce. We feast on Big Macs® and French fries which are 100 calories an ounce. Dominoes® delivers double cheese, thick crust pizzas right to our door at 100+ calories per ounce. Refined flour, sugar, fatty red meats and Wolfgang Puck Four Cheese Pizza® at 85 calories an ounce with its 15 grams of fat are all astoundingly calorie-dense fare compared to the foods of evolution. An Oscar Mayer® Lunchables®[7] pack made with supposedly "lean chicken and turkey" has a whopping 56% of its calories from fat, over 150 separate ingredients and a calorie-to-weight ratio of about 80 calories an ounce—all of which make it a quintessential 21st century food. The way we eat today shocks the body. Every day we consume

9

large quantities of 21st century calorie-dense foods. Is it any wonder we are the fattest generation ever?

Of course, we resoundingly beat ourselves up for becoming plump. We relate our chubby state to a lack of personal discipline. Society reinforces this view. If you are rotund, wear a spare tire or have a bit of a pot belly, society dubs you weak-willed. But, combine calorie-dense foods with the body's *primeval raging appetite (PRA)*, its naturally low metabolic rate when denied food and an infinite capacity to store fat, and what should we expect? Fat's not our fault!

FAT IS THE RESULT OF OUR STONE AGE PRIMEVAL RAGING APPETITE SATED WITH CALORIE-DENSE 21st CENTURY FOODS.

16 NeoCuisine™ FAT-STRIPPING BENEFITS

Stripping fat may not be a panacea for all of life's ills but the rewards for doing so are remarkable: increased self-esteem, more vigor, significantly better health. The benefits of stripping fat and eating a diet rich in fruits, legumes, vegetables and whole grains comes as close to a panacea as we can expect. Look at these benefits. Are any of them important to you?

•CHANCE OF CANCER SIGNIFICANTLY DIMINISHED

The National Cancer Institute (NCI) estimates eating a healthful diet may prevent as many as one-third of all cancer deaths. *The New England Journal of Medicine* has gone so far as to say that upward of 77% of all cancers are preventable with correct diet.[8]

•CHANCE OF STROKE MINIMIZED

Fruits, vegetables, whole grains and beans, NeoCuisine's™ basis, contain thousands of various phytochemicals and flavonoids that help prevent oxidized LDL cholesterol, the bad artery-clogging variety.

•LOWERED BLOOD PRESSURE

Harvard researchers have shown a low-fat diet rich in grains, vegetables and fruits lowers blood pressure by 5% to 10%. Dr. Thomas Moore says, "This is comparable to the effect of some drugs we use in therapy."[9]

•REDUCED HEART DISEASE

Women are six times more likely to die of heart disease than breast cancer. Long known as the primary killer of men, heart disease is almost as deadly for women. When weight rises just 20% above the ideal, the risk of death from cardiovascular disease jumps more than two and a half times.[10] Take excess weight off and heart disease plummets.

●ANXIETY REDUCTION
The gap between how you would like to be and how you are creates stress. Cognitive dissonance, as psychologists like to call it, is the basis for much of life's anxieties. The more distance between how you want yourself to be and actual self-perception, the greater your anxiety. When you become more like you want to be, stress reduces. Lose fat, get thin and align your actual body with your ideal body. You may be surprised how it helps reduce anxiety. This is important beyond mere vanity. *The UC Berkeley Wellness Letter* reports, "There is a large body of evidence showing that depression, hostility, anger and pessimism can indeed have adverse health effects over the years."[11]

●FEEL YOUNGER
By removing that excess 15 or 20 pounds, you will not only be lighter on your feet but, without packing around extra weight, you will feel less fatigue.

●SLEEP BETTER
Snoring is no laughing matter because it may be indicative of sleep apnea, a condition where the air passageway is temporarily blocked, causing highly fitful breathing which in turn raises blood pressure, reduces oxygen to the brain and can leave you fatigued after a night's "rest."[12] One of the most common causes of snoring is fat. Lose the weight and reduce snoring.

●PREVENT ARTHRITIS
The Fred Hutchinson Cancer Research Center at the University of Washington discovered in a study that women consuming more than 2,200 calories a day increased their rheumatoid arthritis risk by 62%. Lower-calorie diets may have a positive effect in arthritis prevention.[13]

●DECREASED DIABETES
Obesity increases your resistance to insulin and is the leading cause of noninsulin-dependent diabetes.[14] Twenty-one million people in this country have impaired glucose tolerance. Like diabetes, it's characterized by high blood levels of glucose. According to the *Tufts University Diet and Nutrition Letter*, weight reduction may prevent or delay diabetes.[15]

●LIVE LONGER
Dr. Roy Walford, noted gerontologist at UCLA and an outspoken advocate of nutrition, has proven "undernutrition" increases lifespans.[16] Animal lifespans can be dietarily increased 50% which corresponds to humans living to 125 years.[17] Mice placed on a low-fat, calorie-restricted diet live three times longer than mice allowed to eat what they want.[18] Here's an interesting statistic. A study of 28,000 women found those who lost 20 pounds or more in a year were 20% less likely to die of any cause in the next 12 years.[19]

To these direct, physical benefits, we can add these, shall we say, luxury benefits:

•A NEW WARDROBE

Now you have that excuse to go out and buy a whole new wardrobe because, with your new lithe body, you deserve to be dressed to the nines.

•INCREASED SELF-APPRECIATION

There is no way to lose that blubber and not feel better about yourself. Your ego will skyrocket. By doing something truly nice and healthful for yourself, self-image rises. People with high self-esteem work better and have better personal relationships. Give yourself a gift and lose that fat.

•MAKE MORE MONEY

One study found fat people make less money, significantly less. For each pound they were overweight, they averaged $1,000 less per year than their peers. Unfair as it is, society judges the overweight harshly.[20]

•FEWER MEDICAL BILLS AND LOWER INSURANCE PREMIUMS

Irrefutably, lower weight means better health which carries with it significantly less expense for you. Health and psychological well-being aside, it costs far less being lean than fat. The expense avoided by waylaying diabetes, for example, measures in the thousands of dollars. Life insurance expenses drop significantly. From a cost-benefit standpoint, being lean is a real moneysaver.

NeoCuisine™ can be the basis for all these benefits. It is exactly what the NCI recommends because it's low in dietary fat, a high consumption of which promotes cancer by stimulating abnormal cell division. NeoCuisine™ is based on high consumption of fruits, vegetables and legumes abundant in antioxidants and phytochemicals which inhibit the spread of malignant cells. NeoCuisine™ puts you in select company because 70% of Americans fail to meet the NCI's guideline of five servings of fruits and vegetables daily.[21]

DIET DEPRIVATION

Psychologist Abraham Maslow dramatically attests to the power of hunger when he says, "Freedom, love, community feeling, respect and philosophy may all be waved aside as fripperies which are useless since they fail to fill the stomach. It is quite true that man does not live by bread alone—when there is no bread."[22] As our most elemental need and motivator, hunger easily outpaces other stimuli, hence the difficulty in controlling its power.

When we're hungry, the *primeval raging appetite* (PRA) does more to dictate our behavior than anything else. No wonder our paranoid bodies are so troublesome to control. The worst time is the 7 to Bed hunger trial. In the late evening, how many of us are overwhelmed with hunger, binging the last hour of the day after a full day of outstanding discipline?

Typical diet recipes are religious in their pursuit of low calories but often fail miserably quantitatively. Itsy-bitsy portions leave you hungry and discouraged. You get a measly three ounces of this, a meager four ounces of that and an inadequate amount of the other thing.

Food manufacturers propagandize us to believe food is life's primary pleasure. Then they mislead us with their calorie information. The artifice of "fat free" and "reduced fat" have fooled many of us. According to the Mayo Clinic, reduced-fat peanut butter compared to its full-fat brother has exactly the same calories. Regular and non-fat pretzels have the same calories. A reduced-fat chocolate chip cookie versus the regular version is only ten calories less.[23]

Manufacturers' "servings" are so tiny that you're guaranteed a small calorie count all right but precious little to eat. A package may say 100 calories per serving but there are three parsimonious servings per container. The so-called "serving amounts" of low-fat cookies, for example, are laughable. Four little wafers for 200 calories hardly satisfies. Sure, you're on a diet of 1,200 calories a day but you also think you're starving. The body doesn't like it. You don't like it.

The Harvard Mental Health Letter explains the possible consequences when it reports psychiatric disturbances are entirely possible for people who feel starved. Furthermore, the *Journal of the American Dietetic Association* states that perceived food restriction "appear(s) to result in eating binges and in psychological manifestations such as preoccupation with eating and food ... dysphoria and distractibility."[24] This comes as no surprise. We've all felt the physiological and psychological discomfort of "dieting."

NeoCuisine™ FIXES

The first goal of NeoCuisine™ is to provide you enough to eat. Research at Tufts University reveals that "It is almost impossible to restrict calorie intake forever, whereas it's relatively easy to follow a low-fat diet indefinitely if it allows you to eat enough to satisfy your hunger."[25] Therein lies the answer to the riddle: low calories and fat but enough to eat.

The following chart contrasts a typical diet food day and NeoCuisine™. Pay particular attention to the regular diet breakfast, a fundamental soft spot for most diets. A dry cereal breakfast portion, normally only an ounce, barely covers the bottom of the bowl. NeoCuisine™ allowed for a more realistic three-ounce cereal portion.

The data on the next page will interest you.

TYPICAL DIET DAY vs *NeoCuisine*™ DAY

	Fat	Calories	Quantity		Fat	Calories	Quantity
BREAKFAST				**BREAKFAST**			
Dry cereal	3.0 gms	330	3 oz	NC amplified			
Skim milk	.5 gms	90	8 oz	breakfast cereal	2.0 gms	300	32 oz
TOTAL	3.5 gms	420	11 oz	TOTAL	2.0 gms	300	32 oz
LUNCH				**LUNCH**			
Broiled chicken breast sandwich w/o fries/salad				Fat-free, sugar-free			
•Bun	3.0 gms	200	2 oz	yogurt	0.0 gms	100	8 oz
•Chicken	5.0 gms	200	4 oz	Orange	0.0 gms	75	8 oz
•Miscellaneous	1.0 gms	50	2 oz	TOTAL	0.0 gms	175	16 oz
TOTAL	9.0 gms	450	8 oz				
DINNER				**DINNER**			
Broiled salmon				Maria deLourdes			
•Salmon	15.0 gms	250	5 oz	Chili Rellenos	0.0 gms	500	38 oz
•Flavored no-fat rice	2.0 gms	200	4 oz	TOTAL	0.0 gms	500	38 oz
•Vegetables	0.0 gms	100	4 oz				
•Roll w/o butter	3.0 gms	100	2 oz				
•Small salad with no-fat 1000 Island	0.0 gms	100	6 oz				
TOTAL	20.0 gms	750	21 oz				
				7 PM TO BED SNACKS/MINI-MEALS			
				•1 gallon air-popped popcorn	4.0 gms	320	4 oz
7 PM TO BED SNACKS/MINI-MEAL NONE				•Rome apple	0.0 gms	75	8 oz
				TOTAL	4.0 gms	395	12 oz

TYPICAL DIET TOTALS

Fat Calories	Calories	Quantity
32.5 gms	**1620**	**40 oz**

NeoCuisine™ TOTALS

Fat Calories	Calories	Quantity
6.0 gms	**1370**	**98 oz**

14

21st Century food vs NeoCuisine™

Big Mac®
71 Calories per Ounce
8 oz. 570 Calories

Domino's®
70 Calories per Ounce
8 oz. 554 Calories

NeoCuisine™ Burger
20 Calories per Ounce
28 Ounces 575 Calories
See page 167

NeoCuisine™ Pepperoni Pizza
14 Calories per Ounce
33 Ounces 469 Calories
See page 189

DIET TORMENT

Millennia of conditioning push us into a rage against perceived starvation. Minimalist portions drive our bodies and psyches wild. When diets deny us quantity, we hurt. We become irritable and aggressive. We are not only difficult to be around, but we abhor the hunger state. Tension mounts. We have difficulty sleeping. We begin to seek any means for relieving the pain. No wonder we hate to diet. Our bodies are placed on full alert. They are ready to fight for their lives.

With such strong incentive, there's little question why most of us are in an emotional mess when we attempt to strip fat. Our bodies tell us absolutely and unequivocally to eat. This order is final. It isn't a "maybe", a "possibility"... quite literally a do-or-die command. Just as we are saddled with a prehistoric fight-or-flight syndrome, the *primeval raging appetite* demands we eat. Diet Deprivation reigns, unless you NeoCuisine™.

The results speak for themselves. For fewer calories, NeoCuisine™ has much more quantity than the typical diet. In its *Health and Nutrition Letter*, Tufts University reported important calorie-to-weight-ratio research conducted at New Zealand's Auckland University. Tufts said, "Your body may be looking not for a certain amount of calories or fat but for a certain amount of weight."[26] **Quantity counts. Hence, NeoCuisine™ rationale: Lots of calorie-frugal food.**

Most 21st century foods burst with 60 to 100 calories per ounce. Factoring in pizzas, burgers, fries, shakes, steak and all the other food which constitutes standard 21st century fare, we can eat an average of about 80 calories per ounce with 30% to 60% calories from fat, much in the form of dangerous saturated fat, the kind that clogs arteries leading to atherosclerosis. Fat (9 cals/gram) has over twice the calories compared to carbohydrates and protein (4 cals/gram).

Our ancient forebears ate 5 to 30 calories per ounce with the exception of the occasional, extremely lean-meat animal they managed to hunt. Man evolved on a diet of about 10% to 15% fat. Today's fat consumption is 300% to 400% that.

THE CORRECT CALORIE-TO-WEIGHT RATIO

THE CALORIE-TO-WEIGHT RATIOS OF MOST CONVENTIONAL "DIET FOODS" RANGE FROM 30 TO 50 CALORIES PER OUNCE. OUR RESEARCH INDICATES THAT A DAY'S AVERAGE OF 20 CALORIES PER OUNCE IS SUFFICIENT FOR QUIETING THE PRIMEVAL RAGING APPETITE (PRA). NeoCuisine™ ENTREÉS ARE 19-20 CALORIES PER OUNCE (SOME LOWER) THUS PROVIDING ANYWHERE FROM 50% TO 100% MORE QUANTITY THAN CONVENTIONAL DIET FOODS. THIS SOLVES THE MOST CHALLENGING PROBLEM: TOO LITTLE FOOD.

Scientists at the University of Sydney determined the satisfaction rating of various foods. The winner was potatoes followed by various fruits, vegetables and proteins. These researchers discovered that fatty foods are much less filling than those high in carbohydrates or protein. Fat is more calorie-dense which results in small portions. Low hunger satisfaction, for example, was scored by croissants, which are fat-loaded.[27]

The research for this book discovered which foods are ideal in achieving high-quantity, low-calorie recipe results. Experimentation led to a specific list of low-fat, low-calorie, high-quantity ingredients. These low-cal, high-quantity foods are called amplifiers. They reduce calorie-to-weight ratios, expand consumption time and add kinesthetic interest for NeoCuisine™ entreés.

Amplifiers include potatoes, apples, mushrooms, zucchini, ultra low-fat tofu and other foods of high-quantity and low-calorie advantage that amplify—expand—dishes resulting in appetite appeasement. They create quantity without adding many calories or sacrificing flavor.

The secret to successful fat stripping is low calorie-to-weight-ratio foods of 20 calories per ounce average.

OSMAZOME PRINCIPLE™

Researchers at Duke University found intensely flavored foods are perceived as much more satisfying. Subjects on low-fat and low-calorie but intensely flavored diet foods tend to lose the most weight and stick to their low-calorie eating plan four to ten times longer than their counterparts who eat ordinary flat-flavored diet food.[28] As we age, we require more flavor intensity. Sure, you can lose weight if you eat a pile of steamed vegetables every meal but who could stand it? NeoCuisine™ is about food you will like.

NeoCuisine's™ experimentation began with the hypothesis that it had to gratify our yearning for predominantly meat-based, richly flavored foods, a predilection that goes back thousands of years. Which brings us to the Osmazome Principle™: Foods taste best when fortified with meat flavors.

In the days of the Grand Hotel, chefs had a plethora of minions scurrying about the kitchen peeling this, mincing that and reducing stocks to their fine osmazome essences. Fortunately, today there are easier ways to get the rich meat flavors. We can buy genuinely excellent meat bases. These are meat essences reduced to thick paste or liquid. They are available at better supermarkets.

The best brand I have found is **Better Than Bouillon®. Call 1-800-429-3663 to order or locate the store nearest you. Buy three beef, three chicken, a clam and a lobster.** Alternatively, look for products that have "meat" or "meat essence" listed in the first three ingredients. Other good brands include Bovril® Liquid, Knorr-Swiss® Liquid and Minors®.

Buy only those brands listing the meat and/or stock as one of the first three ingredients. "Browning sauce," "Maggi seasoning," and Worcestershire are not meat bases. Go to the best grocery or gourmet store in town and buy the most expensive meat bases. Your extra effort in searching out prime meat bases and spending a little more for high quality will pay you mouth-watering dividends.

Osmazome Principle™ meat bases add rich, vertical flavor depth to NeoCuisine™. The subtle seasoning of high-quality meat bases doesn't jump on the palate demanding recognition. Rather, it unifies flavors and adds the deep savor missing from ordinary diet foods and vegetarian fare. Cumulative taste shock is averted because Brillat-Savarin discovered nearly two centuries ago that Osmazome creates great cookery.[29]

Even the best meat bases contain a great deal of salt. Of late, there has been controversy in the role of salt raising blood pressure. Thomas Pickering, M.D., professor of medicine at New York Hospital-Cornell Medical Center and director of the hospital's blood pressure center, says, "Only about half of all hypertensives are salt sensitive."[30] *The UC Berkeley Wellness Letter* reports that "sodium doesn't raise blood pressure significantly in everybody—only about 10% to 20% of Americans."[31] Noted health advocate Dr. Gabriel Mirkin, in his *Healthier Living Report*, states, "going on a low-fat/salt diet is a waste of effort because the vast majority of people will not significantly lower their blood pressure by reducing salt intake."[32] There's even a study showing blood pressure is lower when

two-thirds of salt intake is taken at dinner rather than at lunch.[33] *Nonetheless, NeoCuisine™ does not exceed the USDA 2,400 mg maximum salt intake advisory.*

NeoCuisine™ exploits the taste principle that the sweeter the food, the less salt required. Desserts have little salt, fruits rarely require salt and sweet dairy products, such as yogurt, milkshakes and ice cream, have no salt whatsoever. Yet, the palate is perfectly agreeable to these low- and no-salt sweet propositions.

For example, NeoCuisine™ advises cooked cereals for breakfast liberally sweetened with aspartame, hence requiring no salt. Because NeoCuisine™ breakfasts are so hearty, filling and satisfying, you sail right through lunch when you might enjoy one of 20 no-fat/sugar yogurt choices and one of 50 whole fruit options. The best lunch is NC HiPro Dream™. (See Appendix B.) By evening, 2,000 salt mg are available because salt has not been frivolously squandered through the day.

Culturally, dinner is the reward repast of the day. All our lives, it is the meal we expect to

be most flavorsome. Because it is difficult to create a fully savory, satisfying dinner without salt, NeoCuisine™ "saves up" salt so you get full flavor in the evening just when you expect it. Yet the RDA limit of 2,400 mg maximum daily salt intake is respected.

Those on a severe salt-restricted diet can still take advantage of the Osmazome Principle™ by using canned, salt-free stocks and reducing them to demi-glacé jellies. Also, use nonfat Veg-X, Maggi or Worcestershire in place of the meat bases called for in NeoCuisine™ recipes. Although these alternatives will not give you precisely the same flavor profile as original NC recipes, you will find the results acceptable.

Overall, NeoCuisine™ differs from conventional diets in its clever prevention of diet deprivation. You get enough to eat because of ample portions achieved through amplifiers and discreet ingredient selection. Correct kinesthetic values increase consumption time and provide the proper mouth-feel essential to gustatorial satisfaction. The cumulative taste shock

19

of ordinary diet recipes is circumvented. The Osmazome Principle™, world cuisine fusion and the other NeoCuisine™ flavor force techniques all serve to deliver ample gusto. NeoCuisine™ is simple for ease of preparation. In all, NeoCuisine™ is responsible food that appeases your hunger and pleases your palate.

But the best NeoCuisine™ outcomes cannot be measured simply in terms of ample amounts, delicious flavors and preparation ease. The real payoff is the life-threatening reduction of cancer, heart disease and other illnesses. There are hundreds of studies attesting to the efficacy of the NeoCuisine™ approach. The bottom line is that you feel better, look terrific and enjoy rising self-appreciation.

NeoCuisine™

1 REASONS TO STRIP FAT ARE COMPELLING

Look younger, live longer, feel much better and experience rising self-appreciation.

2 OUR PRIMEVAL RAGING APPETITE (PRA)

Sating it with 60 to 100 calories per ounce 21st century foods make us fat.

3 NEOCUISINE™ AVERAGES 20 CALORIES PER OUNCE

This strips fat by allowing satisfying quantities of calorie-frugal foods.

4 START THE DAY WITH WHOLE GRAIN COOKED CEREAL

Eat all you want. Begin the day entirely satisfied and on the correct calorie-count track.

5 SPARE SALT THROUGH THE DAY

Allow for a fully savory dinner.

6 BUY THE BEST MEAT BASES

Take full advantage of the Osmazome Principle™.

7 STICK WITH WHITE PROTEINS

Turkey breast, crab, lobster, egg whites, scallops, shrimp, chicken breast and ultra low-fat tofu.

8 MANAGE DAY-PART CALORIE CONSUMPTION

This leaves at least 200 7 to Bed calories.

[1] *World History,* Anatole G. Mazour and John M. Peoples, Harcourt Brace Jovanovich, Chicago, Illinois, 1990, pages 3-10, BB241.

[2] *The Serotonin Solution,* Judith J. Wurtman, Ph.D., Fawcett Columbine, New York, New York, 1996, pages 20-21, BB121.

[3] "Fall Is the Mean Season for Overeating," *Men's Health,* November 1996, page 117, BB177.

[4] *Habits Not Diets,* James M. Ferguson, M.D., Bull Publishing, Palo Alto, California, 1988, page 6, BB101.

[5] "Fat-Signaling Hormone Discovery," *Journal American,* August 1, 1996, page C3, BB156.

[6] "Lifelong Weight Loss," Jamie Diamond, *Self,* June 1996, page 152, BB125.

[7] Lunchables® label for "*Lean* Chicken and *Lean* Turkey Breast with Kraft® Cheese," BB372.

[8] "*Can Diet Prevent Cancer?*" *Health News, The New England Journal of Medicine,* February 1999, vol. 5, no. 9, page 4, BB479.

[9] "Varied Diet Lowers Blood Pressure," *Harvard Health Letter,* February 1997, vol. 22, no. 4, page 8, BB223.

[10] *Journal of the American Medical Association,* December 15, 1995, reported in "Pounds and Prevention," *Prevention,* May 1994, page 24, BB162; *Fit Over Forty,* James M. Rippe, M.D., William Morrow Co., New York, New York, 1996, page 19, BB283.

[11] "The Power of the Mind," *UC Berkeley Wellness Letter,* vol. 12, no. 12, September 1996, page 2, BB174.

[12] "More Sure Cures for Snorers," *UC Berkeley Wellness Letter,* vol. 12, no. 12, September 1996, page 3, BB175.

[13] "Fishing for Rheumatoid Arthritis Prevention," op. cit., page 8, B132.

[14] "Weight Control," op. cit., page 2, BB9.

[15] "A Little Known But Widespread Diabetes Risk," *Tufts University Health and Nutrition Letter,* vol. 14, no. 6, August 1996, pages 1-2, BB168.

[16] *Ageless Body, Timeless Mind,* Deepak Chopra, Harmony Books, Division of Crown Publishers, New York, New York, 1993, page 213.

[17] *The 120 Year Diet,* Roy L. Walford, M.D., Simon & Schuster, New York, New York, 1986, page 18, BB166.

[18] *Eat More, Weigh Less,* Dean Ornish, M.D., Harper Collins, New York, New York, 1993, page 28, BB6.

[19] *American Journal of Epidemiology,* June 1995, in *Prevention,* November 1995, page 25, BB172.

[20] Ornish, op. cit., page 5, BB6.

[21] "Cancer: What You Eat Can Affect Your Risk," *Mayo Clinic Health Letter,* September 1995, vol. 13, no. 9, pages 1-2, BB161.

[22] "A Theory of Human Motivation," A.H. Maslow, *Psychological Review,* volume 50, July 1943, pages 370-396, Classics of Organizational Behavior, #40.

[23] "Reduced Fat Snacks" *Mayo Clinic Health Letter,* August 1995, vol. 13, no. 9, page 7, BB203.

[24] "Psychological Consequences of Food Restriction," Janet Polving, Ph.D., *Journal of the American Dietetic Association,* vol. 96, no. 6, June 1996.

[25] "Weight Loss Plan without a Calorie Limit," *Tufts University Health and Nutrition Letter,* vol. 12, no. 6, August 1994, page 2.

[26] "Body Weight Depends, in Part, on the Weight of Your Food," *Tufts University Health and Nutrition Letter,* vol. 17, no. 7, September 1999, page 8, BB480.

[27] "The Satiety Index," *Self,* July 1996, pages 140-142, BB184.

[28] "Fat in Food Is Not the Key to Feeling Full," *New England Journal of Medicine,* vol. 5, no. 9, July 25, 1999, page 5, BB477; "Ask the Experts," *Tufts University Health and Nutrition Letter,* vol. 13, no. 10, December 1995, page 8, BB186.

[29] *The Curious Cook,* Harold McGee, North Point Press, San Francisco, California, 1990, pages 282-3, BB7.

[30] "High Blood Pressure Mistakes Can Easily Be Avoided," Thomas Pickering, M.D., *Health Confidential,* vol. 10, no. 8, August 1996, page 4, BB187.

[31] "Don't Let the Salt News Shake You Up," *UC Berkeley Wellness Letter,* vol. 12, no. 12, September 1996, page 1, BB188.

[32] "Low-Salt Diet Could Actually Harm You," Gabriel Mirkin, M.D., *Healthier Living,* McLean, Virginia, July 1996, page 6, BB189.

[33] "Last Break," Adam Bean, *Runner's World,* January 1996, page 20, BB244.

MUSCLES & LIFE

GOOD FOR HORSES

Years ago, one of my daughters wanted to learn how to ride horseback. So every week we hauled her out to Mrs. Crookshank's Riding Academy where Merissa would go around and around until I was dizzy and she utterly happy. One day, Merissa cantered a little Shetland pony that looked to me to be about 15 years old. Curious, I asked Mrs. Crookshank how old the horse was. She replied, "Pearly is 32 years old." I was, of course, flabbergasted. Seeing my surprise she said, "Let me tell you a story.

"I sold that horse when it was 20 years old to a young girl who rode it for several years and then to be 'humane,' put it out to pasture. They gave the horse

back to me after it had been allowed to run free for about a year and, unfortunately, the horse was almost dead. My solution for that problem has always been the same. Get the horse back in the ring and start running its legs off. In a matter of three months, the horse was slimmed down and frisky. This wasn't the only time something like this has happened. I've sold many horses to young riders through the years and those that I get back always seem to come to me in the same condition—overweight, rheumatic and just about always on the verge of death. My solution is always the same. Exercise."

Mrs. Crookshank seemed to take her message seriously because at age 70 she was a vigorous daily rider and, I might add, she looked terrific. She had enough energy to operate a 35-horse stable with eight riding instructors by herself. There certainly seems to be a lesson in the Crookshank story. If you yet remain unconvinced, horses typically die by age 20.

20 MUSCLE REBUILD™ GIFTS

Exercise is a positive impact on life. It not only helps us lose weight but has a salubrious effect on our psychological state, the cardiovascular system and health in general. Studies show those overweight but fit have lower mortality rates than those who are thin but unfit.[1]

The body responds to exercise in an amazing and positive way. Working the body gives it what it craves—conditioning. The body was never meant to sit idly, wasting away. Exercise is one of the most powerful expressions of our anti-aging attitude. It champions the now. It provides a limitless venue for unfolding our potential. Here are the facts. Look them over and mark the ones most important to you.

•CONTROLLED WEIGHT

Fit men and women burn about 15% to 30% more calories than the unfit.[2] Exercise prevents your body from going into metabolic low gear. When the body senses it's being denied food, it slows its metabolic rate to compensate. This is one of the reasons why dieting alone is not an effective way to lose weight. But exercise prevents this switch into low gear and even boosts the caloric burn rate.[3]

•SUPPRESSED APPETITE

Working out keeps hunger pangs at bay because exercise acts as an appetite suppressor. A good Muscle Rebuild™ session pushes food from your conscious and naturally moderates food cravings.

•CLEARER THINKING

The first thing you may notice from exercising is clearer, quicker thinking. People who exercise consistently score higher in cognitive tests than their sedentary peers. You don't have to run a marathon. Simple walking seems to do the trick. Dr. David Drachman, president of the American Neurological Association, suggests that better blood flow to the brain may be the reason.[4] By the way, not only are cognitive skills improved by aerobic exercise but reaction times and balance are also enhanced due to the brain's improved capabilities.[5]

•BOOSTED OPTIMISM

It has long been known that aerobic exercise increases endorphins, the body's natural mood-elevating hormone. Now researchers at the University of Illinois have found that men who work out aerobically for about an hour four times a week or more are highly optimistic.[6]

•DEEPER SLEEP

Exercise is the mechanism to achieve proper sleep. The body sleeps better when tired. Indeed, the *Harvard Health Letter* says, "exercise is the only known [natural] way for healthy adults to boost the amount of sleep they get."[7] Just make sure to exercise three hours before retiring because working out is a stimulant.

•DYNAMIC HEART

Vigorous exercise works the heart, building its strength. It becomes conditioned to pump out larger blood volumes to meet exercise needs. It becomes more efficient. As well, the reason your maximum heart rate drops with aging is muscles weaken and don't drive the heart as hard as when you were younger. Building muscle jumps your maximum heart rate.[8]

Keep this in mind: According to *The Journal of the American College of Cardiology*, regular exercise increases the number of blood vessels on the surface of the heart. Oxygen and nutrition for the heart muscle come from the outside surface of the heart, not from the blood pumped through the heart's chambers. So if you suffer an obstruction of blood flow to one area of the heart, your heart muscle stays alive by receiving blood from other arteries close by, the result of exercise-induced arterial density increase.[9]

•CLEANER ARTERIES

Dr. Dean Ornish has popularized the fact that fatty deposits in arteries can be reduced by following a low-fat diet accompanied by weight loss and regular exercise. According to the *Harvard Health Letter*, a regimen of a low-cholesterol, low-fat diet and regular exercise works better than surgery which tends to last only a few years before arteries again clog.[10]

•LOWER BLOOD PRESSURE

Increased musculature lowers blood pressure. Studies conducted at Northwestern University showed blood pressure could be reduced with appropriate strength training.[11] The *Johns Hopkins White Paper on Hypertension* states, "increased physical activity lower[s] systolic and dias-tolic blood pressure by an average of 7mm Hg" and "Low to moderate exercise has proven as effective as intensive exercise in lowering blood pressure."[12]

•STRENGTHENED BONES

Bones are lively things and subject to the same atrophy from disuse as muscle. Strength training loads bones, causing them to increase their mass.[13] Exercise physiologists call it Wolf's Law which says bones respond to stress (e.g., resistive exercise) by getting thicker; bone volume actually increases. This is true for people even in their 80s and 90s.[14]

•LOWER DIABETES RISK

Tufts University reports the more muscle mass the body has, the less insulin is needed to get blood sugar into muscle tissue and the less likely the body will be to "run out." This diminishes the likelihood for insulin pills or shots later in life.[15] Let's not pass over this lightly. The pancreas, the body's insulin producer, can eventually burn out its insulin-producing capacity. When that happens, you have diabetes, the leading cause of blindness, foot and leg amputations, and major contributor to heart attacks and strokes.[16] On the other hand, the Muscle Rebuild™ increases muscle mass and sensitizes the muscles to use insulin efficiently.

•DECREASED BREAST CANCER

Moderate and regular exercise lowers the risk of breast cancer by 60% in pre-menopausal women, suggests a study conducted by the University of Southern California.[17] In a huge study of 25,000 Norwegian women, those who exercised lowered their risk of developing breast cancer by 37%.[18]

•CURTAILED ARTHRITIS PAIN

When arthritis is under control, exercise improves health and fitness without hurting joints, reports Dr. John Perkins, medical advisor of the Arthritis Foundation. Exercise may even prevent further joint damage. Arthritic exercisers enjoy improvement in joint mobility, muscle strength and physical conditioning.[19]

•EASED BACK PAIN

Experts like Dr. Jennifer Kelsey of the Yale University School of Medicine say 80% of all men suffer lower back pain.[20] Building back strength is the primary back pain solution. Exercise tones and strengthens back muscles which in turn reduces pain.

•HEIGHTENED ENDURANCE

To do more—increased endurance—you need to burn more fuel. To burn fuel, you need more oxygen. To get more oxygen to the furnaces (cells) where the fuel is

burned, you must move more blood. To move more blood, your heart muscle must be able to do more work. Rigorous exercise makes the heart stronger because a well-trained heart pumps more blood with each beat. Likewise, stronger muscles throughout the body greatly enhance its ability to sustain work over long periods. Fit people go longer because they have larger muscles that store more glycogen, the body's energy which muscles use to do their work.[21] Regular exercise increases the efficiency and "horsepower" of your body.

•IMPROVED COORDINATION

Strong muscles mean improved neural coordination.[22] This is particularly true with free weights, according to research reported by the *Harvard Health Letter.*[23] You may not be able to walk a balance bar as you did when you were 14 but substantial coordination is regained through proper aerobic and strength training. What you thought was lost forever returns in a significant way.

•BETTER SEX

It makes good sense that as one becomes fitter, all his or her functions improve. Research by the Center for Marital and Sexual Studies shows renewed sexual vigor accompanies improved fitness for both men and women.[24] Strength training stimulates testosterone production, the male hormone that promotes sexual interest and muscle gain.[25]

•THE SHAPE OF YOUTH

Less weight and more gently sculpted muscles for women with more pronounced musculature for men translates to improved appearance, the shape of youth. Of all exercise advantages, your improved good looks will be the most obvious change to others. Your new shaped and slimmed body has the look of youth. By the way, strength training (weight lifting) by women does not produce bulky, bulging muscles.[26] The masculine women you see on TV often use steroids. The Muscle Rebuild's™ sensible weight lifting produces softly sculpted muscles in women and a more shapely figure. Skinny arms are supplanted by arms that have appealing definition.

•LIVE LONGER

Let's make it simple. If you are fit, you will live significantly longer than your sedentary friends. Individuals who continue high levels of physical activity have about half the death risk from all causes for individuals between 60 and 84. A large study of 10,000 men conducted by the Cooper Institute for Aerobics Research found fit men between 20 and 82 reduced their mortality risk by 44%.[27]

•ENHANCED SELF-ESTEEM

You're part of an elite population segment. The results from the effort and time you spend on yourself increase your self-appreciation. In the end you are a happier person. Isn't that what it's all about?

All the advantages of fitness sum to substantially increase your self-appreciation. Those who eat well and are physically active comprise less than 10% of the American population, according to the Fred Hutchinson Cancer Research Center in Seattle.[28]

LEGITIMATE CONCERNS

If exercise is so terrific, why don't we all do it? Well, actually, there are a lot of reasons.

"I'm too old."

You can begin strength training at any age. *The New England Journal of Medicine* reports a study where people averaging age 87 more than doubled their muscle strength.[29] Other studies are even more dramatic. People in their 90s can triple their strength and increase their muscle size by 10% after just eight weeks of strength training.[30]

"Exercise takes too much time."

You can get all the exercise you need in 30 minutes every day ... a small expense for the benefits. Even ten minutes a day, studies show, produce positives.

"I don't want a 'muscle-builder's' body."

To look like Arnold Schwarzenegger you would need to spend a couple of hours in the gym every day. The Muscle Rebuild™ is a sculpting program giving musculature pleasing definition. Don't worry. You won't look like the greased-up muscle builders you occasionally see while you're channel surfing.

"I've heard that lifting weights can give you arthritis."

New research shows the opposite is true. Moderate weight lifting actually relieves arthritis pain. It certainly doesn't cause it when exercise is done properly.

"I understand that 'no pain, no gain' is out but I still find exercise too demanding."

If that's the case, then you are still working your muscles too hard and too quickly. A moderate level of exercise is pleasant and enjoyable. Go easy especially when you are starting out. You have the rest of your life for conditioning your body. Relax.

"I've never been inclined toward sports. It just isn't what I like to do."

Conditioning your body is not a sport. Excellent conditioning technique is learned in a few sessions. You don't need a wide technique repertoire to become fit. One the other hand, the sport of conditioning has many nuances, allowing you to learn more about it for years.

"Why bother to exercise when I'm predestined to fathood anyway?"

While genes have an effect on our body makeup, to say you're predestined to be fat is simply incorrect. In studies conducted by Dr. Paul Williams on identical twins, genes were not found to be the determining fat factor. Those twins who exercised tended to be thin while their sedentary siblings (with exactly the same genes) were fat.[31] Don't let the fact that your mother is fat psyche you out. Obesity is a decision, not an immutable fact.

MUSCLE REBUILD™ RULES

You own one of the most remarkable entities in the universe—the human body. It thinks at levels beyond any known physical being; it moves with agility and grace; it can become strong and vigorous; it can be sculpted to shapes you may not have thought possible. We do not, therefore, want to proceed upgrading this elegant entity without first reviewing the basic operating tenets. Read these rules to operate your body correctly. They are important.

1 SEE YOUR DOCTOR

Your doctor is your ally. Most physicians provide full support for those seeking higher levels of physical conditioning. A visit to the doctor assures you do not have a prohibitive medical condition.

2 SET REALISTIC GOALS

The muscle men and women of TV are silly, the result of far too much gym time, unhealthy dieting and oftentimes dangerous steroid use. You will likely never look like them nor would you want to. Your goal is a gently sculpted body—a positive improvement of your current physique.

3 BE KIND TO YOURSELF

If you miss a day or week of exercise, don't worry. Even a month off is not irreparable. The essential thing is to get back to exercise. Getting back is easier than you think. Start at 50% and work up. You have the rest of your life to exercise. Thirty to 45 minutes a day allocated to physical fitness is about all we can afford. Since we're not Olympic competitors, what we really want is to feel better emotionally and physically, strip fat, sculpt some muscle and have fun. Please, no Ironman competitors. Don't make the Muscle Rebuild™ just another emotional stress.

4 TRY COMFORTABLY HARD

You're aiming at comfortably hard exercise effort. On the perceived exertion scale published by the Mayo Clinic, the recommended target intensity is **somewhat hard**. In other words, stay moderate in your effort. Dr. William McCarthy of the Pritikin Longevity Center points out moderate exercisers are twice as likely to stick with it than those who start at high intensity[32]. After exercising you should be energized, not tired.

5 BE PATIENT

You have the rest of your life to exercise. Don't rush your progress. This is the most common exercise mistake. People jump into an exercise program and hammer hard, to their detriment. Ego gets in the way resulting in over-effort leading to serious problems. What could be more serious than discouragement resulting from unreasonable effort levels, sore muscles and general malaise? If you kill your enthusiasm, all the remarkable benefits enumerated above never happen. Start slowly for minimal soreness, no injuries, a lot more fun, zero discouragement and steady conditioning.

Remember, the heart is a muscle. Train it gradually to fitness. Physiologists at the University of Texas recommend starting with ten minutes a day. It may not seem like much time but first establish frequency, then duration and lastly intensity.

Although the amount of exercise increase varies from expert to expert, all agree gradual boosting is imperative. Old-time, muscle-building trainers said it took time when starting out to "stabilize the joints." They were 100% correct. Going slowly gives the tendons and ligaments the chance to strengthen and adjust to the new demands

placed on them. Increase duration and intensity at no more than 5% per week.

6 KEEP IT SIMPLE

Just do it. Many exercise programs place too much emphasis on record-keeping. Charts, graphs, numbers and narratives aren't required for you to accurately track your progress. Here's a good way.

Get a clipboard with a couple sheets of paper and hang it in your exercise area or closet. Record the date, your starting weight for each exercise and walking time. You make another entry only when weight increases or you add walking time. This approach saves endless record-keeping. You write only when something changes or there are observations you wish to memorialize.

This simple technique gives you a progress history. If you like, add your weight reductions in one or two pound increments and the date. But keep in mind that leanness is your goal, not

solely weight reduction. Muscle weighs more than fat but takes up less room.

On the other hand, some people like more thorough records as affirmation of their exercise exertion. It can be a great motivator because it's proof of effort and goal achievement. Tracking workouts likewise stops bogus rationalization. One day off can turn into two and so on unless you confront yourself with the hard data of when you last exercised.

7 EXERCISE IN THE MORNING

You can exercise any time, but mornings are best. You are three times more likely to stick with exercising in the morning than any other time.[33] First of all you burn more fat. "On an empty stomach you'll kick up your metabolic rate and pull energy from fat stores, continuing the calorie burn into the day," explains Edmund Burke, Ph.D., director of the Exercise Science Program at the University of Colorado.[34] Neck and lower back muscles are also strongest in the morning, according to studies published in *Prevention*.[35] These are the muscles you rely on to stabilize your body when strength training. Use them when they are strongest.

Morning is the time of day when there is the least chance to be interrupted. Choosing evening exercise may mean not exercising at all because after a long day, it's hard to motivate yourself. You're tired and want to relax. Having evenings free is always nice. Besides, morning exercise invigorates. Its bolstering effect assists you through the day.

8 WARM UP → EXERCISE → UNWIND AND STRETCH

Successful training follows three distinct steps in this order: warm-up, exercise and stretch. People often confuse warm-up with stretching. For decades, the detrimental protocol has been to "stretch" before exercising. Even today you still see runners stretching prior to jogging, a practice which is downright injurious, according to *The Johns Hopkins Medical Letter*.[36]

WARM-UP

The warm-up is the gentle introduction of exertion to the muscles, including the heart. There are three important reasons to warm-up before exercising. The warm-up has had a place in sports, but only in the last decade has its essential importance been scientifically established. Exercise physiologists discovered that cold muscles readily injure, the incidence of muscle tears rising dramatically with no warm-up (remember the heart is a muscle, too).[37] But that's not the worst of it. Excessively fast-start workouts shunt blood away from glands and organs too quickly, robbing them of vital oxygen. According to respected sports physiologist Dr. Philip Maffetone, M.D.,

this shocks the body and could actually lead to physical damage.[38]

On the other hand, warm muscles perform 30% better than cold. Better performance is the reward of a proper warm-up because it raises the body's temperature and stimulates the flow of oxygen-rich blood. And a good warm-up prepares you psychologically. Knowing that you have to jump right into training can be a put-off. **A warm-up phase adjusts your attitude by preparing you mentally to proceed with energy.**

EXERCISE

Exercise uses the muscles rigorously. Whether walking or strength training, you purposefully challenge your muscles so that they gain strength and vigor. Exercise is the heart of health.

UNWIND AND STRETCH

Unwind after exercise by walking leisurely three to five minutes. This is a must so you don't stress your heart. After exercise, blood still courses rapidly through your body. Your heart is doing a lot of the blood-moving work but so are your muscles. Each time you move, muscles assist blood flow. Blood otherwise pools in the muscles, impeding circulation. Stop abruptly and the full circulation burden dangerously falls on the heart. Besides, keeping on the move for correct unwinding assists in removing from muscles lactic acid (waste) generated by exercise.[39]

Stretch while the body is still warm. Stretching after exercise elongates muscle so your body gains amazing suppleness. You develop flexibility beyond what you may imagine possible, conceivably the best of your life. But, avoid injury by stretching *after* the exercise when you are warm, regardless of what you have been taught. Again, don't confuse warming up with stretching.

9 OVER-DRINK

Call it bloodsweat because most sweat comes from blood. A surprising 70%+ of energy expended during exercise comes from heat loss.[40] That's a lot of sweat.

As blood loses water (and blood gets thicker), the heart works even harder to maintain sweating so your body core with all its vital organs doesn't overheat and start misfiring. Add to this the muscles' demand for more and more oxygen as you exercise and the heart is working exceedingly hard indeed. Hydrate properly for the sake of your heart but also for endurance.

Unbeknownst to most of us, we all tend to be somewhat mildly but chronically dehydrated which causes us to feel fatigued. We don't drink enough fluids because as we age our thirst mechanism becomes less sensitive.[41] Thirst doesn't kick in until dehydration is imminent. This means we must over-drink fluids when

sweating; we must force ourselves to drink while exercising to meet the body's fluid needs. Even if it's cold outside, we still sweat and need plenty of fluid. You'll know you have drunk enough when your urine is clear and not malodorous.

As you become more conditioned, proper hydration becomes more important because you sweat more. This is good. It tells you the body is becoming more sensitive to regulating its temperature. Sweating is good, a prime indicator of a youthful and well-conditioned body.

31

MUSCLES & LIFE

1 MUSCLE REBUILD™ SIGNIFICANTLY ENHANCES STRENGTH, ENDURANCE, BALANCE AND FLEXIBILITY. You can gain its many benefits at any age.

2 SEE YOUR DOCTOR before engaging in any exercise program. It's first-rate insurance.

3 SET REALISTIC GOALS. Be kind to yourself.

4 EXERCISE IN THE MORNING. Follow this order: Warm up or stride, 1•1•2™ (strength training) followed by Macro Deflexing™ (stretching) and Dynamic Balance™ (equilbrium).

5 START BodyRenewal™ AT LOW INTENSITY. Undertrain. Be patient. You have your whole life to exercise.

6 WHEN CONDITIONED, EXERCISE TO COMFORTABLY HARD EFFORT.

7 DRINK PLENTY OF FLUIDS AND POWER BREATHE.

8 SIMPLE RECORD-KEEPING in your BodyRenewal™ journal keeps you motivated.

[1] "Weight Expectations," Colleen Dunn-Bates, *Cooking Light*, November 1996, page 42, BB150.

[2] "Give Your Metabolism a Boost," *UC Berkeley Wellness Letter*, October 1995, page 6, BB31; "Raise Your Rate," Adam Bean, *Runner's World*, November 1996, page 22, BB280.

[3] *Eating for Endurance*, Ellen Coleman, R.D., M.A., M.P.H., Bull Publishing Company, 1992, Palo Alto, California, page 137, BB107.

[4] "HealthFront," *Men's Fitness*, August 1995, page 60, BB35.

[5] "The Thinking Person's Workout," *Tufts University Health and Nutrition Letter*, December 1995, vol. 13, no. 10, page 6, BB35.

[6] "Keep Your Chin Ups," *Men's Health*, December 1995, page 102, BB38.

[7] "Feeling Tired Too Much of the Time," *Harvard Health Letter*, vol. 22, no. 10, August 1997, page 7, BB321.

[8] *Fat Free, Flavor Full*, Gabe Mirkin, M.D., Little, Brown & Company, USA, 1995, page 128, BB388.

[9] *The Journal of the American College of Cardiology*, July 1998, 32 (1): 49-50 from the *Mirkin Report*, September 1998, vol. 9, no. 8, page 6, BB424.

[10] "The Work's Worth It," *Health Beat, Harvard Health Letter*, January 1995, page 8, BB42.

[11]"Inner Tummy Toning," *HealthFront, Prevention,* February 1995, page 44, quoting from the *Journal of American Medical Association,* August 24/31, 1994, BB46.

[12]*The Johns Hopkins White Papers* 1997: Hypertension, Simeon Margolis, M.D., Ph.D., and Michael J. Klag, M.D., Johns Hopkins Medical Institutions, Baltimore, Maryland, pages 34-35, BB289.

[13]*Johns Hopkins Medical Letter,* April 1996, page 8, BB34.

[14]"Bone Density," Michael Yessis, *Snow Country,* February/March 1988, page 87, BB405.

[15]*"Food for Thought,"* op. cit., BB48.

[16]"Little Known But Widespread Diabetes Risk," *Tufts University Health and Nutrition Letter,* vol. 14, no. 6, August 1996, page 1, BB274.

[17]"Fitness," Michael O'Shea, Ph.D., *Parade Magazine,* July 2, 1995, page 13, BB49.

[18]"Study Suggests Exercise Fights Breast Cancer," *New York Times,* from the *Seattle Post-Intelligencer,* May 1, 1997, page A-1, BB279.

[19]"More is More," *Prevention,* February 1996, page 30, BB50.

[20]*Living Longer Stronger,* Ellington Darden, Ph.D., The Berkeley Publishing Group, New York, New York, 1995, page 17, BB53.

[21]*Biomarkers,* William Evans, Ph.D., and Irwin H. Rosenberg, M.D., with Jacqueline Thompson, Fireside (Simon & Schuster), New York, New York, 1991, page 70, BB75.

[22]"Start Strength Training Now to Prevent Muscle Loss," The *University of Texas Health Letter,* March 1996, page 5, BB32.

[23]"Aging Athletes: Keep on Keeping On," Maria A. Fiatarone, M.D., and Leah R. Garnett, *Harvard Health Letter,* vol. 22, no. 5, March 1997, page 5, BB272.

[24]"Conditioning for Getting Physical," *Men's Health,* vol. 10, no. 8, October 1996, page 57, BB275.

[25]*Living Longer Stronger,* Ellington Darden, Ph.D., The Berkeley Publishing Group, New York, New York, 1995, page 177, BB53.

[26]*Parade Magazine,* Michael O'Shea, Ph.D., July 23, 1995, page 11, BB57.

[27]*The Health Letter,* May 1986, vol. 27, no. 9, page 1, BB58.

[28]"Where Do You Fit In?" *Men's Fitness,* August 1995, page 16, BB40.

[29]"Health After 50," *The Johns Hopkins Medical Letter,* September 1991, page 1, BB32.

[30]"Successful Aging: Most Physical Problems are Preventable," op. cit., page 1, BB33.

[31]"Tight-Fitting Genes," *Runner's World,* June 1996, page 19, BB90.

[32]"Big Gains in Weight Loss," *Prevention's Fight Fat 1997,* Mark Bricklin and Gale Maleskey, Emmaus, Pennsylvania, 1997, page 200, BB210.

[33]"A Week's Worth of Fixes," *Runner's World,* July 1996, page 70, BB109.

[34]"Morning Glory," *Prime Health and Fitness,* vol. 4, no. 1, Spring 1998, page 18, BB360.

[35]"Best Time to Do Resistance Training," Mark Golin with Therese Walsh and Toby Hanlon, *Prevention,* November 1995, page 71, BB66.

[36]"Health Tips," *Health After 50, The Johns Hopkins Medical Letter,* February 1996, page 8, BB81.

[37]Evans, Rosenberg and Thompson, op. cit., pages 152 and 173, BB75.

[38]*The High Performance Heart,* Philip Maffetone, M.D., and Matthew E. Mantell, Bicycle Books, Inc., San Francisco, California, 1994, page 49, BB85.

[39]"Focus on Fitness," Gabe Mirkin, M.D., *Mirkin Report,* vol. 8, no. 12, page 6, BB353.

[40]Maffetone and Mantell, op. cit., page 51, BB85.

[41]Evans, Rosenberg and Thompson, op. cit., page 83, BB75.

THE MUSCLE REBUILD™

"...strength training is the closest thing there is to a fountain of youth."
The Harvard Health Letter [1]

The Muscle Rebuild™ (MR) is a complete program including the revolutionary free-weight 1•1•2™ workout, MR striding for cardiovascular enhancement (the heart is a muscle like any other, it benefits from conditioning) and Macro Deflexions™ for youth's litheness. You need all this for the body's 639 muscles.

Muscle constitutes the body's largest component in size, weight and mass, 30% to 50% of the total physique. Its unnecessary, age-related deterioration leads to diminished strength and stamina. Energy drops. We can do less. We get old. It's so unnecessary. Muscle literally begs for conditioning. The proof is its rapid resurgence. You can expect:

- Doubling (possibly tripling) of strength.
- Metabolic rate increases to 30%.
- Muscle size leaping up to 40%.
- Much, much more daily vigor.

In addition to correct aerobic exercise, the best thing you can do for your body is rebuild it with strength training. It's exciting. You're about to commence one of the best things you have ever done for yourself. 1•1•2™ recovers the musculature lost since about age 24. **Unless you regularly weight train, your muscle has shrunk by 20% to 40%—all of which has been hidden by ever-increasing adipose.** That's why aerobic conditioning, while superb for the heart, veins and arteries, is a poor muscle overhaul. Reconstruction of muscle lost through decades of inactivity and body absorption is absolutely best achieved by strength training. Nothing works as well.

1•1•2™ is specialized strength training. Its name derives from the drill itself—1 minute, 1 cycle, 2 times per week. You strength train each muscle for a total of one minute per workout. You do one cycle only, that is, one set of exercises. The "2" means you strength train two times per week. This is your Muscle Rebuild™ formula for all the benefits listed starting on page 23 of Muscles and Life.

Weight training helps everyone. Yet, prejudice toward strength training is still harbored by some women.

A way around women's weight-training hesitancy is understanding women have more to gain than men. Because women frequently diet without exercise, they lose more muscle. Their capacity to regain what has been lost, therefore, is greater. While the incidence of osteoporosis is low in men, it is high in women, something only weight-bearing exercise such as 1•1•2™ corrects.

Still, some women see renewing their bodies using weights as unfeminine. Too bad because shapely arms, legs and buttocks are a good deal more attractive than the typical flab carried by many. Women regain the shaped look of their youth without "bulking up." Don't worry about looking like a "weight lifter." A women's testosterone level is too low for that. If you are a woman, lose the attitude and rebuild your body.

For men, the opposite problem frequently exists. Men don't have an aversion to weight training but plunge into it with a macho attitude that leads to injury and aversion. If the typical male ego can be supplanted with reason, biceps bulge with patience and a long-term program. Building a "magazine body" is impossible in 90 days. On the other hand, a year or two of strength training will lead to the shape of youth. You will not wind up as Mr. America but you will be assuredly proud of your accomplishments.

DON'T DIET WITHOUT 1•1•2™

Many people make the horrible mistake of dieting without strength training. This causes the body to absorb already-debilitated muscle, exacerbating muscle loss[2]. Do not diet without 1•1•2™. You get quicker weight reduction and improved physical and mental well-being by combining NeoCuisine™ with the Muscle Rebuild™.

Keep in mind, when calories are restricted, metabolism slows. It's the body's clever reaction to a dissatisfied primeval raging appetite. In an attempt to save itself, the body drastically slows its fuel burn, making fat stripping exceptionally difficult. The good news is 1•1•2™ and striding (coming up) keep your metabolism humming right along.

If you weigh now what you weighed at age 25 but have not exercised, you are undermuscled and overfat. It means those weight charts issued by insurance companies are wrong. It means every time you get on a scale, you are deluding yourself because weight alone doesn't indicate the lost musculature of your youth. It means your doctor may be shortchanging you. Has he taken your lean-body-mass measurements and satisfactorily explained the pitfalls of muscle loss? Have you been allowed or even encouraged to diet without weight lifting, aggravating muscle loss?

Our goal is sane fat stripping through NeoCuisine™, 1•1•2™ and striding.

1•1•2™ FUNDAMENTALS

Here are 1•1•2™ procedures for optimal results in the shortest time without undue soreness and loss of enthusiasm.

1 START GENTLY— UNDERTRAIN

Doing too much too soon is the worst thing you can do. Your body requires about six weeks' moderate training to adjust to the new demands placed on it. Joints, muscles, ligaments and tendons all need time to adapt. When you hurt you don't look forward to your next workout. Lymph nodes can swell. You feel tired and you are at risk for developing frequent infections and injuries.[3] The secret is to train consistently with no sudden jumps in intensity.

Undertrain for the first two weeks of strength training—about five to ten minutes total. Stop each exercise well short of fatigue. In the BodyRenewal™ chapter coming up you are advised on how to do this. Don't be tricked. The body always thinks the first days of exercise are easy—too easy. As we grow older, some muscle nerve is lost, allowing us to injure more easily because we don't sense damage.[4] So stop well short of fatigue. Even following the undertrain rule, you'll likely feel some soreness. Don't worry about it because a little soreness is good; it shows muscles are responding. But don't get really sore. Once again, you have the rest of your life to exercise. Follow the undertrain rule.

2 WARM UP

As you know, it is essential to warm up prior to exercise so blood gradually shunts from the organs to muscles. Elevated body temperature averts injury. Strength training without proper warm-up can cause irregular heart rhythm even in 17-year-olds.[5] Your goal is to break a slight sweat prior to strength training. Here are some warm-ups:

• Stride. The best way to warm up is by striding (brisk walking), explained in the next chapter.

●Jog in place. Swinging your arms. When first starting out, jog in place for about a minute, rest for 15 to 30 seconds and jog again for about a minute. Work up to five or more minutes.

●March in place. This simple drill works better than you might think. Bring your upper leg parallel to the floor, knees coming high. It's a good heart-starter.

●Skip rope. Buy an adjustable rope and shorten or lengthen it so that the rope (not the handles) comes to your armpits. Jumping rope is a bit of a skill but with a month's practice you get the hang of it. Aim for 70 or more cycles per minute. Hard floors work well. Begin by skipping rope for 30 seconds then marching briskly for 30 seconds. Work up to five minutes and beyond, gradually building to 100% rope jumping. When you make it to 15 minutes, you burn 200 calories.[6]

●Stairclimb. Walk the stairs in your house or apartment building.

●Jumping jacks. Do jumping jacks on a carpeted surface to absorb the shock. The thicker the carpet, the better.

●Light "pre-set." Go through all the exercises at high repetition (up to 15) with light weights (about 20% to 50% of your regular weights). This is not strength training but an excellent warm-up routine preparing you properly for heavier weights.[7]

Regardless of how you choose to warm up, your goal is to break a light sweat. Once you are warmed up, proceed immediately with 1•1•2™.

3 THE MARVEL MINUTE™
This is the most important strength training rule you'll ever learn. It is the first "1" of 1•1•2™. Strength trainers

use the term repetition for completion of one lift or movement. Completing a series of repetitions of one exercise is called a set. But since your muscles don't know how to count, they'll never know how many repetitions or sets you do. Muscles require 50 to 70 seconds constant challenge two times a week to stimulate strength gain. The number of repetitions and sets you do doesn't matter.[8] What counts is **total challenge time (TCT)**. Striding, Macro Deflexions™ and Dynamic Balance™ are all based on the TCT concept, as you will see.

Think about it. A person quickly blasting out two sets of ten reps for a *total challenge time* of 30 seconds accomplishes less than the person doing one set of ten reps for a total of 60 seconds *total challenge time*. What counts is the *total challenge time*, not reps and sets. And, remarkably, the strength gains achieved with the Marvel Minute™ one set versus doing three sets are within 10% of each other.[9]

The Marvel Minute™ takes the guesswork out of strength training. The number of times you lift a weight and how many sets you do is irrelevant provided you accumulate about 60 seconds of high challenge two times a week for each muscle group. If slowly performing five reps yields 30 seconds high challenge, you know another five reps for 30 seconds are necessary. Let the sweep hand of a wall clock determine your training, not repetitions and sets.

It's important not to lock joints. Each 1•1•2™ exercise is designed to keep constant tension on the muscles. Don't come all the way up or down.

Many people find the step-down technique helpful in accumulating the full 60 seconds of the Marvel Minute™. This is done by accumulating X number of seconds (e.g. 35 seconds) with a heavy weight to the point it can no longer be moved (fatigue) and then switching immediately to a lighter weight to complete the balance of the Marvel Minute™. The muscle is challenged for a total of 60 seconds but by switching to a lighter weight, the total 60 seconds is accumulated in one set versus having to perform two or three separate sets. The step-down mode requires a second set of lighter dumbbells be ready but stepping down can be invaluable in facilitating 1•1•2™.

WHEN STARTING OUT: Do not exceed 20 seconds *TOTAL CHALLENGE TIME* per exercise. Add 5-10 seconds a week until you reach the full MARVEL MINUTE™.

4 ONE CYCLE WONDER

Total challenge time is what counts. Completing a series of sets of different exercises is called a cycle. The *one cycle wonder* is the second "1" of 1•1•2™. Rather than thinking of reps, sets of

typical three-cycle workouts, go for the *Marvel Minute*™ and the *one cycle wonder*. Do only one set of each exercise using S-L-O-W reps. Aim for three seconds up and three seconds down, ten reps total for 60 seconds constant effort. Don't come all the way up or go all the way down because it allows a moment's rest. The goal is constant challenge. At the end of 60 seconds, you should not be able to move the weight, which is the *fatigue point* you want to reach.

If you exceed 70 seconds total slow, six-second repetitions, increase the dumbbell weight by one or two pounds. If you can't achieve slow repetitions (six to eight) for at least 45 to 50 seconds, lighten the load.[10] Make sure that the point at which you can no longer move the weight (fatigue) is between 50 to 70 seconds of slow, six-second repetitions.

The *one minute, one cycle* rule preserves your most important asset—time. 1•1•2™ advanced training techniques get you fast results. Rest no more than two minutes between exercises. You want to get done, to keep things moving along. Don't forget to *power breathe*. Bring plenty of air into your lungs as you slowly perform each exercise. *Never* hold your breath; it pushes blood pressure through the roof. Exhale on the lift, breathe in on the descend. For almost every exercise, your back should be straight, shoulders back, chest sticking out and legs in a straight but unlocked position.

5 TWO DAYS STRENGTH TRAINING EACH WEEK
Strength training twice a week reaps 90% of the gains achieved working out three times per week. Since the two-time-per-week versus three-time-per-week outcomes are so close, save time by strength training two times a week; allow a minimum of two days rest between sessions.[11] A strength-trained body part requires time to recover after workout, 72 hours seems ideal.[12] This allows muscle fuel (glycogen) to rebuild and the muscle tissue to repair itself to greater strength. The thorough rest periods resulting from only two strength training sessions per week minimize injury while still maximizing strength gain. And you save time.

6 PERCEIVED EFFORT
No one sticks to harsh conditioning very long. Strength training should be perceived as *comfortably hard*. On a scale of one to ten with one being no effort and ten being *all out*, you should be a six ... *comfortably hard*. Moderately intense exercise is enjoyable. If you aren't enjoying your workouts, you're probably working too hard. After exercising, you should feel energized.

Some people find reducing perceived effort with psychoprophylactics helpful. This positive mental imagery makes 1•1•2™ even easier. Try these:

•**Muscle View**
Imagine seeing your muscles being worked right down to the cell level. Envision muscle cells gaining strength and additional cells being recruited, which in fact happens. See your muscles getting stronger and bigger.

•**"This Is Why I Came"**
When muscle tires is precisely the point when a little more effort does the most good. The Marvel Minute™ requires determination. But remember, fatiguing your muscles is the whole point. Say to yourself, "I want to tire my muscles for great rebuild."

•**Your Body At 25**
When strength training, see your body as it was when you were 25 because that's where you're going. Unless

you were an NCAA swimming champion, you can regain your youth's shape. As you lift, envision the body you had in your prime. That reality is more likely than you may think.

•**Creative Counting**
10%, 20%, 30%, etc.; one/ten, two/ten, three/ten, etc.; ten, nine, eight, seven, etc.; imagine numbered placards changed with each repetition. Invent your own method. Remember, counting is used as a time aid to fulfilling the Marvel Minute™.

•**Positive Self-Talk**
During the Marvel Minute™ talk to yourself positively. Talk to yourself about stronger bones, quicker reactions, higher self-regard, anxiety reduction, growing strength, more endurance and a longer life. Throw in better sex if you like because that happens, too.

•**The Machine Vision**
Olympic marathon gold medalist Frank Shorter imagines his legs as bike wheels, resulting in a smooth, steady pace. Think of your arms and legs as hydraulic pistons, pumping with force and power.

7 PAIN AND SORENESS
If you really hurt, see your doctor right away. 1•1•2™ is not painful and the presence of severe pain indicates injury. Sharp pain in or near the joint that continues to hurt or gets worse indicates a problem with the joint. This is when you should see your doctor. "Good pain" has the sensation of a dull ache located in the muscle and is usually relieved using RICE: Rest, Ice (no more than 15 minutes at a time[13]), Compression, Elevation. Use RICE for a day or two but don't rest too long. Soreness indicates that muscles have been microscopically torn down to rebuild stronger than before. Follow the muscle and joint rehabilitation program advised by Harvard University physiology expert Maria Fiatarone, M.D.

Continue exercising the injured area regularly but at <u>lighter weights</u> well below the pain threshold. The goal is rehabilitation not rest.[14]

The "keep moving" advisory is new to sports science. The old protocol was extended rest which exacerbates an injury through nonuse. Light doses of the exercise causing the original injury is best. Keep moving the muscle and joint through the full range of motion but at a light weight (down to using no weight). Don't rush things. Before jumping up to higher weights, give your body plenty of time to repair itself. One to six weeks is not unusual for healing. Longer than six weeks or for severe pain, see your doctor of course.

You may want to add vitamin E to your supplementation. 400 IU of vitamin E is sufficient to hasten recovery.

8 WIND DOWN AND STRETCH

Allow a cooling-off period so your heart adjusts. Movement helps move blood. Don't put the entire blood distribution load solely on the heart all at once. Keep walking slowly for two to five minutes. After a two to five-minute wind-down (walking period), always stretch. (See Macro Deflexions™ in Striding and Deflexing, in the next chapter.) Macro deflexing returns the full range of motion you possessed in your youth, reduces injuries and feels good.

1•1•2™ GYM

A home gym is superior to joining a health club or working out at a commercial gym. Here's why.

•SAVES TIME
No driving, parking, changing and facing increased traffic on the way home.

•INSTANT SHOWER
Many gyms don't provide shower facilities. For those that do, it means lugging your clothes to the gym. Enjoy privacy and the comfort of your own environment with your home gym.

•NO "ATTITUDE" REQUIRED
You show up at your health club having to promote the "facade of normalcy." At home be as grouchy as you like. But the workout will absolutely lift your mood so you arrive at work in good humor.

•FORGET FASHION
Health clubs appeal to poseurs. The latest Lycra gym wear is *de rigueur.* Your home gym lets you wear exactly what's most comfortable for you. You save poseur money for what you really want.

•OWN HOURS
Exercise exactly when you wish. No sign-ins. No schedule manipulation to "beat the crowd." No lines.

•AUDIO CONTROL
Breathe, grunt, shout as you wish giving no mind to what others think. Express yourself without embarrassment.

On the other hand, the excitement of a Golds Gym® is appealing.

•SOCIALIZING
Many people enjoy the social aspect of being a gym rat. It's fun.

•ARRAY OF MACHINES
There is no question that today's commercial gyms offer a wide variety of

strength-training equipment. Your home gym, believe it or not, can accomplish everything a commercial gym offers. But let's face it. Dumbbells aren't as impressive as $1,000,000 in machinery.

● **MOTIVATION**

If you're paying $500-a-year membership fees, chances are you'll use the gym. Appointments are another spur to exercise.

● **SHOWING OFF**

As you slim your body and become fit, the show-off factor is bound to kick in. Okay, after a few months of 1•1•2™go to a gym. You've earned it.

SET UP

Setting up a home gym is easy. You can achieve a full-body workout in little space and with minimum equipment. Bulk up or sculpt, go aerobic or anaerobic, all at home,

doing as vigorous or gentle a workout as you wish.

Don't worry about space for a home gym because regardless of whether you have a 10,000-square-foot home or a 500-square-foot apartment, you have room. No matter what your impressions, setting up a home gym is entirely doable.

All you need for your home gym is one set of adjustable-weight dumbbells (individual hand weights) also known as free weights. These are superior to any other resistance training equipment. Bill Pearl, possibly this country's foremost strength trainer, simply says "free weights are the fastest way to produce strength and muscle mass."[15]

Prime Health and Fitness magazine researched studies showing free weights increase strength, balance and coordination.[16]

Free weights are small and accordingly don't take up much room. They're inexpensive, convenient, readily weight-adjusted and last forever. They can be worked at various angles and positions. The infinite variety of free-weight workouts keeps exer-

cise interesting versus machines which have significant limits. All muscle groups can be worked using free weights.

Because free weights are lifted a bit differently with each repetition, muscles and joints get a more thorough, balanced workout. Stabilizing (peripheral) muscles are recruited, stimulating improved balance and coordination because you are beneficially challenged. Machines, on the other hand, are too consistent. Their steady up-and-down, side-to-side motions keep muscles, ligaments and tendons in a constant path not equating to real world motions.

Each side of the body is trained proportionally with equal-weight dumbbells. Your left arm will be as strong as your right. Unlike machines, free weights can be used unilaterally, one at a time. Instead of doing bicep curls with both arms at the same time, one arm and then the other can be worked which some people find easier to do.

Because free weights are unrestricted, hands and wrists assume natural positions, rotating comfortably through exercise movements. Into the bargain add what respected magazine *Prime Health and Fitness* has to say: "It's easier to injure yourself on a machine than with dumb-bells."[17]

Visit any store selling free weights. Using your non-dominant arm, find the weight that you can lift (curl) only one or two times. Once this maximum strength measurement is determined (e.g. 10, 15, 20 pounds), buy two dumbbells having weight plates at least 50% more than you lifted a maximum of one or two times. For example, if you found that you could curl 20 pounds, buy two dumbbells having weight plates amounting to about 30 pounds each. Dumbbells having at least four weight plates of one or two pounds are best. This allows for small incremental weight increases, essential for slow, steady progress. Jumping five pounds is often too much. Spend no more than $100. A basic adjustable dumbbell set includes:

- Two dumbbell bars with locks
- Two 10-pound plates
- Two 5-pound plates
- Two 2.5-pound plates
- Two 1.25-pound plates

If you want to use the step-down technique described earlier, you'll need a second set of weight-adjustable dumbbells. Although this investment increases cost, the expense may prove worth it because many people find the step-down down technique ideal for accumulating the Marvel Minute™. But a stool or armless chair is just fine. In any event, depending on your budget and the amount of space you have, buy whatever you wish but at a minimum purchase the weights prescribed above.

The ideal spot for a home gym is your garage or living room. For the garage, go to any carpet remnant store and get two 8' x 10' thick pile carpets. Stack these on top of each other for your exercise pad.

Don't worry about the garage being cold. Dress in layers, including hat or hood and gloves if conditions warrant. As the first couple of exercises warm you up, start removing layers. If you wish, turn on a small electric space heater to take the edge off the chill.

Additional things to consider for organizing your garage:

- Clock: Free weights aside, a large wall clock with a sweep

second hand is your most important piece of equipment. Buy an inexpensive plastic clock that runs on batteries. Then watch it as you accumulate time toward your Marvel Minute™ goal.
- Radio: Studies show that music or an interesting program can get your mind off the workout and actually play a role in reducing perceived exercise effort.
- Water: Drink water before you're thirsty. The Muscle Rebuild™ isn't long enough to require additional carbos so sports drinks are generally unnecessary.
- Tissue: Sometimes noses run when pumping iron.
- Towel and headband: You want to work up a sweat because it shows that you are getting a positive cardio-vascular effect in addition to muscle strengthening.
- Mirrors: See muscles at work while you feel them working. This helps focus the mind. Mirrors also let you check for correct form and allow you to enjoy your gradual appearance im-

provement, boosting motivation.

• Anything else? It's your gym, set it up exactly the way you want. But keep outside distractions to a minimum. This means no phone.

If you don't have a garage, your living room is ideal. It already has the carpet and, by moving the coffee table aside, you have adequate space for exercising. The TV is there anyway; watch while you exercise. With a bit of juggling, your free weights are hidden from sight yet readily accessible, stored neatly behind the couch.

DON'T BE FOOLED

Our culture is built on convenience. It's not a bad thing but: We think we need all manner of gadgets, facilitators and equipment. We buy a wok when our non-stick frying pan works fine. We buy a stair-step exerciser when a brisk walk is better. And we'll buy a space-robbing, expensive exercise machine instead of the two free weights we need.

Buy all the facilitating equipment you wish but your workouts cannot be improved any more than by using simple free weights. The fact of the matter is that all that equipment doesn't make the weights lighter. Fancy gear and expensive machines are fine but what counts most is your effort. The simple weight-training tools advised for 1•1•2™ work best and cost the least for building strength and stamina.

1•1•2™ EXERCISES

1•1•2™ results from an extensive survey of hundreds of drills. Exercise physiologists estimate that there are 4,000 distinct exercises. 1•1•2™ was culled from this overwhelming array of strength-training confusion. Selection criteria included body balance, simplicity and safety, the least equipment and the fastest results with the fewest exercises.

1•1•2™ is a whole-body approach for correct body balance because unequal muscle gain can lead to injury. A good example is working the abdominals without strengthening the lower back. Strong abs pull the vertebrae of the spine forward, misaligning it which pressures back nerves. The result is low back pain. 1•1•2™ evenly conditions opposing muscles such as the front of the arm (bicep) and the back of the arm (tricep). This balances the body. Because 1•1•2™ uses free weights, the right and left sides of the body advance proportionately as do the upper and lower body.

Workouts with unbalanced emphasis leave conditioning half done. For example, many men concentrate on their upper body "beach muscles." Biceps might look great but failing to exercise the legs is a mistake. Not only are the legs the largest muscles of the body and hence the best calorie-burners, but under-trained leg muscles leave you unfit for all recreational sports, not to mention uneven physique development looks odd. Similarly, it's unappealing for a woman to sculpt her upper body without appropriately shaping her legs.

Simplicity and safety are 1•1•2™ factors. 1•1•2™ meets people's real-world needs. The old "no pain, no gain" business is out the door. Too many exercise schemes demand too much too soon at the expense of motivation. There's no need to flog your body.

1•1•2™ works the entire body but places emphasis on the trunk because it houses the abdomen and lower back, common problem areas. There are numerous reasons for back pain but the most effective remedies are weight loss and exercising properly to strengthen the back and stomach muscles. The added bonus is a well-conditioned abdomen holds the stomach in which means you eat less due to heightened fullness perception.[18]

1•1•2™ exercises are ordered in a specific way. You may notice the Back Builder and Tummy Tuck are at the end of your Muscle Rebuild™ routine. There is good reason for this. These muscles help stabilize your spinal column as you perform most exercises. You don't want to fatigue them, therefore, until the end of your workout.[19] Also observe that your largest muscles are exercised first. This time-honored strength-training technique of exercising legs first leaves smaller arm and midsection muscles last. You don't want to attempt large-muscle exercise when you are worn out.

Lastly, you want results. You don't want to spend a year working out without clear improvement. 1•1•2™ combined with NeoCuisine™ gives you visible BodyRenewal™ because 1•1•2™ exercises are efficient for quick effect. The advanced training techniques of one minute, one cycle, two times per week save time and rapidly increase musculature. In all, you'll find 1•1•2™ to be a bit challenging but enjoyable. The muscles were meant to be worked and conditioning them is pleasurable. After completing the 50-day BodyRenewal™, you will know what I mean.

THE THIGH THINNER TUSH TIGHTENER (4T)

Inelegantly known as the squat, the Thigh Thinner Tush Tightener (**4T**) may be your most important exercise. It has been variously described by experts as the single most essential workout of all. Fitness authority Dr. Bob Arnot says that because the **4T** distributes "the load over so many muscle groups in the upper and lower body, it is considered the number one muscle builder of all."[20] *Men's Health* magazine says, "Nothing beats it."[21]

The **4T** absolutely builds strength you can't help but notice. Strong quadriceps (front of the upper leg) and gluteals (butt) contribute to every aspect of life allowing you to move with greater ease and endurance. What you get from the **4T** is significantly better performance in all sports. But possibly the most important **4T** benefit is enhanced knee protection.

The *Tufts University Health and Nutrition Letter* advises that, "many people could prevent osteoarthritis simply by doing simple exercises to keep the quadriceps in good shape." Strong **4T**-strengthened quadriceps control how hard feet hit the ground when walking, reducing knee joint impact. Sixty percent of knee strength comes from muscles of the thighs and therefore are your best hedge against injury.[22]

Knee protection and increased leg strength are fine but what you also want to know is how the **4T** makes you look. "Spot reducing" is an outright fallacy, but overall body-fat reduction slims thighs and reduces butt size. Stripping body fat reveals sculpted muscle and causes sagging buns to shrink. Flabby thighs diminish, revealing long, lean muscle. Don't forget that the thigh and gluteal muscles are the body's largest. Develop them and your metabolic rate rises, burning more calories even while you are at rest.

Not only is the **4T** the most important exercise in your body-strengthening repertoire it is also the most adaptable. Starting with simple and easy 45°-angle wall sit-ups and moving to fully weighted, semi-knee-bends, the **4T** can be executed precisely to your fitness level.

IMPORTANT: Knees are fragile. The best thing you can do for them is to strengthen surrounding muscle. The **4T** does this particularly well. Perform the **4T** with the knee angle at no more than 45° to 50°. Much lower than this puts pressure on the knee itself and may threaten knee injury.

BEGINNING

45° WALL SIT: Lean back against a wall and squat until your upper legs are at a 45° angle to the wall and floor. Hold while tightening your quadriceps (front of the upper leg) and glutes (butt). Keep your knees aligned with your feet. Hold for 20 seconds total challenge time. Work up to the Marvel Minute™.

ADVANCING

BODY WEIGHT: Stand with your feet hip width apart, toes pointed forward, arms out in front of you. Lower your body as if sitting in a chair. Keep your head up, eyes fixed ahead and back straight. Hold onto a chair for balance if you wish. As you become proficient, reduce your chair hold to one finger and then to no chair hold.

Spare your knees by not going much lower than knees to the end of your shoes, 45° being about right. Don't let your knees drift outside of the straight line between your hips and toes; it puts harmful pressure on the knees. Taking a full three seconds, slowly descend only to the point where your upper and lower leg are 45°. Move up, taking a full three seconds. Stop short of locking the knees. Do 10 six-second repetitions for the Marvel Minute™. Remember to keep your lower back in its natural alignment, your chest elevated and your knees above your toes.

Through all 4T free-standing movements, bring your body to just short of knees locking and then back down. Keep steady, constant weight on the thighs and glutes. Push up for three seconds then down for three seconds for approximately ten repetitions totaling the Marvel Minute™. Exhale going up and inhale on the descend.

SINGLE WEIGHT: Hold the end of a free weight in both hands, letting your arms hang straight down. Standing with your feet shoulder width apart, bend your knees until they are at a 45° angle. Keep the weight a bit forward. This keeps pressure off your knees and on your quads,

47

hams (back of the upper leg) and glutes (buttocks) where you want it. Keep your head up, eyes fixed ahead and back straight. Follow the same joint-sparing guidelines given for the Body Weight **4T.**

Keep your weight evenly distributed over your feet with your heels on the floor. Descend for three seconds, rise for three seconds. Don't lock your knees. Keep steady pressure on your gluteals (butt) and quadriceps (front of the leg). Ten six-second repetitions give you the *Marvel Minute*™.

Concentrate on keeping the natural arch of your lower back. Don't let your back or shoulders

round forward. Remember: Don't go beyond a 45° knee angle. This protects your knees.

DOUBLE WEIGHT: This is the big one, performed the same way as the Single Weight but with a weight in each hand at your sides. There is no getting around it, this exercise is challenging but the upside is trimmer thighs and a tighter tush resulting from properly sculpted muscle. Remember as you strip body fat, you reveal beautiful muscle.

Hold the free weights at your sides and somewhat forward to place the weight on your quads, glutes and hams, not

your knees. Sit down, lowering your body until your knees are about 45°. Inhale on the descend. Keep your chest and head up and your back in its natural alignment. If you're not sure how low to go, or are worried about instability at these higher hand weights, put an armless chair or stool behind you. Exhale as you rise, taking a full three seconds. Repeat 10 six-second reps for the *Marvel Minute*™.

HAMSTRING LIFT

The back of the upper leg houses a group of muscles collectively known as the hamstrings or hams. They are difficult to isolate but worth renewing because the ham shapes the back of the leg. The hamstring lift is rated one of the ten overall best exercises by *Men's Health* magazine.[23] It superbly isolates the hamstrings, works the glutes (buttocks) and has many variations, allowing you to pick your best challenge level.

Strong hams facilitate walking, running, stair climbing and any sport requiring leg movement. The ham lift is one routine sure to increase endurance. You're bound to notice the difference because it is the primary "push off" muscle.

BEGINNING

TWO-LEGGED HAMSTRING LIFT: Lie on the floor with the soles of your feet flat on the floor. Slowly push down on your feet exhaling, keeping your back straight and raising your torso until you're resting only on your feet and shoulders. Lift your pelvis as high as you can. Come

down slowly, inhaling, without allowing your glutes to touch the floor. Repeat three seconds up and three seconds down for three repetitions accumulating 20 seconds total challenge time. Go for the *Marvel Minute*™ as your conditioning allows.

ADVANCING

ONE-LEGGED HAMSTRING LIFT: Repeat the same procedure as above but use one leg. To ease intensity, keep the free leg (the one not on the floor) bent and close to your chest. For increased intensity, extend the free leg straight out. You'll notice quite a difference. Do each leg.

TWO-LEGGED CHAIR LIFT: This is the same procedure as before but both feet are resting on a chair. Push up, keeping your feet as flat as possible until your body weight is resting on your shoulders. Allow three seconds up and three seconds down for the full *Marvel Minute*™ of ten repetitions.

SINGLE-LEG CHAIR LIFT: You know the drill. By extending the free leg, you achieve greater intensity. And if that's not enough, cradle a weight across your waist, holding it with both hands, then pushing up with a single leg. This is one of the most difficult 1•1•2™ exercises.

THE BACK BUILDER

The University of Texas reports approximately 90% of all Americans experience back pain sometime in their life. This problem carries with it an estimated $50 billion per year lost-work price tag, not to mention the suffering. The torso deserves special consideration and should be considered as one unit. The back and abdominals really aren't separate but 57 different, interconnected muscles, comprising the most concentrated musculature of the body. The *Tufts University Diet and Nutrition Letter* says that if you train only the abdominals, your back slumps and posture worsens, leading to discomfort.[24] Back pain prevention and cures include:

•Losing excess weight, especially that carried in your abdomen. Although you can't "spot reduce" you can strip fat to the degree that excess weight is removed from the torso.

•Strengthening the abdominals as well as the lower back muscles. Swedish studies show that up to 40% of back strength comes from the abdominals, so they are an important part of the solution.[25]

•Choosing low-impact aerobic exercises like rollerblading, cycling and striding.

•Consistently performing lower back exercises like the Back Builder.

Building your back provides extra strength for all life's activities. Reaching, lifting, bending over, carrying and all sports are improved with a strong back. Here's how to perform the Back Builder.

BEGINNING

FRONT TORSO RAISE: Lie face down on a carpet or exercise mat with a pillow under your abdomen, your feet about ten inches apart. Cross your hands loosely behind your back. Gently raise your head and torso, keeping your eyes aimed at the floor. Use your arms at first to help push your chest off the floor if you need to. Curl up very S-L-O-W-L-Y, one vertebrae at a time. Exhale as you rise. By doing so, you work your lower back more and avoid injury. Raise your chest off the floor as high as you comfortably can. The effort should come from your lower back. Take about three seconds up and three seconds down, doing three reps for a total challenge time of 20 seconds. Inhale

as you descend. Do fewer slow repetitions if you note discomfort. Remember, you have the rest of your life to exercise so don't rush exercise advancement.

ADVANCING

SHIFTING GRAVITY: Once you have worked up to performing the back builder for the full *Marvel Minute*™ with hands at your sides, you may want to add more challenge. Do this by moving your hands to about your shoulder level as shown.

MORE: Accrue greater challenge by moving your center of gravity forward, hence giving the lower back more weight to lift. Use the pillow while resting on your abdomen and stretch your arms straight out forward. You'll notice the difference.

TUMMY TUCK

Nothing shows age quite like a bulging belly. The abdomen makes or breaks the shape of youth. A flat stomach instantly sends the shape and vigor of youth message. Of all tip-offs, a svelte body trunk is the clearest youth signal-sender.

Strong abs not only reduce abdominal girth but facilitate all movement. Getting out of bed or a chair and any lifting benefit from strong abs. Every time you pull a rope or sweep or rake, your enhanced abs are at work, easing your labors.

Internal organs are supported by the abdominal cradle. Think of your body as a chain of linking muscle, from your neck to your feet. Make the notoriously weak abdominals your strong link of the chain. Strong abs also help suppress appetite.[26] A compressed stomach magnifies fullness perception, helping to strip fat, an essential element of tummy tucking.

Since belly fat lies above and below abdominal musculature, stomach flattening demands a weight reduction to 12 to 17% body fat in men and between 19 and 24% for women. The cherished "washboard abs" are realized at between 8 and 10%, not a realistic goal.[27] Shrinking the stomach with the Tummy Tuck, on the other hand, is certainly doable. Plus, removing belly fat is healthful because studies show carrying excess midsection adipose incurs a higher heart attack incidence.

Muscle requires sufficient resistance to stimulate growth.

Doing 100 sit-ups is not what you want. Just as you don't expect biceps to show improvement if you train with dozens of repetitions at a light weight, the Tummy Tuck relies on plenty of resistance during the *Marvel Minute*™. The key to good ab strengthening is a demanding contraction that bends the spine. The primary strength training rule is: Stress muscle to the point you can't move.

Below are six Tummy Tucks, one of which you'll find sufficiently challenging so that the *Marvel Minute*™ can't be exceeded. This is what you want to genuinely build the abs.

BEGINNING

Your goal at this point is to undertrain. Add more total challenge time as soreness abates to achieve the *Marvel Minute*™.

Lie on your back with knees bent and feet flat on the floor, shoulder width apart. Rest hands on the floor, next to your hips.

Concentrating on pulling your rib cage toward your hips, S-L-O-W-L-Y curl (using no momentum) your head and shoulders off the floor two to three inches while exhaling for three seconds. Keep your hips and small of the back firmly on the floor. Hold in your stomach throughout for a superior Tummy Tuck—imagine pressing your navel. Your head should be in a neutral position, not thrust forward or back. You should be able to fit your fist between your throat and chest not pulling or yanking the head forward.

ADVANCING

The Tummy Tuck is infinitely adaptable. Adding more challenge is easy. Remember, you're looking for an exercise with a total challenge time of around a minute. The basic rule is that as you move your hands and arms away from your hips toward your head, Tummy Tucks become more difficult. Hands at your sides is easiest.

For more challenge, bend your spine with your arms crossed on your chest, then lift your shoulders from the floor while keeping the small of your back on the floor.

For more intensity, place your hands at the side of your head. Remember not to yank on your head which could result in neck injury.

Try putting your hands and arms straight back, using them as additional weight.

Last, you can always resort to the ultimate abdominal exercise which is cradling a weight on your chest to maximize your effort. Add weight as needed so you can't exceed the *Marvel Minute*™ with three seconds up and three seconds down for a total of ten reps.

ANYTIME AUGMENT: VACUUMS

Do this exercise every day at least once. The results are outstanding. You make your belly hard and suppress your appetite because the stomach is held in by a strong muscle girdle. Here's how to do *vacuums*.

Suck your abdomen in as far as you can. It's not necessary to hold your breath. Hold it tight for ten or more seconds. Your eventual goal is a total challenge time of 60 seconds. This exercise is especially helpful in targeting the poochy lower abdomen. *Vacuums* can be done anytime you're seated.

BOLDER SHOULDER CHEST BOOSTER

A superb exercise for the chest and shoulders is a modified classic pushup: the Bolder Shoulder Chest Booster (BSCB). This is a put-off for many people—especially women because it's part of the macho image associated with phys ed class and military training. Somehow the BSCB seems old-fashioned but the fact is that it's an outstanding conditioning exercise for the shoulders and chest. It also exercises the abdomen, hips and back which are challenged while moving up and down.

Toning chest muscles enhances breast size for women and chisels pecs for a great look in men. Look at the BSCB as a safe bench press. Every year dozens of people injure themselves with the bench press when the lifter becomes fatigued, allowing the weight to come crashing down on their chest. The BSCB is much more controlled and safe yet just as effective. Doing these S-L-O-W pushups can be remarkably challenging.

BEGINNING

20% BODY WEIGHT: There is no need to panic at the thought of doing BSCB since the 20% bodyweight position is not demanding. Stand two feet from the wall. Lean against it, keeping the body straight. Your body angle will be at the most 45°. Push the body out to almost vertical. Then lean the body again toward the wall, maintaining tension all the while. Repeat S-L-O-W-L-Y three times for 20 seconds accumulation. Go for the *Marvel Minute*™ as your conditioning allows.

OR

30% BODY WEIGHT: Push up pivoting (bending) from the waist.

ADVANCING

50% BODY WEIGHT: With your knees on a pillow, place your hands on the ground, pointing forward, slightly wider than shoulder width. Keep the knees together. Start with your elbows straight, but not locked. Most importantly, keep your body in a straight line from knees to head throughout the entire movement. Don't sag in the middle or raise your buttocks. Push up, exhaling, until just before elbows lock.

Then immediately down, inhaling, to where your chest is within six to ten inches of the floor and upper arms are parallel with the floor.

Move up and down slowly, with the abdominal muscles tight. Don't hold your breath. Remember power breathing: deep breaths inhaling on the descend, exhaling on the rise.

Raise yourself to all but a locked position then immediately begin down again. Again your total challenge time target is three reps for 20 seconds.

Note: Not coming down all the way to the floor is far from wimpy because it spares your rotator cuff while attaining the same muscle-strength gain. Electromyogram analysis shows the pectoralis major (the large chest muscle) tension decreases the more your elbow travels above the shoulder. The poor rotator cuff and other weak, peripheral shoulder muscles are forced to do work God never intended. It is a good way to injure yourself.[28]

66% BODY WEIGHT: This is the classic pushup position.

Legs are fully extended with toes resting on the ground and arms slightly wider than shoulder width. Use the same arm movements described in the 50% total body weight.

BENCHMARKS

- **3** S-L-O-W 6-second reps = **SATISFACTORY**

- **5** S-L-O-W 6-second reps = **GOOD**

- **10** S-L-O-W 6-second reps = **VERY GOOD**

- **15** S-L-O-W 6-second reps = **EXCEPTIONAL**

BICEPS BUILDER
FRONT OF THE ARMS

When thinking of weight lifting, the classic biceps curl comes to mind. Exerting your bicep for 60 seconds total challenge time two times a week sculpts your arm to a pleasing shape. Of all the muscles, the bicep is the most popular because it's the ultimate "beach muscle." Men develop a genuine look of strength. Women add a gentle curvature instead of the stick-thin arms of most "supermodels." Every time you lift a heavy object or open a jar, bicep strengthening will be readily apparent. Yard work, scrubbing and hefting laundry loads will be easier. Have fun. Enjoy.

BEGINNING

First of all, adjust your dumbbells to about 50% of what you can lift one time. Determine this by adjusting your dumbbell, adding weight until you can make just one or two lifts. Rest 3 to 5 minutes between tests. Then start training at half this weight. (An alternative is to start training at 10% body weight.) Stick with this weight for at least two weeks. Remember that your body is adjusting to new demands—UNDERTRAIN.

Be seated. Performing the 1•1•2™ Biceps Builder seated reduces our tendency to swing the arms when lifting the weights. 1•1•2™ Biceps Builder incorporates a twisting action that also strengthens the forearm. Begin with the weights at your side, knuckles facing outward like you were carrying a suitcase.

S-L-O-W-L-Y lift one or both weights for three seconds, exhaling as you bring them to your chest.

For three seconds, S-L-O-W-L-Y return the dumbbells back to a position just below your waist while inhaling. Some people like lifting one weight at a time. Others prefer both weights at once. It's your choice.

Starting out, your goal is 20 seconds total challenge time, three lifts. By lifting the weight to your chest but just short of perpendicular to the floor, tension is maintained. Likewise not bringing your arm all the way down so that it is again not perpendicular to the floor keeps muscle tension high, your objective.

ADVANCING

Work up to 60 seconds total challenge time which is ten 6-second repetitions. Perform repetitions to fatigue, that point where you can no longer move the weight. This may seem like a lot of effort but remember you are rebuilding your body. Musculature rebuilds with challenge so it comes back stronger than before. To achieve this, muscle must be genuinely taxed. If it feels heavy, that's the effect you want.

Don't worry if you haven't lifted weights before because you will be astonished at how rapidly a seemingly heavy weight becomes lighter due to your strength-building endeavors. In a matter of weeks, you will experience a marked difference in how much weight you can lift for 60 seconds.[29]

Moving ahead for continued bicep strength gain is simple. Merely increase the weight used. Do this in one- or two-pound increments because five pounds is usually too much.

If you find your elbow is getting sore, be sure to perform the Bicep Builder at your natural carrying angle. This usually helps. Palms parallel or perpendicular to the floor through the exercise is sometimes a bit too extreme. One free-weight advantage is allowing you to exercise at more natural body angles and positions, a weight at 45° to the floor being a good example.

45°

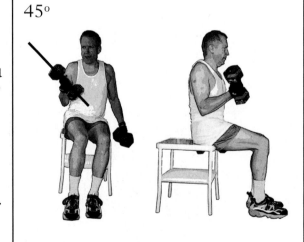

Strength training requires quality protein. Here are the best sources.

FOOD	CALORIES TO WEIGHT FOR 1 OZ	PROTEIN GRAMS PER 1 OZ
EGG WHITE (E.G., EGGBEATERS™)	15 cals	4.5g
NC MEAT LOAF	20 cals (cooked)	5.0g
MOST WHITE FISH (E.G., COD, SNAPPER)	25-30 cals (cooked)	6.0g
ULTRA LOW-FAT TOFU (EXTRA FIRM)	11 cals	2.0g
LOBSTER/SHRIMP	28 cals (cooked)	5.75g
TURKEY BREAST	44.5 cals (cooked)	8.5g
BEEF PLAIN JERKY	75 cals	14.0g
CHICKEN BREAST WITHOUT SKIN	50 cals (cooked)	8.75g
NC HiPRO DREAM	7 cals	1.0g
NO-FAT COTTAGE CHEESE	25 cals	4.0g
TERI TURKEY JERKY	70 cals	11.0g
NO-FAT CREAM CHEESE	25 cals	2.5g
FAT-FREE MILK	11 cals	1.1g
NONFAT YOGURT	15 cals	1.0g

MUSCLE REBUILD™

1 1•1•2™ **MEANS:** One minute total challenge time (TCT) for each exercise done two times per week.

2 ALWAYS WARM UP BEFORE 1•1•2™: Stride, jog in place, skip rope or high knee march in place.

3 UNDERTRAIN: The first two to four weeks, execute no more than half the Marvel Minute™, 30 seconds maximum TCT.

4 DO THE *MARVEL MINUTE*™ TO COMFORTABLY HARD EFFORT but only after four to six weeks training.

5 WHEN SORE, continue to train but moderately with light weights.

6 ALLOW 48 HOURS REST BETWEEN 1•1•2™ SESSIONS (two full days off).

7 INCREASE DUMBBELL WEIGHTS by no more than 20% a month.

8 DON'T DIET WITHOUT 1•1•2™: Restricting calories without strength training depletes muscle, lowering metabolic rate.

9 "ADVANCED TRAINING": You don't need it.

[1]"Aging Athletes Keep On Keeping On." Maria A. Fiatrone, M.D., and Leah R. Garnett, *Harvard Health Letter,* vol. 22, no. 5, March 1997, page 4, BB272

[2]"High-Protein Diets: Why They're Dangerous," Louis Aronne, M.D., *Bottom Line/ Health,* vol. 12, no. 1, January 1998, page 8, BB349.

[3]"Body Language: Everyone Should Listen," Gabe Mirkin, M.D., *The Mirkin Report,* vol. 8, no. 7, page 6, BB292.

[4]"Training Secrets of the Scientists," Larry Mengelkoch, Ph.D., University of Florida, *Runner's World,* November 1992, page 101, BB388.

[5]Ibid., page 176, BB31.

[6]"Skipping Class," Rich Cooper, *Men's Health,* September 1997, page 108, BB312.

[7]"The Ten Rules of Weight Training," Bill Dobbins, *Men's Fitness,* September 1997, page 24, BB313.

[8]"Do More Sets at the Gym," Wayne Westcott, Ph.D., *Men's Health,* September 1997, page 130, BB314.

[9]*Strength Training Past 50,* Wayne L. Westcott, Ph.D., and Thomas R. Baechle, Ed. D., Human Kinetics, Champaign, Illinois, 1998, pages 136-137, BB380.

[10]"Super Slow," Ken Hutchins, *Men's Health,* May 1994, page 51, BB324.

[11]Westcott and Baechle, op.cit., pages 134-135, BB380.

[12]"New Tricks for Old Dogs," Jeff Galloway, *Runner's World,* June 1996, pages 40-41, BB92.

[13]"Injuries on Ice," *Runners World,* vol. 33, no. 2, page 26, BB350.

[14]"Aging Athletes Keep on Keeping On," *Harvard Health Letter,* March 1997, vol. 2, no. 5, BB272.

[15]*Getting Stronger,* Bill Pearl and Gary T. Morten, Ph.D., Shelter Publications, Bolinas, California, page 366, BB74.

[16]"d'Bells are Ringing," Bill Geiger, *Prime Health and Fitness,* vol. 4, no. 4, Winter 1997, pages 42-47, BB321x.

[17]Ibid.

[18]*The New Quick Easy Way to Flatten Your Stomach for Men Over 40,* E. Dugan and editors of *Consumer Guide,* Publications Int'l., Stockie, Illinois, 1985, page 7, BB78.

[19]Westcott and Baechle, op.cit., page 130, BB380.

[20]*Dr. Bob Arnot's Guide to Turning Back the Clock,* Robert Arnot, M.D., Little, Brown & Company Limited, New York, New York, 1995, p. 340, BB33.

[21]"The Best Exercises for Every Part of You," Ken McAlpine, *Men's Health,* October 1997, page 129, BB342.

[22]"Preventing a Common Form of Arthritis With Exercise," *Tufts University Health and Nutrition Letter,* vol. 15, no. 8, page 8, BB355.

[23]McAlpine, op. cit., page 184, BB342.

[24]"A Flat, Sexy Stomach in Five Minutes!," *Tufts University Health and Nutrition Letter,* vol. 14, no. 6, August 1996, pages 6-7, BB352.

[25]"Spine Tingling," *Runner's World,* September 1998, page 45, BB358.

[26]*Lose Weight Guidebook,* Mark Bricklin, editor, Rodale Press, Emmaus, Pennsylvania, 1996, page 181, BB130.

[27]"Viewpoint," George Sheehan, M.D., *Runner's World,* July 1988, page 14.

[28]"The Right Way," Mitch Simon, Ph.D., Personal Trainer's Series, *Men's Health,* page 73, BB345A.

[29]"Weight Training Primer," *Men's Confidential,* July 1996, page 10, BB110.

[30]"Health After 50," *The Johns Hopkins Medical Letter,* December 1995, page 3, BB58.

[31]*The Health Letter,* May 1986, vol. 27, no. 9, page 1, BB58.

[32]"Health After 50," op. cit., page 3, BB58.

LIVING LONG

John Hopkins University says, "Sustained, vigorous exercise prolongs life."[30] A study from Harvard School of Public Health and Stanford School of Medicine reports individuals who continue high levels of physical activity have about half the death risk from all causes for individuals between 60 and 84.★ A large study of 10,000 men conducted by the Cooper Institute for Aerobics Research found fit men between 20 and 82 reduced their mortality risk by 44%.[31] All this makes sense because exercise most benefits the cardiovascular system which considerably reduces heart disease. By the way, if heart disease was eliminated, the average life expectancy in this country would increase by 13.9 years.[32]

★Let's think about this. From all causes? What about car accidents, for example? Yes, even car accidents are reduced. Because fitness improves balance, coordination, reaction time, mental acuity, hearing sensitivity and the plethora of other functions discussed above, fit drivers by definition are better than sedentary drivers. In fact, Formula 1 and Indy car drivers now regularly engage in aerobic and strength training, quite unlike their counterparts of 30 years ago. Indy winner and World Formula 1 champion Emerson Fitipaldi— amazingly competitive in full middle age—relentlessly lifted weights and ran. He readily acknowledged that his high level of physical fitness contributed positively to his driving performance. Why wouldn't it be the same for us mortals in our daily commute?

STRIDING, DEFLEXING AND DYNAMIC BALANCE™

Central to the Muscle Rebuild™ is aerobic conditioning. Now that you understand 1•1•2™, striding, Macro Deflexions™ (stretching) and Dynamic Balance™ (equilibrium training) complete the equation. These three activities build heart strength, increase endurance and produce the litheness of youth.

STRIDING

Done correctly, striding is hard to beat as aerobic exercise. The term "walking" doesn't aptly describe the correct activity. Walking can be leisurely while striding is brisk, hence its aerobic benefit. Striding contradicts the common misconception exercise must be a sweathog proposition. We think

that if we're not jogging, playing tennis or using a Nautilus® at the health club it's not enough. This simply is not true. Studies reported in the *Harvard Health Letter* show that striding (only 3 to 4 mph) three hours a week lowers heart attack and stroke risk a whopping 54% for those who were sedentary.[1] It even battles today's chronic fatigue syndrome plague. In studies conducted by Cathy Y. Fulcher, Ph.D., chronic-fatigue, aerobic-exercise participants felt less tired and had more energy.[2] This isn't surprising because the best time to stride is when you feel listless. When circulation slows or is concentrated on the digestive process, blood to the brain diminishes, causing exhaustion. A brisk walk fixes the problem by oxygenating the brain.[3] Keep it in mind the next time you feel sleepy at work.

Risks are minimal when comparing striding to most sports. Cycling, rollerblading and even running involve falls. Striding keeps you in control and out of the accident zone. Your brisk pace, while aerobically beneficial, still allows plenty of time for your eyes to gaze ahead for obstacles, sidewalk cracks, cars and curbs. The true wonder, though, is striding's smooth, nonjarring motion, making it the model cardiovascular enhancer.

Striding, moreover, offers advantages other aerobics simply can't match. First of all, it is nonthreatening because it's something we all know how to do. It's a private activity, if that's what you wish—no huffing and puffing in front of others.

Striding's pleasurable, whether alone or with a companion. It is cheap and you can do it anywhere at almost any time. But most of all, striding is freedom: Walk anywhere you want to go. Quite simply, it's the easiest way to become active.

EQUIPMENT

•SHOES

When it comes to equipment, striding requires little. Shoes are the most important. Don't worry too much about brands because all well-known manufacturers produce quality products. Buy for price, fit and comfort, not name. Be sure to choose shoes having plenty of toe room. It's far better buying shoes a half or whole size too big than too small. Allow at least one-half inch (1/2") between your toes and the shoe. Keep toenails short so they don't chafe each other and push the end of the shoe. Look for shoes wide at the arch. This increases striding stability.

•DON'T BUY 100% COTTON SOCKS

Buy a sock high in synthetic yarn; polyester is the best. It doesn't bunch up and is effective in wicking away moisture.

•HATS, GLOVES, COATS

When it's cold outside, wear comfortable pants and an inexpensive nylon windbreaker with sufficient layers underneath for warmth. 50% of body heat is lost through the hands and head, so when it's 50° or less outside you may want to consider a stocking cap and gloves.

•SUNSCREEN

Use it on sunny days. Substitute a broad-brimmed hat or baseball cap as you wish. We now know skin deteriorates primarily due to sun rays—protect yourself.

TECHNIQUE

One of the truly nice things about striding is you don't need to read a book on how to do it, hire a coach for training technique or practice ten years before you become good. Here are some tips you may find helpful:

•WARM UP

As you know, warming up makes joints and connective tissue more flexible and less prone to injury. It's a wake-up call to the cardiovascular system, increasing breath and heart rate for oxygenating muscle. Warm up by simply strolling at a leisurely pace for three to five minutes. Then begin striding.

•SLIGHT FORWARD LEAN

From the ankles, not the waist, lean slightly forward. This is the race-walker stance. Leaning from the waist tires the back and makes breathing harder.[4]

•ARM SWING

This makes striding a total body activity. Keep your elbows bent at an 80° to 90° angle and swing from the shoulders, bringing your hands to chest height and back to a forearm position that's parallel to the ground. Keep hands and arms relaxed, crossing the body only slightly, never with an exaggerated side-to-side motion.

•HEEL STRIKE, TOE PUSH-OFF

Don't land flat-footed. Bisect the heel curve. The effect is smooth gliding with almost no impact, a panacea for achy knees and hips. Push off with your toes for added speed and a good calf workout.

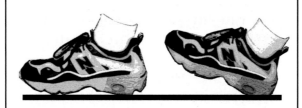

FLAT   BISECT HEEL

•SAFETY

Here are common sense guides to help keep you safe:
- Walk in the daytime or at night in well-lit areas.
- Nightwalk in groups. Notify your local police station of your group's walking time and route.
- Don't wear jewelry.
- Wear headphones only in low-traffic neighborhoods. Keep the volume low.

TARGET HEART RATE

Aerobic exercise's purpose is elevating your heart rate. Because your heart is a muscle just like any other, it profits from conditioning. But because this most important muscle is an internal organ, obviously it can't be strength-trained using weights. The alternative is elevating the heart rate for at least 30 minutes five to six times a week. This makes the heart strong, conditioning it to accrue the many advantages you have read about.[5]

The time-honored method for determining target heart rate is:

220 – AGE =
MAXIMUM HEART RATE (MHR)

MHR x 60% =
MINIMUM STRIDING HEART RATE

NO MATH

Fortunately, you can forget the math and numbers. Research shows perceived effort and talk tests work just as well as counting heartbeats using a watch or wearing a heart monitor. Here are two more important benchmarks to estimate your heart rate:

•60% to 70% MHR = CAN'T SING, CAN TALK
Your pace is sufficiently brisk to where you can't sing but can talk, about 140 steps a minute. You hear yourself breathing. You start sweating in 10 to 15 minutes. Perceived effort is PLEASANT EXERTION.

•70% to 80% MHR = SHORT TALK BURSTS
Ongoing, steady conversation is uncomfortable but short talk bursts are okay. You are breathing hard but are short of air hunger. You feel your heart pumping. You start sweating in five to ten minutes. Perceived effort is COMFORTABLY HARD.

You want to stride between 60% and 80% MHR. Your bottom 60% MHR minimum is: CAN'T SING, CAN TALK and PLEASANT EXERTION. At this level and above, you're pumping blood nicely and doing a good job exercising your heart.

Up to 80% MHR, the heart is still in the aerobic range: SHORT TALK BURSTS and COMFORTABLY HARD EFFORT. This means blood flow still carries plenty of oxygen to the muscles. Do not enter the can't talk, distinctly hard work/pain zones of 80% plus MHR. All below 80% MHR feel like a nice challenge without grinding effort.

Once you master the perceived effort, target-heart-range technique, there's no need to measure a course. Simply stride for 30 or more minutes at your perceived effort target heart range of CAN'T SING, CAN TALK for full aerobic conditioning.[6]

INCREASING INTENSITY

As you become more conditioned, you will find it more difficult to achieve desired perceived effort levels. You'll find striding comes easier. This is called the training effect. It means you must work harder to elevate your heart rate because you are becoming increasingly fit. Congratulations. Here are methods to increase intensity.

•THINK QUICK STEPS
Short, quick steps get you going faster. Your stride spread is likely to be six to eight inches from the front of your trailing foot to the heel of your lead leg. Short, quick steps increase calorie

burn and reduce injury risk.[7] To increase speed, feet should land practically one in front of the other almost in a straight line, race-walk fashion.[8]

•HEAD FOR THE HILLS
Hills are your friends. Seek them out. Striding up a hill is superb for increasing rigor. Most streets incline 10% to 25%. A mere 10% incline increases calorie burn by 50%. A 20% to 25% incline doubles calorie burn and then some. Caution: Head down hills more slowly than you charged up. Take short steps, otherwise joint jarring can cause soreness, especially to the knees.

•PACK SOME WEIGHT
Increasing the weight you bear while walking strengthens bones.[9] The simplest and probably most effective way to add striding rigor is by carrying a weighted backpack. Quality sporting goods stores have ergonomically designed backpacks that effectively distribute load. Use barbell plates for weight. Buy them in no more than five-pound increments because you are subjecting bones, muscle, ligaments and tendons to forces they're not used to. Ratchet up weight slowly. A mere 15-pound backpack at 4 mph increases calorie burn by 20% for a 150-pound person.[10] Weighted vests are effective as well. If you feel inclined, one- or two-pound hand weights are okay but never use ankle weights as they cause injuries.[11]

•SWING YOUR ARMS
You burn 5-10% more calories and get an upper body workout as well when you swing your arms. To reduce fatigue, keep hands unclenched.

•RACE-WALK 90 SECONDS
Occasionally throw in a race-walk sprint of 90 seconds. Race-walking is going as fast you can without breaking into a jog. Stroll for 15 to 30 seconds until you re-cover. Then commence regular striding.

KEEPING IT FUN

With all this talk of frequency, equipment and intensity, it's easy to lose sight of the fact striding is fun. Here are tactics to keep striding entertaining:

•TAKE A FRIEND
Companionship is a fine motivator. Stories, events and good old-fashioned gossip are worthy topics. Scheduling times for regular walks with friends may give you the extra push to get out there. Not all friends are people. Consider getting a dog. You'll learn why the old saw "man's best friend" is true.

•VARY ROUTES
Walk all routes of your neighborhood. Drive to other parts of the city, exploring your town like never before. You'll enjoy the discovery.

•WALK ONE WAY

In terms of a city, walking three or four miles one way covers a lot of city distance. Most metropolises are rarely more than ten miles across. If you decide to walk four miles in one direction, you see half the town. It gives you a pleasant sense of freedom and adventure. Walk one way and take a cab/bus back or call your spouse or friend for pickup. End your walk by having breakfast or lunch.

•WALK TO DESTINATIONS

When on a vacation, consider slowing your pace and doing city travel by walking. While the urban sprawl of cities like LA don't make it a good candidate, most cities are ideally suited to destination walking. You won't gain weight on vacations with sufficient destination walking. Walk that mile or two or more to the restaurant of choice and take a cab home.

Do likewise for trips to zoos, museums and other destinations.

•READ A BOOK

Buy a good, light Walkman® for your favorite music. Better, enjoy a book while striding. Make an agreement with yourself to listen only when striding. Learning what happens in the next chapter is a motivator getting you out the door. Your local library has books on tape for loan. No need to spend your hard-earned money. How long have you wanted to read *Pride and Prejudice, Moby Dick* or *Don Quixote de La Mancha?*

•BUY A HEART MONITOR

It's been just a few years since continuous heart monitoring could be done only in a laboratory. Now, relatively inexpensive heart monitors are available. Use one as your coach to give you striding intensity information. See it as a training partner to motivate you and

assess effort at any moment during your workout. You may find the heart monitor is the best motivator of all. There's something gratifying about knowing precisely where you're at throughout your striding session.

EXERCISE AUGMENTS

A trick to facilitating exercise is learning to lower your perceived effort. Most of us find carving out 10 to 15 minutes a few times a day easier than committing, say, 30 to 60 uninterrupted minutes. Overweight walkers who break up their workouts into two 15-minute bouts nearly double their weekly mileage because they are inclined to go more frequently and faster compared with those who do it in a single 30-minute walk. Likewise, twice as many people stick to several shorter workouts versus a single long one.[12] It makes sense. Wouldn't you rather start exercising knowing that you will be done in ten minutes instead of 60?

The overriding augment technique is: *Throughout the day look for exercise opportunities.* Lists can be boring but look through this one to see if any of these spark interest:

•WALK TO LUNCH
Don't hit the office building cafeteria unless you decide to take the stairs. Better, walk to a restaurant six blocks away. Going each way adds a mile to your physical workout on a daily basis.

•WALK THE STAIRS
Okay, your office is on the 40th floor and you don't want to risk a myocardial infarction, so do this. Take the elevator to the 38th floor and walk the last two flights. It's a terrific workout. Who knows, you may work up to 10 or 20 flights. It sounds like a lot but you'll be surprised what you can do when you're in shape. Take your time, don't run. Make exercise aerobic versus anaerobic and save the sweat.

•PARK A DISTANCE FROM YOUR OFFICE
Don't park in your building parking area. If striding is what you enjoy versus stair-climbing, park a distance from your office and hoof it to work.

George Foreman relates this story: "I remember one time Mohammed Ali was in Archie Moore's training camp, and it drove Ali mad that Archie demanded they rake leaves and wash dishes. But Archie knew little things like that would create muscles."[13] The fundamental equation for paring poundage is: Consume fewer calories while burning more. Our bodies are constructed to accomplish amazing feats of work. But the Industrial Revolution and all that followed has made us sedentary. We view the world from our armchair via TV and the Internet. Great for leisure, bad for the body. The answer is working more physical activity directly into our daily lives.

Augmenting reflects a developing new attitude. You're making exercise fit into, not around, your life. Your life will revolve much more around exercise, not the other way around.

Here are more suggestions. The primary guide is making additional physical activities part of daily living. Yes, it is more work but that's the whole idea. For apropos weight maintenance, additional physical activity is the key instrument for burning unwanted fat. It's the law of nature, irrefutable for those who remain slim and fit. So, in addition to your daily workouts, use these augments.

Not all these augments are for you. But adopting even two or three means faster weight loss and sustained maintenance.

•DO ALL HOME MAINTENANCE
Painting, window washing, car washing, rug shampooing and all the rest not only save you a remarkable amount of money but make you fitter and burn calories.

• DO YARD WORK

Some of us have forgotten the pleasures of gardening and yard work. It's cathartic. You not only burn calories but watch with joy as your yard takes shape and your garden grows.

• CLEAN SOMETHING

Maybe it's time to finally clean the attic, organize that closet or wax that floor. As with yard work, doubling your cleaning activities not only gives you a spotless house but provides a psychologically satisfying sense of control over your environment. Do it for the sake of physical activity and psychological respite.

• DO THE DISHES BY HAND

You're moving your upper body, bending and reaching. You're giving yourself a moderate workout that burns an extra 100 or so calories planting yourself in front of the TV never accomplishes.

• IRON

Just as Archie Moore knew that little things create muscle, ironing accomplishes just that. You stand on your feet, you move your arms, you put clothes away and—maybe most important—you have a sense of fulfillment. It's not high tech but when you iron, you move.

• INCONVENIENT CONVENIENCES

Move the phone so you must walk to the far end of the house or upstairs to get it. Use the farthest bathroom.

• BIKE TO WORK

This might sound hard core to you but in the greater Seattle area, where I live, hundreds do it daily, particularly in the summer. You may even get to work faster.

The point: Work physical activity into your daily routine. The reality is that calories burn according to the Newtonian definition of work ... the expenditure of energy. Without an increased level of physical activity, fat returns with a vengeance.

THE CREATIVITY BOOST

George Sheehan, M.D.—the premier philosopher of exercise—said, "The time I spend alone and in motion sets the creative juices flowing. New ideas and old ideas in new words begin to sweep by my stream of consciousness."[14] The ancient Greeks coupled walking with thinking as a means of mind stimulation.[15] The Greeks knew what they were doing because modern science confirms the creativity-exercise bond. A study published in the **British Journal of Sports Medicine** detailed findings proving exercisers have higher creativity levels than their sedentary peers.[16] You'll be surprised what you discover on your walks.

67

SO YOU DON'T WANT TO EXERCISE?

I t happens. Some days you don't want to exercise. Here are nudges to keep you going. Some sound silly but they work because your resistance is mostly mental.

• **SET OUT YOUR EXERCISE CLOTHES THE NIGHT BEFORE.** Having your set-up ready to go helps spur action.

• **ENVISION HOW GREAT YOU'LL FEEL WITH EXERCISE.** Take a moment to consider all the worth accruing to you in health and well-being. And for a real push, consider your longer, vigorous life.

• **PROGRAM YOURSELF.** Say you'll press on for a certain period (10, 20 minutes) no matter how slowly, then you'll reassess.

• **BRIBERY.** Promise yourself a reward if you complete your exercise, e.g. a skinny double tall Starbucks latté and the magazine of your choice.

• **NEGOTIATE.** Say you'll do half of 1•1•2™ then decide on doing more. Or you'll stride for five minutes and decide to turn around or not.

• **FOLLOW THROUGH.** Work in enough augments where skipping exercise amounts to little, if any, actual lost calorie burn. Decide on which you'll do and follow through.

• **GUTCHECK.** That's right. Sometimes it's a matter of discipline. No cajoling. No psycho-tricks. No excuses. It sometimes boils down to the Nike slogan: "Just Do It." Not too sophisticated maybe, but sometimes if you tell yourself to quit whining, the job gets done quickly and with surprisingly little effort.

• **WHEN YOU SIMPLY DON'T WANT TO DO IT, DON'T.** Take two straight days off but set a clear goal: "Friday walk the park for 45 minutes. I'm marking it on my calendar and laying out my clothes now. Friday is my big day."

POST this page where you'll see it as you duck out the door to avoid exercising.

MACRO DEFLEXIONS™

T he average adult's flexibility declines about 5% every decade.[17] Flexibility is one of the three fitness components which include strength and stamina. Correct, regular stretching increases coordination, agility and expands the body's freedom of movement. Tendons and ligaments grow stronger which helps prevent musculoskeletal injuries.[18] Muscles even grow stronger when stretched.[19] Two studies published in *Behavioral Therapy and Experimental Psychiatry* reveal stretching helps reduce anxiety, muscle tension and blood pressure, and slows breathing rate.[20] Research even suggests that lower back pain, which afflicts millions of Americans, could be eliminated or prevented by stretching the lower back and the hamstrings.[21]

A good stretch is a wonderful way to help your body move more painlessly and easily through all activities at every life's stage. You'll enjoy more freedom that a wider range of motion affords. The term Macro Deflexions™ (MDs for short) derives from the nature of these specialized stretches. MDs are designed to deflex several muscles at once. Just three Macro Deflexions™ are required to stretch your body. The whole MD process only requires about four minutes ... so there's little excuse for not doing them.

Stretch only when warm.

The *UC Berkeley Wellness Letter* says, "cold muscles are more likely to tear than warmer ones, so warming up is an important way to prevent injuries."[22] The warm-up recommendations come from excellent sources and you should follow them—no matter what your high school coach said.

THE PRAGMATIC 30

Muscle tissue responds positively when challenged for one minute two times a week. Stretching muscles out (deflexing) is similar. Thirty seconds stretching—*total challenge time* (TCT)—is about what you need.[23]

How you accumulate 30 seconds deflex time is important. A good cycle is three seconds stretching, three seconds off. If you hold a stretch for a solid 30 seconds your musculature will try to protect itself against overextension. Exercise physiologists prefer short, repeated challenge times. The Macro Deflexion™ rule is:

Hold the MD for three seconds (TCT), then three seconds off. Challenge to mild discomfort.

The to-mild-discomfort advisory is new. It does not mean stretching to the pain threshold. It does mean working muscles, joints, ligaments, tendons and cartilage to a point of heightened body awareness. Stretching to the extent of faint perception does little good. Think about this. The body does not respond to trifling effort. Body response is a function of stimulus. No stimulus, no response. Productive stretching requires a pull on joints and muscles that effectively increases their range of motion. That isn't accomplished with stretches so subtle as to produce no real feeling. Deflexing the body to mild discomfort does something. You feel it working.

Besides being quick and simple, Macro Deflexions™ stretch several muscle groups at once. Your three MDs are the **Cat, Bobsled** and **T-Reach.** Each MD should be done in this order for maximum benefit.

Remember that these stretches are meant to be done after you've warmed up.

CAT

The Cat copies the feline stretch we have seen our pets do. Kneel on the floor as illustrated. With your legs underneath you, reach forward with both arms extended forward while touching your palms to the floor. Reach as far as you can exhaling, holding for three seconds. Relax for three seconds inhaling, then reach forward as far as possible, again holding for three seconds. Repeat for ten cycles, totaling 30 seconds Total Challenge Time (TCT).

BOBSLED

This MD looks like a bobsled. Lie on your stomach and draw your feet toward your glutes. Bring your arms behind and grab your ankles. Exhaling, gently pull your feet to the point of mild discomfort. Hold for three seconds. Relax and inhale for three seconds. Repeat ten times, accumulating 30 seconds Total Challenge Time (TCT).

In time, you'll be ready for the next step which is continuing to hold your ankles as you gently raise your upper body and legs off the floor. This takes some practice.

Repeat the MD hold-relax cycle of three-seconds deflexion by pulling on your legs, then relaxing a bit for three seconds off.

T-REACH

The T-Reach comes from the Hatha yoga twisting triangle. Sit on the floor with your left leg extended and your left foot touching your inner left thigh. Reach forward with your left hand as far as you can. At the same time, twist your torso, reaching back as far as possible with your right arm.

This brings the shoulders into alignment with the stretched-out leg. Swing the torso around as far as possible short of pain but achieving slight discomfort. Hold for three seconds, relax and repeat. You will feel the pull in the back of your legs, shoulders and torso.

Repeat with your right hand to your left foot as shown.

Repeat this MD with the right leg forward and the right hand forward. Try it with the left hand forward to the right foot. Once acclimated, remember to stretch to mild discomfort to achieve full-range motion.

Once you complete a mere four minutes of Macro Deflexions™, the entire body has been gently pulled, accruing all the benefits given before: increased coordination with added range of movement, stronger ligaments and tendons plus reduced anxiety, muscle tension and blood pressure.

DYNAMIC BALANCE™

Every waking moment you employ your sense of balance. You use it constantly when walking, running, driving and playing all sports (golf, tennis, ping pong and pool) to literally stay upright and avoid injury. Your brain continually monitors the position of your head and body with the vestibular system. This inner ear organ senses movement and relays the information to the brain which signals your body to do what is necessary to maintain balance.

As we age, our equilibrium diminishes. Fortunately, we can reverse vestibular system deterioration and even improve it with proper training. Balance practice is important because UCLA gerontologist Dr. Roy Walford says balance " ... is clearly the best among the do-it-yourself biomarker (age) measurements."[24]

Try this Dynamic Balance™ test. Stand on a hard surface (not on a rug) with both feet together. Lift your dominant leg (right leg if you're right-handed) off the ground and slightly bend the other (nondominant) leg. Don't move the foot you are standing on. Close your eyes. How many seconds can you stand this way before putting down your second foot to avoid falling? Score your biological age:

AGE	SECONDS
20	30
30	25
40	15
50	10
60	5
70	4
80	2

Retune your vestibular system with the test you just performed: Dynamic Balance™. Practice standing with bent knee on your nondominant leg. Lift the other, dominant leg and close your eyes. Repeat this exercise until you have accumulated:

- 15 seconds *total challenge time* each exercise session for a month.
- 20 seconds *total challenge time* each exercise session the second month.
- 30 seconds *total challenge time* each exercise session the third month on.
- If you wish, increase your accumulation to 60 seconds.

1•1•2™ also improves balance because it strengthens the stabilizing muscles that keep us erect. Strong gluteals (rear), hamstrings (back of the thigh) and quadriceps (front of the thigh) assist equilibrium. With practice, you will probably be able to stand one-footed with the eyes closed for at least 20 seconds, the equivalent of a 35-year-old.

EVERY TIME YOU MACRO DEFLEX™, DYNAMIC BALANCE™.

STRIDING, DEFLEXING AND DYNAMIC BALANCE™

1 STRIDE
Pace yourself to a point where you CAN'T SING, CAN TALK. Walking briskly, swing your arms.

2 INCREASE STRIDING INTENSITY
Try simply walking faster. Carry barbell plates in a good, ergonomically designed backpack. Throw in an occasional 90-second race-walk sprint.

3 STRIDING IS FUN
Take a friend. Vary routes. Try a one-way trip and cab back. In no/low traffic areas, use a Walk/Discman® for books and music. Buy a heart monitor for maximized feedback.

4 BOOST EXERCISE MOTIVATION
Lay out clothes the night before. Try exercising for five minutes before deciding to stop. Substitute with augments. Simply decide to gut it out.

5 AUGMENT YOUR DAY
If you can't stride, augment for a total of 30 minutes. Augment even when you do stride. Take the stairs. Do your own yardwork and maintenance. Bike or walk all or part way to work.

6 DEFLEX IN ORDER
Start with the (1)CAT, move through the (2)BOBSLED and finish with the (3)T-REACH.

7 3 SECONDS ON, 3 SECONDS OFF
After warming up, deflex to mild discomfort with three seconds challenge and three seconds off.

8 PRAGMATIC 30
When stretching in three-second increments, accumulate 30 seconds *total challenge time.*

9 DYNAMIC BALANCE™
after Macro Deflexing™ by lifting your nondominant leg, bending the standing leg and keeping your eyes closed. Accumulate 30 seconds *total challenge time.*

REMEMBER
You make your decision to enter BodyRenewal™ when you fully understand all its techniques and benefits. Make no judgment until you are entirely apprised and satisfied. Your decision point comes at the end of the Dauntless Spirit of Resolve chapter, ahead.

[1] "Putting One Foot in Front of the Other," *Harvard Health Letter,* April 1997, vol. 22, no. 6, page 6, BB294.

[2] "Battle Fatigue," *Men's Health,* November 1997, vol. 12, no. 9, page 144, BB304.

[3] *Fat, Fat, Fat,* Jack D. Osman, Ph.D., Fat Control, Inc., Towson, Maryland, 1984, page 77, BB84.

[4] "Walking," *Health,* HIC-19L, Boulder, Colorado, 1995, BB299.

[5] *Heart Rate Monitor Book,* Sally Edwards, Polar CIC Inc., Port Washington, New York, 1993, page 99, BB73, and BB331.

[6] "How Hard Are You Working?" *UC Berkeley Wellness Letter,* December 1995, page 6, BB303; "Walking" op. cit., BB299.; "Walk Your Way to Health and Fitness," op. cit., page 50, BB295; *Precision Walking,* Mark Fenton and Dave McGovern, copyright by *Walking Magazine, Inc.,* September 1995, page 5, 16, BB293.

[7] Fenton and McGovern, op. cit., page 39, BB293.

[8] "Four Ways to Test Your Walk," Maggie Spilner, *Prevention,* October 1996, page 118, BB297.

[9] "Tone Your Bones," *Prevention,* November 1996, page 77, BB301.

[10] "Better Walking Workouts," *The Wellness Engagement Calendar, 1998,* Palm Coast, Florida, 1997, Health Letter Associates, page 8, BB302.

[11] "Weight a Little," *UC Berkeley Wellness Letter,* October 1996, page 6, BB333

[12] "Should Your Workout Be Shorter?" Michelle Stanten, *Prevention,* September 1997, vol. 49, no. 9, page 68, from studies presented at the American College of Sports Medicine annual meeting May 1997, BB327.

[13] Fitness with Foreman and FloJo," *USA Weekend,* October 13-15, 1995, page 7.

[14] "The Best of Sheehan," *Runner's World,* August 1995, page 24, BB37.

[15] *Fat Fat Fat,* Jack D. Osman, Fat Control, Inc., Towson, Maryland, 1984, page 78, BB84.

[16] It's Good For the Head," *Runner's World,* March 1998, vol. 33, no. 3, page 25, BB406.

[17] "Stretching Your Health Horizons," Robert C. Adkins, M.D., *Health Revelations,* vol. 5, no. 6, June 1997, page 4, BB361.

[18] *Biomarkers,* William Evans, Ph.D., and Irwin H. Rosenberg, M.D., with Jacqueline Thompson, Fireside (Simon & Schuster), New York, New York, 1991, page 109, BB75.

[19] "Stretching to Get Stronger," *Men's Fitness,* vol. 5, no. 6, June 1999, page 86, BB478.

[20] "Stretching, the Truth," *UC Berkeley Wellness Letter,* November 1994, page 4, BB362.

[21] "To Stretch or Not To Stretch?" *Tufts University Health and Nutrition Letter,* December 1997, page 4, BB363.

[22] "Stretching, the Truth," op. cit., page 4, BB364.

[23] *Physical Therapy,* September 1994, BB363.

[24] *The 120 Year Diet,* Roy L. Walford, M.D., Simon & Schuster, New York, New York, 1986, page 145, BB166.

SURROUNDINGS MANAGEMENT™

Each day, we consciously and subconsciously act on millions of stimuli. The eye sees road curves so we steer through them; a TV ad stimulates us to buy a VCR; we instinctively blow on an especially hot cup of coffee; we buy a magazine at the checkout counter because it's piqued our interest; we empty the container of ice cream because it IS there; and on and on. No matter what our positive intent, surroundings can destroy our BodyRenewal™ because environment is powerful. This reality has dramatic effect on our shape and vigor of youth goals, particularly long term. Diet expert J.T. Cooper, M.D., observes, "Numerous scientific experiments have pointed out time and time again that the surroundings and external influences on fat people have more to do with their problem eating behavior than internal cues of hunger."[1]

Obviously fat stripping isn't completed nor the longterm shape of youth sustained in a vacuum. Physical settings play an appreciable role in fat-stripping achievement and maintenance. Ronette Kolotkin, Ph.D., an obesity researcher at Duke University, says, "I have an arrangement with my husband, who eats sweets on a daily basis, to keep them hidden from me. It's an arrangement that works well."[2] With a little analysis, Dr.

Kolotkin's statement is quite telling. Even as a highly trained professional, she has to plan with those around her to sustain her shape and vigor of youth culture. Now if a Ph.D. in weight management has her husband hide the candy, what must we do to control our environment?

An overload of appealing temptations placed prominently throughout the house (bowls of nuts and candy, half gallons of Dreyer's Grand® ice cream in the freezer, packs of sliced, fatty pastrami in the refrigerator) serve as derailers. A grousing spouse, angry because your fat stripping has disrupted the normal family-eating pattern, does you no service either. Being nettled at work about your little lunches of fruit and yogurt doesn't help. Inadvertently sabotaging yourself by unaware grocery shopping that brings home defeating foods wreaks havoc on your youth connection lifetime body plan.

Fortunately, a measure of planning can positively reconfigure your physical and emotional environments in a way that makes home and work boosts to your shape and vigor of youth lifetime plan instead of banes.

YOU WANT PEOPLE, PLACES AND PROCESSES MOTIVATING YOU TO STAY THE BodyRenewal™ COURSE LIFELONG.

If the people in your life encourage you to seek and maintain the shape and vigor of youth, the odds for a lifetime youth connection are considerably improved. When the places of your life are conducive to sustaining the shape of youth because needless temptations have been removed, you are particularly assisted in your link to the BodyRenewal™. When personal processes like shopping, consciously utilizing the Miracle 20™ and other aids to the shape and vigor of youth are a part of your life, the ease of preserving BodyRenewal™ increases.

Good Surroundings Management™ creates the ultimate basis for your lifetime youth connection. It fills your life with positive people, places and processes. Surroundings Management™ puts you in motion to have the shape and vigor of youth for the rest of your life: improving, changing, learning, practicing and experimenting—unfolding your potential by living in the now and conceding nothing.

It's all a matter of skill. Learn the shape and vigor of youth Surroundings Management™ information to the point of recall. Be patient with yourself as you practice new behaviors. Then, develop self-awareness to monitor behavior. You may do it wrong before doing it right. That's normal. But you will see encouraging progress.

Our values show up in how we use our time and spend our money. If we go back to the same kind of food in the same places at the same times, for sure the weight lost will be regained. Doing the same thing over and over but expecting different results is delusional. A new life's process builds the new shape and vigor of youth culture. Stop thinking about crash diets, faddish exercise machines and the latest pop-psych weight-loss book. Consider these Surroundings Management™ suggestions carefully and choose those that will best suit your needs. Naturally, you can't employ every one of these suggestions when entering the BodyRenewal™ but select those that appeal to you and a few that stretch the envelope, unfolding your potential.

SURROUNDINGS MANAGEMENT™: PEOPLE

You would think all who know you would favor you having the shape and vigor of youth. Surprise. The first time out with family or friends when you order a pizza with no cheese, hilarity will reign. Let's be honest. Ordering a pizza without cheese is funny. Or as a friend said, "What's pizza without cheese? A hamburger without the meat?"

At a party, when you pass on the potato chips and California dip and home in on the veg-

etable tray then take the skin and the buttery *coq au vin* sauce off a chicken breast at dinner, eyebrows will rise. When they then see you dress your chicken with salt, pepper and a bit of juice from the fruit salad, you may encounter more than a few smirks.

There's no getting around it. You may feel odd, deprived and even be the object of jocularity. "Health nut." "Obsessive." "Midlife crisis."

But you have loftier goals in mind. You are in the midst of changing the way you conduct your life. You're forgoing the old, unhealthy behavior for new and unsullied ways of living. You are doing now what they will be doing in five to ten years or they will be suffering the consequences of ill health and amplified aging. Meantime, you can downplay people problems by doing some culture building.

People, as you know, have a huge impact on your behavior. "Over one-third told us their family and friends interfered with their efforts," says Leslie Siegel, Ph.D., co-author of a Yale University study of 224 men and

women dieters. Since family, friends and co-workers are the most influential stimuli of your life, begin Surroundings Management™ with people. It's the best place to start because if your relationships are out of sync with your youth connection goal, attainment is nearly impossible.

> **TO MAXIMIZE YOUR *SHAPE AND VIGOR OF YOUTH*, GET PERMISSION TO PROCEED WITH *Body-Renewal*™ FROM FAMILY AND FRIENDS.**

FAMILY

There might be two cooks in the kitchen and certainly two menus being executed. The family is having macaroni and cheese while you're eating Warm Black Bean Salad. Families develop eating habits cast in concrete. Disrupt them and there is family disruption. So when you start stripping fat, there is disturbance to your family's living patterns. The result is foreseeable. If you get negativity long and loud enough, your fat stripping spins into disarray. Without family support, your program flounders. Your fat stripping and exercise are seen as impositions, stretching family members' patience.

The secret is developing a favorable attitude toward Body-Renewal™. The best way to win over your family is by explaining the plan's advantages from your family's standpoint—not a diatribe on what you get. For example, rather than saying, "I want to have more energy," you might say, "I'll have more energy. It could mean that we can do more things together." The youth connection raises your energy paycheck for the benefit of those around you. Here are more boons others may reap by you achieving the shape and vigor of youth.

●MORE CARING
An improved sense of self-worth can increase your reservoir of kindness and regard, a heightened giving of self.

●INCREASED ENERGY
Increased energy means you are a more lively and productive contributor.

●INCREASED OPTIMISM
As you discovered in the Muscle Rebuild™ benefits, a good conditioning regimen elevates spirits and enhances optimism.

●SOURCE OF PRIDE
A dumpy husband or frumpy wife is not as desirable as a spouse or parent who radiates a flourishing physique. Go ahead and say it, "You'll be proud of me."

●WHOLE-FAMILY REWARD
Why not reward the entire family when you attain your goals? Make it a family win: camping trip, a day at the zoo, a day's shopping spree or (the big one) a trip to Disneyland.

You may think of other reasons to give your family for you seeking the youth connection. Share these. Otherwise,

opposition to your sometimes disruptive behaviors may mount. Thoroughly explain why you're working toward the Body-Renewal™. It makes a difference in others' attitudes.

Once you have shared what you are going to do and why, make clear how your family can help. Here's how:

●BE PATIENT
You may be the source of inconvenience. Food shopping will change; you will be eating differently from the family; and schedules may diverge because you will be getting up earlier than usual to exercise and may be going to bed earlier. These kinds of things are potentially annoying so discuss the patience issue up front.

●NO NEEDLING
This is important. You are the easy target of humor, especially when you sit down to eat. NeoCuisine™ looks good, tastes great, is filling and satisfying, but let's be truthful. Eating a plateful of NC salad doesn't

match most people's idea of dinner.

- **OFFER ENCOURAGEMENT**

What you need is assurance. Support is what keeps you moving forward. It maintains your equilibrium. Remind your family that criticism angers but compliments encourage you to stay the course.

IMPORTANT NOTE: If your mate decides to join you in BodyRenewal™ that's easily accomplished by doubling the NeoCuisine™ portion. HOWEVER, no one should strip fat without exercise. To join you in the Body Renewal™, your partner must engage in the Muscle Rebuild™ for their health's sake. When faced with reduced calories and no exercise, the body absorbs muscle for energy which diminishes the body's metabolic rate. Also, as a father of teenage girls I strongly discourage teenagers stripping fat using NeoCuisine™.

Given their impressionable age and inclination toward anorexia and bulimia, teenagers should diet seriously only under a physician's care.

CO-WORKERS AND FRIENDS

Those other than family also impact your aims. Not everyone needs to know but there are a few who must so they can be a positive influence. Some co-workers will spot your modified behaviors, especially at lunch and after-work happy hours. Explain to them, as you did your family, what you are doing and why. Many benefits that accrue to family can likewise favor friends and co-workers. Tune them into your plan so they become allies. Undue pressure can up calorie intake, scuttling your shape and vigor of youth plan. The last thing you need is heckling or motivation-sapping

indifference.

When you give the reasons why you want to fat-strip your body, be sure to indicate your reasons go beyond vanity and include such laudable goals as better health and more energy. Friends and key co-workers will applaud your efforts toward legitimate self-improvement. The direct solicitation of their help is important because it closes the psychological contract.

SUPPORT PERSON

While you are in the Body-Renewal™, the support person interacts with you, ideally on a daily basis. The phone is an excellent interaction tool. The support person can help by encouraging and praising, suggesting, listening empathetically, withholding judgment or criticism, dining participation and exercising if you both wish.

Your role is to maintain an enthusiastic, success-oriented attitude and to avoid complaining, rejecting suggestions out of

78

hand and consciously or unconsciously seeking permission to backslide. Your support person is there to help; don't trivialize his or her efforts.

SURROUNDINGS MANAGEMENT™: PLACES

Once family, friends and co-workers are part of your youthful shape and vigor culture, it's time to organize your environment. We are not dealing with casual motivations. Breathing aside, we are coping with the most fundamental human drive. Of all our needs, the motivation to preserve ourselves by eating is the most elemental. This primary stimulus compels us to behavior extremes. Take them seriously. If you don't, you simply won't win the fat fight.

Although the following youthful shape and vigor culture-building places list may

appear excessive on some points, it isn't. Read them and use them. You will find that they help control your primeval raging appetite and assist you in attaining the shape and vigor of youth.

You don't need to do all these things but doing as many as are practical helps.

• **SEPARATE FOOD STORAGE**
Preserve your NeoCuisine™ inventory by creating separate food storage. Clean out a cupboard and use it exclusively. Reserve, if possible, an entire shelf of the refrigerator solely for your foods. Your own food storage keeps you organized. Restrict "food hunting" to your areas to minimize temptation.

• **OUT OF SIGHT, OUT OF MIND**
If family members enjoy high-temptation foods like Pepperidge Farm® Chunky Chocolate Chip Cookies, ask that they be put out of sight. Keep that devil's food cake someone brought home in

the cupboard. Conspicuous temptations induce you to have "only one" that we know grows to two and three and so on. This measure may seem overmuch but don't needlessly tempt yourself while on the path to the shape and vigor of youth. As you see, family cooperation is critical to your success.

• **FRESH FRUIT**
Set out a creative bowl of fresh fruit. At any time, your supermarket has four apple varieties, two kinds of pears, oftentimes two or three orange and tangerine varieties plus kiwis and all the rest. Buy every kind of fresh berry in season. Spend a little more buying fruit out of season. Year around hot house raspberries are pricey but NeoCuisine™ is inexpensive so total food expenditure does not rise.

•LEFTOVERS MANAGEMENT

Clear serving bowls from the table right away, putting leftovers in nonsee-through containers. Otherwise those delicious barbecue spare ribs the family enjoyed might start a feeding frenzy by you tomorrow.

•ON THE ROAD

The trouble with traveling is boredom. Since you are confined with little to do, your thoughts can't help but run to food. If you're flying, you are held hostage to what is served unless you take precautionary measures. It's battlefield eating. When booking your ticket, ask the agent what food options are available. Low-cal vegetarian is a good choice.

Traveling by car, you are the captive of roadside mini-marts specializing in fat food. These convenience stores purvey almost nothing good if you are intent on stripping fat. Take proper offensive action: baby carrots, apple varieties, fat/

sugar-free yogurt, jerky (the solid meat strip variety, not the chopped, processed type), an energy bar, air-popped popcorn bag, cherry tomato carton, hard candies, real fruit leather, dried fruits, no-fat tortilla or potato chips or pretzels, diet drinks, a grilled vegetable sandwich and ...

•PARTY VENUES

These are difficult to handle. Here are strategies that can help. If you feel comfortable, call the hostess ahead to assure one or two low-fat alternatives. Simply say certain foods don't agree with you. Another good way to manage these predicaments is eating beforehand so you enter the seductive situation satisfied and in command. Last, if decorum allows, arrive late and leave early. Nibble discreetly, eating just enough to maintain social probity. You may want to increase your calorie allowance for this day only by 200 or 300 calories.

A good way to slow party eating is using your nondominant hand for food and drink because it helps keep you aware of behavior. When reaching for food, you think about it a bit more. Confine eating to what you can hold in that hand, such as shrimp, vegetables, fruit or diet beverage.

•SIGN POINTS

Place visual reminders in strategic areas for daily viewing of what you want and how you're getting it. Three-by-five cards work well. This old chestnut calms emotions, quiets the *primeval raging appetite* and assists you in staying the course. Signs must be changed every week so they retain attention-grabbing quality. Try simply moving them around and changing their colors.

See the next page for helpful sign ideas.

SIGN TOPICS

Your quantified goals

Your favorite three or four pluses of youthful shape and vigor

A picture of you between 21 to 25

Your favorite 7 to Bed preferences

The primary nice thing you are going to do for yourself at your one-year anniversary

Your clothes purchase list when you hit goal weight

What else?

SIGN PLACEMENT

Car dashboard

Bathroom mirror

Inside closet door

Taped to your desk

Refrigerator door

Food storage shelf

On the TV

In your exercise area

On your nightstand

Where else?

•THE CLOSET CLEAN OUT

There are dozens of strategies proposed in Surroundings Management™. This is one of the best. Imagine the emotional uplift of retailoring and swapping out your wardrobe because you've stripped fat. It is one of the most poignant events of Body-Renewal™. It's shedding the past for new, irrefutably.

As you progress in your lean and fit endeavors, clothes become too big. Hallelujah. Celebrate the ritual of taking in your clothes. Whether you do it yourself or have it done by a tailor, the work of tightening up your old fat-clothes is a symbol of your personal victory. Enjoy yourself fully by making clothes-buying trips a celebratory *soiree*.

•RESTAURANTS

Few restaurants favor you with their menu. But any decent restaurant accommodates simple requests.

When staying at a resort or hotel, set up your cuisine requirements ahead of time. Don't go if they can't serve you what you want. Probably the best understood nomenclature for chefs is low-cal vegetarian. Even though Neo-Cuisine™ is not "low-cal vegetarian," telling chefs that's what you want best suits your needs. You may even go so far as to send NeoCuisine™ recipes.

In restaurants, tell order-takers exactly how you want your food. Ask to speak to a chef because waiters almost never get it right. This may strike some as being overly aggressive but in the world of calorie-dense foods, your only defense is a good offense. Tell the chef you want no fat used in your food's preparation. A baked potato with plenty of *au jus* can be flavorsome accented with chopped scallions and fresh ground pepper.

Here's a summary of in-restaurant tactics:

- Eat only clear, noncream soups.
- Ask for your salad to be tossed with about one-quarter the amount of normal dressing. It's enough provided you season with lemon, salt and pepper (yes, really). If you're PRA-prone, order an entree-size dinner "starter" salad.
- Tell the chef to leave cream sauces, butters and gravies off. Ask him to season with herbs, spices and acids (e.g., flavored vinegars and lemon juice) of his choosing.
- Generally, meat-free red sauces and soy-based sauces (e.g., teriyaki) are fat free. Use any of these on a protein in lieu of butter, sauces or gravies. Teriyaki can go on virtually any protein.

- Never order anything sautéed unless a vegetable or meat stock is used as the sauté cooking medium. This is not strictly sautéing, of course, but a stock reduces in the pan creating a nice glacé. Always order the smallest protein available with double or triple vegetables. Be sure they are steamed or stock sautéed.
- Enjoy restaurants fully by focusing on white proteins like lobster, crab, scallops, shrimp white fish and turkey breast.
- Have the chef grill (broil) some vegetables for you.

●AT HOME—DANGEROUS TIMES

Being at home can be restful, peaceful and boring. Having nothing to do on a Saturday or Sunday afternoon can lead to feeling hungry and non-stop noshing. For these week-end afternoons, have an early dinner of Buddhist Vegetable Curry (15 calories per ounce), Maria DeLourdes Chili

Rellenos (15 calories per ounce) or a side of Carlenzoli Steaks (14 calories per ounce). These recipes are coming up.

Arriving home after work is particularly dangerous since you are often hungry and fatigued. Have a snack planned: pears, grapefruit, apples, kiwi, melon, strawberries, ad infinitum. If you are ravenous, eat a yogurt with one tablespoon of no-sugar pectin (soluble fiber to slow digestion) and drink 12 ounces of water, diet pop or decaf iced tea. Fluid must accompany the pectined yogurt.

●VACATIONS

One of the greatest threats to weight loss and maintenance is the vacation. Between that and the holidays, there are pounds to be gained. We work hard, after all, and deserve a vacation as our reward. Our mindset is party. The last thing we want is discipline. Freedom from work, kids and other responsibilities is what vacationing is all about. Unfortunately, vacations seem to center around food and drink. The restaurants are great, drinks delicious and the service relaxed. Local culinary specialties are inviting. These strategies help:

•Resume effort: Make a commitment before you vacation to resume weight-management effort on a particular date afterward. Tell others of your restart date and about your plans for exercising during the vacation. Agree with yourself ahead of time to read at least one inspiring fitness-related book while on vacation.

•The health cruise: More than 20 cruise lines offer healthful shipboard dining options and many also feature comprehensive fitness programs that include aerobics, strength-training instruction and exercise equipment. Ask your travel agent.

•The exercise vacation: Skiing, backpacking, bicycle touring and other action-oriented vacations can help tremendously in minimizing weight gain while allowing you to enjoy more food treats. Although exercise can compensate a great deal, if you eat with abandon you will likely return with some weight gain but a manageable amount.

•Increase exercise: On a non action-oriented vacation, simply increase your standard exercise program. However, brashly increasing your physical exercise (e.g., doubling it) is not advisable. A 10% to 20% increase helps burn calories. You might augment your exercise program with an additional sport such as golfing, swimming or tennis.

•Walk everywhere: Skip cabs: My daughter and I took a trip to Toronto, where we made it a point to walk everywhere. Often city distances are wholly walkable. A mile or two or more walk to a restaurant only takes 20 to 40 min-

utes and allows you to see the sights. We often took cabs home. Result: I never gained a pound and ate with occasional vacation abandon.

•Every third day: Dedicate every third day to a maximum intake such as 1200 or 1500 calories. Prior to a vacation, restrict calories for a week. When you return home, go immediately into weight-gain stripping.

•Cut the booze: No matter how you rationalize it, alcohol is fattening. At 125 calories per ounce of hard liquor, 150 calories per glass of wine and 150 to 250 calories per 12 ounces of brew, booze is tonnage no matter how you calculate it.

SURROUNDINGS MANAGEMENT™: PROCESSES

Good process enhances your youthful shape and vigor culture. It's a matter of skill building: Learning information to recall, self-monitoring awareness and patient practice. If, for example, you learn to switch moderate coffee drinking from the morning to early afternoon, you'll find that it quells typical afternoon hunger. A small point, perhaps, but still a matter of knowledge recall, self-awareness and practice. While some of this advice may appear overzealous, remember you're dealing as always with the *PRA*. Adopt as many of these behaviors as you wish short of placing unrealistic expectations on yourself. The intent is to provide you with a tool list to select those you think will best help in realizing your shape and vigor of youth goal.

● *THE MIRACLE 20™*
The stomach requires two things before it's content. It must be filled to 70% capacity and it needs about 20 minutes for the brain to receive the "it's full" message. When eating, part of food is converted to glucose and blood sugar rises rapidly. This prompts the release of insulin which filters slowly into the spine. When insulin reaches a certain level, the full signal is sent to the brain. It takes about 20 minutes for feelings of fullness to begin. (Unfortunately, insulin enters the bloodstream of a fat person more slowly than it does for a thin person.)[3] If you eat to the point of being just satisfied, in 20 minutes you will feel full.[4]

ALWAYS WAIT AT LEAST 20 MINUTES AFTER YOU HAVE EATEN TO MODEST SATIETY BEFORE DECIDING YOU NEED MORE.

The Miracle 20™ can save hundreds of calories every day. You'll be surprised how effective it is in minimizing calorie intake. If you're hungry in 20 minutes, then have a snack or mini-meal listed in Appendix D. After that, again wait 20 minutes. You will find the raging hunger you had an hour ago satisfied.

● MAGAZINE READING
Periodicals really help power a youthful shape and vigor culture. The right magazines and health letters arriving monthly affirm your intent. Magazines such as *Prevention* (everyone), *Shape* (women), and *Men's Health* all contain valuable information and reinforce your voluntary volition. Getting four or five magazines and health letters each month on different days gives you a store of information to digest. This steady information stream fortifies us. At a minimum, I recom-

mend these magazines. Buy three-year subscriptions. They are superb.

Bottom Line Health
Box 53408
Boulder, Colorado
83322
1-800-289-0409

Prevention
Box 7585
Red Oak, Iowa
51591-2585
1-800-666-1920

Walking
Box 420557
Palm Coast, Florida
32142-8937
1-800-829-5585

Cooking Light
Box 830656
Birmingham, Alabama
35282-9086
1-800-336-0125

Spend ten minutes each day minimum reading magazines. See Appendix C (page 391) for more titles. Read recipes, investigate new weight-training exercises and all else that contributes to your shape and vigor of youth. The ten-minute daily reflection cannot be over-stressed.

●NEW TV GOALS

It makes no difference if your tastes run to talk shows or football games or soaps, now is the time for you to add to your TV preferences. Make an agreement with yourself to watch at least one of the following TV programs:

●Graham Kerr: Good information and fun.

●Other cookery shows: Choose from Asian (but delete the frying oil; use stock instead), vegetarian (delete fats, use nonfat dairy products and apply the Osmazome Principle™) and Italian (delete the olive oil, *sauté* in the microwave or on the stove with stocks. Use no-fat cheese for regular).

●Exercise programs: Watch aerobics and strength-training shows. You learn something every time you make the effort to find a program on exercise. This increases your repertoire and builds your youthful shape and vigor culture.

●BUY VIDEOS

There are many videos that help your youthful shape and vigor culture building. A good way to save money is by exchanging with friends. Large bookstores carry videos with intriguing titles such as *Eating Healthy for Weight Control, Nutrition Counseling at the Next Level* and *Body Trust.* Here is a mail order company:

Exercise Video Catalog
Department EJ4
5390 Main Street NE
Minneapolis,
Minnesota
55421
1-800-378-0333[5]

• WRITE YOUR BodyRenewal™ JOURNAL

I strip fat best when I:

_____

_____

_____

I feel best when I:

_____

_____

_____

The best new behavior I've discovered is:

_____

_____

_____

The top two things I need to work on are:

_____

_____

_____

I am most angry about:

_____

_____

_____

Commit to writing in your journal for a minimum of one year. Don't make long entries unless inclined. Your BodyRenewal™ journal is your private memoranda of your journey. It confirms and encourages.

• EAT ONLY WHEN HUNGRY

Several well-controlled studies show that thin people seem to eat only when hungry. Their internal controls seem to rule them, as opposed to external cues and influences. You probably bear this out from your own observations of your thinner friends and acquaintances. Follow the true dictates of your hunger by eating when you are truly hungry and not simply by: "Oh, it's six o'clock, I must be hungry."

• QUAFF FLUIDS

Here are seven good reasons for drinking copious nonalcoholic, no-caffeine beverages—the best being water:

• They keep blood thin

When you work out, your blood thickens because sweat is drawn from it, increasing blood viscosity. Give your heart a break—drink plenty of fluid.

• They cool the body

Good blood volume through sufficient hydration gives the body enough water inventory to properly cool itself. Sweating keeps you fresh but only if your blood is maintained at adequate volume by enough fluid intake.

• They prevent over-eating

The brain's thirst and hunger centers are close together, so the sensations are easily confused. If you feel hungry, oftentimes you are just thirsty.

• They minimize fatigue

Inadequate fluid intake can make you feel tired.[6] A good start for proper hydration is 64 ounces a day or two quarts. If this seems like a lot, it shows how much you may be shorting yourself. Add at least 50% more if exercising when the weather is hot. Some find it helpful to keep a one-gallon container of water in their refrigerator to track intake.

•**They minimize water retention**

The body only releases fluids and reduces swelling (edema) when it thinks it has enough fluid intake.[7]

•**They help burn calories**

Even slight dehydration drops metabolic rate by 2% to 3%. You burn fewer calories, making it difficult to lose weight. Hydrate to keep your metabolism fully revved.[8]

You should be visiting the restroom every two to three hours and your urine should be light and clear.[9] The more yellow your urine, the more you should increase fluids. You will feel better, reduce water retention, give your heart a break and minimize hunger pangs.

•**LEARN TO RIDE THE HUNGER WAVE**

Dr. James Ferguson, a psychiatrist specializing in weight control and eating disorders, says when you feel the urge to eat, "... 90% of the time if an urge is not responded to within 20 minutes, it will go away. Most urges to eat are transient ..."[10]

Engage in alternate activities like reading a book, having a pre-prepared snack of vegetables, going for a walk, or otherwise engaging your mind.

•**THE CLOTHING CUE**

Tight clothing or belt across the abdomen when eating may cause you to eat less. Not only is your stomach held in, restricting food quantities, but a tight belt is also slightly uncomfortable, prompting a heightened awareness of your lean-body goal.

•**PORTION OUT SNACKS AND MINI-MEALS**

Count the number of graham crackers you are going to enjoy, scoop out the correct portion of fat/sugar-free frozen yogurt you are going to eat and measure the amount of berries you are going to devour. If you eat from original containers that hold an amount larger than the correct portion, you over-consume. Have in front of you only the calorically correct amount.

•**DON'T WATCH TV AND SNACK**

Snacking while watching TV is the great American pastime, but it is a guaranteed way to pack on pounds. Break the TV-food connection. If you feel like a snack, force yourself to sit at the kitchen table, not in front of the TV. As an interim step, eliminate such snacking one day a week.

•SHOP SMART

The grocery store is enemy territory. The modern-day supermarket's primary function is to induce you to buy expensive, fattening, salt-saturated prepared foods. Avoid falling victim.

- •Don't shop when you're H.A.L.T. Hungry, Angry, Lonely, or Tired.
- •Make a list and stick to it.
- •Leave kids at home. They beg for the wrong things.
- •Walk the store periphery as much as possible. That's where the fruits, vegetables and unprepared foods such as beans, bulk whole grains and dairy products are kept.
- •Do not buy prepared foods unless called for by NeoCuisine™.
- •Limit store time.

•DRINK TEA

Drinking tea suppresses hunger. Even decaffeinated tea quells hunger. That's not all. Tea may help keep cholesterol from clogging arteries and protect against cell damage that causes skin, gastrointestinal, liver, pancreatic and breast cancer. Tea contains antioxidants similar to those in fruits and vegetables which, in sufficient amounts, lowers malignant tumor and heart disease rates. It also acts as an anticoagulant which makes a heart attack less likely and less severe if one does occur.[11] Research in Japan indicates that the catechins in tea scavenge brain free radicals.[12] Black tea, green tea and decaffeinated tea all have positive effects. Drinking four or more cups of tea a day seems to be the most beneficial.[13] So, the next time you feel hungry, drink two more cups of tea. It will help. Tea, by the way, has about one-third the caffeine of coffee.

SURROUNDINGS MANAGEMENT™

1 SURROUNDINGS MANAGEMENT™ influences weight loss the same as diet and exercise.

2 WIN OVER FAMILY, FRIENDS AND CO-WORKERS to your shape and vigor of youth goals.

3 NEOCUISINE™ FOOD STORAGE Organize it separately.

4 POST AFFIRMING SIGNS

5 BE ASSERTIVE IN RESTAURANTS Tell them what you want and how you want it.

6 ACTIVATE VACATION STRATEGIES

- Do exercise vacations, e.g. bike touring, skiing, etc.
- Skip the cabs, walk everywhere.
- Every third day, reduce intake to 1,200 or 1,500 calories.
- Cut the booze.
- At the very least, make a commitment before you vacation to resume weight management on a particular date.

7 BUY THREE-YEAR SUBSCRIPTIONS

- *Bottom Line Health* 800-289-0409
- *Walking* 800-829-5585
- *Prevention* 800-666-1920
- *Cooking Light* 800-336-0125

8 YOUR BodyRenewal™ JOURNAL

Write for five minutes every day.

9 THE MIRACLE 20™

Wait 20 minutes before eating more.

10 PORTION OUT meals and snacks.

[1] *The Doctor's Clinic 30 Program,* Sharon M. Cooper, R.N., M.S.N. and J.T. Cooper, M.D., M.P.H., Greentree Press, Erie, Pennsylvania, 1996, page 93, BB386.

[2] *Lose Weight Guidebook,* Mark Bricklin, editor, Rodale Press, Inc., Emmaus, Pennsylvania, 1996, page 28, BB130.

[3] *Maximize Your Body Potential*, Joyce D. Nash, Ph.D., Bull Publishing Company, Palo Alto, California, 1986, page 130, BB127.

[4] "Shrink Your Stomach," Kathy Perlmutter and Michelle Stanten, *Prevention,* July 1996, pages 80-86, BB104.

[5] Magazine ad, BB133.

[6] *Biomarkers,* William Evans, Ph.D. and Irwin H. Rosenberg, M.D. with Jacqueline Thompson, Fireside (Simon & Schuster), New York, New York, 1991, page 83, BB75.

[7] *Living Longer Stronger,* Ellington Darden, Ph.D., The Berkeley Publishing Group, New York, New York, 1995, page 113, BB53.

[8] "Readers Want to Know," Wayne Askew, M.D., University of Utah, *Bottom Line/ Health,* vol. 13, no. 9, September 1999, BB482.

[9] "Don't Let Your Body Run Dry," Marty Munson and Carol Spiciarich, *Prevention,* July 1996, page 91, BB105.

[10] *Habits Not Diets,* James Ferguson, M.D., Bull Publishing, Palo Alto, California, 1988, page 121, BB101

[11] "Reading Tea Leaves for Health Benefits," *Tufts University Health and Nutrition Letter,* October 1995, vol. 13, no. 8, pages 4-5, BB134.

[12] "The Longevity Brew," *Men's Confidential,* Rodale Press, Emmaus, Pennsylvania, pages 6-7, BB254.

[13] "Q&A," *Tufts University Health and Nutrition Letter,* November 1995, vol. 13, no. 9, page 8, BB134.

CONTROL PSYCHOLOGY™

Control Psychology™ is the essential belief processes facilitating our youthful shape and vigor pursuit. *What we believe affects our feelings.* For example, a hunger pang is generally viewed as a negative. But a hunger pang is the body's fat-stripping signal. It means fat cells are shrinking. Knowing this allows us to mentally reframe this experience into a positive. Every time you experience a twinge of hunger realize that you are fat-stripping your body. This powerful visualization dissipates mild to even moderate hunger pangs, the kind most of us occasionally experience.

The best motivation for achieving youthful shape and vigor comes from deeply held beliefs. These beliefs spring from and are nurtured by knowledge. For youthful shape and vigor to be realized, we must possess the right knowledge. The motivation to attain a lean body and high vigor must be deep-seated and the way to begin establishing high incentive is with Control Psychology™.

Control Psychology™ depends on skill-building. Remember that building a skill requires learning for instant recall, self-watching and patient practice. Control Psychology™ works when these axioms are followed.

AXIOM 1: PRACTICE NO PERFECTION

Fat-stripping and exercise require effort. For "relief," we almost want circumstances to intervene which allow us to blow a day or two or more of fat-stripping. Travel, the holidays, impossible goals, a crisis at work seem to afford us an excuse to lay off or quit entirely. These apparent escapes are based on a false notion of perfection—"Oh what the hell, I could never be thin anyway." This is the ideal subterfuge to abandon the path to youthful vigor.

Everyone struggles with the commonplace problems universal to mankind ... ego insecurity ... day in and day out frustrations ... unfulfilled expectations ... all of which lead to the realization of how human we are. The fact is that no one executes perfectly, but a day of backsliding isn't the same as losing the war. *Understand that imperfect execution is the* **norm.**

Too many dieters make rigid rules that are impossible to follow long term. "I'll eat no candy on my diet." "I won't go to the beach until I lose 10 pounds." "I will avoid all social events because they are my downfall." "I plan to stick to my fat-stripping 100%." The real problem with these hopeless goals is that they provide the perfect out. Their violation creates despair which collapses the diet. Don't make silly rules for yourself.

Understanding and rejecting diet perfection eliminates the most common excuse to quit. Missing a day's fat-stripping or exercise goal or even a month's is no pretext to desert your youthful shape and vigor pursuit. If you hold the irrational perfect-execution belief, then a few days' faltering provides an all-too-easy stratagem to chuck your youthful shape and vigor undertaking. Keep in mind that perfectionism may be a cover for perceived shortcomings and feelings of inferiority: We set unobtainable objectives, inevitably fall short, and conclude we're unworthy. It's a no-win, vacuous game.

We flounder because we are human but succeed because we persevere based on the compelling value of our youthful shape and vigor goals. The discipline you need to realize a youthful look and vigor isn't impossible but it does mean that you feel the stretch. You'll do what is required because it enhances your life. The ends are valuable.

I'm committed to something I believe is worthwhile. I know I will pay a price for it. I will not let it take over my life, but I'll make a solid effort. I know I'll make mistakes and lapse but that's okay. I won't be derailed.

AXIOM 2: REREAD BENEFITS AND WIN LIST

An everyday reading of the benefits of being lean and vigorous may strike some as close to a religious novena but goal clarity boosts achievement behavior, especially when the goal makes sense and is desirable. Frequently reconnecting with your shape and vigor of youth positives augments resolve. Spend a moment each day reviewing why you are in BodyRenewal™ by rereading the Muscle Rebuild™ and NeoCuisine™ benefits. Keep your mind on what you want and off what you don't want.

The next thing is to heighten morale and fortify your ego by writing your personal win list. From your earliest recollections, write down the significant wins of your life. It's important to go back to your early life because you have been doing good things for a long time. A well-developed win list has 10 to 30 meaningful life events. Your win list is entirely personal. No one sees it but you, so write exactly what you want. Here's what a list might look like.

Add to your win list by updating it for current wins like "Two weeks straight without a diet lapse." Include other key life wins as you recall them, like remembering that you were also the VP of the debate club.

The win list is your own, personal spirit-booster for your sole private use. Nobody sees it but you so write exactly what you want. Remember, there are no silly personal wins. Write what lifts your mood.

WIN LIST

- The lead in my 3rd grade play. Elected class treasurer in the 7th grade.
- Secretary/treasurer of the Spanish club in my junior year.
- Got into college. Made the Dean's List my junior year.
- Graduated from college.
- Got a good job right out of college.
- Won the Employee of the Month award.
- I'm raising two teenagers.
- I am an excellent gardener.
- I was chosen Most Improved Player on my softball team.
- My spouse loves me.

AXIOM 3: VISUALIZE YOUR YOUTHFUL SHAPE AND VIGOR EVERY DAY

Your best or worst motivator can be self-image. It urges you toward youthful look and vigor goals or stops you cold, depending on perceived strengths and weaknesses. Everyone has self-perception glitches, but now is the time to create a strong, positive self-image, one that spurs you toward your goal of slim and fit. There is a simple, highly effective way to do this.

BREAK NEGATIVE SELF-IMAGE BY PROJECTING AHEAD TO WHAT YOU WILL BE.

By rehearsing a positive future self-image, you change perceived self-worth today because you build on feelings of where you are going, *not what you are.* Forgo current self-concepts and zero in entirely on your future shapely and vigorous self. By so doing, you skip today's detritus to zero in on your new life. You're not cheating but rather using an effective psychological technique which gets you through moments of self-punishment, substituting instead feelings about where you will finish. Medieval theologians called it hope.

PRACTICING VISUALIZATION

Visualization is a remarkable means of preparing for BodyRenewal™. Visualize your new shape and vigor of youth. Just as you can't compete without training or execute a skill without practice, you may not accept your new self without previews sufficient to create self-comfort. Visit your future self with affection, frequency and pride.

Learning visualization requires practice, as with any other skill. Some of us may be natural visualizers but most of us require instruction and repetition to become skillful. Here are the steps in learning to abandon your current self-picture and legitimately move to your new self-image of youthful shape and vigor.

- Get comfortable in a chair.

- Visualize your future shape and vigor of youth in a familiar context such as your home. It makes visualizing easier.

- Don't panic if a clear picture doesn't come through. Remember, visualization is an outcome of practice. You'll definitely get better as time goes on.

- Add complexity as visualization proficiency builds. How warm is the room? Is there a scent in the air? What sounds are there? What new clothes are you wearing? How are others reacting to the new, lean and vigorous you?

- Visualize the correct picture. If you see yourself as fat, "thought stop," rewind the tape and start again. If for some reason you see yourself slurping shakes and inhaling banana splits, stop and rework your motion picture. Visualizing the correct behavior enhances the probability of achieving it.

93

• Practice patiently. Visualization is like any skill. At first, you are self-conscious and unsure. These fade with forbearance and repetition. Shortly, you will see your future best self clearly. This is when excitement begins to build because you know where you're headed. Forget today's hips and double chin. Look to the future for inspiration and motivation.

Future-self focus is no psycho-babble-mumbo-jumbo but a fine tool for your goal achievement. A clear visualization of your future best self establishes a commanding inducement to stay with BodyRenewal™. Your body goal must become so firmly ingrained that non-contributing behaviors feel distinctly uncomfortable. This is classic cognitive dissonance theory and here's how it works.

We all have an idealized self-image, the way we choose to view ourselves. Our ideal self-image is a driving, psychological reality, "the most powerful motivating force for any human being," according to Harvard professor Dr. Harry Levinson.[1] We are not talking here of a mere piffling motivator, but rather our primary psychological impetus. The wish to fulfill our ego ideal guides us through our lives. Cross it, ignore it, violate it and our minds react immediately. We feel pain. We're out of sorts, uncomfortable. We're behaving in ways we shouldn't and it distresses us. The further our behaviors stray from our idealized self, the more discomfort—cognitive dissonance—we experience.

We can use cognitive dissonance force to our full advantage by passionately imagining ourselves the way we want to be. Clearly generate the picture of what you truly want, then use the emotional discomfort caused by untoward behaviors to your benefit. By keeping your goal vision firmly implanted in your mind, counterproductive weight and fitness behaviors serve as stimuli to get you back on track. The better your grip on your ideal self shape and vigor of youth body picture, the greater your willingness to achieve it because the unpleasantness of cognitive dissonance helps keep our proverbial weak flesh in line.

As a means of maintaining your motivation, take two minutes a day to visualize how it will be when you achieve your youthful shape and vigor goals. During this 120-second visualization, appreciate the positive reactions of others. Enjoy the genuine surprise of your friends. Value what you are accomplishing.

Visualize your future youthful shape and vigorous new you for 120 seconds (2 minutes) each day.

AXIOM 4: DISPUTE SILLY FICTIONS

Dr. Albert Ellis says, "getting better almost invariably involves growing up, thinking straighter, and figuring out a method of react-

94

ing on the basis of facts and reality rather than on the basis of silly fictions in your head."[2]

Psychiatrist Aaron Beck came to believe that our moods don't decree our thoughts. It's the other way around. Our thoughts govern our moods. If you think right, you'll feel right. Someone might react to a situation with negative self talk (thoughts) like "This is horrible, I can't stand it." Properly trained, that person might react with "This isn't great but I've faced worse and figured it out"— a more rational and realistic response.[3] In other words, negative thinking (how you talk to yourself) is the pathology.

Thinking is a conversation with self, so talk correctly to yourself and much psychological trash will be swept away.

The technique of countering irrational, negative ideas (self-talk) with more balanced and positive ones is called *disputing.* You can use disputing to effectively protest negative self talk. In effect, good disputing— the result of practice—means you wind up somewhat an optimist. This is important because optimists have fewer ills and evidence suggests that they live longer. Besides, optimistic people are much more successful at achieving the shape and vigor of youth because they persevere.[4]

HOW TO DISPUTE

The fine art of disputing is a skill. It must be prac ticed to gain its full benefits. When you find yourself uneasy, impatient, anxious or simply unhappy about fat-stripping, follow these effective disputing steps:

1 Become sensitive to pessimistic self-talk (thoughts) that deters you from your lean and vigorous, new-you goal. You can't correct gloomy self-dialogue if you don't recognize it.

2 Arrest negative self-talk by mentally shouting STOP! You may even want to shout STOP! aloud to break the negative self-talk cycle.

3 Dispute negative self-talk immediately or write troublesome thoughts down so that you can dispute them later when you have time.[5]

Good disputing has a certain look. It's emphatic and no nonsense. It doesn't allow for those silly fictions Dr. Albert Ellis insists we eliminate. Disputes even have a parental quality to them along the lines of "Grow up," "Get a life," and other unflattering characterizations.

Study the disputing chart on the next page. Some disputes may make you smile, others may make you frown. In the end you know, however, that disputing from the *adult state* is required to win the fat fight.

MY NEGATIVE THOUGHTS	MY QUALITY DISPUTING
•"Becoming lean and fit takes too much work."	•"Anything worthwhile takes work. A little self-discipline won't hurt me. Besides, I am acheiving the shape of youth, considerably better health and elevated self-esteem."
•"It seems unfair that I have to work so much harder today to stay lean and fit."	•"Who said life was fair? It isn't and I know it. The extra work is absolutely worth it because looking better, feeling better and living longer is what quality life is all about."
•"Aging depresses me."	•"Aging is simply a fact of life, but I can rebuild my musculature, become leaner and employ a few face fix tricks and take 5 to 10 years off my looks. That would be fun!"
•"Life is rushing by me."	•"I should be less concerned about time and more concerned about what I do with it. Becoming lean and fit is a great place to start. Besides, between advances in medicine and this commitment of mine, I've probably got 50 more years anyway."
•"Dieting is useless because I always gain the weight back eventually."	•"This time is different! This is doable! With BodyRenewal™ I'm well on my way to a new life process."

The more you practice disputing, the better you get. Continue to challenge your irrational beliefs—your negative self-talk—until you prove them wrong and give them up. Maintain active disputing until you have annihilated the silly notions that bring you pain. Don't stop disputing until you feel 100% better.

AXIOM 5: HAVE MORE FUN

Without a strong hunger drive, we would waste away. Nature has therefore imbued us with an appetite instinct second only to breathing in its force. We manage—not control—the *primeval raging appetite* with NeoCuisine™ technique. But because eating is pleasurable, removing food as a primary pleasure brushes dangerously close to quality-of-life erosion. The last thing any of us want is diminished joy in living. Eating pleasure, fortunately, is something over which we have

some control. If you are clever, you learn to substitute food pleasure. It's called the pleasure compensation principle where overt food pleasure is replaced in part by other gratification forms better comporting with your new life mode.

The pleasure compensation principle should not be taken lightly. Failure to conscientiously use it may lead to dangerous diet deprivation. If we come to sense that stripping fat deprives us of too much, we feel short-changed. Somehow life isn't fair. We pity ourselves. These feelings may lead to anger, despair and even depression. Should this occur, a lapse is imminent or, worse, total abandonment of your Body-Renewal™ efforts.

Replace diet deprivation with compensating pleasure. When you find yourself angry or depressed over perceived satisfaction shortfalls, balance them with offsetting pleasures.

Enhancing enjoyment while in BodyRenewal™ requires planning. Please do plan. The calendar of fun you develop may involve upfront work but take time to organize good times and rewards. Don't let self-pity

throw you off the path to youthful shape and vigor because the remarkable benefits you accrue are a lifelong gift. Planned fun assists you through Body-Renewal™ with greater ease. Be kind to yourself. Here's an idea list.

- See a double feature.
- Play video games.
- Go to two sporting events.
- See a live concert.
- Enjoy boating.
- Take up rollerblading.
- Get cable for 90 days.
- Buy a boom box and listen to the music of our youth.
- Lie on the beach.
- Have your car detailed.
- Get a massage.
- Buy new makeup.
- Enjoy a leisurely walking or bike tour of a part of the city you don't know.
- Enjoy a philharmonic orchestra live.
- Go to a play.
- Visit friends you haven't seen.

- Take up a new hobby:
  - Stamp collecting
  - Model railroading★
  - Kite fighting
  - Model airplane flying
  - Coin collecting
  - Watercolor painting
  - Bonsai miniature tree sculpting
  - Antique apple growing
  - Floral arranging
- Do the public entertainment circuit: museum, zoo and the city's best park.
- Read two of the ten best-selling novels.
- Surf the World Wide Web.
- Take that ceramics class you've promised yourself for years.
- Rent your favorite movie.
- Nap in a hammock.
- Take a bubble bath.
- Make a fire in your seldom-used fireplace.
- Buy something you've always wanted.

★ *Don't laugh. The quality and intricacies of railroad models are exceptional. Go to the city's best hobby store and ask to see German made model Zs. You'll be impressed with their small size and complexity (and price). The point is there are unknown worlds out there for you to explore.*

AXIOM 6: GET MORE SLEEP

It may strike one as odd to use sleep as a Control Psychology™ mechanism but sleep deprivation dampens the immune system (more colds and flus), hampers quality work production and increases the incidence of depression.[6] Studies even link too little sleep with increased appetites and food consumption. "People eat more and they eat more often when they are tired," according to Donald Bliwise, Ph.D., of Emory University.[7] And Dr. Allen Rechtschaffen of the University of Chicago says, "sleep deprivation increases calorie consumption by 10% to 15%."[8]

Society attaches economic and moral value to sleeping as little as possible. We somehow believe we're doing "good" by reducing sleep time. Unfortunately, cheating on sleep increases brain levels of cortisol, a potentially dangerous stress hormone. The adrenal gland releases cortisol in response to stress, preparing the body to take action. Long-term exposure to abnormally high cortisol levels damages brain cells, causing shrinkage in the hippocampus, a critical region of the brain that regulates learning and memory.

When the stress hormone cortisol goes up, two other important hormones—the muscle-building human growth hormone (HGH) and prolactyn, which oversees the immune defense system—go down. Staying awake longer than normal may be at a cost of stress-related memory impairment, increased risk of infection and more flab resulting from decreased HGH.[9]

Rest and exercise go hand in hand. Exercise promotes sleep. Studies reveal those who exercise fall asleep in half the time, sleep sounder, sleep an hour longer and have less daytime drowsiness than nonexercisers.[10] But give exercise a chance because the *Journal of the American Medical Association* reports that the effects of exercise on sleep do not become apparent until after eight weeks of regular conditioning.[11]

1 MAKE SLEEP A PRIORITY

Treat sleep with respect for what it can do for you. Make it a priority in your life. Insist on getting eight hours sleep per night.

2 NO CAFFEINE PAST 3 PM

Caffeine stays in your system about seven hours. Drink none past 3 PM. Don't forget that many soft drinks have caffeine, especially colas and Mountain Dew®. Also remember, alcohol is a sleep disrupter.[12]

3 A HOT BATH

Body temperature drops prior to bed. It's nature's way of signaling the body to sleep. Researchers recommend taking a hot bath 90 minutes prior to retiring because body heat drops rapidly once out of the tub which amplifies the circadian sleep cycle.[13]

4 AVOID AGITATION AN HOUR BEFORE BED

Work, an exciting novel, arguments, stimulating TV can produce agitation which may be sleep-inhibiting.

5 WRITE DOWN TROUBLES

Worries often keep us awake. By writing problems down prior to retiring, they are captured so you don't worry about forgetting them. We are sometimes kept awake by thinking "I must remember to do this" or "I must do that." The Mayo Clinic suggests a worry list where you write down your problems using a two-column format, the left side for problems, the right side for solutions. Knowing that your problems are "saved" is remarkably tranquilizing.[14]

6 KEEP THE BEDROOM DARK

Melatonin, as you know, influences the circadian sleep cycle. Too much light blocks melatonin production.[15]

7 NO CLOCK WATCHING

Watching the clock invites feelings like "Oh my gosh, it's 4 AM and I have to get up in just two hours." This is a surefire way to stay awake. The fix is simple and recommended by sleep specialists. Face the clock so you don't know what hour it is and don't move it. Being unaware of the time makes it easier to fall asleep. Since the ticking of an alarm clock can be irritating and remind you of passing time, place it where you won't hear it, like in a drawer. The alarm is still loud enough to waken you.

8 IF YOU AWAKEN AND CAN'T SLEEP

Get up. But keep the lights low: remember, bright light inhibits melatonin production, our body's natural sleep inducer. Keep the TV off. Rewrite or add to your worry list to be sure that you have captured all that is bothering you. Once you guarantee that information will not be lost, note the calming effect.[16]

9 RISE SAME TIME EACH DAY

Promote your internal circadian cycle by rising at the same time each day. If you sleep in on the weekends, your natural body rhythm is thrown off which inhibits sleep. Create a sleep pattern and stick with it.

11 DON'T WORRY ABOUT A SLEEPLESS NIGHT

Dr. Peter Hauri says that, "Most people can function quite well after a sleepless night." Don't let a poor night's sleep throw you in a tizzy. It won't hurt you.[17]

12 A SLEEP JOURNAL

Try tracking your sleep for a week or two. Use the two-column method. Record quality of sleep on the left side and your day's activities on the right. Doing this may well reveal what's driving your insomnia. Patterns emerge that you can alter. It's a great way of being in charge rather than allowing the environment to dictate your life.

13 BUY AN EXCELLENT MATTRESS

With sleep's many benefits, it makes sense to buy the best quality mattress, one that promotes sound sleep. The investment is small compared to the advantages.

AXIOM 7: PRACTICE GOOD LAPSE MANAGEMENT

Stroll through any mall or airport and you find McDonald's®, Taco Bell®, Mrs. Fields® and a saturation of other temptations which simply don't suit your youthful shape and vigor needs. Walk into an AM/PM® mini-mart or 7-11® and you are deluged with sugary, high-fat temptation foods. Every gas station you go into these days has plentiful candy bars, hot dogs, fried chicken and soft-serve ice cream to throw you off track. There always seems to be some kind of entrapping food purveyor in sight, from small latté stands and miniaturized fast-food outlets in supermarkets to full service restaurants. We walk in a free-for-all fat minefield. Once in a while, we blow our diet.

While experts agree that lapses in eating control are as inevitable as death and taxes, they also agree that a slip isn't an excuse for abandoning your shape and vigor of youth goals. Rampant food rages are eventually reined in as you come to recognize your "occasions of sin" and execute NeoCuisine™, Surroundings Management™ and Control Psychology™. Don't become discouraged. You are unfolding your potential and conceding nothing.

LAPSE FOILS

Since the world seems relentless in its attempt to seduce us with endless temptations, we must have strategies at the ready to counter these inducements. You need fat-fighting weapons, an anti-fat arsenal for the situational temptations.

●PRE-PARTY EATING
Consider what and when you will eat *before* going to a party. Eat NeoCuisine™ to suppress the PRA. By going into a trigger situation satisfied, the likelihood of falling victim to a lapse is considerably decreased.

●IF ... THEN RULE
Use the if ... then rule: "If I don't lapse for a week, then I ... (reward)." Don't make a steak dinner your reward for not lapsing. Buy a book, rent a movie, go fishing, any behavior that isn't food-focused.

●DO A PUNISHMENT REVIEW
Ask yourself, "How will I feel about this tomorrow morning?" "Do I really want to extend my fat-stripping for another week because of this binge I'm about ready to go on?" "Do I need the guilt, discomfort and anger that's going to result from me overeating?" "How will I feel about this binge a day or two from now?"

●SIMPLE ASSERTIVENESS
When Aunt Milly wants to force a huge piece of her delightful devil's food cake on you, insist on just a sliver. Don't let a waiter seduce you into eating the garlic cream scampi that has, assuredly, no less than 1,000 calories. Assert your rights so that you can attain your lean physique. It means sticking up for yourself.

●ENCOURAGE POSITIVE SELF-TALK
"Last week I rode out a wave of hunger; I can do it again." "I have been fat-stripping for two weeks and never lapsed once, no need to start now." "The very first week of fat-stripping I went to a party and did not eat one fatty thing. I know I can exercise self-control if I want to."

●DAY-PART CALORIE CONTROL
One of the most provocative binge stimuli is losing calorie control. This occurs when through the day substantially more calories are consumed than planned. If by dinner you have snacked your way to 1,000 calories, there is ample psychological thrust to simply say the hell with it. Being out of synch with the calorie count does not mean your fat-stripping day is ruined. Create an ultra-low-calorie dinner by having a cooked breakfast cereal dinner.

●READ YOUR LAPSE CARD
Write a lapse card of binge stoppers. Like airline seat pocket cards telling you what to do in the case of an

emergency, your 3x5 reminder card tells you what to do when threatened with a binge. In addition to listing binge negatives, put down the positives, such as your youthful shape and vigor goal. What do you want to weigh? What are your fitness goals? What dress or pant size do you want? Include the phone number of a friend you can call for support. (This isn't extreme advice because if you avoid a 4,000-calorie chocolate truffle odyssey, you've probably saved yourself a half pound plus of adipose.) List your favorite binge stoppers like eating one food only until the palate fatigues, e.g., dill pickles or baby carrots, etc. Keep a lapse card in your wallet and post one in your food storage area. The next time you have the urge to binge, read and consider what you've written.

DURING A LAPSE

Occasionally your body seems to demand a feeding frenzy. We want to respond with huge quantities of high-fat and eminently appeasing foods that lard our hips and clog our innards. The best way to control the feed-frenzie instinct is not with a wide-eyed, white-knuckled self-discipline approach. Don't react to this primal motivation as if it were a life or death situation. Go along with it. If your feeding-frenzy drive is a maelstrom, manage the storm intelligently. You can without destroying your fat-stripping efforts. It's possible to take care of these occasional, wild compulsions and not materially harm your youthful shape and vigor goals. Stick with the following guidelines to manage the unruly feed-frenzy reflex.

If you're clever about it, a carbo binge can be good news. When you eat more carbos or protein than your body needs, the extra energy is stored as the muscle fuel glycogen in the liver and muscles, not as fat. Glyco-gen muscle fuel can be expended in your workouts. (Of course, if you overeat carbos daily, it is converted to fat.) If you must binge, make sure that you do so only on carbos and protein, the two body fuels that are not immediately turned to fat. Provided you do a little extra in your workouts, muscle fuel is "burned"—never converting to dreaded hip fat.

There is virtually no way to defeat the hunger impulse without having the proper foods on hand. If there are no fresh fruit, jerky, salad materials or other hunger-control foods available, you will turn to high-calorie alternatives. If you make it easy to grab the wrong foods, you will.

Your best binge defense is cupboards and refrigerator well stocked with NeoCuisine™. At 9 PM, defenses are down, all of us taking the easy path by gobbling what's readily at hand. That can be four Pepperidge Farms® Chunky Chocolate Chip Cookies (4 ounces for 400 calories) or a Braeburn apple and a peeled, sweet ruby red grapefruit (20 ounces for 150 calories). It depends on your inventory—a critical essential for youthful shape and vigor.

Here are excellent lapse exit strategies. For example, do you really want to lapse? If you ask yourself the question one more time and opt for a pre-binge emergency food, you may go over your calorie allotment by 500 calories but that's substantially less than the 2,000 or 3,000 additional calories you could easily consume.

If the answer is "Yes, I do want/need to do this," then follow this plan:

•ONE FOOD ONLY

A great way to slow and eventually stop a binge is to stick with just one food. This tires the palate and helps you arrive quickly at the point where "I don't think I can eat another bite." If, however, you switch foods, the palate, amazingly, is refreshed and helps spur the *primeval raging appetite* to ever-higher levels. Arrive quickly to food boredom by insisting that you eat only one food-type.

•"GOOD" BINGE STUFF

Eat foods that don't set you back a week. If you overshoot your calorie-consumption goal for the day, make sure it's by as little as possible. Stick with carbohydrates and proteins:
- Baked tortilla chips and salsa
- Baked potato chips
- A whole NeoCuisine™ fat/sugar-free cheesecake
- Fat/sugar-free frozen yogurt
- Oranges or apples
- Order a big, thin crust, no-cheese, double-sauce, triple-vegetable pizza delivered to your house.

•SET A CALORIE LIMIT

Okay, you have decided you are going to eat those Godiva chocolates. But set a limit of, say, 1,000 additional calories. That gives you about 15 chocolates to gobble. But remember: stick only to the chocolates, tiring your palate and reaching the surfeit point apace.

•STOP WHEN DONE

After you have binged and are stuffed, stop. When you are done, you are done. Don't restart. When it's over, it's over. Recognize this.

THIS TIME NEXT TIME

Ironically, lapses are positive. They open the door to self-discovery and, in a sense, unfold your potential. Whereas we often ignorantly proceed through life unaware of what triggers our overeating, you have the opportunity to track and analyze lapse causes. If you don't track it, you can't manage it. Overeating can open the way to renewed commitment and certainly increased self-knowledge. View deviations as opportunities to learn about yourself and how to change your behavior. Remember that weight control is a matter of skill-building.

Use the *next time strategy*. The idea is that, "I may have lapsed this time but next time I will not!" It's the kind of thinking that pushes you forward rather than holding you back. It centers your mind on planning versus lamenting. It reminds us that what really counts is what happens next time because this time is over but there are an infinite number of next times in the future. Such thinking creates a healthy response which concentrates on problem-solving versus self-flagellation, an important lesson as you already well know.

Look for triggers—those events, dates and situations that trigger excessive eating. Sometimes loneliness, boredom, anxiety, sadness and especially the reward syndrome are the triggers for a binge. The reward syndrome is the natural outcome of having worked a long, hard day. It's the powerful notion that "I deserve this." Of the hunger motivations that must be controlled, the reward syndrome is one of the most seductive. The idea that we "deserve some-thing" for our day's efforts is a difficult psychological state.

A good way to master triggers is to track them on the back side of your calorie ToteCard, covered in the next chapter. Some experts advocate using a journal, which is fine, but a 3x5 card is easy to carry and unobtrusive. You're more likely to maintain the records you need for fat-fight success if tracking is kept simple.

Write down the who, what, when, where and why. Be honest. No one reads your notes other than you. Rich-food discomfort and cognitive dissonance usually follow a lapse. Use both as positive motivators for developing the next time plan. Don't waste your time agonizing over a temporary setback. Your youthful shape and vigor goal is not set back more than three or four days even if you eat a whole box of chocolates.

Here are three ToteCard trigger narrative samples.

SCENARIO I

I went to lunch with Harriet. She had a hamburger and I had one, too. After blowing the day, I gave in and ate like a pig until I went to bed.

SCENARIO II

I had a craving for sweets. I said to hell with it, went to the store and bought two packages of Pinwheel cookies and I ate all 24. I just couldn't stop.

SCENARIO III

I was so tired when I got home that I ate my husband's leftover Kentucky Fried Chicken that was sitting in the refrigerator.

As you save your calorie ToteCards, set aside those that record your lapses. Once you have two or more ToteCards narrating your lapses, analyze them. Study additional lapse cards as they collect. Through evaluation, you begin to spot triggers that induce overeating. **With this data, devise your next-time plan.** What is going to be your next-time behavior?

Aim not for perfect control but control that continues steady weight-reduction progress.

By going beyond "this time" and getting on with the "next time," self-retribution is minimized. But most importantly, you devise tactics that manage your future. You are using the now to make the rest of your life conform to your youthful shape and vigor targets. This is good Control Psychology™.

Please, always remember that good Control-Psychology™ skill-building requires patient practice. You may not be an expert at feelings management now but you can be. Be patient with yourself when practicing Control Psychology™. The positive outcomes are worth it. Use the anti-aging cornerstones of continually unfolding your potential, living in the NOW and conceding nothing. Concede nothing to the coming years because BodyRenewal™ boosts your vitality. Age is only a number and a renewed body by your own doing is a wonderful gift to yourself.

CONTROL PSYCHOLOGY™ AXIOMS

AXIOM 1: PRACTICE NO PERFECTION.

AXIOM 2: REREAD YOUR GOALS AND WIN LISTS DAILY.

AXIOM 3: ENVISION YOUR YOUTHFUL SHAPE AND VIGOR EVERY DAY. Seeing yourself svelte and happy makes the goal desirable.

AXIOM 4: DISPUTE SILLY FICTIONS. Self talk like "I can't do this" is nonsense.

AXIOM 5: INCREASE YOUR FUN. Work at having more nonfood fun.

AXIOM 6: SLEEP MORE. Sleep deprivation debilitates. Don't be a victim.

AXIOM 7: PRACTICE GOOD LAPSE MANAGEMENT:
- Have the right foods on hand.
- Write and analyze lapse cards.
- Develop personalized counter-strategies.

[1] *The Great Jackass Fallacy*, Harry Levinson, Division of Research, Graduate School of Business Administration, Harvard University, Boston, Massachusetts, 1993, page 29, BB70, #8.

[2] *Executive Leadership: A Rational Approach*, Albert Ellis, Ph.D., Institute for Rational Living, New York, New York, 1978, page 133, #43.

[3] "Think Your Way Out of Depression," Aaron Beck, M.D., *Reader's Digest,* December, 1980, page 79, A217.

[4] Ellis, op. cit., pages 5, 255, #43.

[5] *Learned Optimism*, Martin Seligman, Ph.D., Alfred A. Knopf, Inc., 1990, pages 71-72, #103.

[6] "Beat Stress and Depression," Michael J. Norton, M.D., *Health Confidential,* January 1996, page 3, BB209; *Dr. Bob Arnot's Guide to Turning Back the Clock,* Robert Arnot, M.D., Little, Brown & Company, New York, New York, 1995, pages 198-199, BB33.

[7] "Overeating? Get Some Sleep," *Tufts University Health and Nutrition Letter*, vol. 12, no. 9, November 1994, pages 1 and 2, BB211.

[8] *Lowfat Living,* Robert K. Cooper, Ph.D., with Leslie L. Cooper, Rodale Press, Inc., Emmaus, Pennsylvania, 1996, page 207, BB370.

[9] *"Lack of Sleep May Cause Aging, Stress, Flab,"* Charles Kotulak, *Chicago Tribune, Seattle Times*, June 7, 1998, page 16, BB410.

[10] "Insomnia: When and How to Use Sleeping Pills," *The Johns Hopkins Medical Letter,* vol. 7, no. 11, January 1996, page 5, BB255.

[11] "Need a Better Night's Sleep?" *UC Berkeley Wellness Letter*, vol. 13, no. 6, March 1997, page 8, BB256.

[12] "Health Notes," *University of Texas Lifetime Health Letter*, vol. 9, no. 3, March 1997, page 2, BB257.

[13] "To Chill Out Before Bed," *The New England Journal of Medicine Health News,* December 9, 1997, page 8, BB411.

[14] "Overcoming Insomnia," *Mayo Clinic Health Letter,* vol. 14, no. 11, November 1996, page 3, BB258.

[15] "Secrets of Serotonin," *University of Texas Lifetime Health Letter*, vol. 8, no. 8, August 1996, page 6, BB212.

[16] *Overcoming Procrastination*, Albert Ellis, Ph.D., and William J. Knaus, Ed.D., New American Library, New York, New York, 1977, page 87, #61.

[17] "Secret of Good Sleep from the Mayo Clinic Insomnia Program," *Bottom Line/Health*, vol. 11, no. 2, February 1997, page 4, BB260.

EXERCISE MOTIVATION

Although not obligatory, many people find careful documentation to be an exercise motivator. It provides proof of your workouts. It's a history of accomplishment and the best basis to compare performances. Your BodyRenewal™ journal is a chronicle for upping striding or increasing weight lifting to more challenging levels. It can trigger good guilt to get you back on track. Sixty seconds writing (the length of a TV commercial) gives you all the information you need: intensity, distance, route reaction, feelings, clothing, shoes, etc.

DAY-PARTS

One of the real fat-stripping secrets is the day-part plan, the skill of minimizing hunger by eating steadily through the day without blowing your calorie count.

This chart gives approximate calorie allotments you will want to observe through the day. The plus/minus sign (±) means "approximate," another way of saying you don't have to hit each day-part calorie accumulation exactly. Just land in the ballpark.

Please don't take it upon yourself to go below about 1,200 calories per day. Nutritional analyses reveal it's impossible to achieve proper nutritional levels below 1,200 calories.

DAY-PART CALORIE ALLOTMENTS

DAY-PART	WEIGHT BELOW 150 LBS.	WEIGHT BETWEEN 150 TO 200 LBS.	WEIGHT ABOVE 200 LBS.
BREAKFAST	(±)300	(±)350	(±)400
LUNCH	(±)200	(±)200	(±)300
2 TO 3 PM LATTE/SNACK	(±)100	(±)100	(±)200
DINNER	(±)500	(±)550	(±)650
7 TO BED	(±)200	(±)300	(±)450
TOTAL	1,300	1,500	2,000

Eating the right foods and right amounts at various day points strips fat simply and easily. The chief day-part objective is not exceeding each day-part calorie allotment. Here's why.

The two primary fat-packing factors are the *primeval raging appetite* and the environment. The PRA pushes us constantly toward eating unless it's cleverly managed while the environment serves to foil our good intent by presenting the seductive foods of the marketplace. The day-part plan gives you a scheme to check intake. Monitoring calorie accumulation gives you control. You can't manage something if you don't track it. Mindful observation regulates the PRA and environment.

Counting for control requires day-parts management. It means that you are eating five or six times a day. In doing so, remember to allow 200 to 300 calories for the *7 to Bed* day-part period, your time of greatest temptation. Here is a time map of someone on a 2,000 calories per day schedule.

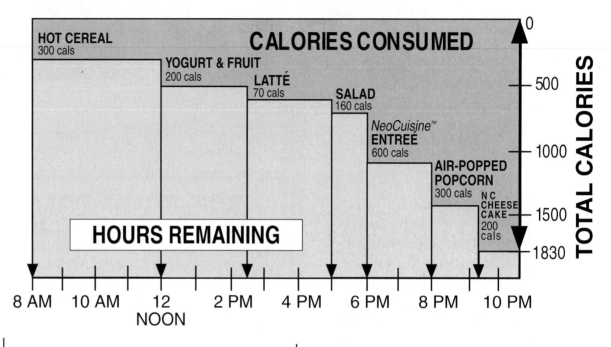

Observe that the day is calorie backloaded. Most calories are consumed in the day's second half. This allows for our subtle discipline fatigue through the day.

Pay no mind to the nonsense that evening calories count more. Energy and its expenditure are an absolute. Timing has nothing to do with it according to scientists at the US Department of Agriculture.[1]

Proper day-part planning assures sufficient evening calories, your time of greatest temptation. After a hard day's work and careful calorie monitoring, the evening presents us relaxation time, rest and reward. The day-part plan conserves sufficient calories to satisfy these legitimate feelings. If you hit 7 PM with zero calories in reserve, a fatigued mind can't dominate the *primeval raging appetite* and reward syndrome. Rather than fighting this tough reality, day-part calorie management assures sufficient calorie reserves for evening enjoyment without relying on pure discipline.

Your goal is to have at least 200 calories available for the 7 to Bed day-part. Nothing is worse than a day of careful calorie accounting that is ruined in the last hours before bed by not having enough calories in reserve to ward off the primeval raging appetite.

Day-part plan calorie management is a skill. You recall that skill-building means learning to recall, self-monitoring the skill behavior and practicing patience. Devoting a little time to studying this section gives you the knowledge for day-part plan success. Following up with self-observation and patient practice builds the skill you need for handling the *primeval raging appetite* and reward syndrome.

THE QUICK CAL COUNT

You need to know counting calories is something you will do the rest of your life. Before you sigh in disgust, let me quickly add that it is far easier than you might imagine. Calorie counting becomes second nature and the body adjusts well to lower energy intake.

As you now know, the body's fundamental drive is to become fat. Your body's biology stacks on fat to assuage its starvation paranoia. If you don't watch what you eat, you will get fat. You may not like this reality but reality it is, nonetheless. Fortunately, tracking calories isn't maddening.

Most "weight watching" systems are complex. Who of us can really track exchanging this for that and continually look up the calorie counts in a book for various foods? We are told to eat so many calories in this and that category. Why, it's not only confusing but downright antagonizing. There is an easier way.

USING QUICK CAL COUNT

Make several copies of the Quick Cal Count in Appendix E. Put one in your wallet and post the others, say, on your refrigerator door and inside your food storage cupboard. Over the next 60 days, refer to the Quick Cal Count chart at every meal. By the time 60 days is up (if not sooner) you will memorize the nutrition generalizations that dispose you toward the best foods for your life. This is better than relying on calorie books, continually looking up statistics and trying to figure out if you're eating too much fat.

Dining out or eating in, you become adept at estimating food quantities. The Quick Cal Count uses only four sizes: one cup (the size of your fist), one bread slice, a tablespoon and a deck of cards, the last of which, interestingly enough, almost perfectly equals 4 ounces of any protein such as chicken or fish.

As you go through the day, you make estimates as to the size of the portions you are eating. To sharpen size recognition, study a cup, a standard bread slice, a deck of cards and a tablespoon. Commit these measures to memory. You'll be quite surprised at how accurate you become. Professional chefs eyeball measure when they estimate various quantities such as a tablespoon or cup. By simply pouring a dry ingredient into the palm of their hand, they readily estimate its volume. You can become a good quantity estimator just as professional kitchen personnel readily learn sizes without having to haul out measuring cups and spoons for every recipe.

QUICK CAL COUNT IN THE ORDER OF CONSUMPTION PREFERENCE

- VEGETABLE:
  UNLIMITED.
  - Leaf (e.g. chopped lettuce, cabbage): 0 calories per cup
  - Regular (e.g. broccoli, carrots): 50 calories per cup
  - Starch (e.g. potato, peas, winter squash): 100 calories per cup

- FRUIT:
  EAT ABUNDANTLY.
  - 75 calories per whole piece or cup

- DAIRY:
  EAT A LOT.
  - 1 cup no-fat/sugar dairy (e.g. yogurt, no-fat milk): 100 calories
  - 1/2 cup no-fat, concentrated dairy (e.g. no-fat cheese, no-fat ice cream): 100 calories

- BEANS AND LENTILS:
  EAT A LOT.
  - 200 calories per cup

- COOKED WHITE PROTEIN:
  EAT SOME.
  - Skinless chicken breast, white fish, shrimp, etc: 50 calories per ounce, 4 ounces cooked equals a deck of cards
  - All other meats: **RESTRICT.** 100 cals/ounce

- BREAD/RICE/PASTA:
  LIMIT.
  - 75 calories per standard bread slice (1 ounce)
  - White rice, white pasta: 200 calories per cup

QUICK CAL COUNT LOGIC

Vegetables are divided into three categories. As you see, leaf vegetables such as lettuce and cabbage are allotted zero calories. Of course they do have a caloric content but it's so low studies find it a waste of time estimating calories. A whole head of iceberg, for instance, is only about 70 calories. The real calorie content of salad is in its dressing and accoutrements such as cheese, meat and so on. Regular vegetables such as eggplant, zucchini and asparagus run about 40 calories per cup. Starchy vegetables like peas, winter squash and potatoes are about 100 calories per cup.

Although fruits vary somewhat in their calorie content, 75 calories per whole fruit piece like apples, oranges, pears, grapefruits is comparable to their actual calorie count. Using your imagination, it is possible when eating a fruit salad to figure the number of cups you're consuming. That times 75 will give you a close approximation of the fruit salad's actual calorie content. A two-cup fruit salad, for instance, is 150 calories.

All the dairy products you eat should be nonfat. Eat a lot of them (skim only) for protein and important calcium. The old adage of three cups of milk per day is still a good gauge for calcium intake. It equals the minimum daily requirement of 800 mg. calcium. More is better. You get it in fat-free cottage cheese, fat/sugar-free yogurt, fat-free cheese and so forth. Dairy products (fat-free) are your best calcium source.

No-fat milk and no-fat/sugar regular and frozen yogurt are about 100 calories per cup. Concentrated forms of no-fat dairy products, such as no-fat cheese, salad dressing, cream cheese, etc., should be counted at 100 calories per half cup. Hence, a quarter cup of creamy, no-fat salad dressing is about 50 calories. (A quarter cup no-fat, creamy dressing with a quarter cup vinegar mixed with a packet of aspartame and pepper to taste yields a tasty, satisfying dressing at half the calories.)

To simplify protein calorie count, it's divided into white and other. The white cooked proteins such as skinless chicken or turkey breast, red snapper and halibut run about 50 calories per ounce. Although it may appear too simple, other cooked proteins actually run about 100 calories per ounce. Following this clear guide assesses calories quite accurately.

If there was a case of creative accounting, it's with breadstuffs, given their wide range of size, density and fat content. Here's how to use your mind's eye in estimating with fair accuracy the calorie count of baked goods. A standard bread slice is one ounce and runs about 75 calories. From this starting point, assess the baked good's size and density. For example, although a bagel appears to be equal to about one and a half or two bread slices, it is a dense bread product. Compensating for density, you can envision a bagel equaling three or four bread slices for 225 to 300 calories. A four-ounce bagel equals 300 calories, a fairly standard bagel size. Graham crackers run between 60 and 70 calories per 2-1/2 inch by 5 inch cracker. With a little fancy, you can picture one cracker equaling a compressed bread slice. Since the exact calorie count for a graham cracker is about 65 calories, you are close at estimating 75 calories using the Quick Cal Count. Bread products are the toughest to estimate but use your imagination.

Remember, all baked goods are calorie-dense and best avoided in quantity.

Fats and sugars are the most calorie-dense of all foods. A little fat and sugar are harmless and tasty. But a little goes a long way in loading calories. A tablespoon of any fat is 125 calories. Sugar runs about half that or around 60 calories per tablespoon. For purposes of stripping fat and calculation ease, simply avoid straight fats and sugars. See the NeoCuisine™ Cookbook (coming up) for great no-fat/sugar desserts.

In general, other cooked protein like pork, beef, lamb, salmon, etc. runs about 100 calories per ounce. So when you're dining out, a standard eight-ounce steak is about, believe it or not, 800 calories. The best way to judge protein size is the Mayo Clinic way by imagining a deck of cards, which equals approximately four ounces.[2] Picture how many decks of cards an eight-ounce steak is. Yes, you do have to use your mind's eye but it is surprisingly easy to come quite close to actual weights. You'd likely estimate an eight-ounce steak to be two card decks large which would put your calorie approximation at 800 calories, right on the money.

QUICK CAL COUNT PRACTICE

To become proficient at Quick Cal Counting, practice. You are otherwise at the mercy of food propaganda luring you into the fat trap. **Maintain control of your food intake through the day by being aware of your calorie consumption using the Quick Cal Count and noting calorie quantities on your ToteCard.** If not, others will determine your fat or lean destiny. You must be in control. What follows may seem like a lot of work but it isn't. Once you get the hang of it, the Quick Cal Count is a breeze, far easier than the "exchange" method.

1st SIZE STUDY

Get a deck of cards, tablespoon and one-cup measure. Put these in a prominent place and study them for a moment each day for a month. You must learn these measures so well that you can look at food and gauge its card-deck/cup/tablespoon quantity. Helpful hints: A tablespoon is the size of your thumb, a deck of cards is about four ounces and a cup is approximately the size of a baseball.

2nd ESTIMATIONS

Using the portable Quick Cal Count (Appendix E) and your quantity-estimation skills, assess the quantity and total calories of what you're eating. At first this may seem hard but once you're adept, a whole plate of food can be quantified in 20 seconds or less.

3rd RECORD

Use a 3x5 card (ToteCard) each day to record your calorie intake estimations. On the back side of the card, record triggers that threw you off your day's calorie plan. As you identify, track and study your triggers, you begin to spot patterns, events and situations that push you off your lean-and-fit course.

Once you have mastered the Quick Cal Count (practice for 30 days), you can be anywhere, eating anything, and know your approximate calorie intake. With practice, you can estimate just about any meal to within 10 to 15% of its actual calorie count. Sometimes you may be a bit high and other times you may be a bit low but overall you will be able to estimate fairly correctly your total day's calorie intake. It's a valuable skill because it puts you in control of your fat or lean destiny. Otherwise, you are at the benevolence of the environment notoriously unkind to the flourishing-physique minded.

COUNTING IS CONTROL

With the Quick Cal Count (QCC) estimates, you don't need to carry books or charts because memorizing the six calorie categories by simply using the QCC condensed table for a few weeks makes it easy. Once you have memorized it, tracking calories through the day is effortless using the ToteCard. Until you become adept, use the QCC table. Remember to jot down your calorie counts on your 3x5 Tote-Card for breakfast, lunch, dinner and snacks. This will help you track your intake until you learn to do it mentally. *Eventually you'll be able to follow your calorie intake through the day wholly from memory.* It's easy. I do it daily.

DAY-PART PLAN ADJUSTING

The BodyRenewal™ day has five parts: Breakfast, lunch, afternoon snack, dinner and 7 to Bed. Provided your day's total calories equal your daily total calorie allowance, almost any calorie allotment through the day works. You may find, for example, that you wish fewer calories at breakfast and more at lunch. The one over-riding rule is that at the end of the day you have at least 200 calories remaining for 7 to Bed. When you are tired you are at greatest risk for blowing your fat-stripping endeavors. Actively manage caloric intake through the day so your 7 to Bed calorie reserve leaves you satisfied. Hunger at night is a sleep disrupter.

TOTECARD

Simply and effectively track day-part calorie count by carrying a 3x5 card. A ToteCard fits in a wallet or pocket. Make an entry each time you eat and maintain a running calorie total.

There may be those desiring quicker weight loss than afforded by the recommended calorie categories. The reasons for losing weight slowly, however, are compelling. Provided you exercise, the BodyRenewal™ strips fat at the rate of one to two pounds per week. Don't lose weight more quickly because:

- Facial wrinkles increase when skin contracts slower than fat lost[3];
- A nutritionally complete diet below 1,200 calories is impossible[4];
- Rapid weight loss lowers cognitive function[5];
- Rapid weight loss promotes gallstones[6];
- Rapid Weight loss exacerbates muscle loss.[7]

Moderate, weekly weight loss is the healthful approach. You have plenty of time to strip fat. The purpose of the BodyRenewal™ cycle is to introduce you to lifelong habits. Lose all the weight you want at about four to eight pounds per month. Take your time. You have the rest of your life.

Since calorie restriction can lead to vitamin deficiencies, it is wise to take a quality multivitamin every day, your insurance policy for complete nutrition. A restricted diet can also create calcium deficiency. The average person only gets about 750 mgs of calcium per day, which is about half the amount you need for healthy bones. A calcium supplement of 600 to 700 mgs per day is recommended.[8] The decision to add antioxidants E, C and beta carotene plus others like selenium and omega-3 is a personal decision.[9]

NeoCuisine™ BREAKFAST

- **BELOW 150 LBS: 250 CALS**
- **150 TO 200 LBS: 350 CALS**
- **200+ LBS: 400 CALS**

NeoCuisine™ breakfasts of cooked whole breakfast grains have superb calorie-to-weight ratios of only 10 to 12 calories per ounce versus the egregious 110 calories per ounce of the typical boxed cereal. This is extremely important. WHEN YOU START THE DAY FULL, WITH PLENTY OF ENERGY FOR ONLY 250 TO 350 CALORIES, YOU SUCCESSFULLY PRESERVE CALORIES FOR THE REST OF THE DAY. Your day-part plan is off to a great start. Starting anything correctly, as you know, is the way to success.

BREAKFAST COMPARO

FOOD	CALORIES	WEIGHT	CALS/1 OZ.
•Ham, eggs and hash browns	600 to 800	8 to 10 ounces	70
•Typical 3 oz. breakfast cereal and 1 cup milk	460	11 ounces	50
•French toast	700 to 800	8 to 10 ounces	100
•NeoCuisine™ WHOLE BREAKFAST GRAINS	250 TO 350	30 TO 40 OUNCES	10

Unlimited breakfast greatly improves diet attitude and stops the bogeymen of diet deprivation: self-pity, anger, hunger pangs and diminished motivation. The NeoCuisine™ cooked-cereal, whole-grain breakfast provides an excellent low-calorie-to-high-weight (quantity) ratio, complete satiety and bountiful energy, a must for successful NeoCuisine™ day-part calorie management. If you don't eat a correct NeoCuisine™ breakfast, you may overeat at lunch, throwing off NeoCuisine™ day-part calorie management. By 7 PM you'll be yearning for calories that aren't there because you've overeaten through the day.

Many of us are out of the breakfast habit. Some even find food repulsive in the morning. I know because I was one. But the pluses are too many to ignore. Learn to eat breakfast again. Do this by first making breakfast easy to prepare. Put grains in hot water the night before for rapid morning cooking in about a third the time. In ten minutes, breakfast is ready.

Since whole breakfast grains are fibrous, starting small is okay. Work up to large portions because your goal is sailing through the morning to lunch without hunger pangs. Be sure to buy a wide variety of breakfast grains. If you stick with rolled oats only, you'll soon tire of breakfast and forgo it.

Keep in mind that winning the shape and vigor of youth results from skill-building. Be patient because in a matter of months you will be looking forward to breakfast with enthusiasm. The body wants and needs morning nourishment. Soon it encourages you to eat generously. The hackneyed advisory—breakfast is the most important meal of the day—is true. To strip fat and enjoy full vigor, a nutrient-rich breakfast of flavorful cooked cereals is essential. Learn to eat breakfast and enjoy significant boons, including hunger elimination through your morning.

One important directive. Save your coffee allotment for the early afternoon. By conserving your safe two to three-cup-per-day consumption for early afternoon, you benefit from caffeine's hunger-stifling qualities. There's not one medical condition linked directly to coffee consumption.[10] Besides, coffee increases clearheadedness, happiness, friendliness and calmness.[11] All qualities needed for that afternoon work run.

Here are simple instructions to give you copious, low calorie-to-weight-ratio breakfasts of 10 to 12 calories per ounce, the best calorie-to-weight ratio in NeoCuisine™. This literally means you can eat all you want for breakfast.

OATS

The king of cooked breakfast cereals is oats in all varieties. Do not buy instant oats. Buy only whole grain oats that require cooking. If you like a nutty flavor, roast dry oats first in a 350° oven, stirring occasionally until they turn dark golden. Put in plenty of cooking water for a fluid consistency, not a dry mush result.

AN ALTERNATIVE

If there's no way you can see yourself eating oats at all (shame on you), there is a tasty satisfying alternative. Turn to page **389** and review the NC HiPro Dream. A pure protein breakfast is amazingly filling and is a remarkable energy charger. Catecholamines are released with the ingestion of a high protein meal. This neurotransmitter is a natural attention sharpener, one you will assuredly notice. So if cooked cereals are just not your inclination, substitute an NC HiPro Dream of 200 or 300 calories for a tasty alternative. Be sure to follow the directions closely for best results.

●WHOLE ROLLED OATS
The most common of all oat varieties. Start by putting them in hot water to soak overnight with the lid on. Add up to 100% more water than package instructions call for. You want a creamy cereal.

●STEEL-CUT OATS
These are delicious, nutty and slightly crunchy. Begin the cooking process by putting them in hot water for an overnight soak with the lid on. This makes for quick cooking of ten minutes in the morning. Increase specified water by up to 100% for creaminess.

●OAT BRAN
Don't be afraid of it because I guarantee you will like it. It cooks to an exceptionally smooth and delicious cereal. One of oat bran's best features is its quick cook time of only a few minutes. No need to soak overnight. Oat bran is rich in soluble fiber which lowers cholesterol.[12]

●FLAVORED OATS
Do not buy instant, flavored oatmeals. They are loaded with sugar and calories. You can have oatmeals in more than 20 varieties. Simply mix no-fat/sugar yogurt with your favorite oatmeal type for delicious flavors. Mix,

for example, blueberry yogurt with cooked steel-cut oats for delightful blueberry oatmeal. Try black cherry oatmeal. Oat bran mixes well with all fruit yogurts. Try raspberry. Remember to use no-fat/sugar yogurt only.

WHEAT

Cooked wheat breakfast cereals have a more pronounced flavor than their oat brothers. Rolled wheat, cracked wheat and farina (such as Cream of Wheat®) are all flavorsome. Farina accepts up to 100% over recommended cooking water amounts. Rolled and cracked wheat breakfast cereals accept up to 50% above recommended amounts of water. To speed morning cooking for rolled and cracked wheat, add hot water the night before, stir and lid for heat retention. This cuts cooking time by half.

•ROLLED WHEAT

Rolled wheat can be roasted, like oats, prior to cooking for heartier flavor. Long cooking is essential for good flavor so be sure to start with a lidded, hot water soak the night before. It is possible to cook cereal overnight but stoves vary so much that you'll need to experiment to see if your stove's heat goes low enough.

•CRACKED WHEAT (BULGUR)

Cracked wheat is particularly hearty. The same cooking directions apply as for rolled wheat.

•CREAM OF WHEAT

Here is a light cereal you probably haven't tried in years. It isn't whole grain but it's filling nonetheless. One of the wonderful things about farina is that it accepts a wide variety of flavors. Make a fruit pureé. Swirl it in for dramatic effect and fine flavor. With Cream of Wheat®'s flavor versatility, you are limited only by your imagination. Try yogurt, flavoring extracts and fruit purees.

•"PANCAKES"

Remember that wheat makes pancakes and pancakes have a natural affinity for maple flavor. Try maple extract in rolled or cracked cooked wheat followed by I Can't Believe It's Not Butter® spray for an inviting NeoCuisine™ pancake-like flavor.

COOKED CEREAL BLENDS

Don't get stuck in an oatmeal rut. Try everything. If you do, you'll be delighted with the cooked-breakfast-cereal habit. I recommend that you have no fewer than six types, yes six, on hand. Mix it up to maximize enjoyment. Try blending your own cereals. The combinations are endless. Start with a base of oats or wheat and add brown rice or whole, hulled barley or corn meal or flax seed or any combination.

The *Harvard Health Letter* says, "whole grains are probably a better investment in one's health than taking dietary supplements."[13] With that endorsement and the added benefits of low calorie-to-weight ratios, whole grain breakfasts are the best way to start your day. Low fat, unlimited breakfast quantities and slow digestion for even energy release with no insulin spike are also pluses.

To keep salt consumption and calories in line, aspartame is essential for sweetening cooked breakfast cereals. Remember that Equal®, NutriSweet®, NatraTaste® and all the other brands of aspartame are simply a protein and utterly harmless.[14] Even the conservative American Cancer Society approves aspartame.[15] So rest easy. Use all the aspartame you want to sweeten your cooked cereals. I say this because the number of aspartame packets needed for desired sweetness may surprise you (but it's no more than a can of diet soda). Count on two to ten packets plus for each bowl. Pleasantly sweet, cooked cereal boosts enjoyment. Using low-sodium Molly McButter® also adds flavor without undue salt.

COUNTING CONTROLS CALORIES.

Fill in your ToteCard.

NeoCuisine™ LUNCH

- BELOW 150 LBS: 200 CALS
- 150 TO 200 LBS: 200 CALS
- 200+ LBS: 300 CALS

NC lunches are quick; this allows time for a walk during your lunch break. Walking before lunch acts as a mild appetite suppressant, accumulates exercise and refreshes you for afternoon work by elevating the heart rate, oxygenating the brain.

NeoCuisine™ lunches are designed so you don't get ahead of the day-part calorie count. They also include protein which boosts mental sharpness.[16] Simple NC lunches are also low salt, saving it for your savory NC dinner.

Here are NeoCuisine™ lunch options. After lunch you have a snack or cafe latté for more protein and a welcome caffeine boost.

- RECOMMENDED: Have a NC HiPro Dream™. (200 to 300 calories.)

- RECOMMENDED: NC leftovers from the night before.

- RECOMMENDED: Ultra-low-fat tofu shake. Use one 12-ounce tofu container, 1 cup chopped fruit, non-fat milk to thin, 1 teaspoon vanilla and 10 to 15 aspartame packets. Blend. (225 calories.)

- Fresh fruits are too much of a forgotten delight. Somehow the "eat a piece of fruit a day" advice lacks appeal. On the other hand, sliced bananas, juicy ripe strawberries, succulent raspberries, or fresh-picked blackberries served with aspartame-sweetened no-fat sour cream sound delicious.

- Eight ounces fat-free, sugar-free yogurt (100 calories) and a large apple/orange (or two small) (100 calories) or banana (100 calories). (200 calories total.)

- Two eight-ounce containers of fat-free, sugar-free yogurt. (200 calories total.)

- Three ounces skinless, chopped, cooked chicken breast (50 calories per ounce for 150) over six ounces lettuce with no-calorie dressing stretched with balsamic vinegar for salt sparing.

- Two ounces skinless teriyaki (no extra sauce to minimize sodium) chicken breast (100 calories) over one cup rice (170 calories). (270 calories total.)

- Four ounces fat-free, skinless turkey slices (30 calories per ounce) on Wonder® Lite bread (40 calories per slice) garnished with lettuce, tomato, a shave of onion and plain yogurt with plenty of pepper. (Approximately 225 calories total.)

- A salad as big as you like with no-cal dressing stretched with rice vinegar and aspartame to taste to minimize salt. Adding sweetness eliminates the need for additional salt. (100 calories.)

Look at the 7 to Bed list. See Appendix D. Many items are suitable for lunch.

2 TO 3 PM LATTÉ OR SNACK

- BELOW 150 LBS: 100 CALS
- 150 TO 200 LBS: 100 CALS
- 200+ LBS: 100 CALS

Now for the two- to three-cup-per-day coffee allotment you saved for the early afternoon. Most experts agree that two or three cups a day is harmless unless otherwise advised by your physician. Caffeine has hunger-dulling qualities suitable for the afternoon. Caffeine also heightens mental acuity and is a great headache fix with ibuprofen.[17] Provided coffee is drunk by 3 PM, at 10 PM caffeine is out of your system.[18]

A latté is recommended not because it is stylish but because it happens to provide—in addition to hunger-squelching caffeine—a healthy dose of protein, about eight grams and 70 mg of calcium in the milk. In the standard 12 ounce latté you get a net of around six ounces milk for less than 60 calories. Be sure to order skim milk. A double shot gives you a nice caffeine buzz and more mental horsepower for the long afternoon while helping rein in your *primeval raging appetite*.

If there are no latté stands nearby, make a classic *café au lait* by combining equal amounts of fresh, strong, hot coffee and skim milk heated in a microwave. Flavor it with vanilla powder, nutmeg, cocoa powder, cinnamon or what have you. Of course, if you like straight coffee best, enjoy it. The point is to squelch the PRA with a little caffeine.

If you don't drink coffee, allow a 100-calorie snack, preferably protein: no-fat/sugar yogurt, steamed flavored milk, frozen no-fat/sugar yogurt, turkey breast slices or a 100 calorie HiPro Dream.

COUNTING CONTROLS CALORIES.

Fill in your ToteCard.

NeoCuisine™ DINNER

- •BELOW 150 LBS: 500 CALS
- •150 TO 200 LBS: 550 CALS
- •200+ LBS: 650 CALS

You have been working all day keeping your calorie count in line. When you arrive home, you're tired and famished and you want a little reward. Fruit is an excellent starter or a small version of a NeoCuisine™ salad or one of the tofu-augmented salads like Dilled Tuna Tomatoes (page 326) or Hi Protein Chicken Salad with Fruit (page 327). By having something ready to go, you're not sucked into the common mistake of grabbing whatever's handy. Eating four SnackWell cookies may taste good but they throw your calorie count off by 200 calories. RULE: Have food prepared for your homecoming snack. Good pre-dinner starters are:

- •Apple
- •Grapefruit
- •Orange
- •No-sugar yogurt
- •A big mug of steamy decaf tea
- •Starter salad✦

Dinner is when NeoCuisine™ really delivers. Because you have been sparing salt all day long, you can now enjoy a fully savory dinner of substantial quantity. The NeoCuisine™ calorie-to-weight ratio of 20 calories per ounce provides you much more food to enjoy than the typical 21st century cuisine calorie-to-weight ratio of 60 to 100 calories per ounce. The diet deprivation perception is soothed because you have enough to eat. Portions are quite large so if you can't always finish dinner, so much the better.

✦As you recall, lettuce is not counted on ToteCards. Packaged greens are the way to go. Make no-cal salad dressings taste considerably better by adding aspartame. Stretch those dressings by adding your vinegar of choice to lower salt useage. You'll find that adding sweetness cuts the acids and smooths the flavor profile. Or simply buy quality balsamic vinegar to sprinkle on your salad.

Because NeoCuisine™ uses amplifiers, it is the best calorie-frugal, high-quantity, tasty cookery you've ever enjoyed. The Osmazome Principle™, combined with other flavor force principles such as adequate salt and plenty of seasoning, means you indulge in flavor-packed dinners. Most NeoCuisine™ dinners can be prepared in 20 minutes or less. The process can be speeded up, of course, by doing prep work in the morning. Stews, chilis and meat-loafs are particularly suited to doubling up.

If you are on the 1,300-calorie-a-day program, plan on leaving about 20% of your food on the plate. This will put you in the 500-calorie range.

7 TO BED

As you know, the most difficult fat-stripping time is from about 7 PM to bedtime because you are tired, the least motivated and therefore the most susceptible to a slip that ruins your entire day's efforts. You have been diligent the day through in recording calorie intake. You meticulously stuck to calorie-count management and you resisted many fattening temptations.

Now comes the evening and resolve starts fading. You begin to think about how much work it is stripping fat. Naturally, you feel a trace of self-pity. Diet deprivation begins to rear its ugly head. You realize that when you go to bed hungry you won't be able to sleep, a legitimate concern.

BodyRenewal™ day-part plan allows almost a third of the allotted calories from 7 PM on. There has been misgiving about night eating but this relates to those consuming 75% of their calorie intake after 6 PM.

Studies indicate night eating has little, if any, effect on weight gain.[20] It still comes down to total calorie intake versus total calorie expenditure. An elevated resting metabolic rate—achieved through the Muscle Rebuild™—strips fat regardless of calorie-consumption timing.

Because eating at night is okay, don't be fooled by the sugary, fat-free and low-fat desserts now widely available. To replace flavor lost from fat reduction, manufacturers use more sugar, making "fat-free" desserts a poor calorie bargain. A small chocolate chip cookie has 80 calories while its "reduced-fat" brother has almost the same number at 70. A half-cup of regular instant pudding has 160 calories while the fat-free version has 140 calories. A serving of regular potato chips (17) has 160 calories while the fat-reduced type has 150 calories, and for you pretzel lovers, the fat and no-fat versions are virtually the same.[21]

So if it isn't four Snack-Well® sandwich cookies (less than two ounces) in the evening for 220 calories, what is it? The old saw "have a carrot when you're hungry" doesn't sound too appealing. The idea of chomping carrots instead of reveling in a hot fudge sundae sounds awful, but wait. When was the last time you had a fresh carrot? Reading about carrots is suspect but actually eating one is something quite different.

Carrots are sweet. They have a crunch you probably haven't experienced in years. Their flavor is pleasing and aroma clean and fresh. Every time you eat one, you're nourishing your body with vital beta carotene, flavonoids and phytochemicals. They are a powerhouse.

The same goes for much-maligned celery. Let's be honest, you haven't had a celery rib in a decade. The only thing you remember are those peanut butter-slathered celery sticks our moms insisted on putting in our lunch boxes, but let's do celery justice. First of all, celery is juicy. It snaps when you bite it. Its flavor is reminiscent of absinthe and, interestingly, has pleasing palate-anesthetizing qualities. Aromatically, celery is

spring. When you try it, concentrate on what you're tasting, fully experiencing it.

Beyond carrots and celery, the 7 to Bed list has variety, including jerkies (terrific chew value and rich in protein), delectable NeoCuisine™ desserts like Sugar-Free, Fat-Free Pumpkin Cheesecake and a gallon of butter-flavored popcorn at only 320 calories.

A few observations and suggestions are in order. The secret for a 7 to Bed guilt-free snack time is having the right inventory. Although self-evident, your cache of 7 to Bed delights can only be enjoyed if you have them in your larder. The fact is you eat what's on hand. If what you have on hand is fatty and fattening, that's what you eat.

To maintain calorie control, never eat from original containers. Portion out the correct amount called for on the 7 to Bed list. This is important because we tend to miscount calorie intake in our favor. Eating from the no-fat Cracker Jack® container means that we will probably eat the whole seven

ounces for 700 calories, the temptation being overwhelming.

The 7 to Bed evening selections are in Appendix D. The wide range of delicious, hunger-shackling evening alternatives may help you decide to enter the BodyRenewal™.

COUNTING CONTROLS CALORIES.

Fill in your ToteCard.

ILL WINDS

Before going further we must discuss the subject of, huh, flatus or as it was more delicately characterized in Victorian England, "an ill wind from behind."[22] Any carbo-rich diet has oligosaccharides that our enzymes can't accommodate but intestinal bacteria thrive on, producing our much-feared digestive wind.[23] I say "our" because studies show that the average adult flatulates from 8 to 20 times every day.[24] Its commonality, however, does not lessen the social embarrassment emanating, as it were, therefrom. Why, even Hippocrates investigated flatulence. Benjamin Franklin, too, lent studious thought to a cure for "escaped wind"—possibly because he spent so much time closeted in stuffy rooms with overfed patricians whose occasional venting set his wig standing on end. So what is a body to do? Here are science's best fart fixes to date:

- There are two enzyme products on the market that work well. Try Beano® or Be Sure® with the first couple of bites of food.

- Thoroughly rinse canned beans. This washes away much indigestible sugar.

- Gastroenterologist Steven Peikin, M.D., recommends activated charcoal tablets. He advises not to take them within two hours of medication because they can sweep drugs from the body.

Though harmless, they turn stool black.[25]

- Much gas and stomach rumbling comes from lactose intolerance. Stick with fermented milk products such as no-fat cheese and yogurt or use Lactaid®.

- Carbonated beverages and gulping food put more air into the stomach and hence into the intestines. Slow down, chew your food thoroughly and enjoy dinner without wolfing it.

Whatever you do, don't go light on fiber because it helps prevent cancers of the colon, prostate and breast, and minimizes diverticulitis, appendicitis, hemorrhoids and varicose veins. High fiber keeps cholesterol levels down, lowers the risk of heart attacks and helps you lose weight.[26]

DAY-PARTS

1 SELECT YOUR CALORIE GOAL: If your weight is below 150 pounds, aim for 1,300 calories per day. At 150 to 200 pounds, aim for 1,500 calories per day. Above 200 pounds, allow 2,000 calories a day.

2 COUNTING CONTROLS CALORIES: THE TOTECARD. Keep a Quick Cal Count table (Appendix E) in your wallet. Use daily. Note calories on your ToteCard. You can't manage what you don't track. Be careful about getting ahead: 200 calories maximum at any time.

3 EAT WHOLE GRAIN BREAKFASTS: This puts you on the right day-part calorie-control track by filling you up with minimal calories.

4 SUPPLEMENT: Take a quality MULTIPLE VITAMIN and at least 750 mgs CALCIUM supplement every day. Investigate other supplements like vitamin E and low-dose aspirin with your physician.

123

5 BOOST PROTEIN: Enjoy a NC HiPro Dream™ for lunch (Appendix B). Eat white proteins. Half your weight is your daily protein goal in grams, e.g. 150 pounds equals a 75-gram protein requirement.

6 ALLOW AT LEAST 200-300 CALORIES FOR 7 TO BED: This is the peak temptation. Track your time calories through the day. Don't get ahead. ToteCard so you know your accumulation.

[1]Special Report; *Tufts University Health and Nutrition Letter,* October 1999, vol. 17, no. 8, page 4, BB486.

[2]"Food Servings," *Mayo Clinic Health Letter,* April 1997, page 7.

[3]*Total Health for Men,* Neil Wertheimer, editor, Rodale Press, Emmaus, Pennsylvania, 1995, page 566, BB245.

[4]"Weight Control: What Works and Why," Medical Essay, supplement to *Mayo Clinic Health Letter,* Mayo Foundation for Education and Research, Rochester, Minnesota, June 1994, page 5, BB9.

[5]"A Thinner Brain," *Men's Fitness,* April 1997, page 50, BB266.

[6]"Yo-Yo Weight Can Be Harmful to Your Health," *Healthier Living,* vol. 2, no. 2, March 1997, page 5, BB267.

[7]*The Serotonin Solution,* Judith J. Wurtman, Fawcett Columbine, New York, New York, 1996, page 14, BB121.

[8]"Nutritional Supplements: What You Really Need for Optimal Health," Jeffrey Blumberg, Ph.D., *Bottom Line/Health,* vol. 11, no. 1, January 1997, BB247.

[9]"Facts and Fiction about Vitamin E," *Harvard Health Letter,* vol. 22, no. 1, November 1996, pages 1-4, BB246.

[10]"The Supreme Bean," Kristina Koszmovszky, *Men's Health,* January/February 1997, page 107, BB226.

[11]Psychopharmacology, vol. 199, 1995, pages 66-70, from "Lift Your Spirits with a Cup of Joe," *Men's Confidential,* December 1995, page 6, BB227.

[12]"Amazing Grain, How Sweet It Is," *Harvard Health Letter,* vol. 22, no. 5, March 1997, page 7, BB264.

[13] Ibid.

[14] "What You Should Know About Aspartame," The International Food Information Council Foundation, reviewed by the American Academy of Family Physicians Foundation; "Aspartame Consumption Found Safe in New Studies," *Food Insight,* January/February 1990, BB145.

[15]"FDA: Sweetener Is Safe," *Restaurants and Institutions,* vol. 107, no. 5, February 15, 1997, BB224.

[16] Bricklin, op. cit., page 205, BB130; "Protein Primer," op. cit., page 25, BB136; "Older Adults May Not Be Getting Enough Protein," *Tufts University Diet & Nutrition Letter,* vol. 14, no. 11, January 1997, page 2, BB198; *Prevention's Lose Weight Guidebook 1996,* Mark Bricklin, Rodale Press, Emmaus, Pennsylvania, 1996, page 10, BB130.

[17]"Caffeine Helps Tension Headaches," *Health News,* vol. 3, no. 5, April 15, 1997, page 5, BB265.

[18]"Sleep Lab Instructions," *Neurological Associates of Washington,* Bellevue, Washington, 1997, BB215.

[19]Low Fat Beats the Sun," *UC Berkeley Wellness Letter,* August 1995, page 2, BB169; "Low-Fat Diets Reduce Skin Cancer Risk," *Health Confidential,* Homer S. Black, Ph.D., Baylor College of Medicine, *The New England Journal of Medicine,* October 1996, BB170.

[20]"Watch What You Eat After Dark," Holly McCord, R.D., *Prevention,* January 1996, pages 57-58, BB199.

[21]"Reduced Fat Snacks," *Mayo Clinic Health Letter,* Rochester, Minnesota, August 1995, page 7, BB203.

[22]*"A Digestive Wind," Food in History,* Reay Tannahill, Crown Trade Paperbacks, New York, New York, 1988, page 193, BB103.

[23]*On Food and Cooking,* Harold McGee, Macmillan Publishing Co., NY, NY, 1984, page 258, BB25.

[24]"Gut Reactions," Michael Castleman, *Men's Fitness,* August 1996, page 122, BB111.

[25]Wertheimer, op. cit., page 206, BB245.

[26]"High Fiber Diet and Preventative Medicine," Gerard Guillory, M.D., *The Little Black Book of Secrets,* Boulder, Colorado, 1996, page 15, BB248; *Journal of the American Medical Association,* February 14, 1996, page 18, from "An Apple a Day Keeps the Cardiologist Away," *Prevention,* June 1996, page 17, BB249.

"The Dauntless Spirit of Resolve . . ."

—Shakespeare

YOUR ABILITY TO CHANGE

You are now at the most important point in the process of stripping fat, becoming stronger and living longer: BodyRenewal™. You read about the *primeval raging appetite,* the NeoCuisine™ solution, the 20 benefits of exercise, the power of Control Psychology™ and the Surroundings Management™ of people, places and processes. You are aware that NeoCuisine™-style eating and regular exercise cut lung and heart diseases, cancer, strokes, pneumonia and flu deaths by 25% to 50%.[1]

Now be aware of your potential to change. Believe and know it is in you to proceed gladly and with self-trust. Once aware, you will be all right. Your potential to change your life's mode exists. Believe it. Each of us carries with us a unique set of qualities to power us forward. Draw upon these for your success.

125

If you have failed at weight loss attempts in the past, view them as learning experiences rather than seeing them as failures. Consider all you have learned. You are far wiser now for having tried than not having tried at all. The fact is that you had the wrong strategies. Change your strategies and success is probable.

When you say that you are not the kind of person who can lose weight and become fit, what you are really saying is this: Up to this time I haven't become fit or lost weight. Growth and change are things people do every day.

Human beings naturally avoid hard tasks. But maturity helps us understand that avoidance is simply a form of immaturity. Tough words, maybe, but true. Achieving the shape and vigor of youth requires a level of maturity that's emancipating. As an adult, you have the ability to forgo current pleasures for future rewards.

The dauntless spirit of personal resolve embraces voluntary volition (your own personal act of free will), good timing (no life crises), recognizing and accepting elemental effort (yes, there's work in achieving the shape and vigor of youth) and answering yes to all the key gateway questions (coming up). The next several pages cover these topics and help create your personal resolve to enter the Body-Renewal™.

VOLUNTARY VOLITION

When Shakespeare spoke of "the dauntless spirit of resolve," he understood the power of one who has made up his mind. *Voluntary volition* is crucial to long-term success. It carries the notion of "I don't like the way I look and I'm not going to stand for it any more!" It is a huge affirmation of self. Voluntary volition means that you are fed up to the point where you want to change and never go back. There is a part of your mind that simply says, "I will never again be fat." You'll know when it happens because it is gut felt. You know that the time for achieving the shape and vigor of youth is at hand. Yes, entering a new life's phase is always fraught with trepidation but your voluntary volition has qualities of joy and relief. You have at last decided after much time, thought and even agonizing.

YOU WANT THE SHAPE AND VIGOR OF YOUTH FOR <u>YOU</u>.

You are renewing your body to become stronger, healthier, happier, live longer and look great. You are deciding for a more positive life for you.

Your voluntary volition springs not from fear and pressure but from happiness for all the benefits accruing to you. The strength, positivism, good feelings, endurance and the many other life-enriching blessings of regaining the shape and vigor of youth energizes your voluntary volition. The negative psychology of "have to" is replaced with affirming incentive for extracting the most out of life because you want health, stamina and high self-appreciation.

Hippocrates, the father of modern medicine, believed that each person experiences favorable moments during which healing most likely occurs. He knew favorable moments resulted from time and effort. You are now at a favorable moment. You have read and contemplated. You realize that achieving the shape and vigor of youth is more than a mere diet. It's a life-mode change.

Just how powerful is voluntary volition? The desire for independent decision making is innately strong. Jefferson, Washington and the other Founding Fathers realized that freedom of choice is one of the most powerful human motivations, sufficient to create a country. If voluntary volition is potent enough to create the United States of America, it is ample to propel you through the BodyRenewal™.

TIMING YOUR BodyRenewal™

The first aspect of timing your BodyRenewal™ is being sure you have contemplated your new life's mode. You want to anticipate your new way of life. The contemplation period preceding BodyRenewal™ should have advanced to a commitment of eating NeoCuisine™-style the rest of your life. You agree that some television will give way to striding, 1•1•2™, deflexing and Dynamic Balancing™.

Maybe most important is that you have spent time examining the benefits of Body-Renewal™. By thinking about them, you have gone beyond the moment's inspiration and into *I really need to do this for my life's sake.*

There is a long-standing school of psychological thought that all people have self-control limitations. This principle suggests the BodyRenewal™ cycle be started when there is low stress in your life. Most of us don't realize how much self-control we exercise on any given day: getting out of bed, controlling our temper when somebody makes us angry, getting to meetings on time, living within budget, constantly running errands and the many tasks required in daily life. So it makes good sense, then, to begin the BodyRenewal™ when you're emotionally composed. Tackling too many things at once overwhelms us and provides the perfect excuse to forgo the plan. Pick a time in your life to commence BodyRenewal™ when you are relaxed.

Limit goals, too. Please don't promise yourself to lose ten pounds and run 20 miles the first week. Remember that starting when you are relaxed and limiting your goals is not a sign of weakness. It has more to do with being intelligent and managing yourself accordingly.

ELEMENTAL EFFORT

I would be less than candid if I told you that maintaining a positive attitude, preparing NeoCuisine™ and rebuilding your body require little effort. Just as the sun and earth did not stand still for the Beethovens, DaVincis and Edisons of this world, you likewise cannot expect miracles. Understandably, it is challenging to accept giving up present pleasures for future shape and vigor of youth gains. *But it is not too hard.* Discipline always requires some degree of sacrifice but it's not awful or terrible. It is simply how life works.

Dr. John Kabat-Zinn says, "People stay on their diets because the diet is seen in a larger framework. It's part of working on one's self to develop one's inner capacity to be whole."[2] This insight alludes to the fact that a diet and exercise are not simply pursuit of vanity but development of our physical and psychic potential. The discipline required and results gained make us better people. We can do and share more. Our increased self-appreciation elevates our capacity to love. Our heightened vigor means greater contribution. We have developed ourselves to a higher level. It is not conceit that drives us to the shape and vigor of youth, it's our intent to attain our potential.

Here is a good way to test elemental effort. Imagine yourself at 85 looking back over your life, recounting its high points to your 12-year old, wide-eyed grandson or granddaughter. Consider what you would remember in your career, your relationships and about yourself. Visualize what you would like to look back on. Then ask yourself: "Am I living a life that will allow me to look back and smile?"

Think how at 85 you could still possess in large measure the shape and vigor of youth through regular exercise and eating NeoCuisine™ style. It's a reality you create right now provided your timing is right, you have voluntary volition to move ahead and you readily embrace the elemental effort required.

GATEWAY QUESTIONS

Thus far you realize that you are making the Body-Renewal™ decision entirely on your own, the timing is right because you're not stressed and elemental effort is okay. Here is a list of gateway questions to move you along in your Body-Renewal™ decision:

1 I am willing to adopt the anti-aging attitudes of self-actualization, living NOW and conceding nothing.
Yes ____ No ____

2 I get energized when I think about the unbeatable benefits of attaining the shape and vigor of youth.
Yes ____ No ____

3 I don't mind cooking NeoCuisine™ for 15 to 30 minutes every day.
Yes ____ No ____

4 I'm ready to spend the $100 to $200 and time required to set up a home gym.
Yes_____   No_____

5 I'll make the time for 30 to 60 minutes of exercise five to six days a week.
Yes_____   No_____

6 I'm pretty sure I can manage my environment and win over family and friends.
Yes_____   No_____

7 The idea of having to make elemental effort doesn't much bother me.
Yes_____   No_____

8 In my heart I feel I have a desire to change my life.
Yes_____   No_____

The answer to all these questions should be yes. If you find yourself hesitant, it doesn't mean that you won't decide for BodyRenewal™ one day—it simply means that the timing is not right. On the other hand, if you answer these questions with a determination to proceed, chances are very, very good that you will prevail.

YOUR FUTURE: THE SHAPE AND VIGOR OF YOUTH

Here is where you begin breaking current negative self/body image by projecting ahead to what you will be. Rehearse your positive future self and leave current self-image behind. Build positive feelings for where you are going by completing this exercise. Write in pencil because you may want to make changes as you go through BodyRenewal™.

1 My weight will be (keeping in mind you are trading fat for muscle, not necessarily huge weight loss): _____

_____

2 My clothing size will be: _____

_____

3 My shape will be (e.g. when I was 25 or 30): _____

_____

4 When people say, "How thin you are" (meaning how fat you once were) I will cope by saying: _____

_____

_____

5 How will everyday future life be different (e.g. climb stairs without huffing and puffing, going to the beach without embarrassment, etc.): _____

_____

_____

6 My new feelings about myself will be: _____

_____

_____

7 My home life will change to: _____

_____

8 My spouse/partner and I will: _____

_____

_____

9 My social life will be: _____

_____

_____

10 The sports/activities I engage in will be (e.g. hiking, water skiing, a two week cycle tour, etc.): _____

_____

_____

_____

NOW THAT YOU HAVE WRITTEN YOUR GOALS, TRANSFER THE THREE MOST IMPORTANT TO THREE 3X5 CARDS. PLACE THEM WHERE YOU FREQUENTLY ARE SUCH AS YOUR CAR, BATHROOM AND REFRIGERATOR.

130

REWARDS

Right now, write down the positive rewards for achieving your desired weight. Welcome rewards for yourself because winning the fat fight requires cunning in a world beset with attractive pitfalls, each designed to derail your shape and vigor of youth achievement. Create an agreeable combination of incentives motivating you in staying the course. List your accomplishment rewards on several cards, posting them where you can see them daily. CONSIDER:

HALFWAY
- A one-hour full body massage.
- Take a day off from work to do what you want to do.
- Buy two best-sellers.
- Buy a decor treasure from an antique store.
- Call in sick. Take a day off.
- Spend 10 minutes really thinking about your

positive progress. Reflect on how much better you're beginning to feel ... emotionally and physically.

- Visit a nearby special place. Consider the advances you are now making in your life.
- Give yourself a week of NC celebration dinners.

- _____
- _____
- _____
- _____
- _____
- _____

FINAL

- Buy that CD player that you want.
- Buy the new wardrobe you need because of the weight loss.
- Catch one of those cheap air shuttles to Las Vegas or Reno to enjoy the bargain rooms and entertainment. Skip the gambling and stick to the salad bars.

- Buy a new car. Every time you make a payment, remind yourself how you earned it and the import of the lean and fit life.
- Have a gathering of friends to celebrate your victory over fathood. Serve an NC celebration dinner.

Now it's your turn to list the rewards you plan to give yourself when you realize your final diet goals. Be generous with yourself and be clever.

- _____
- _____
- _____
- _____
- _____
- _____
- _____
- _____
- _____
- _____

- _____
- _____
- _____
- _____

So what can you expect emerging from the Body-Renewal™? First, you will have the shape of youth. Your body will be leaner and more muscular than it has been for years. You will begin to see pleasing body definition reminiscent of your youth.

You will be more vigorous due to enhanced strength, added endurance and increased flexibility resulting from the Muscle Rebuild™. Added energy will indeed be a part of your life.

Mentally, you will notice a more optimistic, positive and enthusiastic attitude. You have, after all, stripped fat, added muscle and begun a new life's process which will doubtless add vigorous years to your life. As a result, your self-appreciation rises markedly, your thought processes clear, and your overall health and well-being improve dramatically.

PERSONAL RESOLVE

1 MORE THAN ALL ELSE, POSITIVE CHANGE RESULTS FROM RESOLVE.

2 *VOLUNTARILY* ENTERING BodyRenewal™ INCREASES YOUR SUCCESS.

3 MAKE A FLOURISHING PHYSIQUE ONE OF YOUR LIFE'S PRIORITIES.

4 START BodyRenewal™ AT A CRISIS-FREE TIME.

5 EXPECT ELEMENTAL EFFORT. It's okay.

6 ANSWER YES TO ALL THE GATEWAY QUESTIONS.

7 PURSUE REALISTIC GOALS, e.g, a one- to two-pound loss per week. Impossible expectations disappoint and lay the foundation to quit, e.g. "ten-pound loss per week."

FOOD AND THE POPULATION EXPLOSION

Food availability correlates directly to population explosions. At 10,000 B.C., the world's population numbered but 3 million. But after 7,000 years of farming—3,000 B.C.—world population exploded to 100 million.[1] Likewise with the introduction of the New World's maize, potatoes and peanuts to China in the 18th century, its population zoomed from 150 million to 450 million in a mere 150 years.[2] And my, how quality food has made us bigger. In 1986 Japan, the average 17-year-old boy grew two inches taller than his 1962 counterpart. In China over the last 30 years, height increased at the rate of one inch every ten years![3]

But all is not well. Today we eat too much, resulting in 60% of the U.S. population being overweight. NeoCuisine™ is the solution with a third the calories of conventional 21st century slow-kill food.

[1]*Food in History*, Reay Tannahill, Crown Trade Paperbacks, New York, New York, 1988, page 33, BB103.

[2]Ibid., page 264, BB103.

[3]Ibid., page 371, BB103.

[1]"How Healthy Are We?" Mark Clements and Diane Hales, *Parade Magazine*, September 7, 1997, pages 4-7, BB287.

[2]*Healing and the Mind*, Bill Moyers, Doubleday Inc., New York, New York, 1993, page 135.

BodyRenewal™

Plunging a life into a swirl of immediate change is not a good idea. BodyRenewal™ is accordingly organized in phases for minimal disruption. It accounts for the difficulties in changing longstanding habits. Each week you are discreetly conditioned to the behaviors of your new life and NOW is the time to begin. To quote Patrick Henry, "When should we be stronger? Will it be next week, or next year?"[1]

Over the next 50 days as you are judiciously introduced to BodyRenewal™, you will not achieve your goal weight. It is a 50-day instruction to control fat for the rest of your life. The aim now is to gradually initiate you to BodyRenewal™ technique, allowing your body to adjust. Weight loss with BodyRenewal™ is steady and consistent. There is no flash reduction.

Once acclimated you continue BodyRenewal™ until you achieve your desired weight. At the end of 50 days you're "in the groove" to continue stripping fat, become stronger and engineer your flourishing physique. At 50 days, you have the cuisine, psychology, environmental practices and physical training processes for lifelong fat control. Once your goal weight is realized calories are gradually added back, but more on that later. Our true objective is setting a lifelong course.

BodyRenewal™ begins with Surroundings Management™. The first thing you want to get straight is your environment. It makes good sense. The first week you rework your surroundings for BodyRenewal™ harmony.

BodyRenewal™ also launches you immediately into NeoCuisine™ to develop a pattern of eating calorie-frugal foods. When you see how easy it is to modify eating habits, you'll be encouraged because each recipe serves ONE. Portions by design are large. Your past lifestyle may have included for dinner salad with an oily vinaigrette, plenty of bread with margarine and a serving of meat alongside buttered vegetables and a starch of pasta or potato. This was followed later in the evening with ice cream or possibly (for the sake of conservatism) six or eight

SnackWell® cookies. Your evening repast easily ran 1,500 calories or more. All this is altered to more salubrious approaches.

Human beings are genetically programmed for rapid single-food satiety. In other words, satisfaction is reached quickly after eating enough of one food with particular characteristics—flavor, appearance, mouth feel and so on. You've experienced this: The third Snickers® bar never tastes as good as the first. Purdue University Nutritionist Richard Mattes, Ph.D., says, "The monotony becomes so overwhelming that you lose interest in eating."

Man has a built-in disposition to eat a variety of foods. The body learned this to help ensure adequate nutrient intake. We are genetically hardwired to seek a variety of foods. This can work against us. Food scientist Susan Roberts, Ph.D., of the Human Nutrition Research Center at Tufts University has verified that the broader the array of people's food choices, the more calories they consume. But as food choices narrow, less eating

naturally results stemming from rapid single-food satiety. Eating one kind of food (even pepperoni pizza every night) fatigues the palate. You tend to eat less.[2]

The single-food satiety effect guides NeoCuisine™ logic. You will note that most NeoCuisine™ entreés are one-dish dinners. You are not presented five-course meals for the reasons given above. NeoCuisine™ strategy includes not only calorie-frugal foods but one-entreé dinners so the single-food satiety effect works in your behalf. Eat as much as you like knowing that no matter how good that first bite tastes, it will be difficult for you to overconsume calories not only because NeoCuisine™ is calorie-frugal but also because of the single-food satiety effect. Now you have more reasons to relax.

YOUR BodyRenewal™ JOURNAL

Ken Blanchard, Ph.D., and Spencer Johnson, M.D., say in their famous book *The One Minute Manager*, "Clearly the number one motivator of people is feedback on results."[3] BodyRenewal™ success is enhanced by keeping your own BodyRenewal™ journal. Use a simple spiral notebook. Bear in mind that this is private, nobody's business but yours. Your best feedback motivator is contrasting now with the past, particularly your before photo. Keep it handy. Begin your BodyRenewal™ journal with these basics:

- Current weight
- Waist measurement
- Before picture

- Maximum non-dominant arm curl∗ See page 56
- Your starting feelings/ morale∗∗
- Dynamic Balance™ test results∗∗∗

As you go through your BodyRenewal™, you'll want to record personal insights like hunger patterns, binge triggers and discoveries found in books, magazines and learned from friends. Write anything you wish that is a service to you.

There are a couple of last important points. Begin BodyRenewal™ by reminding yourself that carrying too much fat is not your fault. The body's primary

---

∗ This will be used as a strength progress indicator. You will be surprised at how rapidly you progress.

∗∗ Because one of BodyRenewal's™ goals is feeling better about life, write a five- or six-sentence feelings profile. You probably feel encouraged and optimistic because you have made a decision. It almost comes as a relief because you have finally decided. But whatever your feelings profile is today, it will be better once you fully engage BodyRenewal™. Numerous studies point to the exercise-optimism connection.

∗∗∗You will make that connection. You will find that balance improves considerably through the course of BodyRenewal™.

goal is to get fat because it was the body's best survival insurance. We've evolved over 3 million years but only had a consistent food supply for the last 150 years due primarily to cheap, extensive railroad transportation. Fat is the result of our stone age *primeval raging appetite* sated with calorie-dense 21st century foods. To the rescue comes Neo-Cuisine™. As you know, it's based on foods of 20 calories or less per ounce which gives the ideal calorie-to-weight ratio for allaying your hunger versus 21st century typical foods of 60+ calories an ounce.

So be kind to yourself. The extra weight you carry is not the result of personal weakness. Stop blaming yourself because you are the victim of evolution's cruel trick:

OUR BODIES ARE PARANOID.

We are saddled with a naturally prodigious appetite, nature's way of protecting us from the starvation of times past. NeoCuisine™ handily fools Mother Nature with copious quantities of low calorie-to-weight ratio foods.

135

Here's more good advice. Don't compare. It's witless. Most magazines use 25 year-old female models with breast implants and greased up professional male weight lifters browned with too much self tanner. You will wind up looking good but it's doubtful you'll be on the cover of *Cosmo* or *Muscle*. Would you really want that?

One last thing. Don't put your life on hold during Body-Renewal™. Never say that you won't go to the beach until you've lost ten pounds. Don't say you won't get a good bike until you're "in shape." Don't say you'll forego social events until you have "things under control." Because you're committed with voluntary volition, you'll do just fine. Body-Renewal™ is not monkish asceticism. You continue to have a life but with revolutionary changes that strip fat and increase your endurance and vigor.

THE BodyRenewal™ SCHEDULE

BodyRenewal™ eases the logistical demands of buying the right food, setting up your gym and body acclimation. By the end of your Body-Renewal™ segue, for example, you spend anywhere from 30 to 45 minutes daily creating your flourishing physique. It's a small investment for the returns: enriched self-regard, amplified vitality and a longer life.

DAY	DAILY	CYCLE	TIME
MONDAY	TC,BRJ	S,MD, & DB	35 min
TUESDAY	TC,BRJ	S	30 min
WEDNESDAY	TC,BRJ	1•1•2™, MD & DB	15 min
THURSDAY	TC,BRJ	S	30 min
FRIDAY	TC,BRJ	S	30 min
SATURDAY	TC,BRJ	S, 1•1•2™, MD & DB 45 min	
SUNDAY	TC,BRJ	OFF	0 min

LEGEND

TC = TOTECARD
BRJ = BodyRenewal™ Journal
S = STRIDE
MD = MACRO DEFLEX™

DB = DYNAMIC BALANCE™
1•1•2™ = ONE MINUTE *TOTAL CHALLENGE TIME*, ONE CYCLE, TWICE A WEEK

CUSTOMIZING

It is unlikely that you will like every NeoCuisine™ recipe. Don't give it a second thought. You may substitute NeoCuisine™ recipes as you wish. Look at Appendix A, the Neo-Cuisine™ cookbook. You have a nice variety of recipes to choose from: salads, NeoCuisine™ meat-loaves, stews, stir-fries and so on. Choose what you like because all meet the 20-calorie-per-ounce criterion. Do try all food varieties, however, because you may surprise yourself by preferring a particular approach that initially you may not have considered appealing. The only way to know is by giving each dish a trial run.

To some the BodyRenewal™ schedule may appear too structured or doesn't conform to their time needs. Every person is different. Use the suggested instructions as a model to be customized by you. You may, for example, wish to start 1•1•2™ before beginning striding. This works fine. Accommodate your-self as necessary. Feel free to change starting times for beginning NeoCuisine™, striding and so on. If you customize Body-Renewal™, change timing, not content.

If you are already exercising, your introduction to strid-ing, deflexions and 1•1•2™ may seem somewhat slow. Using your good judgment, go immediately to the more challenging 1•1•2™ levels if you are already strength training. Proceed to 4 mph strid-ing if you already walk or jog. If you stretch frequently, go imme-diately to full deflexing and add additional stretches as you wish. However, if you are a neophyte to strength training, striding, deflexing or Dynamic Balance™, follow BodyRenewal™ in the steps suggested. You'll less suffer 1 soreness and no discour-agement. The trick to good physical training management is gradual introduction which cir-cumvents injury and despair.

If you do customize, there are only a few rules cast in con-crete:

- •DON'T LEAVE OUT ANY ASPECT OF BodyRenewal™. ALL ARE IMPORTANT.
- •STRIDE FIVE DAYS A WEEK.
- •DO NOT INCREASE 1•1•2™ INTENSITY FASTER THAN RECOMMENDED UNLESS YOU ARE WELL CONDITIONED.
- •NEVER SKIP THE WARM-UP PRECEDING 1•1•2™.
- •MINIMUM 48 HOURS REST (TWO FULL DAYS) BETWEEN 1•1•2™.
- •CONCLUDE 1•1•2™ WITH MACRO DEFLEX™ AND DYNAMIC BALANCE™.
- •YOU CAN SWITCH ANY RECIPES YOU WISH PROVIDED THEY ARE NeoCuisine™.

CHECKLIST

❏ Voluntary volition: 100% your choice
❏ BodyRenewal™ journal
❏ Doctor check-up
❏ Weights
❏ Before picture
❏ No self-blame
❏ Small food scale in ounces
❏ BUY:

•Quality meat bases (meat concentrate listed in the first three ingredients): two beef, two chicken, one lobster and one clam or call: **For the Better Than Bouillon® (meat bases) source nearest you: 1-800-429-3663.** Buy any meat base you wish provided meat concentrate is among the first three ingredients. This assures quality.

•Ultra low-fat tofu (no more than 1/2 gram fat per ounce) or call: **Mori-Nu®** (low fat tofu) **For the source nearest you: 1-800-669-8638.** Buy a case of extra-firm lite tofu.

•Good whey (or soy) protein powder (expensive but worth it).

•Fill/stock your larder. Set space aside in your pantry and refrigerator for your NeoCuisine™. Having your own inventory area set aside makes it easy to find ingredients rather than dashing about the kitchen. Keep NeoCuisine™ specific ingredients in one place in the refrigerator and pantry.

For years all of us have shopped with impulse. It's not our fault really. Marketers spend their days getting us to reach for what we hadn't planned to buy. Impulse buying (it looks interesting, colorful and pleasurable) is now habit. Breaking it is a good way to reduce calorie consumption because unnecessary temptations never make it into your house. Here are tips to help break the great American impulse buying tradition:

•Shop less: Write your list and stick to it. Control what is brought into the house and placed in your larder. If you have the good stuff available, that's what you eat.

•Shop the perimeter: Grocery stores are organized so the most expensive and cal-dense foods are in the center aisles. The outer perimeter of grocery stores is where you want to linger, particularly in the vegetable, bulk food and fish sections. This is where you find the most NeoCuisine™ foods.

BodyRenewal™
SURPRISE BENEFITS

MORE COMFORT

As fat accumulates, it crowds space occupied by your organs. Obese people often can't sit comfortably because of the fat accumulated in their abdomens. Thin people are more comfortable. Sitting is easier because the 90° angle of the torso does not cause the innards to be pressed by the excess fat. Belts don't feel as tight. Summer isn't as sticky. Losing weight likewise reduces strain on your lower back, hips and knees.

LOOK YOUNGER

Lean is young. Be lean, look young. It sounds simplistic but when I ran a marathon with Johnny Kelly, the legendary 80-year-old, two-time Boston marathon winner, he had the butt of a 19-year-old. I know because I had to follow him too often in the training runs when he decided to hotfoot it for short sprints. There's nothing quite like 19-year-old buns on an 80-year-old man.

SLEEP BETTER

One of the most common causes of snoring is fat. Lose the weight and reduce snoring. By the way, snoring is no laughing matter because it may be indicative of sleep apnea, a condition where air passageways temporarily block, causing highly fitful breathing which in turn raises blood pressure, reduces oxygen to the brain and can leave you fatigued after a night's "rest."[5] If for no other reason, lose the snoring for the sake of your mate.

VIRTUE & HAPPINESS

Aristotle said, "... those who are happy spend their time most readily and continuously in virtuous activities."[4] Aristotle was big on virtue but he did have a point. If BodyRenewal™ leads to better health, less stress and more discipline, then you are pursuing virtue. Aristotle correctly states it leads to happiness which the ancient Greeks said was man's purpose.

FASTER HEALING

Being overweight carries odd consequences, many you would never imagine. Mayo Clinic, for example, reports, "Complications following surgery occur more often in overweight people versus those who aren't. Wounds don't heal as fast or as well. Infection is more common."[6]

139

MONDAY, DAY 1

Welcome Your Family

Your action today for the shape and vigor of youth is encouraging your family to help you strip fat and exercise. Revisit Surroundings Management™ to remind yourself how to sell your new life to your family. You can't achieve the shape and vigor of youth in a vacuum.

APPROACH YOUR FAMILY WITH THE BENEFITS OF YOUR GOALS:

- Increased optimism.
- Source of their pride.
- Whole family reward.
- If you love yourself more you can do better loving them.
- Increased energy.

REMIND YOUR FAMILY WHAT THEY CAN DO TO HELP:

- They must be patient because if it took 20 years to put the fat on, it can't be stripped in a month.
- Please don't raid your NeoCuisine™ inventory.
- No teasing or joking, please.
- Entreat them to offer encouragement.

EXPECT:

ANYTHING

Reactions vary. But remember this is your decision. As you progress, your family acclimates. Fervor (enthusiasm/pessimism) moderates.

HOMEWORK:

YOUR FEELINGS

Today you begin your Body-Renewal™ journal. Write a five- or six-sentence feelings profile. You probably feel encouraged and glad because you have made a decision. It almost comes as a relief because you have finally decided. But whatever your feelings profile is today, it will be better once you fully engage in 1•1•2™, striding and deflexing.

NeoCuisine™

As you voyage through the BodyRenewal™ cycle, feel free to peruse Appendix A, the NeoCuisine™ cookbook. Switch recipes as you wish.

CACCIATORE CON POLENTA

Cacciatore served with polenta in place of pasta, a nice touch indeed. Whereas pasta is just water-boiled wheat, polenta is flavored with stock for much more flavorful results.

• **Serves one.**

Calories: 587
Net Weight: 31 ounces
Prep time: 20 minutes
Cook time: 20 to 25 minutes
Calorie-to-weight ratio: 19 calories per ounce

- *2 cups chicken broth, fat skimmed*
- *1/3 cup polenta*
- *4 ounces chicken breast, boned and skinned*
- *1/2 cup fat-free (lite) pasta (marinara) sauce*
- *1 cup sliced fresh mushrooms*
- *1/4 cup onion, chopped*
- *1/2 cup whole baby carrots— smallest size*
- *10 to 12 ounces frozen petite green beans*

In a medium saucepan bring chicken broth to a boil. Stir in polenta with a wire whisk. Return to full boil, cover, reduce heat to medium-low and cook until thickened, about 3 to 5 minutes. Remove lid and continue to cook over low heat 20 to 25 minutes, stirring occasionally. Polenta should be very thick.

Meanwhile, cut chicken breasts into 1/2" to 3/4" cubes. Sprinkle with salt, pepper and garlic powder. Cook in a nonstick skillet over medium-high until browned on all sides. Add pasta sauce and 1/4 cup of water and stir to deglaze pan. Simmer for 5 minutes.

Microwave mushrooms, onions and carrots in a microwavable container, e.g. lidded glass, for 3 minutes. Add to pasta sauce and cook for 1 to 2 minutes.

Microwave green beans in a microwavable container (e.g. lidded glass) for 6 minutes. Put on a serving plate. Add salt and pepper to taste and 3 to 4 sprays of "I Can't Believe It's Not Butter."® Place polenta on serving plate, top with pasta sauce and serve with a quarter-lemon.

TUESDAY, DAY 2

Welcome Co-Workers and Friends

Co-workers and friends have almost as much impact on BodyRenewal™ follow-through as your family. It helps if they buy into your Body-Renewal™ efforts. People tend to do things because they see it as being in their best interest. Their benefits are:

- As with your family, you can love friends better if you love yourself more.★
- More cooperation can result because higher self-appreciation diminishes your need to "win" in all situations.
- A robust whole augurs more energy and increased productivity.
- You have fewer "down days" because striding and 1•1•2™ decreases depression, builds optimism and enhances the immune system.
- Who knows, you may inspire some near you to start striding or do a little strength training.

A co-worker/friend conversation might sound like this:

"I've been carrying extra weight for some time and I'd like to make a change in my life. To tell you the truth I'm a little nervous because it's going to require work. I could use your encouragement. You'll see me eating what looks like odd foods and trying to stay on the straight and narrow. I'll be eating vegetables for snacks, not my favorite donuts, and trying to avoid the other stuff that packs on pounds. You can help me out by maybe offering some encouragement along the way."

EXPECT:

A LITTLE NEEDLING
It may happen. But you may also get lucky and hear an encouraging word or two.

HOMEWORK:

HAVE A FRIEND JOIN YOU
If you can get a friend to join you in BodyRenewal™ (provided he/she's resolved to change), mutual support is a strong impetus. Meet weekly and talk about anything that helps. Walking together is good talk time.

★ This is often a difficult concept to understand because we sometimes don't acknowledge friendship as a form of love. Much of your ability to contribute is based on your self-appreciation. You must see yourself as having something to give. If you don't love yourself, it's difficult to love others.

SHRIMP QUICHE *

A high-protein, tasty quiche. Quiche is another scare word but, yes, men eat it. Enjoy this large serving, sure to quiet your primeval raging appetite.

•
Serves one.

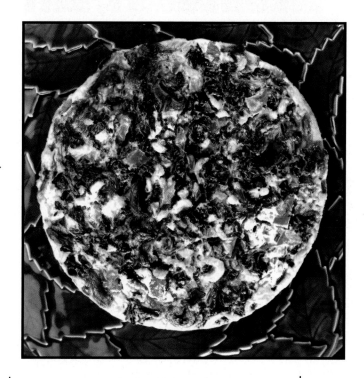

Calories: 604
Net Weight: 32 ounces
Prep time: 15 to 20 minutes
Cook time: 40 to 45 minutes
Calorie-to-weight ratio: 19 calories per ounce

- *2 cups fresh mushrooms, sliced*
- *1 cup tomato, diced*
- *10-ounce package frozen chopped spinach, thawed and lightly squeezed (should be "juicy")*

- *1 teaspoon lemon zest*
- *1 generous teaspoon quality lobster base (refer to page 138 for ordering information) or 1/2 teaspoon salt*
- *1 cup bay shrimp*
- *1/4 cup quality grated Parmesan cheese, e.g. Reggiano*
- *1/4 teaspoon pepper or more*
- *Three 4-ounce (1-1/2 cups) containers fat-free egg substitute, e.g. EggBeaters®*

Combine all ingredients. Spray pie tin with nonstick vegetable spray and add quiche mixture. Bake at 350° for 40 to 45 minutes.

★ The *UC Berkeley Health Letter* recently had an article titled "Keep Shrimp on the Team." The point was that shrimp's a source of high-quality protein and low in *saturated* fat, the real culprit in high cholesterol.[7]

WEDNESDAY, DAY 3

NeoCuisine™ Breakfast Start

Breakfast is the most abused meal of the day. We're too rushed to do it right. So, we settle for Pop Tarts®, Eggo® waffles or a fatty brand muffin at some latté stop. What you wind up getting is too much sugar, insufficient quantity and lousy nutrition. NeoCuisine™ vastly improves that scenario by providing you with a steaming bowl of whole grain breakfast cereal.

• QUICK-COOK OATMEAL.

It's the simplest way to introduce yourself to a quality, nourishing breakfast because it's recognizable and easy. But for the sake of variety, evolve to the more interesting oatmeal types and other grains reviewed in Day-Parts.

• START WITH SMALL PORTIONS

Learn to eat as little as a cup of oatmeal or Cream of Wheat® or any whole grain breakfast cereal of choice. Eat as much as you can. Your goal is to fill up so you go all the way through to lunch.

• EXPERIMENT

Try no-fat/sugar fruit yogurt mixed into your hot cereal. It's delicious. Fresh or whole individually quick-frozen (IQF) fruits are available at your supermarket and although a little pricey, add flavor variation.

• MAKE AN NC HI PRO DREAM™

See Appendix B. Start with a half recipe. Or, make a whole recipe drinking half for breakfast and the other half for lunch. Accompany your NC Hi Pro Dream™ lunch with whole fruit or a fruit salad for total breakfast and lunch calories of only 300 to 400.

EXPECT:

EATING BREAKFAST TO FEEL STRANGE

Give yourself a couple of weeks to adapt. Eating a good breakfast shortly becomes second nature.

HOMEWORK:

NeoCuisine™ LUNCHING

Tomorrow you start NeoCuisine™ lunching. This is a good time to start experimenting with NC Hi Pro Dreams™. See Appendix B. You will find NC lunching saves you both time and money. Instead of going to a restaurant, you can eat on the job or, better, stride after your quick NeoCuisine™ lunch. You begin striding on Monday, Day 8. The point here is that a quick lunch allows for a nice lunchtime stride, the ultimate wake-up strategy for the afternoon.

ALL AMERICAN MEATLOAF

Meatloaf, potatoes and ketchup on a diet? You can have it the NeoCuisine™ way at 1/3 the calories of the old fatty original.

•

Makes 2 meatloaf servings.

Calories per serving: 482
Net weight per serving: 36 ounces
Prep time: 15 to 20 minutes
Cook time: 45 minutes
Calorie-to-weight ratio: 18 calories per ounce
(Calorie count includes Button Mushroom Gravy or Sugar-Free ketchup.)

- *3/4 pound (12 ounces) 1% fat very lean ground turkey*
- *1 Tablespoon quality beef base*
- *1 teaspoon garlic powder*
- *1 teaspoon pepper*
- *1 teaspoon red wine vinegar*
- *1/2 cup onion, finely diced*
- *18-20 ounces (1-1/2 packages) extra-firm, ultra-low-fat tofu*
- *1 recipe Garlic Mashed Potatoes (see page 352)*

- *1 recipe Button Mushroom Thyme Gravy: 39 calories (see page 345)*
  or
  1 recipe Sugar-Free Ketchup: 36 calories (see page 343)

Combine first six ingredients. Set aside.

Crumble tofu thoroughly into blender and pureé until smooth, about 30 to 45 seconds. You will need to stop blender and stir twice or more. Add to meatloaf mix and stir well to incorporate all ingredients. Pour into 8" x 3" loaf pan. Bake at 350° for 45 minutes.

Make Garlic Mashed Potatoes. Make Button Mushroom Thyme Gravy or ketchup. Pour off excess juice (this is not fat) after loaf is baked. Divide loaf in half and save half for later use. Slice second half and top with Button Mushroom Gravy or Sugar-Free Ketchup. Serve mashed potatoes on the side.

NeoCuisine™ meatloaves are white proteins and are naturally light in color. Brown them if you wish with this heated dip: 1/2 cup hot broth (the same meat base flavor as used in the loaf) and 1 Tablespoon Kitchen Bouquet®.

145

THURSDAY, DAY 4

NeoCuisine™ Lunch and 2 to 3 PM Nosh

Ideally you sail through the morning without a snack because the NeoCuisine™ whole-grain breakfast is so filling and satisfying. Around 11, you may notice you're hungry. By noon you're really ready for lunch. If you work, packing lunch may be something you haven't done in years but is advisable for complete control. The NC Hi Pro Dream™ is the perfect lunch because a dose of quality protein for the afternoon lifts mental acuity and does a superb job stanching the PRA. Other NeoCuisine™ lunches are simple, straightforward affairs usually consisting of fruit and yogurt. Look for lunch ideas in the Day-Parts chapter.

Use dinner leftovers from the night before for lunch if you have them. NeoCuisine™ entreés are sizable, as you now know. Leftovers heated in the microwave make a nice lunch and carry the guarantee you are eating properly.

Finally, remember you have a 2 to 3 PM latté or snack with 100 calories allotted. A little caffeine suppresses the PRA, wakes you up and is harmless. By 10 PM, it's completely out of the system and won't interfere with sleep. If you don't like coffee try tea with modified "tea sandwiches" made with water crackers spread with herbed no-fat cream cheese. Don't forget about fruit, especially fresh grapefruit wedges which are calorie-frugal and good. Also try this sometime. Hi-Pro Hot Chocolate: To a preheated blender add: 2 heaping Tablespoons (one scoop) chocolate whey protein mix; 1 teaspoon instant coffee; 1 packet no-fat, low-cal hot chocolate mix, e.g. Swiss Miss® of 20 cals; 4 packets or more aspartame; and 1-1/2 cups of boiling water. Blend one minute. (100 calories)

EXPECT:
STRANGE CO-WORKER LOOKS
Coming to work with Tupperware® tubs isn't what they expect but you know you're on your way to the shape and vigor of youth. And think of the money you're saving.

HOMEWORK:
STRIDING ARRANGEMENTS
On Day 8 you begin striding so purchase your gear today or tomorrow if you haven't already done so. You need to have your shoes, clothes, time-of-day schedule and a two-mile loop course (use your car). These logistics sound like a lot on paper but in a matter of just weeks, dressing correctly, lacing up and heading out the door for 30 or 45 minutes of brisk striding will be second nature. Striding is a great stress reducer. That's why striding at lunch is so helpful. It calms you down by metabolizing stress hormones and wakes you up with a nice pump of fresh oxygenated blood to the brain.

ANY MEATLOAF SANDWICH

NeoCuisine™ meatloaves have an excellent shelf life of a week plus in the refrigerator and two months in the freezer. Here's a toothsome way to use leftovers.

•

Serves one.

Calories: 427
Net weight: 21 ounces
Prep time: 10 minutes
Calorie-to-weight ratio: 20 calories per ounce

- *Sugar-Free Ketchup (see page 343)*
- *Yellow mustard*
- *2 slices light bread (e.g. Wonder® Lite)*
- *2 slices red onion*
- *1/4 recipe meatloaf of choice, sliced*
- *1/2 medium tomato, sliced*
- *2 to 3 leaves of lettuce*
- *1 Side dish of choice: slaw, fries, yogurt, etc.*

Spread Sugar-Free Ketchup and mustard to taste on both slices of bread. For easiest assembly, layer in order: bread, onion, meatloaf, tomato sprinkled with salt and pepper to taste, lettuce and second slice of bread. Serve with your choice of side dish. This sandwich tastes great with the meatloaf heated. Try slicing it off and dry frying it in a good nonstick pan. All NeoCuisine™ meatloaves brown nicely.

OTHER GREAT MEATLOAF SUGGESTIONS
- Accumulate NeoCuisine™ leftovers for a smorgasbord night.
- Enjoy NeoCuisine™ leftovers for lunch the next day.

- You will generate the most second dinners from NeoCuisine™ meatloafs which provide you a variety of delicious opportunities. Consider these options:
- Make the Anyloaf Sandwich (see above). Vary it with different mustards such as tarragon Dijon and Gouldings® deli mustard. Use different vegetable accoutrements such as a no-fat coleslaw.
- Cut meatloaf slabs and fry them for hot sandwiches using either the Celebration or Puyallup Fair Burger recipes on pages 285 and 289.
- Crumble meatloaf and scramble with egg substitute adding frozen chopped spinach and other vegetables for a marvelous frittata.
- Use any pizza polenta recipe with a cooked meatloaf center to make a tamale. Use the Molé Sauce listed on page 346.
- Slice cold meatloaf slabs and fry them as an accompaniment to steamed vegetables and Carlenzoli Steaks (page 351).
- Replace the beef in the Szechuan Beef and Vegetable Stir-Fry with crumbled meatloaf of choice.
- Get crazy and fry meatloaf slabs, dousing them with NeoCuisine™ Sugar-Free Ketchup (page 343).
- See the French Countryside Sandwich, page 341.

147

FRIDAY, DAY 5

Pre-Dinner Appetizer

Arriving home you may be hungry. Have something ready to go, as simple as fresh baby carrots (40 calories). A quick sliced tomato basil salad with balsamic, salt and pepper takes no time (50 calories). Eat an apple (90 calories). Enjoy a peeled grapefruit (60 calories). Keep pre-dinner snacks to 100 calories or less because shortly you will enjoy a large NeoCuisine™ dinner.

You may be surprised (even slightly awed) at NeoCuisine™ portions. Relax. Eat what you like, being sure you get enough. If you can't eat it all, so much the better because you are left with more calories for 7 to Bed. Leftovers make the perfect tomorrow's lunch. Put them in Tupperware® to microwave at work the next day or save leftovers from two or three meals, having them later as a no-work smorgasbord.

EXPECT:

PALATE ACCLIMATION
You've been saturated with fats and sugar your whole life owing to their addition as cheap, tasty ingredients. Expect a shift (not a drop) in flavor impact. It's a minor transition. A NeoCuisine™ pizza isn't the same as a fatty, aorta-clogging original but good nonetheless. Satisfying the palate with flavor force and particularly the Osmazome Principle™ helps acclimation but, the truth be told, you do experience an adjustment. Imagine going from 2% milk to fat-free. NeoCuisine™ takes a little getting used to but in no time you adjust.

TIP: Suspend judgment on NeoCuisine™ taste until after the third bite.

HOMEWORK:

BodyRenewal™ Journal
Start writing if you haven't already done so. Be sure to include your starting weight and a before picture. You are going to be pleasantly surprised with your progress. Bear in mind that your BodyRenewal™ journal is entirely private. Memorialize thoughts you want to save: recipe changes, snack ideas, behavioral changes, e.g. making lunch the night before, good disputes like, "Why does this have to seem like work?" because "Every worthwhile thing in my life required effort. How could I otherwise appreciate it?"

Keep your BodyRenewal™ journal simple: a spiral notebook, five minutes a day and total freedom to write what you wish about this new life's experience.

BACON PINEAPPLE POLENTA PIZZA

Pizza is pretty much a no-no for any diet. Yet, with some doing, the NeoCuisine™ researchers evolved polenta using the Osmazome Principle™ that produces a credible pizza. Just think of it as a soft, thick crust pizza, rich in flavor because of the chicken stock. This pizza will remind you of its step-brother from the local pizza parlour. Enjoy the experience without clogging your arteries.

• Serves one.

Calories: 555
Net Weight: 30 ounces
Prep time: 15 minutes
Cook time: 30 + 30 minutes
Calorie-to-weight ratio: 18 calories per ounce

- 3 cups chicken broth, fat skimmed
- 1/2 cup polenta
- 1/2 cup NeoCuisine™ Red (see page 347)
- 1/2 cup Kraft® fat-free shredded cheddar cheese
- 1/8 teaspoon red pepper flakes or more
- 1/2 cup crushed pineapple (in own juice), squeezed and drained
- 2 ounces fat-free Canadian bacon, diced small

In a medium saucepan bring chicken broth to a boil. Stir in polenta with a wire whisk. Return to full boil, cover, reduce heat to medium-low and cook until thickened, about 3 to 5 minutes. Remove lid and continue to cook over low heat 20 to 25 minutes, stirring occasionally. Polenta should be very thick.

Pour cooked polenta into ungreased deep dish pie plate and refrigerate 1 to 2 hours or overnight.

Put NeoCuisine™ Red on top of polenta and spread to edges. Top with cheese. Add red pepper flakes to pineapple and put on pizza. Add Canadian bacon. Bake at 350° for 1/2 hour.

149

SATURDAY, DAY 6

7 To Bed

7 to Bed is the final phase of Day-Parts and likewise the most dangerous. When we're tired, discipline ebbs. Temptation creeps into our psyche. By convoluted logic we destroy our day's fat-stripping efforts by indulging in a calorie-packed mollification. The reward syndrome rampages full force. What the heck, we've worked all day and deserve our just rewards. And you do.

Outwit the *primeval raging appetite* and reward syndrome. Study Appendix D for your 7 to Bed options. Finish NeoCuisine™ dinner leftovers. If you're short of protein, now is the time to catch up with beef jerky or, more tempting, a slice of No-Sugar/Fat NC Cheesecake at a mere 90 calories and 5 grams protein. If you're really short on protein have an NC Hi Pro Dream™. (Pure protein wakes you up.

Drink it at least two hours before bedtime.)

Whatever you eat, this is the day's final intake. Time your 7 to Bed calorie allotment in steps. Have a few pretzels or what have you at 7 and later a slice of No-Fat/Sugar NC Berry Pie. Eat your final nosh no sooner than 8 PM so you don't go to bed hungry. Having a bit of carbohydrate before retiring helps you sleep. Play it right and you will end the day with enough to eat while not exceeding your total calorie goal.

PRIMEVAL RAGING APPE-TITE™ STRATEGY: Occasionally your *PRA* storms out of control. The best hunger stancher of all is a 300-calorie portion of oatmeal. This emergency therapy has little appeal as you read it now but on those occasions where the primordial tapes unreasonably urge you to eat, a steaming bowl of oats is quite welcome.

Also, try air-popped popcorn and a huge mug of steaming decaf tea with milk.

EXPECT:

TO FINESSE 7 TO BED WITH AWARENESS

Fatigue spurs binge eating. Forewarned is half-saved, as they say.

HOMEWORK:

PREPARE YOUR GYM SPACE

On Day 9, you begin Dynamic Balancing™ and Macro Deflexing™. These require a space about 8 feet by 10 feet. A living room works with the coffee table moved aside but better is your garage with a double or triple layer of carpet. Wherever you choose, ready your space.

CHINESE-FRIED CHICKEN NOODLES

Classical ingredients including the requisite ginger to make you believe you ordered in Chinese. But, NeoCuisine™ stir-fries reduce calories by almost 1/2.

• *Serves one.*

Calories: 582
Net weight: 30 ounces
Prep time: 5 to 10 minutes
Cook time: 5 minutes
Calorie-to-weight ratio: 19 calories per ounce

- *1 cup cooked whole wheat spaghetti*
- *2 ounces chicken breast, boned and skinned*
- *16 ounces stir-fry vegetables, thawed and drained*
- *1/4 cup low-sodium soy sauce*
- *1 Tablespoon white wine vinegar*
- *1/8 teaspoon crushed red pepper flakes*
- *1/2 teaspoon garlic powder*
- *1/2 teaspoon ginger*
- *1 teaspoon quality chicken base*
- *8 to 10 ounces (4 to 5 cups) shredded cole slaw cabbage*
- *1/2 teaspoon lemon zest*
- *2 packets aspartame*

Prepare spaghetti according to package directions. While spaghetti is cooking, prepare chicken and vegetables.

In a large nonstick skillet or wok, brown chicken over high heat. Add soy sauce, white wine vinegar, red pepper flakes, garlic powder, ginger, chicken base and cole slaw. Deglaze pan and cook for 3 minutes.

Add drained vegetables, lemon zest, spaghetti and aspartame. Reheat and serve immediately.

151

SUNDAY, DAY 7

COUNTING IS CONTROL:
THE TOTECARD

Start your ToteCard today, a simple listing of foods consumed and calories. Using the quick cal count (see Day-parts), you can easily estimate calories. Tracking what you eat is quite important so that you have 200 or more calories available for 7 to Bed, your period of greatest temptation.

The tried and true management dictum you can't manage it if you don't track it is undeniable. Your ToteCard is a focusing device for monitoring calorie intake. It works because it creates short-term goals—something you do that day.

Working a ToteCard through the day reminds repeatedly not to eat haphazardly. Research clearly shows that those who track calories by writing them down lose weight while those who estimate gain weight.[8]

EXPECT:
AMBIVALENCE
Recording calorie intake (everything) can be a bit annoying in the beginning. But put your mind aright. Your ToteCard is an indispensable management tool leading to the shape and vigor of youth.

HOMEWORK:
TOTECARDING; STRIDING LOOP
Appendix E has a small quick cal count card. Copy it for your purse or wallet. Use it in conjunction with your ToteCard to capture calories consumed. Weigh, measure and estimate all food. Use the back of your ToteCard for observations on what does and doesn't work for you: favorite yogurt flavors, fruits you want to try, notes on avoiding coffee break jelly doughnuts and so on. Save information in your BodyRenewal™ journal.

You begin *striding* tomorrow. Have a plotted course loop of two miles. You eventually work up to four miles an hour (15 minutes per mile) so you can cover the route in approximately 30 minutes.

Feb 15		
BREAKFAST OATS		250
LUNCH: Yogurt 100		
Apple 75		175
		375
2 PM Latte		75
		450
5 PM Fat Free Potato		
Chips 1 oz. +		100
		550
NC Pepperoni Pizza		
(75%)		410
		960
7 PM NC Hi Pro Dream™		200
		1,160
8 PM NC Berry Pie		200
		1,360

SHRIMP OR CRAB LOUIE

The sugar/fat-free NeoCuisine™ Thousand Island dressing mimics its fatty sibling so well, you'll likely not notice any difference. But the NeoCuisine™ version has only 15% the calories. Wow.

•

Serves one.

Calories: 483
Net weight: 36 ounces
Prep time: 25 minutes
Calorie-to-weight ratio:
13 calories per ounce

- One 12- to 16-ounce prepared salad greens, chopped to a maximum of 1" x 1" by you
- 1 NeoCuisine™ recipe Thousand Island Dressing (see page 306)
- 6 ounces fresh frozen crab or shrimp meat (3 ounces cooked chicken breast julienned can be substituted)
- 1 medium tomato, cut into 4 wedges
- 2 hard-boiled eggs, whites only, quartered
- 2 Tablespoons olives, sliced
- 8 canned/fresh cooked and chilled asparagus

Put lettuce on a serving plate. Place dressing over top of lettuce. Arrange crab, tomatoes, eggs and olives. Top with asparagus spears. Serve with 1/4 lemon wedge.

MONDAY, DAY 8

TODAY: STRIDE 30 MINUTES

Striding (Strolling) 30 Minutes

Today you begin striding. Strolling, actually, which is a relaxed easy pace of two miles per hour. By now you have your gear ready and your route planned. You're ready to go. Start slowly. This means two things. Allow your body to warm up by casually walking a couple of minutes before challenging it. Second, the loop course you laid out is about two miles in length so you can eventually stride at four miles an hour for 30 minutes. For your first day, however, stroll for 30 minutes total by turning around after 15 minutes into your course. Yes, this is strolling, not striding because you want to acclimatize: break in new shoes, test your gear, allow joints and muscles to adjust. You have your whole life to exercise. Please go easy.

This week, add about two minutes to your time each day so that by the week's end you are strolling 40 minutes. The overall work-in plan to full striding looks like this:

1st WEEK	2nd WEEK	3rd WEEK	4th WEEK	5th WEEK
•30 min	•40 min	•35 min	•30 min	your
•1 1/2 mi	•2 mi	•2 mi	•2 mi	choice

By the 2nd week you will be strolling two miles. In the 3rd week you shorten your time by about five minutes to 35 minutes for your two-mile loop course. By the 4th week you are striding at 4 miles per hour for two miles. This is a brisk pace: CAN TALK, CAN'T SING. In your 5th week the option is yours to increase striding time. The criteria isn't so much distance and speed as elevated heart rate and time. Our goals are to work the heart muscle and adjust properly to striding stresses.

EXPECT:
RELAXATION AND FUN
Enjoy yourself when striding. See the sights, architecture, storefronts, landscaping, and gardens. Look around. Wave to friends. Make your time outside a bond with reality.

HOMEWORK:
STROLL FOR 30 MINUTES
Take a quick look at Striding, Dynamic Balance™ and Macro Deflexions. You won't be using all the techniques immediately but an information refresher will prove helpful in the days to come.

CHILI VERDE FRIJOLES NEGRO

Mild green Anaheim (California) chilies add interest to this black bean-stuffed potato. More chili powder increases flavor.

• Serves one.

Calories: 496
Net weight: 27 ounces
Prep time: 15 minutes
Cook time: 25 minutes
Calorie-to-weight ratio: 18 calories per ounce

- *Cold baked potatoes totaling 16 ounces*
- *1/2 cup mild, canned chopped green chilies*
- *1/4 teaspoon garlic powder*
- *1/2 to 1 teaspoon chili powder (be brave)*
- *1 teaspoon quality chicken base*
- *1/2 teaspoon dried Italian herb seasoning*
- *1/4 cup chicken broth, fat skimmed*
- *1/2 cup black beans, drained*
- *1/2 cup <u>fresh</u> salsa (mild, medium or hot to taste; find in deli case)*
- *2 slices no-fat Swiss cheese singles*

Microwaving: Microwave potatoes in the morning. Wash them, put in a microwavable container, e.g. lidded glass, and microwave for 8 to 10 minutes, turning once. Let sit in the microwave until you're ready to use in the evening. For potato skins that give more toothsome, crispy gratification, bake conventionally. Conventional oven: In the morning, wash potato(es) and bake in oven at 500° for 10 to 15 minutes. Turn off and let potatoes sit in the oven until ready to use in the evening.

Cut potatoes in half. Scoop out the meat and mash. Reserve shells.

Add green chilies, garlic powder, chili powder, chicken base, Italian herb seasoning and chicken broth to mashed potato meat and mix. Add black beans and mix gently.

Fill potato shells with mixture and top each half with Swiss cheese and salsa. Place on nonstick cookie sheet and bake at 400° for 15 minutes.

TUESDAY, DAY 9

TODAY: STRIDE 32 MINUTES

Visualize Your Future Shape and Vigor

Break negative self-image by projecting ahead to what you will be. See where you are going, not where you are now. You know that today's shape is temporary, soon to pass. Build on that imagery. Quash negative thoughts by indulging in the visualization of yourself with your shape and vigor of youth. Imagine to the point of almost touching it. If you allow yourself, it is a dream that becomes reality.

This simple psychological technique is one of your best motivators. Visiting your future self with clarity, however, is a function of skill. You would think conjuring up images of your shape and vigor of youth would be straightforward but, unfortunately, it is not. Like all of life's proficiencies, visualizing your future shape and vigor of youth requires practice.

For a moment each day, fantasize your future. It's really more than a fantasy, though. With each visit to the future, you build engagement. Each reflection encourages you. After a week or two of practice, you really can see yourself with the shape and vigor of youth. Good. This is where you want to be. The vision is quite real and obtainable. Let yourself believe it because you have the voluntary volition and all the BodyRenewal™ tools you need for accomplishment.

EXPECT:

IMAGINING YOUR FUTURE SHAPE AND VIGOR OF YOUTH TO BE ASSURING

Allow it to affect you this way. That is the purpose of the exercise.

HOMEWORK:

VISIT YOUR FUTURE BEST SELF

Make a commitment to visit your future best self for a couple of minutes every day. This is not a protracted drill. Do it for a moment while driving or during commercials on TV or whenever you wish. Close your eyes (not while driving for goodness sake), relax and dream your future shape and vigor of youth. Embrace the visualization as a reality soon to be yours. With persistence you learn to form a picture to your liking. Hang on to it. This is where you are going. It is the equilibrium of forward motion. Enjoy.

BOEUF BOURGUIGNONNE

As tasty as the classic French presentation in half the time with 1/3 the calories and fat.

Serves one.

Calories: 595
Net weight: 28 ounces
Prep time: 20 minutes
Cook time: 30 minutes
Calorie-to-weight ratio: 21 calories per ounce

- *4 ounces top round, rough chopped in 1/4" pieces*
- *One 14.5-ounce can beef broth, fat skimmed*
- *1 teaspoon quality beef base*
- *1 cup drinking quality red wine [FYI: All the alcohol boils out.]*
- *8 ounces potatoes, 1" dice*
- *2 cups whole baby carrots*
- *2 cups small whole mushrooms*
- *1/2 teaspoon dried thyme*
- *1/2 cup fat-free (lite) pasta (marinara) sauce*
- *1/4 cup frozen peas*

In a large nonstick skillet brown meat. Add beef broth, beef base, red wine, potatoes, carrots, mushrooms and thyme. Bring to a full boil and cook uncovered for 20 to 25 minutes, or until about 1/2 cup of liquid remains.

Reduce heat and add pasta sauce and pepper (1/8 teaspoon) to taste. Cook 3 to 4 minutes. Add peas. Serve. (No-fat sour cream optional.)

157

WEDNESDAY, DAY 10

TODAY: STRIDE 34 MINUTES • MACRO DEFLEX™ AND DYNAMIC BALANCE™ 15 SECONDS TCT⋆

MACRO DEFLEX™/ DYNAMIC BALANCE™

Today Macro Deflex™ and Dynamic Balance™ after striding. Flexibility is one of aging's needless losses. Proper deflexing makes you remarkably lithe. Enjoy a body having freedom of movement because you Macro Deflex™ two times a week. There are many advantages.

Well-designed studies confirm that proper stretching helps tendons and ligaments grow stronger, reduces anxiety and lowers blood pressure. You'll also find stretching assists striding. As we age the body loses its range of motion causing shorter steps. Deflexing elongates your stride making you faster which helps elevate your heart rate.

See page 70 for the Cat, Bobsled and T-Reach. The logic of Macro Deflexing™ is to stretch several muscle groups at once. In the beginning you spend only 30 seconds total for each Macro Deflex™. Deflex five times for three seconds on, three seconds off. The Total Challenge Time (TCT) is 15 seconds: 5 three-second holds. **Caution: Do not stretch to mild discomfort when starting out. Go only to the "I can feel it" point.**

Spend a few moments after Macro Deflexing™ doing Dynamic Balance™. Equilibrium affects our ability to walk, run, play sports, drive and the many other activities essential to our lives. Good balance boosts confidence. You navigate with aplomb. Cracks in the sidewalk, steps, curbs, skiing, tennis, golf, bowling and anything else requiring movement depend on deft balance.

Review Dynamic Balance™ on page 71. To start, shoot for 15 seconds TCT accumulation. For example, if you can stand one-legged, eyes closed for five seconds at a time, repeat the Dynamic Balance™ exercise three times for a TCT of 15 seconds.

Tuning your equilibrium can literally shave decades off this crucial age indicator. In fact, if you eventually work your way up to a full 30 seconds Dynamic Balance™ (eyes closed on one foot without falling)—you have the balance of a 20 year old! Practicing scrupulously, your time may exceed a full minute's balance, a truly exceptional feat.

EXPECT:

MACRO DEFLEXIONS™ AND DYNAMIC BALANCE™ TO FEEL A BIT ODD
After all, how many of your friends do one-foot balance exercises? On the other hand, flexibility and balance are important BodyRenewal™ elements, increasing your range of behavioral options.

HOMEWORK:

COMPLETE YOUR GYM

⋆ TCT means Total Challenge Time. It's the time spent during the exertion (challenge) phase of strength training, i.e. the "lifing" phase. The concept is also used for Macro Deflexion™ *on* vs *off* phases. The TCT concept is likewise used to track Dynamic Balance™.

CRAB AND ARTICHOKE FRITTATA

This likable dish has a pleasing complexity of flavors and no fancy egg-pan work required because this frittata is baked. The list of ingredients is longer than usual but it goes together quickly.

•

Serves one.

Calories: 551
Net Weight: 29.5 ounces
Prep time: 20 minutes
Cook time: 30 minutes
Calorie-to-weight ratio:
19 calories per ounce

- 4 ounces fresh frozen crab, thawed
- 1 cup zucchini, chopped (1/2" maximum)
- 1 cup canned artichoke hearts (not marinated) chopped (1/2" maximum)
- 1 cup fresh mushrooms, sliced
- 1/4 cup onions, chopped (1/2" maximum)
- Three 4-ounce (1-1/2 cups) containers fat-free egg substitute, e.g. EggBeaters®

- 3 Tablespoons quality grated Parmesan, e.g. Reggiano
- 1 teaspoon quality chicken base or lobster base
- 1/2 teaspoon anchovie paste
- 1/4 cup nonfat sour cream
- 1 Tablespoon Miracle Chop (see page 346)

Combine crab, zucchini, artichoke hearts, mushrooms, onions, fat-free egg substitute, Parmesan cheese, chicken base and anchovie paste. Add pepper (1/8 teaspoon) to taste.

Spray an 8" x 8" pan (or comparable size, e.g. 6" x 10") with non-stick vegetable spray and add omelet mixture. Bake at 400° for 30 minutes. Frittata is done when sides are firm but center is still soft.

Combine sour cream, Miracle Chop and salt and pepper to taste. Microwave for 30 seconds. Plate omelet and top with sour cream mixture.

If crab is unavailable, substitute fresh frozen shrimp, lobster or langostino. DO NOT use canned seafood.

159

THURSDAY, DAY 11

TODAY: STRIDE 36 MINUTES

AGAIN, COUNTING IS CONTROL

Hidden diet busters lurk everywhere, sabotaging your calorie control. Inadvertently eating calorie-dense foods throws your day's cal count into a tailspin because by 8 PM you have used your entire calorie allotment but feel famished. Careless munching is the very thing triggering binges. Successful fat-stripping wastes no calories through the day. Remain leery. Avoid baked goods (cal dense at 80 to 120 calories an ounce), pasta and rice (the same cal density as bread), sports drinks and juices (eat the whole fruit for a much better calorie-to-weight ratio) and be cautious about "fat-free" foods because they are often calorie-jammed owing to their sugar and refined flour content, e.g. SnackWell® cookies.

Estimating size isn't tricky. Your thumb is about the size of a tablespoon, for example. A one-cup portion is about the size of your fist, an apple or baseball. Cooked beans and rice are 200 calories a cup. Green vegetables are 50 calories a cup while starchy vegetables (e.g. potatoes) are 100 calories a cup. Keep in mind that a deck of cards equals about 4 ounces cooked white protein, 200 total calories or 50 calories an ounce.[9] Get the rest of your calorie counts from food labels. With every meal, snack or nosh, note the cal count on your ToteCard.

EXPECT:

CONTINUED NeoCuisine™ FAMILIARIZATION

Switching to sun foods after years of a red meat-centered diet doesn't become customary in two weeks. The first thing you observe is more bathroom trips and gas. This is due to the increased fiber in your diet. But the body adjusts and you learn to modulate fiber intake to levels best suited to you.

Next you may perceive a flavor difference, not less taste mind you, but a character change because fat is now replaced with flavor force. A diet with copious sun foods, lots of white protein and little saturated fat in the form of ice cream, cake and candy is bound to make you noticed. Don't take the attention the wrong way. Others probably admire your efforts.

HOMEWORK:

NeoCuisine™ ACCLIMATING TIPS

Remember these three simple things. First, allow three bites of any NeoCuisine™ entreé before passing judgment. Your palate is acclimating. Second, project ahead to what you will be. Vigorous. Robust. Lean and conditioned. Third, remember you will live longer and better than those eating slow-kill 21st century foods.

¡CARAMBA! CON MOLÉ

Makes 2 meatloaf servings.

This Mexican meatloaf (reminiscent of tamale) is somewhat complex but the ¡sabor! The Molé sauce is quite good and should not be skipped. Since it's mild, add more of those ingredients suggested for enhanced flavor.

Calories per serving: 584
Net weight per serving: 32 ounces
Prep time: 20 to 25 minutes
Cook time: 45 minutes
Calorie-to-weight ratio: 18 calories per ounce
(Calorie count includes Chili Masa and Molé)

- 3/4 pound (12 ounces) 1% fat very lean ground turkey
- 1 Tablespoon quality beef base
- 1 teaspoon garlic powder
- 1 teaspoon pepper
- 1 Tablespoon chili powder
- 1 teaspoon cumin
- 1 teaspoon red wine vinegar
- 1/2 cup onion, finely diced
- 4 to 6 ounces canned diced green chilies, drained

- 18-20 ounces (1-1/2 packages) extra-firm ultra-low-fat tofu
- 1 recipe Molé (see page 346)

CHILI MASA
- 1-1/2 cups chicken broth, fat skimmed
- 1/4 cup polenta
- 1/4 cup Kraft® fat-free shredded cheddar cheese
- Rounded 1/4 teaspoon red pepper flakes

Combine first 9 ingredients. Set aside.

Crumble tofu into blender and pureé until smooth, about 30 to 45 seconds. You will need to stop blender and stir twice or more. Add to meatloaf mix and stir well to incorporate all ingredients.

Pour into 8" x 3" loaf pan. Bake at 350° for 45 minutes.

In a medium saucepan bring chicken broth to a boil. Stir in polenta with a wire whisk. Return to a full boil, cover, reduce heat to medium-low and cook until thickened, about 3 to 5 minutes. Remove lid and cook over low heat 20 to 25 minutes, stirring occasionally. Stir in cheddar and red pepper flakes.

Pour off excess juice (this is not fat) after loaf is baked. Divide loaf in half and reserve remainder for later use. Slice and top with Molé. Serve with Chili Masa on the side.

NeoCuisine™ meatloaves are white proteins and are naturally light in color. Brown them if you wish with this heated dip: 1/2 cup hot broth (the same meat base flavor as used in the loaf) and 1 Tablespoon Kitchen Bouquet®.

161

FRIDAY, DAY 12

TODAY: STRIDE 38 MINUTES

PRACTICE NO PERFECTION

Perfection is a goal breaker because it's unachievable. We set unobtainable (perfectionistic) goals which "prove unworthiness" by our inevitably falling short. We're provided with an "out." A few days' faltering provides an all-too-easy excuse to chuck your shape and vigor of youth undertaking. It's a vacuous no-win.

Everyone struggles with the commonplace problems universal to mankind ... insecurity ... day in and day out frustrations ... unfulfilled dreams ... all of which lead to the realization of how human we are. But the fact is that no one executes perfectly and a day or week of backsliding isn't the same as giving up. Understand that imperfect execution is the norm. We flounder because we are human but succeed because we persevere based on the compelling value of our youthful shape and vigor goals. Backslide all you want but don't quit. A day or a year's layoff is not irreparable. Repeat this often:

I'm committed to something worthwhile. I make mistakes but that's okay. I WON'T GIVE UP.

EXPECT:

EDGY EVENINGS

7 to Bed is a challenging time. Discipline ebbs, the reward syndrome imposes itself and you can't help but wonder why life is sometimes so much work. Today's homework helps.

HOMEWORK:

7 TO BED LIST

If you haven't already done so, buy everything on the 7 to Bed list. Try all the suggestions to see what you like best. The minimum you should have on hand is:

- Pears and hard apples
- Unsweetened applesauce
- Teriyaki or regular beef jerky (solid meat only)
- Carr's® water crackers
- 20-calorie-per-cup diet cocoa
- Dill pickles
- Diet Jell-O®
- A variety of peppers
- Hot air-popped popcorn
- No-fat/sugar puddings
- No-fat/sugar yogurt
- No-fat/sugar frozen yogurt★
- Peeled grapefruit and oranges
- NC Hi Pro Dreams™, Appendix B
- Variety of diet pop
- NC Desserts, page 378

If you don't have the right foods on hand, you opt for calorie-dense fare at hand that ruins your calorie count and all your hard work through the day. It's a pity to waste a day's effort by stuffing Snickers® at 10 PM.

★ Read the label to avoid mannitol and sorbitol. Anything containing these artificial sweeteners upsets the GI track. A little (no more than one cup) might be okay but more can cause cramping, diarrhea and excess gas. This applies to "sugarless" candies, most of which contain one or both of these ingredients.

SHRIMP CHOP SALAD

Reminiscent of a shrimp Caesar but with the added complexity of basil and red kidney beans. It sounds unusual but the result is delicious.

Serves one.

Calories: 549
Net weight: 33 ounces
Prep time: 15 to 20 minutes
Calorie-to-weight ratio: 17 calories per ounce

- *1 recipe NeoCuisine™ Vinaigrette (see page 307)*
- *2 teaspoons dried basil, rubbed between fingers to release flavors*
- *1/2 teaspoon anchovie paste*
- *6 ounces medium to large shrimp, cooked and shelled*
- *1/2 to 3/4 head iceberg lettuce, chopped (4 to 6 cups)*
- *1 cup canned red kidney beans, drained, rough chopped*
- *1 small tomato, diced*
- *1/4 cup quality grated Parmesan cheese, e.g. Reggiano*

Combine dressing, basil and anchovie paste. Add shrimp and marinate for 30 minutes or more, up to 8 hours.

Combine all ingredients. Toss. Serve.

SATURDAY, DAY 13

TODAY: STRIDE 40 MINUTES • MACRO DEFLEX™ AND DYNAMIC BALANCE™ 15 SECONDS TCT

STRIDING BENEFITS

Striding is full-on aerobic exercise. You may not think so right now with your beginning adaptation but in due course you will be increasing striding rigor. Patience. Meanwhile know that quality aerobic exercise like striding is your best respiratory, heart, reflex, endurance and mental acuity improvement strategy. The heart's a muscle benefiting from exercise like any other. Of all wake-up expedients, a brisk stride sends oxygen to the brain refreshing your mind for high output, not to mention that seeing the sights and enjoying the outdoors are pleasures in themselves.

EXPECT:

TO PRACTICE THE MIRACLE 20™

You remember that it takes the brain 20 to 30 minutes to register the "I'm-full" feeling. Practice by eating to a point where you are not entirely satisfied, there remains trace of hunger. Stop. Wait 20 to 30 minutes and observe your feelings. Chances are that your brain registers satiety. To be honest, this is a difficult skill to master but if you can, you'll save hundreds of calories a day.

HOMEWORK:

STROLL VS STRIDE 40 MINUTES

Continue a strolling pace versus striding. If you are unused to physical activity your body is still acclimating. By now you should be striding (strolling) 40 minutes and completing your two-mile loop. Intensity is easily increased by walking faster, which is coming up.

Don't forget to Macro Deflex™ (MD) and Dynamic Balance™ (DB) 15 seconds total challenge time (TCT). The permanent MD and DB days are Wednesday and Saturday.

FUSION STEW

Beautiful hard winter cracked wheat—bulgar—makes this Russian-Italian fusion hearty and filling. The use of quality balsamic in the amalgam sets off the stew's flavor.

Serves one.

Calories: 557
Net weight: 38 ounces
Prep time: 5 minutes
Calorie-to-weight ratio: 15 calories per ounce

- One and a half 14.5-ounce cans chicken broth, fat skimmed
- 1/2 teaspoon quality chicken base
- 1/3 cup uncooked bulgar
- 1/2 can (14.5-ounce can) redi-cut Italian recipe tomatoes, undrained
- 2 teaspoons balsamic vinegar
- 1 medium zucchini, halved lengthwise, thinly sliced
- 4 ounces frozen corn
- 1/2 can (15-ounce can) white beans, drained and rinsed
- 1 scant teaspoon dried Italian herb seasoning
- 1 teaspoon Miracle Chop (see page 346)

In heavy medium saucepan over medium-high heat, bring broth and chicken base to a boil. Stir in bulgar, tomatoes, balsamic vinegar and pepper (1/8 teaspoon) to taste. Return to boil, reduce heat to medium-low, cover and cook for 15 minutes.

Add zucchini, corn, beans, Italian herb seasoning and Miracle Chop. Cover and return to boil, then reduce heat to medium-low and cook 3 to 4 minutes or until bulgar and zucchini are tender. Serve.

165

SUNDAY, DAY 14

TODAY: OFF FOR EXERCISE

"THE CLUB"

You have been in Body-Renewal™ for two weeks. Maybe a few of those people around you have noticed. Some may have asked about BodyRenewal™. These are prime "club" candidates because you may have been an inspiration. Remind yourself that a "club" can be simply two people talking about their mutual Body-Renewal™ interests. Take advantage of their curiosity and ask if they would like to join you. Take the "edge" off the club by agreeing at the outset to its limited life. Big commitments deter. Say that you will plan to meet for three to six months but do set a limit so the obligation isn't onerous.

Meet as often as you wish but usually more frequently is better, two times a week not being too much. Keep "meetings" informal. Chatting over coffee is ideal. There are recipes, exercises, found restaurants serving calorie-frugal foods and most importantly idea and feelings sharing. Communicating perceptions on mutual difficulties is not only cathartic but helps problem-solve. A few people offering mutual support work wonders in stripping fat and motivating Muscle Rebuilding™. Why not ask a few friends, colleagues or family members about their BodyRenewal™ interest?

EXPECT:

YOU MAY BE UNEASY ASKING FRIENDS ABOUT A "CLUB"

Relax. It's not obligatory. However, many people are looking for a nudge to get them started. Your query might very well be welcomed.

HOMEWORK:

ASK SOMEONE YOU THINK MIGHT BE INTERESTED TO JOIN YOU

Identify and casually ask a few people if they might be interested in BodyRenewal™. If so, let them borrow this book. You may make an ally or two in your BodyRenewal™ effort. That's the idea.

CELEBRATION BURGER

WITH JO-JO FRIES AND SLAW

This celebration dinner includes a downright scrumptious THICK (4") burger, a big stack of fries with plenty of ketchup and a generous portion of slaw. It's a great celebration. A similar McDonald's® burger has twice the calories, ten times the fat and 75% less quantity by weight.

• Serves one.

Calories: 575
Net Weight: 28 ounces
Prep time: 20 to 25 minutes
Cook time: 5 to 7 minutes
Calorie-to-weight ratio: 20 calories per ounce

• 4 ounces 1% fat very lean ground turkey breast
• 2 ounces (1/2 cup) fresh mushrooms, finely chopped
• 1 teaspoon quality beef base
• 1 Tablespoon fat-free mayonnaise

• 1 recipe Sugar-Free Ketchup (see page 343)
• 1 teaspoon yellow mustard
• 2 Tablespoons dill pickle, finely chopped
• 1 packet aspartame
• 1 hamburger bun ("light" or reduced calorie if you can find it)
• Lettuce
• 1 tomato slice
• 1 red onion slice

• 1 recipe Fruit Slaw (see page 350)
• 1 recipe Roasted Flavor Fries (see page 354). Use option 1.

Mix turkey, mushrooms and beef base and form into a patty to fit the bun. Salt (1/4 teaspoon) and pepper (1/8 teaspoon) to taste. Cook patty in a nonstick skillet over medium-high heat until browned and cooked through, about 5 to 7 minutes.

Meanwhile, make hamburger sauce by combining mayonnaise, 1 Tablespoon Sugar-Free Ketchup, mustard, dill pickle and aspartame.

Toast the bun in the skillet and spread sauce on the toasted bun. Add the turkey patty, lettuce, tomato and red onion. Plate slaw and serve with Roasted Flavor Fries. Use the remaining ketchup for dipping.

167

MONDAY, DAY 15

TODAY: STRIDE 40 MINUTES

ABSOLUTIST VS PRACTICALIST

NBC Medical correspondent Dr. Robert Arnot wrote the best seller *The Breast Cancer Prevention Diet.*[10] He came under quick criticism from the medical community because he alleged that breast cancer could be minimized through diet, exercise and supplements. "How could you say that!" the scientific community protested. "We haven't proved proper diet, exercise and supplements stop breast cancer."[11]

To fathom the scientific community's overreaction, you must understand that it is *absolutist*. Scientific method demands that experiments be replicable. The absolutist (scientist) insists on perfect proof. There can be no room for subjectivity, the tiniest amount of error or doubt. It is indeed a laudable stance. It demands considerable rigor and is, in fact, the highest standard of proof.

But Arnot is not coming from the typical absolutist framework. He is being a *practicalist*. We are practicalists. If we waited for perfect proofs nothing would get done. Each day we conduct our lives in the inscrutable world of probabilities. We don't know for sure how our kids will turn out, whether or not we will have an auto accident, what illnesses we will contract or what today's decisions precisely mean for tomorrow. If we waited for perfect proofs, we couldn't live.

Dr. Arnot simply makes a good case that exercise, correct supplements and a diet rich in soy tends to reduce breast cancer. He is propagating good to the world. Similarly, this book is practicalist because it presents creditable know-how corresponding with life's realities. Since we can't wait for perfect proofs, we must go with research as it stands. Final, ultimate medical proofs sometimes take decades. We can't wait. Let's act on what we know now.

EXPECT:

DOUBT FROM OTHERS

Skeptics abound. Don't worry about it.

HOMEWORK:

REREAD

"The dauntless spirit of resolve ..." Remind yourself that you have made a decision. Don't let the doubt and cynicism of others sway you from your worthwhile goals.

CHILI'D CHICKEN STIR-FRY

Noted for its fiery hot food, Szechuanese cookery didn't get chili peppers until the 16th century. Portuguese traders brought the New World chilies to their Macau colony and from there, chili's popularity spread like wildfire, so to speak. The culinary arts of the world were literally turned upside down from the spread of New World foods like chilies, cocoa, potatoes, tomatoes and all the rest.

Make this dish as hot as you like with additional red chili pepper flakes.

• Serves one.

Calories: 550
Net weight: 28 ounces
Prep time: 10 minutes
Cook time: 5 minutes
Calorie-to-weight ratio: 20 calories per ounce

- 1 cup instant rice
- 1 cup low-sodium chicken broth, fat skimmed
- 2 ounces chicken breast, boned and skinned, cut in 1/4" ribbons
- 16 ounces stir-fry vegetables, thawed and drained of excess water
- 1/4 cup soy sauce
- 1 Tablespoon white wine vinegar
- 1/8 teaspoon crushed red pepper flakes
- 1/2 teaspoon garlic powder
- 1 teaspoon dark sesame oil
- 1 teaspoon quality chicken base
- 2 packets aspartame

Prepare rice according to box directions (do not use salt or butter) using chicken broth for the liquid. While rice sits, prepare the chicken and vegetables.

In a large skillet, brown the chicken over high heat. Add soy sauce, white wine vinegar, red pepper flakes, garlic powder, sesame oil and chicken base. Deglaze pan.

Add drained vegetables and aspartame and stir until heated, but do not cook.

Put on one side of serving plate with rice alongside and serve.

169

TUESDAY, DAY 16

TODAY: STRIDE 40 MINUTES

1•1•2™ REMINDERS

Tomorrow you start 1•1•2™. Overwhelmingly the most common mistake made by strength training beginners is going at it too hard. This is an error because over-sore muscles are a real discouragement that may cause you to forfeit BodyRenewal™. There couldn't be a worse outcome. Quitting denies you Body-Renewal's™ merits. Intensity comes soon enough. Please, acclimate first.

When starting, accumulate only 18 to 20 seconds *total challenge time,* about three repetitions at three seconds up and three seconds down.

As you have been advised, the body is easily tricked when starting out by doing more than it should. Beginning slowly is one of the key elements to long-term BodyRenewal™ success.

The second imperative is warming up before exercising. Use one of these alternative techniques for three to five minutes:
- March in place.
- Brisk, brief stride around the block.
- Do jumping jacks on soft carpet no more than 45^0 to 50^0.
- Jog in place on your gym rug.
- Jump rope.
- Go through several exercises with light weights.

Studies show you can actually lift about 30% more weight after you have warmed up than when starting cold.

EXPECT:
SORENESS
Even with a reduced 1•1•2™ you are likely to feel soreness. This is to be expected and is a positive indicator you are starting to rebuild muscle. One of 1•1•2's™ advantages is its 48-hour minimum rest (two full days) between sessions. Do not shorten this rest period because it allows the body plenty of time to rebuild itself so you are thoroughly refreshed and regenerated for your next 1•1•2™. You'll note soreness dissipating over the two- or three-day rest period.

HOMEWORK:
TOMORROW YOU BEGIN 1•1•2™
Be sure your weights are adjusted to only 50% your maximum weight one-time bicep curl, you have your 1•1•2™ space set aside and 1•1•2™ facilitators are in your workout area: radio, tissue, workout gloves (any inexpensive leather work glove with finger tips cut off) and anything else you wish, e.g. water, mirrors, sweat band and so on.

WARM BACON SALAD

A huge salad, enough to satisfy the most demanding primeval raging appetite. Tasty and piquant, this hearty salad sates with punchy flavor.

• Serves one.

Calories: 450
Net Weight: 33 ounces
Prep time: 15 minutes
Calorie-to-weight ratio: 14 calories per ounce

- 6 ounces fat-free Canadian bacon, cut in julienne strips
- 1/2 onion, diced
- 3/4 cup rice vinegar
- 1/2 cup red kidney beans, drained
- 2 Tablespoons red bell pepper, diced small
- 1/4 teaspoon garlic powder
- 3 packets aspartame
- 16 ounces Romaine lettuce, chopped

Combine bacon, onion, vinegar, beans, red bell pepper, garlic powder, salt (a generous 1/4 teaspoon) and pepper (1/8 teaspoon). Microwave to a boil, 4 to 6 minutes, stirring once. Remove from microwave and add aspartame.

Put chopped romaine in a large warm bowl or plate. Pour dressing over romaine. Serve.

WEDNESDAY, DAY 17

TODAY: 1•1•2™ 20 SECONDS TCT • MACRO DEFLEX™ AND DYNAMIC BALANCE™ 20 SECONDS TCT

STARTING 1•1•2™

Always warm up before 1•1•2™ by marching in place, jumping rope or a quick stride around the block for three to five minutes. You know you're ready to strength train when you feel your heart beating a little more rapidly and you're beginning to power breathe. You may notice a trace of sweat. Perform 1•1•2™ by turning to page 46 of The Muscle Rebuild™ chapter for 1•1•2™ exercises. Go in this order:
1. Thigh-Thinner-Tush-Tightener (4T)
2. Hamstring Lift
3. The Back Builder
4. Tummy Tuck
5. Bolder Shoulder Chest Booster
6. Biceps Builder

As advised in the Muscle Rebuild™, begin each exercise at an easy level for you. Start bicep building at 50% your maximum one-time lift weight. Starting maneuvers using body weight or light dumbbells may seem too comfortable but intensity comes quickly. Our goal is to first establish consistency, gradually working toward greater challenge.

As you recall, 1•1•2™ means one minute total challenge time (TCT), one exercise cycle, two times per week. You don't start at a one-minute TCT because it's too much in the beginning. You want to allow muscle, tendon, ligament and joint acclimation, gradually working up to longer TCTs and greater weight for more rigor. Follow the one-cycle (do each exercise one set only) twice-a-week workout instruction. This never changes whereas weight and TCT increase with time.

When starting, accumulate 18 to 20 seconds TCT per muscle group, about three to four repetitions at three seconds up and three seconds down.

EXPECT:

1•1•2™ TO BE TOO EASY
It isn't. Learning 1•1•2™ is a little frustrating, perhaps, but not too easy. Starting slowly prevents excessive muscle tissue tear and allows joint, ligament and tendon adaptation. Intensity will build.

HOMEWORK:

MACRO DEFLEX™ AND DYNAMIC BALANCE™ 18 TO 20 SECONDS TCT WITH 3 OR 4 SIX-SECOND REPETITIONS
Today begin holding your Macro Deflexions™ for 18 to 20 seconds TCT. The advisory is still three seconds on, three seconds off for three or four repetitions. Deflex to "I can feel it," no more. This is what stretches your musculature, making you supple and lithe. We are slowly working our way to more aggressive stretching but for now, stay with the "I can feel it" advisory.

See if you can accumulate a total of 18 to 20 seconds Dynamic Balance™ TCT. Retraining your vestibular system regains the marvelous balance of youth.

PALERMO POTATO

This is an excellent example of the Ozmasome Principle™ delivering deep vertical flavor to an all-vegetable entreé. The Sicilian gusto is here.

• Serves one.

Calories: 513
Net Weight: 25 ounces
Prep time: 20 minutes
Cook time: 25 minutes
Calorie-to-weight ratio: 20 calories per ounce

- *Cold baked potatoes totaling 16 ounces*
- *1/4 cup zucchini, diced*
- *1/4 cup red bell pepper, diced*
- *1/2 cup onions, diced*
- *1 cup fresh mushrooms, sliced*
- *1/2 teaspoon dried commercial Italian herb seasoning*
- *1 teaspoon quality chicken base*
- *1/4 cup quality grated Parmesan cheese, e.g. Reggiano*
- *2 Tablespoons black olives, sliced*
- *1/4 to 1/3 cup chicken broth, fat skimmed*
- *1/4 cup NeoCuisine™ Red (see page 347)*

Microwaving: Microwave potatoes in the morning. Wash them, put in a microwavable container, e.g. lidded glass, and microwave for 8 to 10 minutes, turning once. Let sit in the microwave until you're ready to use in the evening. For potato skins that give more toothsome, crispy gratification, bake conventionally. Conventional oven: In the morning, wash potato(es) and bake in oven at 500° for 10 to 15 minutes. Turn off and let potatoes sit in the oven until ready to use in the evening.

Cut potatoes in half. Scoop out the meat and mash. Reserve shells.

Microwave zucchini, red bell pepper, onion, mushrooms and Italian herb seasoning for 2 minutes. Add chicken base, parmesan and olives to vegetables, mix and add to mashed potatoes. Add chicken broth. Careful—too little and mixture will be dry. Put mashed potato/vegetable mixture into shell. Top each potato with NeoCuisine™ Red.

Place on nonstick cookie sheet and bake at 400° for 15 minutes.

173

THURSDAY, DAY 18

TODAY: STRIDE 40 MINUTES

FEELING SORE

It's inevitable that sedentary muscles feel a little sore beginning 1•1•2™. Don't let it bother you because it's a good sign. It shows that the body's musculature is being worked to its benefit. You're calling upon your body to do what it has not done, possibly, for years. Muscle tissue is challenged so that it is "torn down" to be rebuilt stronger than before. Soreness is your body's signal that it's headed in the right direction.

Excessive soreness—where you really ache—means you've done too much. You should feel soreness but not pain. There is quite a difference. Soreness means you feel slight achiness, but pain is altogether different. If you feel sore, simply continue on track as advised in the coming days. If you feel pain, do these things:

- Reduce advised total challenge time by half: two repetitions.
- Reduce free weights weight by half for the Bicep Builder
- Go back one or more levels where body weight is used as the resistance mechanism: the Hamstring Lift, the Back Builder, the Tummy Tuck and Bolder Shoulder Chest Booster.

You will be pleasantly surprised how two full days off (48 hours) allows the body to repair itself. Your next 1•1•2™ is scheduled for Saturday. By then you will find most (not all) soreness dissipated to a comfortable level. It might be wise for you to read the 1•1•2™ recommendations for Day 31. This advisory counsels you to take it easy. You have the rest of your life to exercise.

EXPECT:

SORENESS BUT NOT PAIN

If you feel pain you are definitely doing too much. Ease back to the levels suggested above. Note, however, that in a remarkably short time you will be moving ahead to higher levels of difficulty. When you feel no soreness and 1•1•2™ seems "too easy," it's time to increase your resistance weight and total challenge time.

HOMEWORK:

SUBSTANTIALLY REDUCE MUSCLE REBUILD™ EFFORT IN THE EVENT OF PAIN

A GOOD BOWL OF RED

Simple to make and dandy flavor. Eggplant adds, surprisingly, to the chili flavor. You'll like this bowl of red.

Serves one.

Calories: 650
Net Weight: 33.5 ounces
Prep time: 20 minutes
Cook time: 30 minutes
Calorie-to-weight ratio: 19 calories per ounce

- 1/2 onion, chopped
- 1 clove garlic, minced
- 1/2 green bell pepper, chopped
- One 14.5-ounce can diced tomatoes, undrained, chopped
- 1 teaspoon quality beef base
- 1/2 teaspoon chili powder
- 1/2 medium eggplant, unpeeled, cut into 1/2"cubes
- One 15.5-ounce can kidney beans, undrained

Combine all ingredients in a pot. Bring to a boil and simmer for 25 to 30 minutes or until the eggplant is soft. Serve.

175

FRIDAY, DAY 19

TODAY: STRIDE 40 MINUTES

DISPUTING SILLY FICTIONS

We often entertain silly fictions. Sometimes thinking (self-talk) destroys our motivation on the basis of utter nonsense we allow ourselves to believe. Here are typical silly fictions:

- "I know my friends think I'm wasting my time."
- "Oh what the hell, being fat isn't that bad."
- "This is too hard."

The fine art of disputing rids our minds of motivation-destroying notions. Free your mind of unnecessary emotional travails by seeing self-talk falsehoods for what they are. Use these steps:

1 Pay attention to what you're telling yourself.

2 Demand that you stop nonsense talk.
3 Tell yourself the real truth.
4 Be prepared to tell yourself the real truth. Here are disputes for the foolish fictions above.

- "My friends probably admire my efforts."
- "Being fat isn't a moral issue. BodyRenewal™ is about extracting the most from life."
- "BodyRenewal™ isn't too hard. Dying young is what's hard."

EXPECT:

THE ART OF DISPUTING TO BE WORK

You have to recognize the falsehoods knocking around your brain. Then, you must take time to recognize their logical inconsistencies. Last, you must explain the correct rationale to yourself again and again. (See Homework.)

HOMEWORK:

DISPUTE CARDS

Sometimes it helps to write down on 3x5 cards ongoing silly fictions and their disputes. Keep these handy and review them often. Here's an example:

FICTION: "Renewing my body is just too hard."
REALITY: I have been packing around too many pounds for too many years. I haven't exercised. I need this. When I follow NeoCuisine™ I have enough to eat. My primeval raging appetite stays pretty well in control. The walking isn't that hard either. I see the sights and have the chance to get outdoors. 1•1•2™ is beginning to condition my muscles. This isn't too much work. I've done harder things than this in my life.

Right now, write one dispute card for your most frequent silly fiction. Read it often. If you like the technique, write more in the coming weeks. It's a good way to have ready answers at hand.

SALADE NICOISSE IRENE

Named for its creator, a marvelous cook and friend, Irene Mulroy. The fun is in eating ingredients alone and together. Try wrapping the shrimp in the bell pepper, mix tomato and potato. Try mushrooms and zucchini.

• Serves one.

Calories: 500
Net Weight: 33 ounces
Prep time: 30 minutes
Cook time: 7 minutes
Calorie-to-weight ratio: 15.5 calories per ounce

- 8 ounces red potatoes, unpeeled, large dice
- 1 cup small whole fresh mushrooms
- 1 large or 2 small zucchini, 1/4" lengthwise slices
- 4 cherry tomatoes, halved
- One 14.5-ounce can plain (unmarinated) whole artichoke hearts, drained and rinsed, halved
- 8 black olives, large

- 1/2 cup prepared roasted red bell peppers
- 4 ounces medium to large shrimp, precooked
- 2 recipes NeoCuisine™ Vinaigrette (see page 307)
- 2 Tablespoons Miracle Chop (see page 346)
- 4 sprays olive oil: 2 seconds total. Buy an aerosol can.

Microwave potatoes in a microwavable container, e.g. lidded glass, for 3 to 4 minutes or until cooked.

Microwave mushrooms and zucchini about 2-1/2 to 3 minutes or until cooked.

Combine all ingredients except Miracle Chop and olive oil in dressing and marinate in refrigerator 4 hours or more. Assemble, spray olive oil, and sprinkle Miracle Chop.

177

SATURDAY, DAY 20

TODAY: STRIDE 40 MINUTES • 1•1•2™ 20 SECONDS TCT • MACRO DEFLEX™ AND DYNAMIC BALANCE™ 20 SECONDS TCT

MIRACLE 20™

It takes about 20 minutes for the brain to register the full feeling. If you train yourself to eat to an initial feeling of modest satiety, in 20 minutes you will feel satisfied. If you eat to complete satisfaction and fullness, in 20 minutes you will likely feel too full.

The Miracle 20™ requires self-training. Our natural inclination is to eat, eat, eat. We eat to complete fullness without thinking about it. With practice we learn to stop short of full satiety knowing that shortly we will feel agreeably full. To stop our lifelong eat-eat-eat habit, we must make a conscious awareness effort. Do this. Make the Miracle 20™ an affirmation for several days: "Follow the Miracle 20™." Repeat it frequently through the day. It may seem rather witless but this reinforcement can magnify your fat-stripping purpose.

EXPECT:

MIRACLE 20™ AWARENESS TO BE CHALLENGING

To guarantee self-awareness sufficient to stop eating at modest satiety versus our lifelong habit of eating to complete fullness, plan on elemental effort. The idea of stopping eating before we're completely full is counter to our habits. Charles Dickens' dictum holds true: "A long pull, a strong pull, and a pull all together." If you can train yourself to follow the Miracle 20™, it's a guaranteed fat-stripper.

HOMEWORK:

EAT TO MODEST SATIETY

Try this tonight. Consciously eat to the point of modest satisfaction. Then stop. Note the time and wait 20 minutes. Observe your reduced hunger level. You will be pleasantly surprised to discover you feel fuller after the Miracle 20™ than you did when you stopped eating. The point is to always wait 20 to 30 minutes before deciding you want more to eat. If you do eat more, do so modestly in keeping with your true appetite.

SATIETY COCKTAIL

If you have continued problems managing your *primeval raging appetite*, try a Satiety Cocktail. Researchers at the University of Southern California Medical School found the soluble fiber in pectin increases feelings of fullness because food passes out of the stomach more slowly. Mix 1 Tablespoon reduced calorie pectin with 8 ounces of tomato or grapefruit juice (no orange juice). Drink 30 minutes before eating.[12] It should help.

PAISANO

MAKES 2 MEATLOAF
SERVINGS.

A fine Italian meatloaf, that you'll swear is made of veal, rich with traditional ingredients like sun-dried tomatoes, sweet red bell pepper and finished with heady red sauce.
Served with delicious browned Basil Parmesan Polenta.

Calories per serving: 565
Net Weight per serving: 28 ounces
Prep time: 15 to 20 minutes
Cook time: 45 minutes
Calorie-to-weight ratio: 20 calories per ounce
(Calorie count includes Basil Parmesan Polenta and NeoCuisine™ Red.)

- *3/4 pound (12 ounces) 1% fat very lean turkey*
- *1 Tablespoon quality beef base*

- *1 teaspoon garlic powder*
- *1 teaspoon pepper*
- *2 teaspoons dried basil*
- *1 teaspoon red wine vinegar*
- *1/2 cup onion, finely diced*
- *3/4 cup fresh mushrooms, sliced*
- *9 dry (no oil) sun-dried tomato halves, quartered*
- *2 Tablespoons prepared, roasted red bell pepper, chopped*
- *18-20 ounces (1-1/2 packages) extra-firm ultra-low-fat tofu*
- *1 recipe NeoCuisine™ Red (see page 347)*
- *1 recipe Basil Parmesan Polenta (see page 350)*

Combine first 10 ingredients. Set aside. Crumble tofu into blender and pureé until smooth, about 30 to 45 seconds. You will need to stop blender and stir twice or more. Add to meatloaf mix and stir well to incorporate all ingredients. Pour into 8" x 3" loaf pan. Bake at 350° for 45 minutes.

Make polenta and NeoCuisine™ Red. Pour off excess juice (this is not fat) after loaf is baked.

Divide loaf in half and save half for later use. Slice second half and top with NeoCuisine™ Red. Serve with Basil Parmesan Polenta on the side.

179

SUNDAY, DAY 21

TODAY: OFF FOR EXERCISE

SURROUNDINGS MANAGEMENT™:

RECOMMENDED PROCESSES.

• Write for a few minutes every day in your BodyRenewal™ journal. Record what works for you. In the end you have your own custom information repository.

• Understand that when you are hungry, you are not starving. Starvation takes 30 to 40 days of eating nothing. Learn to ride out the occasional hunger pang.

• Tight clothing is a good fat-stripping body mnemonic. The slight discomfort is a reminder.

• Always portion snacks and meals. Two "reduced fat" Oreo® cookies turn to ten if the package is within reach.

• Drink tea, especially green tea which is loaded with advantageous phytochemicals unequivocally shown to reduce cancer according to studies published in the respected British medical journal *Lancet*.[13]

• Kill hunger pangs by tightening your stomach muscles and slowly counting to 10. This helps curb the flow of stomach acid that causes the hunger sensation.[14]

• Learn to eat breakfast: One of the best ways to start "eating breakfast" is with a protein shake because it's an easy to make and a proven wake-up food. Yes, it really works. Today buy a high-quality whey protein powder and other ingredients listed in Appendix B for the NeoCuisine™ HiPro Dream™. You want the highest quality whey protein mix because cheap brands don't taste very good. Buy small containers to experiment until you find a brand you like. When made in the morning an NC Hi Pro Dream™ can be shaken or reblended for an enjoyable lunch.

EXPECT:

EFFORT IN RULING THE *PRIMEVAL RAGING APPETITE*

Some Surroundings Management™ processes may strike you as extreme but you are, in a sense, fighting three million years' evolution. More than all else the body wants to get fat to save itself from starvation. It doesn't know that in America today, death by starvation is virtually nonexistent. The body estimates its needs by the events of 250,000 years ago. It readily accepts all the fat and simple carbohydrates (sugars) you feed it. Greasy pizza, dripping hamburgers, fatty French fries, sugary Snickers® and all the rest of our slow-kill 21st century foods are its favorites. You must literally command the body's urgings.

HOMEWORK:

EXPERIMENT WITH SURROUNDINGS MANAGEMENT™

Try a new Surroundings Management™ process today. And keep trying them until you discover which work best for you.

WINE-GARLIC SCAMPI SAUTÉ

The Tadich Grill in San Francisco serves its version at twice the calories. The truth be told, this NeoCuisine™ rendition has an entirely respectable flavor profile so close to the classic sauté you don't miss a thing.

•

Serves one.

Calories: 550
Net weight: 24 ounces
Prep time: 20 minutes
Cook time: 5 minutes
Calorie-to-weight ratio: 23 calories per ounce

- *13 ounces medium to large raw unpeeled shrimp (9 ounces peeled)*
- *1/4 teaspoon garlic powder*
- *1/4 teaspoon dried thyme*
- *1/2 cup chicken broth, fat skimmed*
- *1/2 cup instant rice, uncooked*
- *10 to 12 ounces frozen petite whole green beans*
- *1/2 cup drinking quality white wine [FYI: All the alcohol boils out.]*

- *1 Tablespoon red bell pepper, chopped*
- *1 Tablespoon scallions, green parts only, chopped*
- *"I Can't Believe It's Not Butter"®*
- *2 sprays olive oil, aerosol can*

Remove shells from shrimp. Devein and butterfly (use a knife to split down the outside curve 1/2 to 3/4 of the way through the shrimp). Remove black line (vein). Season with salt (1/4 teaspoon) and pepper (1/8 teaspoon) to taste. Sprinkle with the garlic powder and thyme.

Bring chicken broth to a boil. Stir in rice, cover, remove from heat and let sit 5+ minutes or until liquid is absorbed. Microwave green beans in a microwavable container, e.g. lidded glass, for 5 to 7 minutes. Drain.

Meanwhile, in a nonstick skillet, bring wine to a full boil. Reduce by 50% to 75% (this takes 5 to 10 minutes). Add shrimp and cook over medium heat until shrimp turns pink and flesh is white, 1 to 2 minutes. Meanwhile, add red bell pepper and scallions to rice.

Plate shrimp, rice and green beans. Season green beans with salt, pepper and "I Can't Believe It's Not Butter"® spray. Spray shrimp with olive oil.

MONDAY, DAY 22

TODAY: STRIDE 35 MINUTES

THE 20-YEAR ADVANTAGE

Robert Goldman, M.D., Ph.D., Chairman of the American Anti-Aging Academy says, "People who are physically fit, eat a healthy, balanced diet and take nutritional supplements can measure up to 20 years younger biologically than their chronological age." He describes exercise as "the anti-aging pill" because it:

• Improves immune system function substantiated by a review of 629 studies summarized in The International *Journal of Sports Medicine.*
• Improves posture.
• Relieves tension headache pain.
• Increases the density and strength of ligaments and tendons.
• Improves short-term memory.

• Sharpens dynamic vision and helps control glaucoma.
• Moderates the rate of joint degeneration (osteoarthritis).
• Helps alleviate depression which (among other things) lowers the risk of coronary heart disease.
• Improves blood circulation resulting in better organ function including the brain.
• Improves balance and coordination.
• Improves overall life quality.[15]

EXPECT:

BOOSTED OPTIMISM

Every time you rebuild muscle it makes a life deposit in your flourishing physique account. Your body realizes this and sends positive signals to the brain boosting your spirits.

HOMEWORK:

35-MINUTE STRIDE

You strided (strolled) this last week for about 40 minutes per day. Now decrease your striding time to 35 minutes using your entire two mile loop. You will hear yourself power breathing. Your perceived effort is pleasant exertion.

• Warm up by strolling for three to five minutes.
• Lean slightly forward.
• Swing your arms to help activate your heart.
• Stride onto your heel, push off with your toes.
• Enjoy yourself.

PRIMAVERA ALFREDO

At less than 1/2 the calories of the fatty original, this delicious dish is a praiseworthy substitute.

• *Serves one.*

Calories: 541
Net Weight: 29 ounces
Prep time: 20 minutes
Cook time: 20 minutes
Calorie-to-weight ratio: 20 calories per ounce

- *2 ounces uncooked whole wheat spaghetti*
- *One 16-ounce bag frozen stir-fry or mixed vegetables of choice (not to exceed 150 calories)*
- *2 cups fresh mushrooms, sliced*
- *3 dry (no oil) sun-dried tomato halves*
- *1 teaspoon balsamic vinegar*
- *1/2 cup (4 ounces) fat-free cream cheese*
- *1/4 cup nonfat milk*
- *1/2 teaspoon garlic powder*
- *2 teaspoons quality chicken base*
- *Scant 1/4 teaspoon pepper*

Cook spaghetti according to package directions.

Microwave vegetables 6 to 10 minutes in a microwavable container (e.g. lidded glass) turning once and draining. For the last 3 minutes of microwaving: in a separate lidded glass container, add mushrooms and sun-dried tomatoes mixed with balsamic vinegar and 1 Tablespoon water. Microwave both containers.

Make Alfredo sauce by combining cream cheese and milk in a small saucepan over low heat until cream cheese is soft. Add garlic powder, chicken base and pepper. Whisk until smooth.

Chop sun-dried tomatoes. Combine with spaghetti, vegetables and sauce. Toss. Squeeze lemon over the top for added zing.

TUESDAY, DAY 23

TODAY: STRIDE 35 MINUTES

HAVE MORE FUN

Behavior tends to pursue happiness, whether it is as subtle as honoring an ideal like community service, or a more obvious pleasure like attending a football game. Since the happiness-pursuit guides our actions so much, we readily realize when we are being deprived.

The pleasure compensation principle means we intuitively seek restitution for perceived self-denial. Diet deprivation can throw us into self-pity. Rather than repaying ourselves with food, it's important to spend a little more time having fun. BodyRenewal™ does not mean putting your life on hold.

- Buy a lovely house plant.
- Treat yourself to a fresh bouquet of flowers every week.
- Get a new hairstyle.

- Have your nails done.
- Scout garage sales.
- Drive to another city for a one-day holiday taking advantage of a hotel's coupon rate.
- Buy the best tea you can find.
- Make arrangements to spend a day with a friend.
- Catch a cheap flight to Las Vegas and watch a show or two.
- Hire a college student to paint your kitchen (under your close supervision).
- Drive out of town with a friend for a walk in the forest.
- Go to a large book store and buy three magazines on subjects you love: fashion, travel, home decor, fishing, garden, etc.

- List the clothes you are going to buy when you achieve the shape and vigor of youth.
- Plant a rose.
- Buy rollerblades.
- Get that CD you want.
- Have your car detailed.

EXPECT:
TO WORK AT COMPENSATING PLEASURES
No one else makes your life fun and enjoyable but you, as you know. Put effort into your happiness-pursuit.

HOMEWORK:
LIST COMPENSATING PLEASURES
Spend a few moments right now jotting ideas for having more fun.

JERK BBQ SPUDS

Caribbean cooks invented jerking. The name derives from the lusty use of heady spices and particular cooking technique. Using open flame, the Calypso cook jerks food from the fire at its precise moment of perfection. Our cookery is conventional but the flavors are real. Add red chili pepper flakes to the BBQ sauce if you like heat.

•

Serves one.

Calories: 594
Net Weight: 28 ounces
Prep time: 10 minutes
Cook time: 7 minutes
Calorie-to-weight ratio: 21 calories per ounce

- 4 ounces chicken breast, boned and skinned, cut into 1/4" ribbons
- 1 Tablespoon soy sauce
- 1 teaspoon ground allspice
- 1/4 teaspoon garlic powder
- Hot baked potato(es) totaling 16 ounces

- 1/3 to 1/2 cup chicken broth, fat skimmed
- 1/2 cup BBQ sauce (see page 343)
- Yogurt fruit slaw (see page 349)

Combine chicken, soy sauce, allspice, garlic powder and pepper (1/8 teaspoon) to taste in a Ziplock® bag and refrigerate.

Microwaving potato(es): Wash potato(es), put in a microwavable container, e.g. lidded glass, and microwave for 8 to 10 minutes, turning once. Conventional oven: Wash potato(es) and bake in oven at 400° for about 45 minutes. Check with fork.

Discard marinade. Reserve chicken. In small nonstick skillet brown chicken over high heat. Remove chicken. Add 1/3 to 1/2 cup chicken broth to deglaze pan.

Fork mash potato(es) to fill the plate. Pour chicken broth over. Potato(es) should be saturated. Top with chicken and BBQ sauce. Serve lemon slaw on the side. (Enjoy the rest of the yogurt later in the evening or the next day.)

185

WEDNESDAY, DAY 24

TODAY: 1•1•2™ 30 SECONDS TCT • MACRO DEFLEX™ AND DYNAMIC BALANCE™ 20 SECONDS TCT

BOSS YOUR MOUTH

Food is everywhere. Latté stands purvey bran muffins under the guise of "low fat," gas stations feature Dunkin Donuts® and Taco Bells®, malls dedicate huge areas to their "food courts," and grocery stores tempt you with snazzy fatty take-home meals.

You can feel like you aren't part of the group if you aren't eating like everyone else. You may get odd looks. Companions can be difficult with their ribbing. By any reckoning this is stressful. Shrug off your friends' nettling in favor of clean arteries for your head and heart.

Eventually you come to the realization that you are the boss of your mouth. What you eat is your decision. Blaming others for being overweight is a way of avoiding personal responsibility. No one's force-feeding you. Remember you decided to lose weight because you are a wonderful person, not to become one. Take charge of your mouth and your surroundings.

Try this exercise for a few days. Keep a record in your BodyRenewal™ journal of the calories you didn't eat. These are self-discipline wins. Did you skip the doughnut at the committee meeting? That's 300 calories you didn't eat. For lunch, did you go for the 1/2 turkey sandwich instead of whole and dress it with Dijon instead of mayonnaise? Did you replace the potato chip bag with a little fruit cup? If you did, you avoided another 300 calories. These little victories matter because they show you are building self-control skills. Dietary changes like these are the difference between stripping fat and being portly. An extra 100 calories a day over what you metabolize converts to an additional 10 pounds body fat a year!

EXPECT:

CONSCIOUS EFFORT

Avoiding pitfalls in the fat battlefield require your attention.

HOMEWORK:

1•1•2™ 30 SECONDS TCT ... 5 SIX-SECOND REPETITIONS

You have been strength training for one week. Now up total challenge time to 30 seconds, about 5 six-second repetitions. If you can't quite manage 30 seconds, do what you can. Observe the time and come back for a second cycle to achieve 30 seconds total challenge time. Or lighten your weights.

On days you don't stride always warm up for three to five minutes before 1•1•2™. Jump rope, stride, march in place, dance fast—your choice. You decide but achieve rapid breathing and a trace of sweat.

BUDDHIST VEGETABLE CURRY

Don't let the words curry or vegetable scare you. This is a delicious dish.

•
Serves one.

Calories: 475
Net weight: 32 ounces
Prep time: 15 minutes
Cook time: 12 to 17 minutes
Calorie-to-weight ratio: 15 calories per ounce

- *One 14.5-ounce can chicken broth, fat skimmed*
- *2 teaspoons quality chicken base*
- *16 ounces of potatoes, diced*
- *1/2 cup onions, diced*
- *1 Tablespoon sliced scallions, green part only*
- *1 teaspoon curry powder (Spice Islands® is excellent)*
- *8 ounces frozen cauliflower*
- *2 ounces frozen peas*
- *Juice of 1/4 lemon*
- *12 canned (unsweetened) Mandarin orange sections*

In a medium saucepan combine chicken broth, chicken base, potatoes and onions. Bring to a full boil and cook uncovered 10 to 15 minutes or until potatoes are done. Meanwhile, slice scallions.

Add curry powder and cauliflower. Cook 2 minutes. Add peas. Remove from heat and add lemon juice. Put on serving plate and garnish with Mandarin orange sections and scallions.

THURSDAY, DAY 25

TODAY: STRIDE 35 MINUTES

BRIDLE DEPRESSION, LIFT OPTIMISM

One strength-training advantage is its anti-depressant effect. Studies at the University of Washington suggest that weight lifting is as effective in reducing depression as some medications.[16] Research irrefutably links high optimism and exercise, but common sense already tells you it's true. Physical activity releases endorphins, the body's own morale-lifting hormones. Exercise metabolizes adrenaline, naturally relaxing you. As we lose weight and sculpt our bodies, self-approval rises. Maybe the simplest explanation is that 1•1•2™ accords with the body's natural intent. Working muscles pleases the body which signals its satisfaction with amplified feelings of contentment.

EXPECT:

TO FEEL BETTER

You deserve payback for your estimable efforts. Take a few moments after exercise, noting how good you feel. Value your rising self-appreciation. You deserve it because you are, after all, on the path to considerable accomplishment. Anticipate a flourishing physique. Expect a trim body, one you possess with pride. Take a moment to reflect on where you're headed. Use projecting ahead to what you will become to build confidence and self-admiration.

HOMEWORK:

FEELINGS PROFILE, ANOTHER LOOK

Write in your BodyRenewal™ journal observations on how you feel at this point. Chances are you feel better than your feelings profile written at the beginning of BodyRenewal™.

BodyRenewal™

SURPRISE BENEFIT: PREVENT DIABETES. Obesity increases your resistance to insulin and is the leading cause of noninsulin-dependent diabetes.[17] Twenty-one million people in this country have impaired glucose tolerance. Like diabetes, it's characterized by high blood levels of glucose. According to the *Tufts University Diet and Nutrition Letter,* weight reduction may prevent or delay diabetes.[18]

PEPPERONI PIZZA

Imagine after having stripped ten pounds of fat with another ten to go that you can enjoy a nice, gooey pepperoni pizza. This NeoCuisine™ masterpiece indulges you with just about all the flavor you get from a Domino's® gut bomb but with 1/4 the calories.

• Serves one.

Calories: 469
Net Weight: 33 ounces
Prep time: 15 to 20 minutes
Cook time: 30 + 30 minutes
Calorie-to-weight ratio: 14 calories per ounce

- 3 cups chicken broth, fat skimmed
- 1/2 cup polenta
- 1/2 cup NeoCuisine™ Red (see page 347)
- 1/2 cup Kraft® fat-free shredded cheddar cheese
- 1/4 cup onions, chopped
- 1/2 cup sliced mushrooms
- 1/3 green bell pepper, diced small
- 9 slices reduced fat pepperoni, diced small

In a medium saucepan bring chicken broth to a boil. Stir in polenta with a wire whisk. Return to full boil, cover, reduce heat to medium-low and cook until thickened, about 3 to 5 minutes. Remove lid and continue to cook over low heat 20 to 25 minutes, stirring occasionally.

Pour cooked polenta into ungreased deep dish pie plate and refrigerate 1 to 2 hours or overnight.

Put NeoCuisine™ Red on top of polenta and spread to edges. Top with cheese. Add onion, mushrooms, green bell pepper and pepperoni. Bake at 350° for 1/2 hour.

189

FRIDAY, DAY 26

TODAY: STRIDE 35 MINUTES

NeoCuisine™ BENEFITS

The phrase is so tiresome we ignore it: You are what you eat. Twenty-five years ago this was merely good guesswork. When Denham Harmon, M.D., Ph.D., pioneered the free radical theory decades ago, he was viewed by peers as somewhat of an oddball. Thanks to his research, the free radical theory has come to be the central theory of aging.[19] Think of free radicals as rogue atoms ravaging the molecular structure of your body. Not good.

The chief defense against free radicals is antioxidants. Vitamin supplements provide some antioxidants, but there are so many phytochemicals, supplementation simply can't provide them all. Nothing takes the place of a diet rich in a wide variety of fruits, vegetables and whole grains—the sun foods. Hundreds of studies verify that diets of the NeoCuisine™ type reduce cancer, heart disease, cut fat and keep it off while helping you live longer with greater vigor. These are wide-ranging claims but prove to yourself you feel better. Stay with NeoCuisine™ for 90 days. Then make your own assessment. You will find that you have stripped fat and you have an overall sense of improved well-being. Make your own decision.

EXPECT:
RISING SENSE OF FLOURISHING PHYSIQUE

In as little as three weeks you begin perceiving that you're feeling better emotionally and physically. It's not your imagination. Your body is reacting to favorable treatment.

HOMEWORK:
TAKE A QUALITY MULTIPLE VITAMIN AND AT LEAST 750 MG CALCIUM DAILY

Despite sun foods' superior phytochemical antioxidant availability, taking a good multi is wise insurance. Calcium supplementation is smart, too.

Ask your doctor about additional E, selenium, low-dose daily aspirin and other options. The day is long past to forego some form of rational supplementation.✶

✶Although expensive, a superior all-encompassing multiple supplement is Life Extension Mix: 1-800-544-4440. Be prepared for sticker shock.

SZECHUAN SHRIMP WARM SALAD

A snappy dressing accentuates this interesting salad which includes noodles and shrimp flavored with Chinese five-spice.

•

Serves one.

Calories: 525
Net weight: 30 ounces
Prep time: 15 minutes
Cook time: 15 minutes
Calorie-to-weight ratio: 18 calories per ounce

- 1 recipe Szechuan Dressing. Add more red pepper to taste.
- 4 ounces medium or large cooked shrimp*
- 1 cup of whole wheat spaghetti (1/3 cup dry) cooked in 1 cup clam juice* *
- 1/4 cup red bell pepper, diced
- One 12- to 16-ounce package of American salad mix, chopped
- 1/2 cup scallions, tops included, chopped

*Scallops, lobster or crab can be substituted.
**Buy or make with clam base.

SZECHUAN DRESSING
- 1/4 cup soy sauce
- 2 Tablespoons white wine vinegar
- 1 teaspoon dark sesame oil
- 1 teaspoon sesame seeds
- 3 packets aspartame
- 1/2 teaspoon garlic powder
- Scant 1/4 teaspoon ginger
- 1/4 teaspoon red pepper flakes or to taste
- 1/8 teaspoon Chinese five-spice or 1 pinch each anise and cinnamon

(Combine ingredients.)

Heat Szechuan Dressing in a small nonstick skillet to first sign of boil.

Add shrimp and cooked spaghetti; return to boil. Remove from heat and pour over lettuce, red bell pepper and scallions.

Toss and serve.

191

SATURDAY, DAY 27

TODAY: STRIDE 35 MINUTES • 1•1•2™ 30 SECONDS TCT • MACRO DEFLEX™
AND DYNAMIC BALANCE™ 20 SECONDS TCT

AFFIRMATIONS

Focusing devices keep us on track. Signs we post are worthwhile focusing devices. Affirmations can serve us well also. These are short pithy statements of intent repeated silently through the day to build resolve. Yes, they do work because they grab your conscious mind. Learn to overwhelm negative thought with these powerful statements. The choice is yours. Allow your mind to wander where it will or manage your self-talk using affirmations as one of your prime tools. Try these plus creating your own affirmations:

- "BodyRenewal™ leads to high self-appreciation."
- "My resolve is rising."
- "I already feel more vigorous."
- "I will not be fat."
- "I already feel better."
- "I'm adding 20 years to my life."
- "My strength is growing."
- "My fat-stripping skills keep getting better."

EXPECT:

AFFIRMATIONS TO FEEL A LITTLE AWKWARD

You may sense that "you're trying too hard" or affirmations "are a little silly." Don't be thrown off track by affirmation simplicity. Self-talk (thinking) management is one of the tricks to effective fat-stripping.

HOMEWORK:

BUILD ONE OR TWO AFFIRMATIONS

Repeat these through the day. Write an affirmations card to carry with you. Keep it in a pocket you reach into frequently, even a front pants pocket. Every time you touch it, remind yourself to repeat your affirmations. Take it out and read it if you like. Be sure to write affirmations confirming self-worth for the sake of your positive mental health. Consider: "Damn I'm good." You laugh because you are and getting better every day.

LONE STAR BAKED BEANS

Baked beans done right with nice, smoky Canadian bacon. The surprise ingredient is the addition of tart, green apple like Granny Smith. Add more ardor by mixing in fresh, chopped jalapeños.

•

Serves one.

Calories: 604   Net weight: 34.5 ounces
Prep time: 25 minutes
Calorie-to-weight ratio: 17 calories per ounce

- *1/2 red bell pepper, diced*
- *1/2 green bell pepper, diced*
- *1/4 onion, diced*
- *One 15-ounce can white beans, including liquid*
- *One 14.5-ounce can diced tomato, drained*

- *2 ounces Canadian bacon, diced*
- *1 teaspoon quality beef base*
- *1 teaspoon Worcestershire sauce*
- *1/4 teaspoon dry mustard*
- *1 tart green apple, such as Granny Smith or pippin, peeled and diced*
- *1 recipe Sugar-Free Ketchup (see page 343)*

Microwave bell peppers and onions in a microwavable container, e.g. lidded glass, for 3 to 4 minutes.

Meanwhile, combine the rest of the ingredients in a saucepan. Add peppers and onions and cook uncovered over medium heat for 15 to 20 minutes.

SUNDAY, DAY 28

TODAY: OFF FOR EXERCISE

THE BodyRenewal™ JOURNAL

Your BodyRenewal™ journal is an engagement tool. The more involved you are in the BodyRenewal™ process, the greater your chances of success. The mere act of writing deepens engagement. It is another effective way of reinforcing your positive intent. With the *primeval raging appetite* constantly urging overeating, multiple reinforcements are imperative.

Recording data in your BodyRenewal™ journal measures your progress. It's your history of improvement. Moving, for example, from a 20-second total challenge time to 30 seconds is an accomplishment. You are encouraged. Tracking advances gives you a solid record of how well you're doing.

Use your journal to capture discoveries—insights that foster BodyRenewal™. Think of your BodyRenewal™ journal as an information repository. Have you learned that going into the empty conference room at lunch, sitting quietly and visualizing your flourishing physique future for a few minutes galvanizes your motivation? Have you ascertained that after-work drinks are a surefire binge starter? Have you determined that prepping NeoCuisine™ dinners the day before or in the morning allows for an early dinner when you are most hungry? Make a record of what works for you.

EXPECT:

SELF-CONSCIOUSNESS WHEN WRITING

Thoughts put to paper or into the computer may look odd. Remember, though, these insights are written solely for you. What helps you best? Don't worry about format, neatness or what you write. Later, highlight what you like for ready reference.

HOMEWORK:

YOUR BodyRenewal™ JOURNAL IS A TOOL

If you have not started a BodyRenewal™ journal or have been neglecting it, start again today. Spend five minutes (more is better) penning your progress, memorializing your right ideas and listing worthy disputes.

Feelings fluctuate during change. You know how to restrain the roller coaster with Control Psychology™, your best tool being disputing silly fictions. Write them down. Refine them. Refer back to them: "I'm so tired of all this." Dispute: "Hold on. Am I really too imposed upon? No! My life filled with vigor and high self-appreciation is worth the effort required of me."

Last thing. Recording your BodyRenewal™ activities shows you in black and white hard copy whether you're advancing or backsliding. Either way it's a good energizer.

194

MUSHROOM BORDELAISE FILET MIGNON

**WITH GARLIC POTATO CAKE
AND VEGETABLES DU CHEF.**

• Serves one.

Calories: 525
Net weight: 26 ounces
Prep time/Cook time: 30 -
35 minutes
Calorie-to-weight ratio: 20
calories per ounce

- *One 14.5-ounce can beef broth, fat skimmed*
- *1/4 cup red wine (FYI: All the alcohol boils out.)*
- *2 cups fresh mushrooms, sliced*
- *6 ounces hash browns, shredded, fat-free*
- *5 ounces filet mignon net, fat trimmed*
- *1/2 Tablespoon Miracle Chop (see page 346)*
- *1 teaspoon red wine vinegar*
- *1/4 teaspoon dried thyme*
- *1/4 teaspoon garlic powder*
- *1 teaspoon cornstarch mixed with 1 teaspoon water*
- *10 to 16 ounces fresh asparagus or vegetable of choice*
- *1 medium tomato, sliced*
- *1/2 teaspoon balsamic vinegar*
- *1/4 teaspoon Miracle Chop (see page 346)*

In a small saucepan combine beef broth, red wine and mushrooms. Bring to a boil and cook over high heat until fluid reduces by 90%. Reduction takes 20 to 25 minutes so don't stand over it. Meanwhile, microwave hash browns in a microwavable container, e.g. lidded glass, 6 to 7 minutes until softened. While microwaving hash browns, preheat oven to 150°.

Cook steak in a small nonstick skillet over highest heat until dark crust forms on both sides. It will smoke but that's okay. Remove filet one degree before desired doneness (if you want medium rare, remove at rare). Test for doneness by making small slits in meat with a knife.

Keep steak warm in oven while preparing the rest of the meal. Steak will cook slightly while in the oven. Reserve skillet for potato patty.

Combine 1/2 Tablespoon Miracle Chop, red wine vinegar and salt/pepper to taste. Mix and add hash browns. Form into one 3" to 4" patty. In the same skillet used for the filet, cook potato patty over medium-high heat until browned and crusty on both sides.

Stir mushroom sauce occasionally. During the last five minutes of cooking, add thyme, garlic powder and pepper to taste and the stirred cornstarch/water mix. Stir. When sauce is thickened set aside.

Meanwhile, trim asparagus. Microwave asparagus or green beans in a microwavable container, e.g. lidded glass, for 6 to 8 minutes. Spray with "I Can't Believe It's Not Butter."®

On a plate, place filet on potato patty. Place asparagus. Top the filet with the mushroom sauce. Put sliced tomatoes on the plate and sprinkle with balsamic vinegar then top with 1/4 teaspoon Miracle Chop. Serve.

195

MONDAY, DAY 29

TODAY: STRIDE 30 MINUTES

MORE STRIDING CHALLENGE

Today you have been striding for three weeks. Over the past week, you've strided your two-mile course in 35 minutes which is a little over 3 miles per hour. Now is the time to pick up the pace. You want to go at a speed where about after ten minutes you CAN'T SING, CAN TALK. You will hear yourself breathing. Your perceived effort is pleasant exertion. You should complete your two-mile course in approximately 30 minutes, a speed of 4 miles per hour.

Now that you are striding faster, remind yourself to power breathe. Keep your blood enriched by bringing in plenty of oxygen. Train your lungs' chief respiratory muscle, the diaphragm, by working it with vigor. It gets in better shape as time goes on. Bear in mind that the lungs are analogous to a balloon. The more you blow up a balloon, the easier it gets.

Breathing has marvelous psychoprophylactic qualities. Displace discomfort by focusing on breathing. Striding is made easier by developing a breathing pattern. Try inhaling with every two steps and then exhaling two steps. When going up a hill, try breathing in and out with each step. Concentrate on filling your lungs.

EXPECT:

A TRUE CARDIO WORKOUT

You are now striding at four miles per hour, a speed that activates your heart. You'll feel it, which is the intent.

HOMEWORK:

STRIDE 30 MINUTES

Remember these simple striding rules:

- Warm up by strolling for three to five minutes.
- Lean slightly forward.
- Swing your arms to help activate your heart.
- Strike with your heel and push off with your toes.
- Enjoy yourself.

For Even More Striding Info Visit Us @ bodyrenewalpast 40.com

CHOPPED SALAD CUCINA

The garbanzos and basil do taste tricks. Great calorie-to-weight ratio and splendid flavor.

• Serves one.

Calories: 459
Net Weight: 36 ounces
Prep time: 15 to 20 minutes
Calorie-to-weight ratio: 12 calories per ounce

- *1 recipe NeoCuisine™ Vinaigrette (see page 307)*
- *2 teaspoons dried basil, rubbed between fingers to release flavors*
- *1/4 cup scallions, chopped, green parts only*
- *2 ounces chicken breast, boned and skinned*
- *1 cup garbanzo beans, drained*
- *1/2 to whole head iceberg lettuce (depending on its size and your PRA), chopped*
- *1 small tomato, finely chopped*
- *1/4 cup quality grated Parmesan cheese, e.g. Reggiano*

Combine dressing, basil and scallions.

Brown chicken in nonstick skillet over high heat. Reduce heat and cook until done, about 1 to 2-1/2 minutes. Cool and chop into 1/4" dice.

Mash 2/3 of the cup of garbanzo beans and rough chop the remaining 1/3 cup.

Combine dressing mix with lettuce, chicken, tomato, beans and Parmesan cheese. Toss and serve.

TUESDAY, DAY 30

TODAY: STRIDE 30 MINUTES

BODY MNEMONICS

We respond to millions of stimuli a day. There is so much mind-traffic, it's a wonder we remember to do anything. We have so many inputs vying for our attention that it's troublesome to remain fixed on our fat-stripping aims. We require prompting through the day to channel our thoughts toward our shape and vigor of youth resolution. It is far too easy to grab a ubiquitous Snickers® on the fly versus a small carton of strawberries.✦

You will recall the clothing cue from Surroundings Management™ with its recommendation that you wear tight clothing or a snug belt to heighten the shape and vigor of youth goal awareness. The mild discomfort of tight clothing or a belt serves as a focusing device called a body mnemonic to assist you in staying on track.

A body mnemonic is simply a minor irritant causing you to notice it several times during the day, a physical prompter reminding you of your shape and vigor of youth goal. Its value comes in associating the reminder with your fat-stripping aspirations. Best-known body mnemonics of legend and fancy are tying a piece of string on a finger and a pea in the shoe. They sound daft, something out of a Grimm's fairy tale, perhaps, but the fact is they work. Every time a body mnemonic jogs your memory you can repicture where you are going. This spurs the mind toward right thinking. You may for example forego deep-dish pepperoni pizza for lunch if you're reminded of your fat-stripping goal because your belt's a bit tight. That tight belt may also remind you to skip a pastrami sandwich the next time and go for double large garden salad with balsamic vinegar. Body mnemonics include:

- A piece of tape on the inside of your wrist.
- Switched rings and/or watches to the other hand.
- A paper dot affixed to your watch dial.
- A Scotch® tape ring put on daily for a week.
- A new ring on your little finger.
- Rubber band on the wrist.✦✦

EXPECT:
BODY MNEMONICS TO HELP FOCUS YOU

But as with all aspects of BodyRenewal™, no single approach is the solution. It takes a comprehensive plan. Body mnemonics can be a helpful part of the puzzle.

HOMEWORK:
OVER THE NEXT WEEKS TRY BODY MNEMONICS AT LEAST TWICE

You'll feel slightly awkward but each time you notice your prompter, activate yourself by recalling the numerous BodyRenewal™ advantages accruing to you or visualizing your future best shape and vigor of youth or ...

✦This example illustrates the magnitude of change coming to your life. You may almost be taken aback at the idea of trading a Snickers® for strawberries (somewhat extreme?) but you will be surprised how much you come to enjoy juicy fresh fruit at one-third the calories and infinitely better body betterment owing to the phytochemicals and no saturated fat.

✦✦ Snapping it once in a while may appear a little idiotic but sharp sensory input brings the mind to attention.

CABO SAN LUCAS BOWL

If you enjoy lively entreés, this Mexican fish medley has plenty of action.

•

Serves one.

Calories: 581
Net Weight: 38 ounces
Prep time: 15 minutes
Cook time: 11 minutes
Calorie-to-weight ratio: 15 calories per ounce

- *1 medium zucchini, shredded*
- *1 stalk celery, cut into 1/4" slices*
- *1/2 cup green bell pepper, diced*
- *8 to 10 ounces clam juice*
- *One 14.5-ounce can Mexican recipe stewed tomatoes, undrained*
- *1 cup black beans, drained*
- *1 teaspoon chili powder*
- *1 teaspoon anchovie paste (All you anchovie phobes relax. The anchovie taste disappears.)*
- *1/2 cup frozen corn*
- *1 packet aspartame*
- *6 ounces filet of sole or other white fish, cut into 1" pieces*

Microwave zucchini, celery and green pepper in a microwavable container, e.g. lidded glass, for 3 minutes.

In a serving bowl, combine all ingredients. Cover with plastic wrap and microwave 5 minutes.

Stir. Don't break fish. Cook an additional 3 minutes. Salt (1/4 teaspoon) to taste. Serve.

199

WEDNESDAY, DAY 31

TODAY: 1•1•2™ 45 SECONDS TCT • MACRO DEFLEX™ AND DYNAMIC BALANCE™ 30 SECONDS TCT

1•1•2™ RECOMMENDATIONS

The start of strength training is somewhat like walking through a tempting buffet: Our eyes are bigger than our stomach. During the first sessions of 1•1•2™ you will probably feel that you can do more, maybe much more. Now is when you want to use discretion. You're probably motivated to higher 1•1•2™ rigor despite feeling a little sore. Heed the 18- to 20-second total challenge time, starting at an easy body weight resistance position and the 50% one-time dumbbell lift maximum advisories because your body is not yet conditioned. You'll soon be ratcheting up.

There is one other instruction worth repeating. When performing the Thigh-Thinner-Tush-Tightener (4T), observe the 45° angle warning. Never allow your knee angle to reach a right angle (90°) because it is too demanding on the knees. You superbly strengthen quadriceps (front of the leg), hamstrings (back of the legs) and gluteals (butt) by

going no lower than a 45° or 50° knee angle. You should always be able to see your toes.

EXPECT:

MORNING EXERCISE ADJUSTMENT

You are not used to morning exercise and probably don't like it. Patience please. Habit is just weeks away.

HOMEWORK:

UP 1•1•2™ TO 7 SIX-SECOND REPETITIONS. AND MACRO DEFLEX™ AND DYNAMIC BALANCE™ TO 30 SECONDS

You have been 1•1•2™ strength-training for two weeks. Using the same weights and body weight resistance positions of the past weeks, up your repetitions to seven (3 seconds up, 3 seconds down). This builds more muscle, which increases metabolic rate and thus fat burn. Because you are maintaining your same calorie intake, you're slimming down. Don't forget the five-minute warm-up so your muscles are ready.

Increase deflexion to ten three-second holds in the "I can feel it" range, not to mild discomfort. You complete this entire Macro Deflexion™ routine in just four minutes. That's quick for all the advantages. See if you can increase total Dynamic Balance™ to 30 seconds. You probably won't be able to accumulate this amount of time in one try. That's okay. Several time-accumulating Dynamic Balances™ are fine.

THE POGETTI SAN FRANCISCO FRITTATA

This fines herbes omelet is inspired by San Francisco master chef John Pogetti, who put on his restaurant menus: "If you don't see it on my menu, ask for it and I'll cook it."

•

Serves one.

Calories: 574
Net weight: 35 ounces
Prep time: 10 minutes
Cook time: 35 minutes
Calorie-to-weight ratio: 16 calories per ounce

- 1 cup zucchini, chopped (1/2" maximum)
- 1 cup onions, chopped (1/2" maximum)
- 1 cup fresh mushrooms, sliced
- 1 cup chopped canned tomato, drained
- Three 4-ounce (1-1/2 cups) containers fat-free egg substitute, e.g. EggBeaters®
- 1/4 cup quality grated parmesan cheese, e.g. Reggiano

- 1 teaspoon dried Italian herb seasoning
- 2 teaspoons quality chicken base
- 1 cup fat-free (lite) pasta (marinara) sauce

Combine all ingredients except pasta sauce.

Spray an 8" x 8" pan (or comparable size, e.g. 6" x 10") with nonstick vegetable spray and add frittata mixture. Bake at 400° for 35 minutes. Frittata is done when the sides are firm but the center is still soft.

Heat the pasta sauce and serve over frittata, garnishing with a teaspoon of parsley flakes.

201

THURSDAY, DAY 32

TODAY: STRIDE 30 MINUTES

MORE SLEEP, BETTER SLEEP

By now the positive effects of exercise are beginning to make themselves known in your sleep patterns. As your exercise becomes more rigorous, quality sleep increases. You want sound sleep because proper rest helps strip fat. A properly rested body and mind produces clear-headed eating and exercise decisions. You exercise better when rested and, plainly, you feel better. Here are the points experts say assure good rest:

- Make sleep a top priority in your life.
- Buy the best mattress you can afford.
- Keep your bedroom dark, cool and quiet (consider ear plugs or a white noise machine).
- "Hide" your clock so you don't say, "Oh my gosh, look how late it is."
- Develop a sleep pattern, rising every day at the same time even on the weekends.
- Don't drink liquids for two hours before bed so you don't wake in the night for too many bathroom trips.
- Before retiring, write down your problems so they are captured. We all fear losing information. This will save it for later resolution. You'll be amazed how effectively it calms the mind.
- If you take supplements, take your calcium and magnesium, baby aspirin and vitamin E at night. Calcium is a natural muscle relaxant, aspirin alleviates minor pain and vitamin E calms restless leg syndrome.

EXPECT:
IMPROVED SLEEP

HOMEWORK:
ALLOW YOUR BODY THE REST IT WANTS
In other words, don't strangle your new slumber patterns with late nights. Let your body enter a new circadian cycle beneficial to your health. Good sleep is a privilege you have earned through exercise. Enjoy it.

SOUTHERN SMOTHERED CHICKEN LOAF

WITH REDEYE GRAVY AND HOME FRIES. MAKES 2 MEATLOAF SERVINGS.

Redeye Gravy is alleged to have come about when General Andy Jackson won the battle of New Orleans. The morning after his victory he ordered his hungover cook, who'd celebrated all night, to make "a mess o' biscuits and gravy as red as your eyes."

Calories per serving: 512
Net Weight per serving: 30 ounces
Prep time: 15 to 20 minutes
Cook time: 45 minutes
Calorie-to-weight ratio: 17 calories per ounce
(Calorie count includes Redeye Gravy and Home Fries.)

- 3/4 pound (12 ounces) 1% fat very lean ground turkey
- 1 Tablespoon quality chicken base
- 1 teaspoon garlic powder
- 1 teaspoon pepper

- 1 teaspoon red wine vinegar
- 1/2 cup onion, finely diced
- 1 teaspoon Bacobits®
- 18-20 ounces (1-1/2 packages) extra-firm ultra-low-fat tofu
- 1 recipe Flavor Fries (see page 354) Use option 3.

REDEYE GRAVY
- 1 cup chicken broth, skimmed of fat
- 1 Tablespoon quality chicken base
- 1 Tablespoon flour
- 1 teaspoon paprika
- 1/4 teaspoon dried thyme

Combine first 7 ingredients. Set aside. Crumble tofu into blender and pureé until smooth, about 30 to 45 seconds. You will need to stop blender and stir twice or more. Add to meatloaf mix and stir well to incorporate all ingredients.

Pour into 8" x 3" loaf pan. Bake at 350° for 45 minutes.

Prepare Flavor Fries of choice. Combine Redeye Gravy ingredients. Bring to a boil. Pepper to taste (1/4 teaspoon). Set aside.

Pour off excess juice (this is not fat) after loaf is baked. Divide loaf in half and save half for later use, up to a week. Slice second half and top with gravy.

203

FRIDAY, DAY 33

TODAY: STRIDE 30 MINUTES

DO I REALLY NEED ALL THIS?

ToteCards, journaling and all the rest must seem like a lot of reinforcement. Visualizing, disputing and win lists may strike one as "too much management." It adds up to a fair amount of structure, enough to make one wonder.

If it appears to be a lot, let's briefly recount our challenge. Breathing aside, we are dealing with our most fundamental survival mechanism—eating. The body becomes, you might say, insane in its efforts to stay alive when it perceives food shortage. Some of life's strongest urges are eating. Shrewd management of these primordial motivations offers our only hope. This is why BodyRenewal™ presents so many tools for con-trolling these overarching impulses.

Factoring in time availability, use as many follow-up and reinforcement tools presented in Surroundings Management™ as you can handle. You cannot do all of them, but do select those you can fit into your schedule. Recommended are:

- Magazine subscriptions
- Portion all snacks and mini meals
- 10-minute daily reflection for weight control reading
- Drink tea
- The Miracle 20™
- Fresh fruit bowl with three apple varieties and plenty of grapefruit
- Eating slowly
- Quaffing no-cal fluids
- Signs
- Writing daily in your Body-Renewal™ journal

EXPECT:
CONTINUOUS SELF-MANAGEMENT
There are no days off when stripping fat.

HOMEWORK:
YOU WANT TO BE CLEVER IN MANIPULATING THE PRIME-VAL RAGING APPETITE
The processes above can help. Review the processes list and select at least one new one for your use.

WARM BLACK BEAN CILANTRO SALAD

The concept of using a meat base in a salad may strike you as curious but the taste outcome tells the story. Here is the Osmazome Principle™ at work, making flavor that won't quit. You'll not notice that this is fat-stripped with 1/3 the calories of your favorite tacqueria taco salad.

• Serves one.

Calories: 490
Net weight: 35 ounces
Prep time: 15 minutes
Cook time: 4 to 5 minutes
Calorie-to-weight ratio: 14 calories per ounce

- 1-1/2 cups canned black beans, including liquid (stir before measuring)
- 2 teaspoons chili powder
- 2 teaspoons red wine vinegar
- 1 teaspoon dried cilantro, rubbed between fingers to release flavor
- 1 teaspoon quality beef base
- 1/4 cup frozen corn, thawed

- 1 packet aspartame
- 12- to-16 ounce package of American salad mix, rough chopped
- 1/2 cup red onion, chopped
- 1 ounce (about 20) fat-free baked tortilla chips, slightly crushed
- 1/2 cup tomato, diced
- 1/4 lemon wedge

Combine black beans, chili powder, red wine vinegar, cilantro, beef base, corn and aspartame. Mix and microwave until hot but not boiling, about 4 to 5 minutes.

Add hot dressing mix to salad mix, onion and chips. Toss. Add tomato to top or side. See photo. (The scallion mariachis are strictly optional.)

Squeeze lemon over salad (important for flavor) and serve.

SATURDAY, DAY 34

TODAY: STRIDE 30 MINUTES • 1•1•2™ 45 SECONDS TCT • MACRO DEFLEX™
AND DYNAMIC BALANCE™ 30 SECONDS TCT

IMPROVE YOUR MIND

One of the surprising advantages accruing from the Muscle Rebuild™ is mind improvement. The studies are incontrovertible. MacArthur Foundation researcher and University of Michigan professor emeritus of psychology Robert L. Kahn, Ph.D., notes that laboratory animals exercised regularly have higher levels of nerve growth factor which stimulates development of new brain cells.[20] People who exercise consistently score higher in cognitive tests than their sedentary peers. The International Society of Sports Psychology reports aerobic exercise to be as effective as some forms of psychotherapy.[21] Even levels of creativity may rise.[22] But you know firsthand how exercise reduces tension and relaxes you. You just feel better.

You are invigorated. All good reasons to continue Muscle Rebuilding™.

EXPECT:
RISING POSITIVE ATTITUDE

Take a moment to note the change in your psyche. Compare your morale now with when you started. Chances are you feel better, the result largely of your Muscle Rebuild™. Exercise improves your spirits.

HOMEWORK:
AN INTELLECTUAL CHALLENGE

For weeks you have been exercising and eating correctly. You've done it for your body without giving much consideration about how it is affecting your mental efficiency. It's time for you to discover your improved cognitive capacity. Choose an intellectual challenge: A novel by Joseph Conrad, learn a new computer program, take a class at the Learning Annex®, or community college, write that letter to the editor, read a self-help book. Choose something because your mind is clearer now than it has been in years. You can feel it. Take advantage of your new cognitive fitness.

SHEPHERD'S PIE

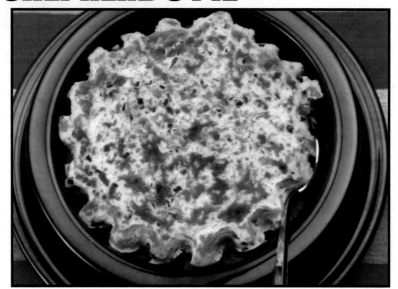

This is a no-fat version of the classic. It takes a little extra time to prepare, but the results speak for themselves.

• Serves one.

Calories: 569
Net weight: 36 ounces
Prep time: 25 minutes
Cook time: 15 minutes
Calorie-to-weight ratio: 16 calories per ounce

- *One 14.5-ounce can beef broth, fat skimmed*
- *6 ounces small baby carrots*
- *2 teaspoons quality beef base*
- *Scant 1/2 teaspoon dried thyme*
- *1/2 teaspoon garlic powder*
- *1/4 cup tomato paste*
- *2 cups sliced mushrooms*
- *1 scallion (chop green and white parts separately)*
- *1 medium zucchini*
- *16 ounces peeled potatoes, diced large*
- *1/4 cup peas*
- *2 Tablespoons fat-free cream cheese*

In a medium saucepan, combine 3/4 of the can of beef broth (reserve the rest for the crust), carrots, beef base, thyme, garlic powder, tomato paste, mushrooms, white part of scallion, zucchini and pepper (1/4 teaspoon) to taste. Bring to a full boil and cook until liquid is reduced by 1/3 to 1/2, 10 to 15 minutes.

Meanwhile, microwave potatoes in a microwavable container, e.g. lidded glass, 6 to 8 minutes until cooked through. Put half of the potatoes and the peas plus the saucepan ingredients into an oven-proof casserole.

Mash remaining potatoes, adding cream cheese and the green part of the scallion. Add 1 to 2 Tablespoons of the beef broth to smooth the mixture. Put mashed potatoes on waxed paper and form into a shape to cover the entire top of the casserole. Invert spud crust onto top of casserole.

Put under broiler 1 to 2 minutes or until potato crust is browned. Serve.

SUNDAY, DAY 35

TODAY: OFF FOR EXERCISE

FOCUSING DEVICE: SIGNS

As you've learned, experts say we exposed to three million stimuli a day. To help keep us stay goal-oriented, focusing devices are helpful, especially signs.

Review *Surroundings Management*™ for sign tips, topics and posting places (page 81).

There are a couple of things you need to know about signs. The first and most important rule of good sign management is they get old fast. In other words they quickly blend into our surroundings. To avoid this, make new signs weekly or, at the most, monthly. At the bare minimum, move sign locations. Do this during Body-Renewal™ and for 60 days thereafter. Every time you change a sign it renews as a goal reinforce-ment. Change sign colors and shapes. Yes, this does seem like fussing, but bear in mind we need a host of cues to breach our barrier of consciousness. With hundreds and hundreds of thousands of stimuli bidding for attention, we require focus management. Signs help.

EXPECT:

TO SENSE THE JOY OF MOVING FORWARD

You know you're making progress. It makes you feel good. Stop and savor the experience.

HOMEWORK:

MAKE THREE SIGNS FOR POSTING

You don't need to spend a lot of time or make them elaborate. Use a simple pen and standard 8-1/2 x 11" paper or 3 x 5" cards. Make one sign with a quantified goal (e.g., dress size, weight, waist measurement, etc.), your top three shape and vigor of youth benefits and the three nice things you are going to do for yourself when your goals are reached.

PAGO PAGO PINEAPPLE PORK

South Seas inspired, this melange of flavors is an eminent celebratory dinner. The South Sea islands are a world crossroads making its cookery outstanding world flavor fusion.

•

Serves one.

Calories: 568
Net weight: 28 ounces
Prep time: 15 minutes
Cook time: 20 minutes
Calorie-to-weight ratio: 20 calories per ounce

- *8 ounces pork tenderloin, trimmed of fat*
- *5 ounces whole baby carrots*
- *12 ounces fresh broccoli, cut into spears*
- *1/4 cup water chestnuts, drained*
- *1 teaspoon red bell pepper, chopped*
- *1/2 can (8-ounce can) crushed pineapple packed in its own juice, squeezed of liquid*
- *1 Tablespoon scallions, green parts only, chopped*

- *Pinch red pepper flakes or a dash red pepper sauce*
- *2 Tablespoons rice vinegar*
- *1 packet aspartame*
- *1/2 teaspoon sesame seeds*
- *1 recipe Teriyaki Dressing (see page 307)*✶

Rub pork liberally (don't be stingy) with salt, pepper and garlic powder. Sear pork in a nonstick skillet over high heat. Reduce heat to medium-low and continue cooking 15 to 20 minutes or until cooked medium-well. ✶✶

Meanwhile microwave carrots and broccoli in a microwavable container, e.g. lidded glass, for 8 to 10 minutes. Add water chestnuts the last minute microwaving.

Microwave red bell pepper in a microwavable container, e.g. lidded glass, for 30 seconds. Combine bell pepper, pineapple, scallions, red pepper flakes, vinegar, aspartame and 2 pinches of salt. Microwave 15 to 30 seconds until warm.

Slice tenderloin in 1/4" slices. Arrange in an overlapping circle. Place pineapple salsa in center. Add vegetables to plate and sprinkle with sesame seeds. Pour Teriyaki Dressing over pork and vegetables. Serve.

✶ If you wish, you may thicken the Teriyaki Dressing. If you do, reserve aspartame. Mix 1 Tablespoon cold dressing and 1 teaspoon cornstarch. Reserve. Bring dressing to boil. Add cornstarch/teriyaki mix. Stir. Turn off the heat. Let stand a couple minutes. Then add aspartame.

✶✶ Medium-well with a trace of pink brings pork to its best flavor and an internal temperature of about 160°+, the U.S. Federal standard.

MONDAY, DAY 36

TODAY: STRIDE 30 MINUTES

MUSCLE REBUILD™ REMOTIVATION

There are those days you just don't want to exercise. It's important, though, to maintain exercise frequency because if you don't, a day off or two turns into a week and then possibly a month until you eventually abandon Muscle Rebuild™ entirely. Go back to Striding and Deflexing and reread the strategies that keep you exercising steadily, page 68. Bear these points in mind:

- New is motivational. From your magazines have two or three new approaches ready to go on a moment's notice. This might be a completely new set of exercises, light jogging instead of striding, or anything else that appeals to you like yoga stances or isometrics.
- Visualize positive muscle benefit. Imagine what's happening internally: Blood rushing into your muscles, cells responding to the challenge, nerves firing and muscles screaming, "This is what's saving me!" Visualizing muscle getting stronger makes 1•1•2™ easier.
- Remember exercise is a privilege. Your body works in an exhilarating reality-touching way. You connect with consciousness by learning about your body with 1•1•2™, Macro Deflexing™ and Dynamic Balancing™. Think about how one of life's pleasures is striding out of doors and all the people who can't.
- "Resistance training is the only type of exercise that can slow and even reverse declines in muscle mass, bone density and strength that were once considered inevitable results of aging." *The Harvard Health Letter.*[23]
- Miriam Nelson, Ph.D., Tuffs University, simply says of her pioneering reasearch, "After one year of strength training, subjects' bodies were 15 to 20 years more youthful."[24]

- Have a brand-new workout video or two to pop into the VCR.
- Maximize cross-training. This means doing something else. Instead of striding consider:
  - Bike riding
  - Waterskiing
  - Rollerblading
  - Tennis
  - Basketball
  - Racquetball
  - Swimming
  - No-cart golfing

EXPECT:
EXERCISE REMOTIVATORS TO BE ENERGIZERS
They can work for you.

HOMEWORK:
HAVE AN EXERCISE REMOTIVATOR LIST READY TO GO
A remotivator might be an entirely new lifting routine or a new striding route. Tear out pages from your magazines, putting them in a file.

DIJONNAISE CHICKEN PANINI

A pan-grilled chicken sand-wich stuffed with balsamic seasoned eggplant slices and zesty red onion. The mix of no-fat mayo, horseradish and Dijon set piquant nuances.

• *Serves one.*

Calories: 500
Net weight: 21 ounces
Prep time: 25 minutes
Cook time: 20 minutes
Calorie-to-weight ratio: 19 calories per ounce

• *12 ounces chicken breast, boned and skinned*
• *1/4 teaspoon garlic powder*
• *1/4 teaspoon commercial Italian herb seasoning*
• *Two 1/2" round slices eggplant, peeled*
• *2 teaspoons balsamic vinegar*
• *1 recipe sandwich Dijonnaise (see page 346)*
• *2 slices whole grain light bread (e.g. Wonder® Light)*
• *1/4 cup prepared roasted red bell pepper*
• *2 slices red onion, 1/8 to 1/4" thick*

• *1 slice fat-free Swiss cheese single*
• *1 recipe Cottage Cheese Kiwi-Pineapple Salad (see page 348)*

Place chicken breast between two pieces of plastic wrap. Pound gently to flatten to 1/2" thick (use bottom of small sauce pan or wooden mallet). Rub chicken with garlic powder, Italian herb seasoning, salt (1/8 to 1/4 teaspoon) to taste and a pinch of pepper.

Cook in a nonstick skillet over high heat 2 to 3 minutes or until bottom is well-browned and crusty. Turn once and cook 1 minute more. Don't overcook. Cool and slice into thin strips.

While chicken is cooling, sprinkle eggplant with balsamic vinegar and microwave in a microwavable container, e.g. lidded glass, until cooked, about 2 minutes.

Layer in this order, spreading a little dijonnaise on each layer: wheat bread, eggplant, red bell pepper, onion, chicken strips, Swiss cheese, wheat bread. This makes a juicy sandwich.

Place sandwich in nonstick skillet. Cover and cook over medium-low heat, turning once, until heated through and cheese is melted, about 3 to 5 minutes per side. Serve with Cottage Cheese Kiwi-Pineapple Salad.

TUESDAY, DAY 37

TODAY: STRIDE 30 MINUTES

CLOCK HUNGER VS EATING WHEN HUNGRY

One of our most ingrained habits is eating by the clock instead of eating when we are hungry. Eating by the clock means we observe the time and judge our hunger on that basis. The power of belief is enormous. For example, we may be paying little mind to hunger until we discover it's 7 PM. Our immediate reaction is, "Oh, it's seven. Time to eat." We all do it. Researchers allowed subjects to think it was late in the day. Seeing the late hour subjects believed they were hungry. The later subjects thought it was, the hungrier they got. Likewise, subjects told it was earlier than it actually was weren't as hungry.[25]

The clock hunger response counters evolution. The hominids of 100,000 years ago obviously didn't eat by the clock because there were no clocks. They had a rough sense of the time of day but no clocks to tell them that at precisely 6 PM dinner is served. They ate when hungry, evolution's preferred hunger response.

Our solution is simple but challenging owing to lifelong clock-watching: Learn to eat when hungry versus time of day. It may well cut hundreds of calories daily.

You now know that hunger quite literally won't kill you. You've gained a new level of discipline which can stay with you the rest of your life. You've discovered how to cope with that hunger pang by having a cup of coffee, mugs of tea, diet pop or glasses of water. You've become skilled. You have learned how to ride the hunger wave, putting it gently to rest.

EXPECT:
SURPRISE BY HOW YOUR EATING IS CLOCK-REGULATED

HOMEWORK:
EXPERIMENT TODAY EATING BY HUNGER, NOT TIME
Delay eating by not clock-watching. The later you have your meals, the more you have for 7 to Bed. Learn to build calorie reserves you don't entirely use. Dropping only 100 calories a day strips 10 pounds a year.

BLACK BEAN CHILI IN EGGPLANT

Although eggplant may not be everyone's favorite vegetable, this dish will surprise you. Neutral in flavor, eggplant picks up the redolent native Sonoran spices of cumin and chilies. Eat the skin, too, you'll be surprised how much you enjoy it.

• Serves one.

Calories: 399
Net weight: 28 ounces
Prep time: 15 minutes
Cook time: 10 minutes
Calorie-to-weight ratio:14
calories per ounce

- 1 pound eggplant
- One 14.5-ounce can black beans, drained
- One 14.5-ounce can redi-cut Italian tomatoes, drained
- 1 Tablespoon quality beef base
- 1 Tablespoon chili powder (add more or less as personal tastes dictate)
- 1 Tablespoon cumin powder
- 1 packet aspartame
- 1/4 cup Kraft® fat-free shredded cheddar cheese
- 2 Tablespoons onions, chopped

Cut eggplant in half, cover each half with plastic wrap and microwave for 8 minutes (or until done), turning once.

While eggplant cooks: Combine black beans, tomatoes, beef base, chili powder and cumin. Bring to a boil. Remove. Add aspartame.

Open eggplant meat in shell to form a well. Fill with half the chili mixture (Save the rest for another day).

Garnish with cheddar and onion. Serve.

WEDNESDAY, DAY 38

TODAY: 1•1•2™ 60 SECONDS TCT • MACRO DEFLEX™ AND DYNAMIC BALANCE™ 30 SECONDS TCT

CONCEDING NOTHING

Since the dawn of recorded history about 15,000 years ago, the average human lifespan was 40 years. In fact, in 1900 people rarely lived past 50. So it's not surprising that little is known about the capabilities of the human body past 50. A few apocryphal stories aside, little has been known of our speed, strength, endurance and agility potential during the second half of our lives. There have been few studies, rare role models, and certainly no encouragement toward living a vigorous, physically demanding life beyond 50.

The running and fitness boom, kicked off by Dr. Kenneth Cooper and his 1968 book *Aerobics* changed the game. The message preached by Dr. Cooper is one of lifetime fitness. Baby boomers are true pioneers in proving the body's remarkable potential. Although he's not exactly a baby boomer, a grand example of the body's true capabilities is Paul Reese.

Over a period of 124 days, Reese ran 25 to 26 miles each day. His goal? To run across the United States without taking a day off. He made it. But that's not the amazing thing. **Paul Reese was 73 years old.** Reese says about aging and the body.

"... the human body, I've learned through years of running, is a remarkable piece of machinery—capable of more than the guy who holds the warranty on it generally realizes. I remained in action for 124 days, never taking a day off—which again, is another manifestation that senior citizens have more physical stamina than they are credited with."[26]

That should do it. No more excuses. If Paul Reese can run 26 miles a day to cross the United States without taking a day off at age 73, you can certainly stride five days a week and pump a little 1-1-2™ iron.

EXPECT:
TO DO MORE THAN YOU EVER IMAGINED

HOMEWORK:
1•1•2™ TO 60 SECONDS ... 10 SIX-SECOND REPETITIONS AND MACRO DEFLEX™ TO MILD DISCOMFORT

PHO
(pronounced FAW)

This is the famous national dish of Vietnam. Rather than have you run all over town for purple-tipped basil and mung bean sprouts, the recipe has been altered for ingredients readily at hand, with no loss of flavor.

• *Serves one.*

Calories: 521
Net Weight: 33 ounces
Prep time: 20 minutes
Cook time: 20 minutes
Calorie-to-weight ratio: 16 calories per ounce

- *Two 14.5-ounce cans beef broth, fat skimmed*
- *1 teaspoon quality beef base*
- *1/8 teaspoon red pepper flakes*
- *4 ounces uncooked whole wheat spaghetti*
- *1 Tablespoon Hoisin sauce*
- *2 teaspoons dried cilantro*
- *2 rounded teaspoons dried basil*
- *1 Tablespoon fresh lemon juice*

- *1/2 cup scallions, chopped, white and green parts*
- *1/2 packet aspartame*
- *3 cups iceberg lettuce, shredded (or mung bean sprouts)*

Combine beef broth, beef base, red pepper flakes and spaghetti in a medium saucepan. Boil until spaghetti is done.

Add Hoisin sauce, cilantro, basil, lemon juice, scallions and aspartame. Return to a boil and remove from heat.

Put lettuce in a large serving bowl. Pour spaghetti and broth over lettuce. Mix and serve. Eat immediately with chopsticks and soup spoon.

215

THURSDAY, DAY 39

TODAY: STRIDE 30 MINUTES

CALORIE SQUANDERING SABOTAGE

Hidden diet busters lurk everywhere, sabotaging your efforts. Many so-called "fat-free" foods are calorie dense. Adding 200 to 300 additional calories by inadvertently eating calorie-dense foods throws your day's diet into a tailspin because by 8 PM you have used your entire calorie allotment but feel famished. Careless munching is the very thing that triggers binges.

Somehow the word "bran" justifies consuming hellaciously cal-dense muffins. Even the "fat-free" varieties are 80 to 100 calories per ounce. Bagels are no better. The worst cal-dense offender is dry breakfast cereal at 110 calories per ounce. Because of the calorie concentration, most baked goods are off limits.

Pasta is supposed to be great diet food but it's one of the secret weight loss saboteurs. Each cup of cooked pasta (about five ounces) is good for 200 calories. With two cups the minimum serving, then adding sauce, you are looking at 500 to 600 calories for a paltry 12 to 14 ounces food for a calorie-to-weight ratio of 40 to 50 calories per ounce—not terrible, perhaps, but out of the range to satisfy the PRA without cal overload. Recognize that pasta is nothing more than boiled flat bread and bread is the great calorie squanderer at 100 calories an ounce (about one bread slice).

Unless you're working out at high levels for more than an hour at a time you don't need the extra calories of sports drinks. Sixteen ounces of Gatorade is 160 calories plus. In the simplest terms, they are nothing more than sugar and salt. Drink water. As for juices, you are better off eating the whole fruit. OJ, for instance, is cal-dense at 90 calories per eight ounces with a pint easily consumed for almost 200 calories. A whole orange is only about 70 calories and provides needed fiber. Of course never drink sugared sodas as they average 150 calories per can.

EXPECT:

CAL SQUANDERING SABOTEURS EVERYWHERE

Maybe you've been drinking classic Coke® or having a McDonald's® bran muffin or eating a "vegetarian" burrito for lunch laden with fatty cheese and larded frijoles. Take a close look because you can avoid hundreds of calories a day.

HOMEWORK:

DELETE CAL SQUANDERING SABOTEURS

Substitute fat-free sugar-free ice cream, diet pops and make a NeoCuisine™ dessert or two in Appendix A instead of eating calorie squanderers.

LASAGNE FIRENZE

A marvelous characteristic of good lasagne is it bakes to a melding of flavors for an integrated whole. This dish tastes unlike its individual ingredients. Morning: Thaw spinach.

•

Serves two.

Calories: 594
Net Weight: 32 ounces
Prep time: 30 minutes
Cook time: 50 minutes
Calorie-to-weight ratio: 18 calories per ounce

- 1 Tablespoon red wine vinegar
- 2 recipes NeoCuisine™ Red (see page 346)
- 4 medium zucchini, cut in 1/4" or less lengthwise slices
- Two 10- to 12-ounce packages frozen chopped spinach, thawed and lightly squeezed
- 2 cups fat-free ricotta cheese (or fat-free cottage cheese)

- 2 teaspoons quality chicken base
- 2 Tablespoons Miracle Chop (see page 346)
- 6 sheets Ronzoni® oven-ready lasagne noodles ✷
- 2 Tablespoons quality grated Parmesan cheese, e.g. Reggiano

Add red wine vinegar to NeoCuisine™ Red. Salt and pepper zucchini. Microwave in a microwavable container, e.g. lidded glass, for 8 minutes or until cooked, drain. Meanwhile, lightly squeeze spinach of excess water.

Combine spinach, ricotta cheese, chicken base and Miracle Chop.

Spray two 8" x 3" loaf pans with nonstick vegetable spray. Layer each pan equally in the following order:

1st	zucchini
2nd	1 lasagne noodle
3rd	1/2 spinach ricotta mix
4th	1 lasagne noodle
5th	1/2 spinach ricotta mix
6th	1 lasagne noodle
7th	NeoCuisine™ Red
Top	Reggiano Parmesan cheese

Cover one pan with aluminum foil and bake at 350° for 45 minutes. Freeze the second pan.

✷ These have been pre-cooked which means you don't have to. Regular lasagna noodles that need to be cooked work as well, but add time.

217

FRIDAY, DAY 40

TODAY: STRIDE 30 MINUTES

REREAD YOUR WIN LIST

Control Psychology™ Axiom 2 directs you to write a *win list*. It's in the form of an order because it's a necessary drill reminding you of the good things you've accomplished in your life. Maybe you wrote a great essay when you were a junior in high school. Perhaps you overcame a difficult time at age 23. Possibly you were promoted at age 34. These point to the goodness of your character. Recall and record your wins. Your aim is to boost your morale, to evidence your worthiness, to show you have strength of character. Review your *win list* to see how good you really are.

EXPECT:

YOUR MORALE TO BE HIGHER AFTER REREADING YOUR *WIN LIST*

HOMEWORK:

YOUR GRATITUDE LIST

Anthony Robbins, one of the world's most successful motivational speakers, says that cultivation of gratitude is the path to enlightenment: "When you're grateful, fear disappears. When you're grateful, lack disappears. When you're grateful, self-significance disappears. You feel a sense that your life is uniquely blessed ..."[27] Robbins has a point. We spend too much looking at what others have and not enough time appreciating what we have.

Your homework is to list all for which you are grateful. Like the *win list*, the *gratitude list* is psychic balm erasing envy, self-pity and gnawing need. Done well, you can truly see how blessed you are. Prompter questions:

- Did you wake up today?
- Can you stride a two-mile course?
- Are you slowly but surely making your way toward a flourishing physique?
- Can you pump free weights?
- Do you have a mind that can think?
- Do you have people in your life who love you?
- Do your eyes see?
- Are your kids healthy?
- Do (did) your parents love you?
- Do you like music?
- If you wanted to, could you study for another career?
- If you take good care of yourself, you will have a long life.

Now consider all the people in the world who do not have one or more of the advantages you have itemized on your *gratitude list*.

KUSHI YAKI CHICKEN SALAD

French-inspired wilted lettuce, Japanese-based sauce and Italian noodles combine for a tasty world fusion salad.

•

Serves one.

Calories: 498
Net weight: 24 ounces
Prep time: 5 minutes
Cook time: 10 minutes
Calorie-to-weight ratio: 21 calories per ounce

- *3 ounces chicken breast, boned and skinned.*
- *1 recipe Teriyaki Dressing (see page 307)*
- *1 cup cooked whole wheat spaghetti*
- *One 12- to 16-ounce package mixed salad greens*
- *1/4 cup red bell pepper, diced*
- *1/2 cup scallions, tops included, chopped*

Brown chicken breast in non-stick skillet over high heat. Lower heat and cook until done, about 1 to 2 minutes. Remove.

Add dressing to skillet, warming it and scraping up any chicken bits. Slice the chicken into 1/4" strips and return to skillet with the spaghetti. Reheat.

Remove from heat and pour over lettuce. Add red bell pepper and scallions. Toss. Serve.

SATURDAY, DAY 41

TODAY: STRIDE 30 MINUTES • 1•1•2™ 60 SECONDS TCT • MACRO DEFLEX™
AND DYNAMIC BALANCE™ 30 SECONDS TCT

COMFORTABLY HARD

You want to stride at a COMFORTABLY HARD perceived effort. This is the best aerobic level. Pay attention to what your body is telling you. Try singing. If you can, up your exertion a notch or two. EXERTION is the purpose of striding. It reshapes your body and builds endurance, the foundation of vigor. You feel your heart pumping and begin to sweat after 10 to 15 minutes. Striding at a comfortably hard perceived effort means you are power breathing. At striding's end you should sense a little fatigue, the result of exertion.

EXPECT:

EXERTION REQUIRES ELEMENTAL EFFORT
In other words, comfortably hard demands some work.

REMEMBER THIS

Some people who exercise tend to reward themselves by resting and relaxing more. As a result, the net change in total 24-hour calorie expenditure may be virtually unchanged.

KEEP MOVING!

HOMEWORK:

EXERT YOURSELF TO A *COMFORTABLY HARD* LEVEL
Power breathe. You have been Muscle Rebuilding for almost five weeks and its value is making itself apparent. Your joints are strengthened and lung capacity enhanced. Aerobic endurance is elevated. Aerate muscles with power breathing. Flow air deeply into your lungs. The more you oxygenate your blood, the easier the exercise.

HAM N' CLAM CHOWDER

It's hard to imagine that a good-tasting chowder can be part of a diet, but this is an especially good one. Here's where you put your quality clam base to excellent use.

Serves one.

Calories: 585
Net weight: 36 ounces
Prep time: 15 to 20 minutes
Cook time: 5 to 8 minutes
Calorie-to-weight ratio: 16 calories per ounce

- 8 ounces potatoes, peeled, diced 1/2"
- 1/2 cup celery, diced small
- 1/2 cup onion, chopped
- 1 cup skim milk
- 12-13 ounces extra-firm ultra-low fat tofu
- 2 teaspoons quality clam base
- 1/4 teaspoon thyme
- 1/4 teaspoon garlic powder
- 2 Tablespoons prepared roasted red bell peppers, fine diced
- 1 ounce Canadian bacon, fine diced
- Two 6.5-ounce cans minced clams, drained
- 2 teaspoons fresh lemon juice
- 1/4 packet aspartame

Microwave potatoes, celery and onion in a microwavable container, e.g. lidded glass, 8 to 10 minutes.

Meanwhile, combine milk, tofu, clam base, thyme, garlic powder and 1/8 teaspoon pepper in blender and pureé until well blended and smooth, about 1 minute. Put in saucepan. Add red bell pepper, Canadian bacon, clams and lemon juice. Bring to a simmer. Add microwaved vegetables. Cook 1 to 2 minutes. Add aspartame and stir. Serve.

221

SUNDAY, DAY 42

TODAY: OFF FOR EXERCISE

PATIENCE

It took you 20 or 30 years to become weakened and a bit too fat. After all this time the body deserves fair play. Don't expect immediate satisfaction—despite today's predilection for instant gratification. A 20-year downward spiral can't be reversed in a week or two despite the absurd claims made in TV infomercials. Take your time, you have the rest of your life. The body and mind become stressed if pushed too fast.

You are beginning to see results, nonetheless. If you have reached a plateau, don't think you've reached the end of the road. You're only in a traffic jam. Sometimes, you stay at the same weight for one, two or even three weeks, but you are making progress. Eventually the light changes to green and things get moving again. Weight comes down.

Noted nutritionist Ellen Coleman points out that sedentary women who begin exercising can lose two pounds of fat but gain two pounds of muscle while dropping a dress size.[28] Leanness is what counts, not necessarily body weight. Go by clothing size, not what you weigh. Hang in there and be patient because fat is melting away.

EXPECT:

WEIGHT PLATEAUS

These are common. Eventually, though, fat melts away if you maintain consistent calorie shortfall.

HOMEWORK:

LIST YOUR PERCEIVED IMPROVEMENTS

If you find yourself becoming faintly deterred, pause and reflect on the affirming advantages passing to you. You are replacing fat with muscle. Your physique is beginning to flourish. Your mood is improved. Your stamina is bettered. Note in your BodyRenewal™ journal the best benefits you notice since beginning BodyRenewal™. Increased energy? A heightened sense of well-being? What are they?

LOBSTER THERMIDOR

Here is NeoCuisine™ Lobster Thermidor with rich flavor at 1/3 the calories.

•

Serves one.

Calories: 549
Net weight: 26 ounces
Prep time: 20 to 25 minutes
Cook time: same
Calorie-to-weight ratio: 21 calories per ounce

- *10 to 12 ounces gross weight lobster tail ("little slipper" tails are inexpensive), net meat 4 to 6 ounces*
- *1/2 cup white wine [FYI: All the alcohol boils out.]*
- *2 cups water*
- *1-1/4 to 1-1/2 pounds gross weight butternut squash (2 cups or 1 pound after cooking), cut in half lengthwise*
- *1/8 teaspoon dried thyme*
- *1/2 teaspoon quality chicken base*
- *1 cup sliced mushrooms*
- *1 Tablespoon sherry [FYI: All the alcohol boils out.]*
- *4 ounces fat-free cream cheese*
- *1/4 teaspoon Dijon mustard*

- *1/2 teaspoon garlic powder*
- *1 teaspoon fresh lemon juice*
- *1 Tablespoon quality grated Parmesan cheese e.g. Reggiano*
- *8 ounces frozen petite green beans*
- *10 sprays "I Can't Believe It's Not Butter"®*

Boil lobster tail uncovered in wine and water. Remove lobster when cooked, 6 to 8 minutes. Remove lobster meat and throw shells back in stock. Return to a boil and cook until reduced by 75%, about 20 minutes. Chop lobster into 1/2" to 3/4" chunks.

Meanwhile, cover squash halves with plastic wrap and microwave 10 to 15 minutes. Remove seeds. Scoop out meat and measure 2 cups or 1 pound. Mash squash. Add thyme, chicken base and pepper (1/8 teaspoon) to taste. Add chicken stock as necessary to smooth.

Microwave mushrooms in a microwavable container, e.g. lidded glass, for 3 to 5 minutes. Remove shells from stock reduction. Add sherry. Add cream cheese to reduction and turn heat to low. Whisk until smooth. Add Dijon, garlic powder, lemon juice, Parmesan cheese, mushrooms and pepper (1/8 teaspoon) to taste. Add lobster.

Microwave green beans in a microwavable container, e.g. lidded glass, for 4 to 5 minutes. Drain. Add salt (1/4 teaspoon) and pepper (1/8 teaspoon) to taste.

Serve lobster over squash. Plate beans and spray with "I Can't Believe It's Not Butter."®

223

MONDAY, DAY 43

TODAY: STRIDE 30 MINUTES

SHORT STRIDING SESSIONS

Forty percent of all adults are completely sedentary with the average American glued to the tube 4.5 hours a day.[29] Each year 300,000 people die from obesity-related conditions.[30] Despite these statistics, we continue to resist exercise because we find it "too hard."

The trick to facilitating exercise is learning to lower perceived effort. For example, most of us find carving out 10 to 15 minutes a few times a day easier than finding, say, 60 uninterrupted minutes. In one study, overweight walkers who broke up their daily workouts into two 15-minute sessions nearly doubled their weekly mileage because they were inclined to go more frequently and faster compared with those who did it in a single 30-minute walk. Likewise, twice as many people stuck to several shorter workouts versus a single long one.[31] It makes sense. Wouldn't you rather start exercising knowing that you will be done in ten minutes instead of 60? Your goal is 10,000 steps a day at striding pace, three to four miles an hour. Five, ten and fifteen-minute stridings add up and make you fit.[32]

•**STRIDE TO THE STORE:** Your store may be too far to stride the entire distance, so drive to within a good stride distance of the store and park. Your upper body will get a superb workout from carrying the groceries back to the car.

•**STRIDE TO LUNCH:** Don't hit the office building cafeteria unless you decide to take the stairs. Better, walk to a restaurant six blocks away. Striding each way adds a mile to your workout on a daily basis.

•**WALK THE STAIRS:** Okay, your office is on the 40th floor and you don't want to risk a myocardial infarction so do this. Take the elevator to the 38th floor and walk the last two flights. Take your time, don't run. Make exercise aerobic versus anaerobic and save the sweat. Work up to 10 or 20 flights. It sounds like a lot but you'll be surprised what you can do when you're in shape.

•**PARK A DISTANCE FROM YOUR OFFICE:** If striding is what you enjoy versus stair climbing, park a distance from your office and hoof it to work.

EXPECT:

THAT A BODY FULL OF MUSCLES (WE HAVE MORE MUSCLE THAN ANYTHING ELSE) MUST BE WORKED

HOMEWORK:

EXPERIMENT WITH TWO OR THREE STRIDING SESSIONS A DAY

ROSEMARY CHICKEN STROGANOFF

This heart-saving rendition of the old and heavy beef stroganoff version is nonetheless palate rewarding.

Serves one.

Calories: 563
Net Weight: 30 ounces
Prep time: 15 minutes
Cook time: 5 minutes
Calorie-to-weight ratio: 19 calories per ounce

- *Hot baked potatoes totaling 16 ounces*
- *2 ounces chicken breast, boned and skinned, cut into 1/4" ribbons*
- *3 cups fresh mushrooms, sliced*
- *1/4 cup red bell pepper, diced*
- *1/4 teaspoon dried rosemary*
- *2/3 cup nonfat plain yogurt*
- *1/4 cup scallions, finely chopped, green parts only*
- *2 teaspoons quality chicken base*
- *1/2 packet aspartame*
- *1/3 cup or more chicken broth, fat skimmed, hot*

Microwaving: Wash potato(es), put in a microwavable container, e.g. lidded glass, and microwave for 8 to 10 minutes, turning once. Conventional oven: Wash potato(s) and bake in oven at 400° for about 45 minutes. Check with fork.

In a medium nonstick skillet, brown chicken, mushrooms, red pepper and rosemary over high heat about 2 minutes or until any liquid is absorbed. Add yogurt, scallions, chicken base, aspartame and pepper (1/8 teaspoon) or to taste and cook until hot.

Pour chicken broth over fork-mashed potatoes. Potatoes should be well saturated. Add more broth if necessary. Top with chicken mixture.

TUESDAY 44

TODAY: STRIDE 30 MINUTES

OVERTRAINING, WRONG TRAINING

You have been consistently advised to avoid overtraining and stick with what works. A good example of doing it the wrong way is one of our favorite people, Oprah Winfrey. *Prevention* Magazine reported that she runs five to ten miles, spends 45 minutes on the Stairmaster® and does 250 sit-ups each day.[33] Despite its impressive statistics, this is not a good regimen. First of all, doing 250 sit ups is neither aerobic (because the abdominal muscles are relatively small and don't get the heart pumping) nor particularly muscle building (because only strength training using weights builds muscle). Oprah's back probably hurts from all the overwork, God bless her. Running more than 20 miles a week is also not a good idea because studies consistently show running more than 15 miles a week increases injuries. Short of going to the Olympics, this is a program no one could stick with long-term.

Stay with the Muscle Rebuild™: 1•1•2™, striding, Macro Deflexing™ and Dynamic Balance™. This does great things for the body, conditioning it properly. Allied with rebuilding muscle, NeoCuisine™ provides plenty to eat while restricting calories correctly.

EFFECTIVE STRATEGY: Rather than overtaxing the body by trying to "run fat off," it is better to appropriately manage calorie intake (NeoCuisine™) and engage in long-term practical exercise you stick with the rest of your life (Muscle Rebuild™).

EXPECT:

MUSCLE REBUILD™ TO BE "WORK" BUT NOT AWFUL Don't overtrain. See the homework.

HOMEWORK:

CHECK YOURSELF FOR OVERTRAINING You spot it by observing that one or more joints is chronically sore. This should not be the case. Be sure to allow a full two days rest (48 hours) between 1•1•2™ workouts. If you find that you despise exercise you are doing too much. Cut back to lighter weights, slow your striding pace and deflex with a little less vigor. Take it easy and enjoy what you do. You are not conditioning yourself for world class competition. You're aiming for a realistically fit physique resulting from a pragmatic program perpetuable lifelong.

RED SNAPPER CIOPPINO

You'll think you're at Fisherman's Wharf in San Francisco. If you're inclined, add a pinch or more of saffron.

• Serves one.

Calories: 522
Net Weight: 32 ounces
Prep time: 20 minutes
Cook time: 20 minutes
Calorie-to-weight ratio: 16 calories per ounce

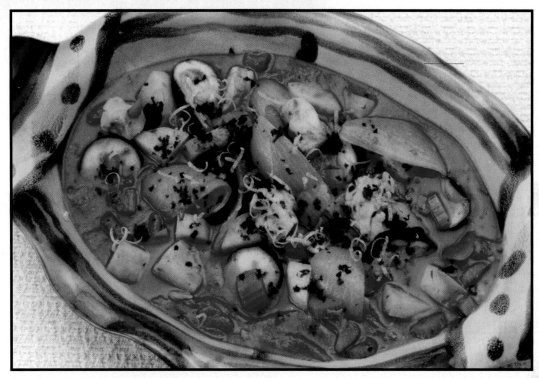

- 1 can clam juice (8 to 12 ounces)
- 1/2 medium onion, chopped
- 6 ounces potatoes, 1/2" to 1" dice
- 1 stalk celery, cut in 1" chunks
- 1/2 cup Chardonnay wine [FYI: All the alcohol boils out.]
- 1 cup NeoCuisine™ Red (see page 347)
- 1 zucchini, cut in 1/2" coins
- 1 teaspoon anchovie paste
- 8 ounces red snapper (or other white fish), cut in 1/2" to 1" chunks
- 1 heaping teaspoon dried parsley flakes
- 1/2 teaspoon lemon zest

In medium saucepan combine clam juice, onion, potato, celery and wine. Bring to full boil and cook uncovered for 10 to 15 minutes.

Reduce heat and add NeoCuisine™ red, zucchini and anchovie paste. Add salt (1/4 teaspoon) and pepper (1/8 teaspoon) to taste. Add fish, parsley and lemon zest. Simmer 2 to 4 minutes or until fish flakes.

Remove from heat, add parsley and lemon zest. Serve.

WEDNESDAY, DAY 45

TODAY: 1•1•2™ 60 SECONDS TCT • MACRO DEFLEX™ AND DYNAMIC BALANCE™ 30 SECONDS TCT

MUSCLE REBUILD™ SUMMARY

As you know, the entire Muscle Rebuild™ (striding, 1•1•2™, Macro Deflexions™ and Dynamic Balance™) is founded on the concept of *total challenge time*. When striding, you energize the body for 30 minutes. With 1•1•2™, your goal is a full minute of muscle challenge. Your Macro Deflexion™ goal is 10 three-second stretches to mild discomfort for 30 seconds TCT. Even Dynamic Balance™ is measured using time: 30 seconds of balance accumulation.

Muscle Rebuilding™ results from muscle total challenge time, not number of repetitions (you can lift a light weight many times for small positive effect) or how far you walk (you can cover long distances but at a leisurely pace resulting in little heart benefit) or the number of times you stretch (it does little good unless it's 30 total seconds to mild discomfort) or incorrect balance practice (it is of small worth unless it's with eyes closed for proper vestibular stimulation). Total challenge time is the best criterion for rebuilding muscle.

EXPECT:
TOTAL CHALLENGE TIMES TO BECOME SECOND NATURE

HOMEWORK:
FOLLOW TOTAL CHALLENGE TIME RECOMMENDATIONS, AVOIDING THE TEMPTATION OF THINKING YOU HAVE TO DO MORE

LIMBER ARTERIES

As people age, blood vessels lose some elasticity, becoming more rigid. But a study conducted by Johns Hopkins University Medical School found fit, active people were much better off than their sedentary peers, with arterial stiffness measuring 26% to 36% lower. If a training program can keep your knees and back flexible, it may well have the same effect on your blood vessels which lightens the load on your heart.[34]

MARIA DeLOURDES CHILI RELLENOS

My first restaurant was Mexican and Maria DeLourdes Mecedo-Orosco was my Mexican food tutor in the fine art of Sonoran cookery. This dish is about 1/3 the calories of the traditional fried chili rellenos version for a great calorie-to-weight ratio of 15 calories per ounce.

• Serves one.

Calories: 525
Net Weight: 36 ounces
Prep time: 10 minutes
Cook time: 35 minutes
Calorie-to-weight ratio: 15 calories per ounce

- Three 4-ounce (1-1/2 cups) containers fat-free egg substitute, e.g. EggBeaters®
- 1 cup onion, chopped
- 1 cup mild green chilies, e.g. Ortega® brand, diced (one 7-ounce can or two 4-ounce cans)
- 1 cup tomatoes, diced
- 1/2 cup nonfat cheddar cheese, shredded, e.g. Kraft®
- 1/2 Tablespoon chili powder
- 1/2 teaspoon garlic powder
- 1 teaspoon quality beef base
- 1 cup salsa

Combine all ingredients except salsa. Spray an 8" x 8" pan (or comparable size, e.g. 6" x 10") with nonstick vegetable spray and add mixture. Bake at 400° for 35 minutes. Rellenos are done when the sides are firm but the center is still soft.

Garnish with salsa.

THURSDAY 46

TODAY: STRIDE 30 MINUTES

INCREASING STRIDING INTENSITY

Yesterday, you were advised to take it easy. On the other hand, some find striding too easy. It isn't challenging enough. The simplest way to increase rigor is by simply going faster. Try race walking for a minute or two, then back off to your normal pace. This is just like sprinting (called interval training by professionals) without the debilitating jarring. Try tip-touching where you touch the ground with your fingertips every five or ten paces. This is harder than it sounds and gives your quadriceps (front of the leg) a real workout.

The ultimate is running. It has not been advised because it pounds joints. But your ability to run actually rises through time because of weight reduction and body strength enhancement. As you approach your ideal weight, the probability of running without injury increases because joints (especially knees) are subjected to less stress. There are many factors relative to running injury-free such as your weight (the lighter the better), height (shorter is better) and past history (football injuries) that determine ultimately whether running is right for you. Before you run, try the striding intensity tricks. They work and keep you in the safest type of cardio exercise.

EXPECT:

TO ENJOY THE SCENERY AS YOU STRIDE
Make it a point to look around and gather in the sights. Spring is especially delightful because the scene changes daily. Paying attention to your surroundings disassociates you from the physical demands of brisk striding, a marathoner's trick used to make time fly.

HOMEWORK:

TRY ZIPPING UP YOUR STRIDING TO: *CAN'T SING, SHORT TALK BURSTS OKAY*
Without going overboard, the heart muscle, lungs and arteries are strengthened by elevating your heart rate.

BBQ BEEF LOAF

MAKES 2 MEATLOAF SERVINGS.

Here is a grand BBQ substitute without the fat or cancer danger. It tastes great which is important because a steady diet of regular BBQ is off limits. It's too fatty and carries carcinogens in the form of polycyclic amines, the brown crust of long-roasted meats. You'll hardly miss those baby back ribs, seriously.

Calories per serving: 570
Weight per serving: 30 ounces
Prep time: 15 to 20 minutes
Cook time: 45 minutes
Calorie-to-weight ratio: 20 calories per ounce
(Calorie count includes BBQ Sauce and Roasted Flavor Fries.)

- *3/4 pound (12 ounces) 1% fat very lean ground turkey*
- *1 Tablespoon quality beef base*
- *1 teaspoon garlic powder*
- *1 teaspoon pepper*
- *1 teaspoon red wine vinegar*
- *1/2 cup onion, finely diced*
- *1 teaspoon Bacobits®*
- *18-20 ounces (1-1/2 packages) extra-firm ultra-low-fat tofu*
- *1 recipe Oven Roasted Beef Fries (see page 354)*

NeoCuisine™ BBQ Sauce
- *1 recipe Sugar-Free Ketchup (see page 343)*
- *1/4 teaspoon liquid smoke*
- *1/2 teaspoon chili powder*
- *1/4 teaspoon dry mustard*
- *1/2 teaspoon quality beef base*

Combine first 7 ingredients. Set aside.

Crumble tofu into blender and pureé until smooth, about 30 to 45 seconds. You will need to stop blender and stir twice or more. Add to meatloaf mix and stir well to incorporate all ingredients. Pour into 8" x 3" loaf pan. Bake at 350° for 45 minutes.

Make Oven Roasted Beef Fries. Make BBQ Sauce by combining all ingredients.

Pour off excess juice (this is not fat) after loaf is baked. Divide loaf in half and save half for later use. Slice second half and top with BBQ Sauce. Serve with Roasted Flavor Fries.

NeoCuisine™ meatloaves are white proteins and are naturally light in color. Brown them if you wish with this heated dip: 1/2 cup hot broth (the same base flavor as used in the loaf) and 1 Tablespoon Kitchen Bouquet®.

231

FRIDAY, DAY 47

TODAY: STRIDE 30 MINUTES

AUGMENTATION: OUR BODY IS MUSCLE.

The fundamental equation for paring poundage is: Consume fewer calories while burning more. But there is something more important. The body is primarily muscle which should send you a clear message that movement, action and activity are what bodies do. Our body IS muscle. Of our 70 trillion body cells, we have more muscle than any other tissue,

Inactivity dissipates the body to disease and, ultimately, failure. Death by dissipation is the common way to die. The hell of it is that dissipation is painless. As you sink into infirmity, everything feels okay until you bottom out. We don't feel our muscles wasting away, we simply die of high blood pressure, atherosclerosis, myocardial infarction and the other garden variety 21st century killers.

Don't opt for the *after* plan: Doctors, pills, tests, time and money. Go for the *before* plan: Cheap, simple, time-efficient and even fun.

1•1•2™, striding and the other formal Body Renewal™ techniques are now important factors in your new life. They reflect your new attitude of exercise being a part of your life, not a willy-nilly addition to it. But despite our best intent we sometimes get sidetracked. Augmentation is additional physical activity used to fill in missed exercise. Even moderate augmentation helps tremendously. A study published in the *Journal of the American Medical Association* compared walking, climbing stairs and around-the-house chores to structured and demanding gym workouts. The findings are encouraging. Researchers report that there are, " ... no significant differences in the degree of improvement between the two groups."[35]

Some of these augments may strike you as empty-headed but movement is the goal.

- Change TV channels manually.
- Wash your car.
- Do dishes by hand.
- Clean and organize your attic, garage or closet.
- Do your own yard work.
- Do your own ironing.
- Help someone with their work.
- Home maintenance: painting, carpet cleaning remodeling, etc,
- Skip the cabs: anything up to two miles can be walked in 30 minutes or less.

EXPECT:
TO SEARCH FOR AUGMENT POSSIBILITIES
We're so used to cars, escalators, elevators and for-hire services that we must consciously seek opportunities to work our bodies.

HOMEWORK:
FIND AT LEAST ONE AUGMENT TODAY

SHRIMP WOK

Rockefeller University in NYC discovered shrimp is great for the heart. Although high in cholesterol, shrimp contains low saturated fat, the real culprit in blood cholesterol elevation. Shrimp is also rich in omega 3s which play a beneficial role in preventing heart disease.[36]

•

Serves one.

Calories: 495
Net weight: 28 ounces
Prep time: 5 minutes
Cook time: 5 minutes
Calorie-to-weight ratio: 18 calories per ounce

- 1 cup instant rice
- 1 cup clam juice
- 1/4 cup low-sodium soy sauce
- 1 Tablespoon white wine vinegar
- 1/8 teaspoon crushed red pepper flakes
- 1/2 teaspoon garlic powder
- 1 teaspoon dark sesame oil
- 1 teaspoon quality chicken base
- 2 packets aspartame
- 2 ounces large shrimp, cooked (not little popcorn shrimp)
- 16 ounces frozen stir-fry vegetables, thawed and drained of excess water

Prepare rice according to box directions (do not use salt or butter) using clam juice for liquid. Meanwhile, prepare rest of dish.

In a large skillet or wok, add soy sauce, white wine vinegar, red pepper flakes, garlic powder, sesame oil and chicken base. Bring to a boil. Reduce heat and add aspartame, shrimp and drained vegetables. Stir until heated, but do not cook. Put on one side of serving plate with rice alongside or as shown in picture. Serve.

233

SATURDAY, DAY 48

TODAY: STRIDE 30 MINUTES • 1•1•2™ 60 SECONDS TCT • MACRO DEFLEX™ AND DYNAMIC BALANCE™ 30 SECONDS TCT

UNFOLDING POTENTIAL OUTRACES AGING

Freud thought psychotherapy did little good after age 40 because the personality froze as we grew older, unable to change. This idea has long since given way to the reality that we change, improve and grow all our lives. BodyRenewal™ is part of your unfolding. It isn't the oversimplification of "losing weight" but rather a change in how you have decided to live.

You have resolved to minimize slow-kill 21st Century foods, renew your body through 1•1•2™, striding and deflexing and commit to a life mode that revitalizes your entire being. It's something you feel great about. It's your reward for unfolding your potential.

The act of becoming is life's great experience. But don't stop with renewing your body. Now that you are approaching ever-higher levels of reinvigoration, why not pursue more personal development? Consider BodyRenewal™ a platform for other accomplishments. There are classes to be taken, skills to advance, games to be played, hobbies to be pursued and the world to be known. *You can't feel old when you're growing.*

EXPECT:
UNFOLDING POTENTIAL TO BE THERAPEUTIC
One of life's grand adventures is working toward actuating your latent skills, talents and capacities. Enjoy the journey.

HOMEWORK:
CHOOSE A SKILL TO DEVELOP

• New, tougher striding route.
• Invent new NeoCuisine™ dishes.
• Enroll in a class.
• Study the countries you plan to visit.
• Start again practicing your long neglected musical instrument.
• Take up car racing.

With this last suggestion we leave the self-actualization list because the flamboyant possibility of amateur car racing reflects the freedom of thought you should apply to unfolding who you are.

RED PEPPER CANADIAN BACON GRILLED GRINDER

Shaved Canadian bacon accented with roasted red peppers and butternut squash slices then grilled with cheese. Tasty.

• *Serves one.*

Calories: 521
Net weight: 31.5 ounces
Prep time: 15 to 20 minutes
Cook time: 6 to 10 minutes
Calorie-to-weight ratio: 17 calories per ounce

- *3 to 4 slices (4 to 6 ounces total with skin) butternut squash*
- *2 Tablespoons fat-free Ranch salad dressing*
- *2 slices whole grain light bread (e.g. Wonder® Lite)*
- *1/4 cup prepared roasted red bell pepper*
- *2 slices red onion*
- *2 ounces fat-free Canadian Bacon, shredded*
- *1 slice fat-free cheddar cheese single*

- *White Bean Salad (see page 349)*

Microwave butternut squash (with skin on) 5 to 6 minutes. Remove skin and slice.

Layer in order, drizzling a little Ranch dressing on bread and on top of each layer: bread, red bell pepper, red onion, butternut squash, Canadian bacon, cheddar, bread.

Place sandwich in a nonstick skillet, cover and cook over medium-low heat, turning once, until heated through and cheese is melted, about 3 to 5 minutes per side.

Serve with White Bean Salad.

SUNDAY, DAY 49

TODAY: OFF

THE HERE AND NOW

Here is a small essay that gives us wisdom for beginning each day.

TODAY

This is the beginning of a new day. God has given me this day to use as I will. I can waste it or use it for good. What I do today is important because I'm exchanging a day of my life for it. When tomorrow comes, this day will be gone forever, leaving in its place something I have traded for it. I want it to be a gain, not a loss; good, not evil; success, not failure—so I shall not regret the price I paid for it.—Anonymous

Call to mind that your record for the day can include the pursuit of joy. The BodyRenewal's™ aim is a better life and more happiness for you. Never lose sight that fun is crucial to your well-being.

If your interest in striding occasionally lags, get a bike or a dog or a walking machine. Do something.

If you want exciting new flavors, order *Saveur* magazine at 1-877-717-8925. NeoCuisinize its recipes by cutting out the fats, "sauteing" using stocks, doubling the vegetables, cutting the red meat by two-thirds and always using the Osmazome Principle™ by adding meat bases instead of salt. *Saveur* is one of the best magazines for a truly in-depth look at cuisines worldwide. See Appendix C.

If 1•1•2™ is going stale, study your new magazines for stimulating new exercises.

EXPECT:
MORE FUN
You're more vigorous and capable of greater gladness. Your range of potential behaviors is expanded. Walks and hikes you'd never consider in the past, trips you'd not take and the rest of the world out there now await you.

HOMEWORK:
A NEW EXERCISE(S)
Pick something in Muscle Rebuild™ where you're going stale. Give it the change antedote.

TENDERLOIN WITH CARLENZOLI STEAKS, DEMI GLAZED EGGPLANT TOURNEDOS and TEPIDINDA

Who says you can't have opulent dining while fat-stripping? Here is a superb presentation of mouth-watering tenderloin steak married with the deep, rich flavor of Carlenzoli portabello mushroom steaks and eggplant tournedos. Completing the meal is a delightful butternut squash Tepidinda. It's hard to imagine enjoying a lovely dinner like this, guilt-free.

Serves one.

Calories: 515
Net weight: 28 ounces
Prep time: 20 minutes
Cook time: 30 minutes
Calorie-to-weight ratio: 18 calories per ounce

- *1 recipe Carlenzoli Steaks and Eggplant Tournedos (see page 351)*
- *1-1/4 to 1-1/2 pounds gross weight butternut squash*
- *(1 pound or 2 cups after cooking), cut in half lengthwise*
- *1/2 teaspoon quality chicken base*
- *1/8 teaspoon dried thyme*
- *Pinch to taste nutmeg*
- *1/8 to 1/4 cup chicken broth, fat skimmed*
- *5 ounces filet mignon (buy a 6- to 7-ounce filet to net 5 ounces meat when trimmed of all fat)*

Start Carlenzoli steaks and Eggplant Tournedos (see page 351).

Cover squash halves for the tepidinda with plastic wrap and microwave 10 to 15 minutes. Keep working on Carlenzoli steaks and eggplant tournedos while squash is microwaving.

Tepidinda assembly: When squash is cooked, remove seeds. Scoop out meat and measure 2 brimming cups. Mash. Add chicken base, thyme, nutmeg and pepper (1/8 teaspoon) to taste. Add chicken stock as necessary to smooth.

Sprinkle filet with salt, pepper and garlic powder. Put filet in nonstick skillet. Cook slowly, 5 to 10 minutes per side, to desired doneness.

Serve filet atop mushrooms. Top squash and filet with reduced Carlenzoli steak glaze. Plate eggplant and top with tomato and Miracle Chop relish.

237

MONDAY, DAY 50

TODAY: STRIDE 30 MINUTES

HOW LONG DO YOU WANT TO GO?

You are now fully introduced to BodyRenewal™. Stay with the plan as long as you wish to strip fat. How do you know you're done? This question is answered in the next chapter. Meanwhile, stick with BodyRenewal™.

Now that you've had a taste of NeoCuisine™, repeat your favorite recipes. Also look in back at the NeoCuisine™ cookbook for more recipes and technique. Eventually you'll be cooking all recipes NeoCuisine™ style. In fact, you will become so adept that you'll convert most conventional recipes to low-fat, calorie-frugal entreés.

You're now on an excellent exercise track. Stay with it. As you read the recommended magazines (*Prevention, Walking, Cooking Light* and *Bottom Line/ Health*) try new workouts. Go ahead. Change maintains interest. Eventually, you will develop an entirely customized approach to obtaining and maintaining your flourishing physique. Don't be afraid to experiment.

Continue writing in your BodyRenewal™ journal. It contributes in many ways. As an information repository it saves personal ideas and those strategies learned from reading, your experience and friends. When frustration kills motivation, writing is cathartic. Capture your exercise statistics so you know your progress. Record your weight loss progress. In sum, save any information you wish.

Finally, maintain your spirit. The word maintain is crucial because having a positive attitude requires effort. Always remember where you are going (the flourishing physique) and the benefits accruing thereto (the shape and vigor of youth).

EXPECT:
CONTINUED WEIGHT LOSS WITH PLATEAUS ALONG THE WAY

HOMEWORK:
READ THE FINAL CHAPTER

LOMBARDY POLENTA PIZZA

Hamburgers aside, pizza is America's favorite food. Pizza is also the prototypical 21st century fat food because it is loaded with saturated fat and has a calorie density well over 80 calories an ounce ... out of reach for the robust-whole minded. However, after two years of researching and experimentation here is NeoCuisine's™ pizza solution. Enjoy. It's surprisingly tasty.

• Serves one.

In a medium saucepan bring chicken broth to a boil. Stir in polenta with a wire whisk. Return to full boil, cover, reduce heat to medium-low and cook until thickened, about 3 to 5 minutes. Remove lid and continue to cook over low heat 20 to 25 minutes, stirring occasionally.

Calories: 474
Net Weight: 33 ounces
Prep time: 15 to 20 minutes
Cook time: 30 + 30 minutes
Calorie-to-weight ratio:
14 calories per ounce

- 3 cups chicken broth, fat skimmed
- 1/2 cup polenta
- 1/2 cup NeoCuisine™ Red (see page 347)
- 1/2 cup Kraft® fat-free shredded cheddar cheese
- 1/4 cup onions, chopped
- 1/2 cup fresh mushrooms, sliced
- 2 Tablespoons sliced black olives (Kalamata if possible)
- 1 Tablespoon capers (optional)

Pour cooked polenta into ungreased deep dish pie plate and refrigerate 1 to 2 hours or overnight.

Put NeoCuisine™ Red on top of polenta and spread to edges. Top with cheese. Add onions, mushrooms, olives and capers. Bake at 350° for 1/2 hour.

[1]"Liberty or Death," Patrick Henry, from *The Book of Virtues,* William Bennett, Simon and Schuster, New York, New York, 1993, page 519, BB115.

[2]"Special Report: Dietary Variety Loses Favor as Nutritionists Find it Causes Weight Gain," *Tufts University Health and Nutrition Letter,* vol. 17, no. 5, July 1999, page 4, BB475.

[3]*The One Minute Manager,* Ken Blanchard, Ph.D. and Spencer Johnson, M.D., Berkeley Publishing Group, a division of Penguin Putnam Inc., New York, New York, 1981, 1982, page 48, #25.

[4]*The Pocket Aristotle*, edited by Justin Kaplan, Washington Square Press [Pocket Books], Division of Simon and Schuster, New York, New York, 1988, page 175, #77.

[5]"More Sure Cures for Snorers," *U.C. Berkeley Wellness Letter,* vol. 12, no. 12, September 1996, page 3, BB175.

[6]"Fishing for Rheumatoid Arthritis Prevention," *Harvard Health Letter,* Boston, Massachusetts, vol. 21, no. 11, October 1996, page 8, BB132.

[7]"Keep Shrimp on the Team," *U.C. Berkeley Wellness Letter,* vol. 13, no. 6, March 1997, page 1-2, BB251.

[8]*Obesity Research*, May 1998, vol. 6, no. 3, page 24, BB473.

[9]"How Much Are You Eating?" *Men's Health,* March 1999, page 56, BB452.

[10] "Advice/How-To/Misc.," What's Happening, *Seattle Post-Intelligencer,* Friday, November 20, 1998, page 21, BB452.

[11]"Wishful Thinking About Diets and Breast Cancer," *UCB Wellness Letter,* vol. 15, no. 6, March 1999, pages 1-2, BB458.

[12]*The Super Start Fat Attack Plan,* Annette D. Natow, Ph.D., R.T., and Jo-Ann Heslin, M.A., R.D., Rodale Press, Emmaus, Pennsylvania, 1995, pages 2-4, 9 and 11, BB143; "Fill Up, Not Out," Adam Bean, *Runner's World,* November 1996, page 22, BB137; *Maximize Your Body's Potential,* Joyce Nash, Ph.D., Bull Publishing Co., Palo Alto, California, 1986, pages 159-161, BB127.

[13]"Fit to a Tea," *Prevention,* May 1996, page 97, BB428.

[14]"Nine Ways to Beat the Fat," *Men's Health,* September 1998, page 159, BB427.

[15]"Exercise—The Ultimate Anti-Aging Pill," Robert Goldman, M.D., Ph.D., *The International Journal of Anti-Aging Medicine,* vol. 1, no. 1, page 11; "Depression May Increase Heart Risk," *The Johns Hopkins Medical Letter,* vol.10, issue 10, page 1, December 1998; "Boosting Winter Immunity," Dr. Andrew Weil, *Self Healing Journal,* November 1998, page 1; All BB449.

[16]"Strength," David Buchner, Deputy Director, Northwest Prevention Effectiveness Center of the University of Washington School of Public Health and Community Medicine, *Over Fifty and Fit,* vol. 3, no. 2, page 20, BB433.

[17]"Weight Control," op. cit., page 2, BB9.

[18]"A Little Known But Widespread Diabetes Risk," *Tufts University Health and Nutrition Letter,* vol. 14, no. 6, August 1996, pages 1-2, BB168.

[19]*Life Extension,* September 1998, BB431.

[20]"Successful Aging: Lessons for All from the Country's Leading Study on Aging," Robert L. Kahn, Ph.D., University of Michigan, *Bottom Line/Health,* vol. 12, no. 8, page 5, BB438.

[21]"Exercise Combats Lifestyle Diseases," *Over 50 and Fit,* vol. 1, no. 6, October 1998, page 7, BB37.

[22]"It's Good for Your Head," *Runner's World,* vol. 33, no. 3, March 1998, page 25, BB406.

[23]"Stronger Longer with Weight Training," *Harvard Health Letter,* vol. 23, no. 12, October 1998, page 1, BB435.

[24]*Strong Women Stay Young,* Miriam Nelson, Ph.D., with Sarah Wernick, Ph.D., Bantam Books, New York, New York, 1998, p. 36, BB418.

[25]*Habits Not Diets,* James M. Ferguson, M.D., Bull Publishing, Palo Alto, California, 1988, page 47, BB101.

[26]*10 Million Steps,* Paul Reese and Joe Henderson, WRS Group Inc., Waco, Texas, 1993, pages 181, 196, 212.

[27]"Excellence is Not Enough," Craig Hamilton, *What is Enlightenment?,* issue 15, Spring/Summer 1999, page 29, BB474.

[28]*Eating for Endurance,* Ellen Coleman, R.D., M.A., M.P.H., Bull Publishing, Palo Alto, California, 1992, page 132, BB107.

[29]"From Eating to Pets, Statistical Abstract Has Facts of U.S. Life," *Seattle Post-Intelligencer*, Randolf Schmid, AP, December 5, 1997, BB345.

[30]"My Best Advice on How to Live a Longer Life," C. Edward Koop, M.D., *Health Confidential,* Winter 1996, page 1, BB326.

[31]"Should Your Workout Be Shorter?" Michelle Stanten, *Prevention,* vol. 49, no. 9, September 1997, page 68, from studies presented at the American College of Sports Medicine annual meeting May 1997, BB327.

[32]"Squeezing Physical Activity Into Everyday Life," *Tufts University Health and Nutrition Letter,* vol. 17, no. 1, March 1999, page 8.

[33]"Celebrity Size-Up," *Preventions Fight Fat 1997,* Mark Bricklin and Gale Maleskey, editors, Rodale Press, Emmaus, Pennsylvania, 1997, p.209.

[34]"Keeping Your Arteries Limber," *UC Berkeley Wellness Letter*, July 1994, page 7, BB44.

[35]"Exercise: Gain Without Pain," *New England Journal of Medicine: Health News,* vol. 5, no. 3, February 25, 1999, page 2, BB462.

[36]"Keep Shrimp on the Team," op. cit., BB251.

STAYING THE COURSE

"The greatest pleasure in life is in doing what people say you cannot do."

Walther Bagehot

Fifty days of BodyRenewal™ have wrought worthwhile behavior modifications. You've made substantial progress because you have translated knowledge into behavior. This is a huge leap. You are on your way. Let's review.

You now know you get along just fine with less food. You don't even mind slight hunger. The "eat-now" reflex is more relaxed. You are more in touch with your true physiological rhythms and not overtly compelled to eat, eat, eat with each *primeval raging appetite* demand. You understand that hunger and true physiological needs don't necessarily correlate.

You've learned about the nature of food: fat content, calorie-to-weight ratios, the Osmazome Principle™ and all the rest. You have become skilled at coaxing marvelous flavor out of food without butter, cream or other fats. You've likely broadened your tastes to include East Indian, Vietnamese, Moroccan, Szechuan and others. Why, even your appreciation of wonderful fresh foods has risen. Amazingly, you likely now enjoy raw vegetables without much adornment.

You know more about yourself. You understand the

241

power of resolve's dauntless spirit. You recognize what triggers a binge and what to do about it. You understand something about restructuring perceived negative incoming information through practiced *disputing*.

You are making Muscle Rebuild™ an integral part of your life. 1•1•2™, striding, Macro Deflexions™ and Dynamic Balance™ are becoming more routine, a given in your life. You just flat feel better and stronger. You're excited because you know there's more to come.

But most of all, you have increased confidence. Your self-admiration has rightfully risen. You realize you can lose weight at will. You appreciate that strategies are at hand for lifelong weight management. You have gained a higher level of self-assurance because of your attainments. You are in the enviable position of seeking the shape and vigor of youth not out of fat fear or ego but for the sheer joy of living. By any measure, you've begun the long-term plan that achieves the shape and vigor of youth, that removes the fear of aging and charges you with hope.

Perfection is for Angels

University of Rhode Island psychologist Dr. James O. Prochaska says that change proceeds through five steps. First, we become aware of a new behavior (precontemplation). Then we consider the desirability of this behavior (contemplation— sometimes this takes years). As we contemplate new behavior we may become convinced of its worthiness. If we decide to change, we plan for the change (preparation) and, next, we dive into action: BodyRenewal™. Last, we enter a maintenance phase.[1]

You've completed steps one through four: awareness, contemplation, preparation and action. Now you are into maintenance— staying the course—the most challenging aspect of protecting and enhancing your shape and vigor of youth. Don't be disheartened. There are a wealth of resources for the upkeep and nurturing of your marvelous current and future accomplishments.

This chapter unlocks the secrets of staying the course lifelong. You will master skills guaranteeing a lifetime of well-being. You discover *Sustaining Forces™*.

Through all this, you will not execute perfectly because perfection's for angels. We're no angels. Perfection is reserved for the spirits of heaven. Numerous studies confirm, however, that repeated exposure to information about the desired life change increases its probability of success. You still have a ways to go but you are on track. It won't go perfectly, but you will achieve your aims.

You may be, nonetheless, a little disappointed because the weight has not come flying off. You say to yourself, "After all that work only five pounds lost?" But the lesson is clear. As you gain experience, execution becomes easier. The first 50 days are the hardest. If you have come this far, you have survived—indeed prospered. You are advancing by degrees.

Bear in mind you may have altered your body's shape without changing your weight. Muscle takes up about 20% less space than fat so building musculature results in a leaner physique.[2] If you have used 1•1•2™ and strided, your body is altered. You have doubtless exchanged fat for muscle even while keeping the same weight. Even slight improvement helps prompt shape and vigor of youth behaviors.

What Next?

You can lose all the weight you want. Fundamental, however, is that you address each of the key weight loss realms: food (NeoCuisine™), exercise (Muscle Rebuild™), environment (Surroundings Management™), and mental equilibrium (Control Psychology™).

Continue to eat NeoCuisine™. Try all the recipes to find your favorites. Then experiment with adapting some of your own favorite recipes. Instructions for converting recipes to NeoCuisine™ is at the front of the NeoCuisine™ cookbook, Appendix A.

Maintain relatively salt-free eating through the day so you can enjoy a fully savory dinner. This means the whole grain breakfast or Hi-Pro Dream™ advisories are your best bet for a filling and satisfying start to your day. Remember the sweet-to-salt principle: the sweeter the food, the less salt required. Also enjoy plenty of fat-free/sugar-free yogurt and fresh fruit for lunch plus a 2 PM snack of your choosing. Don't forget that the NeoCuisine™ HiPro Dream™ is a superb meal replacement for breakfast, lunch or afternoon.

Maintain your Muscle Rebuild™ schedule. Stride, 1•1•2™, Macro Deflex™ and Dynamic Balance™. Arrange your schedule any way you wish but be sure to get in your physical activity. Your body is predominantly muscle and must be worked. Without physical activity, the body is not properly preserved. There is simply no way for you to enjoy a flourishing physique without recognizing and acting upon the fact that the body demands action. If you want to replace striding with rollerblading, swimming, jogging, racquetball

or what have you, feel free to do so. But be sure your activities pass the **can't sing, can talk** test for full aerobic benefit.

Surroundings Management™ continues to be an imperative. Allies in your BodyRenewal™ journey are fundamental to your success. Keeping your home free of needless temptation helps eliminate binges. Practicing Surroundings Management™ processes aid in keeping you focused. You master the *primeval raging appetite*, provided your Surroundings Management™ stays at the level you realized during the BodyRenewal™ cycle.

And last we come to your mental equilibrium. So much of your success depends on your frame of mind that Control Psychology™ remains a main aspect of your continued fat-stripping success. You are continually propagandized by the clever Madison Avenue manipulators. Succumbing to their seduction is a no-brainer. Right now, take a quick look at the Control Psychology™ summary on page 105.

Know When You're at the Right Weight

Throughout BodyRenewal™ the enduring question is: "When do I stop stripping fat and cruise into maintenance?"

Here is the Body Mass Index chart issued by the National Center for Health.[3] Find your height and then your weight. The number at the top of the chart is your Body Mass Index (BMI). You want a BMI of no more than 23.

This handy reference helps but like all weight assessment methods, it's only approximate. For example, the *Nutrition Action Health Letter* notes that serious bodybuilders can have BMIs in the 40s—normally a category called "morbidly obese." What make strength-trainers like yourself a little heavier is increased muscle mass, not fat.[4] Muscle, which never reads as fat, makes you strong and burns more calories.

According to the Mayo Clinic, even using "reliable methods" such as skin fold measurements, infrared interactance, bioelectrical impedance or underwater weighing only give you a ballpark figure.[5]

MAYBE THE BEST TEST IS THE "PINCH AN INCH." Using your thumb and forefinger, pinch the flesh at your waist, then on the side of your thigh and back of your upper arm. If there's much more than an inch of pinch in any areas, you probably still have a little too much body fat.[6]

BODY MASS INDEX

	BEST			OVERWEIGHT					OBESE		
	21	22	23	24	25	26	27	28	29	30	31
5'0"	107	112	118	123	128	133	138	143	148	153	158
5'1"	111	116	122	127	132	137	143	148	153	158	164
5'3"	118	124	130	135	141	146	152	158	163	169	175
5'5"	126	132	138	144	150	156	162	168	174	180	186
5'7"	134	140	146	153	159	166	172	178	185	191	198
5'9"	142	149	155	162	169	176	182	189	196	203	209
5'11"	150	157	165	172	179	186	193	200	208	215	222
6'1"	159	166	174	182	189	197	204	212	219	227	235
6'3"	168	176	184	192	200	208	216	224	232	240	248

THE ULTIMATE WEIGHT ARBITER IS YOUR FEELINGS AND DECISION.

Just how lean do you want to be? Keep in mind that a little fat is good for you because it supplies an energy reserve, cushions vital organs like the kidneys, liver and intestines, acts as insulation and synthesizes estrogen and other hormones. The ultimate marker of knowing when to stop fat-stripping is emaciation. You don't want it; being too thin is unhealthy.[7] A "skin and bones" body is ugly while shape and definition are a source of pride.

Adding Back Calories

Once you have achieved the shape of youth you want, it is time to start slowly adding back calories. Clearly you can't go back to the same pre-BodyRenewal™ calorie level. This is what made you fat in the first place. Begin adding calories at the rate of about 100 per week. Give your body time to adjust.

You want to wind up at a calorie level of about 13 times your ideal weight.

When, for example, you achieve your ideal weight of 125 pounds, then you want to add back calories of 50 to 100 a week until you are consuming about 1,625 calories (13 x 125 = 1,625) per day.

If you exercise beyond Muscle Rebuild™ minimum recommendations, you may require additional calories. A 15 times body-weight factor might be appropriate. At 125 pounds, the daily calorie allowance would be 1,975 calories (15 x 125 = 1,975) per day. Your best strategy, though, is to use the 13 times body-weight factor as your starting point. If you continue to lose weight, add more calories.

If you are particularly active, you may require up to 15 times your ideal weight.

Bear in mind that if you choose 21st century calorie-dense foods, the *primeval raging appetite* will not be sated without calorie overdose. There aren't many guarantees in life but one you can count on is: consume "modern food" and gain weight. There is virtually no way to keep weight off if you return to pizza, pasta and burgers. The quantity of 21st century food allowed at 13 to 15 times your body weight is small, so you will assuredly be victimized by restriction. You will feel hungry. It does not work. Study after study confirms that quantity restriction leads to long-term weight gain because it is impossible to maintain the protocol. Again quantity restriction does not work. Eat according to the NeoCuisine™ pyramid. You get enough food to feel full. More on this coming up.

Staying the Course Lifelong: The Challenge

The positive part of guaranteeing the shape and vigor of youth is that it's a straightforward proposition: Burn calories consumed. Once a weight goal is reached, however, a person can have a curious reaction. Despite his goal realization, there can be psychological slump. Susan J. Bartlett of the Johns Hopkins Weight Management Center says, "The research is pretty convincing that for most people a dip in motivation appears as early as four months. Most people find the things they've put on the back burner become a higher priority, suddenly making demands on their time."[8] The groundbreaking book *Biomarkers* says, "Once a goal is reached, the average person experiences a let down, even depression, a kind of postpartum blues."[9] This seemingly unlikely reaction results from the fact that a filled need is no longer a motivator.[10] In a sense, reaching a goal is a loss. The stimulus urging you forward is gone. No wonder we tend to react ambivalently when finally accomplishing what we set out to do.

If the postpartum fat blues weren't enough, we live in an unsafe environment. The last two centuries have moved us so far from the body's inherent design that fathood is almost inevitable. The world is crazy with pitfalls. Physical activity has been exchanged for ease. We don't walk, we ride. We don't climb stairs, we elevate. Little in the modern world demands the work the human body requires for strength maintenance. We laze too much. All of today's unparalleled labor-saving devices rob us of our strength. The body's plain purpose is action. Its strong bones and powerful muscles were never intended to sit at a desk the day through, ride in a car home and then plop in front of the TV for 4.4 hours, the national average.[11] The body can't take it. It breaks down. It falls apart. It gets old.

We have paid dearly for ignoring the body's action purpose. Our leisure plus fatty, high-sugar, calorie-dense foods have produced startling heart and cancer death rates. The miracle of modern medicine does much to shore up our contrarian body-blueprint transgressions but drugs, laser surgery and organ replacements cannot counter the body's natural negative reaction to the 21st century's leisure and food onslaughts. Medical advances cannot compensate for our blatant disregard of the body's design. Dr. Charles Hennekens, chief of preventive medicine at Brigham and Women's Hospital in Boston, says, "The U.S. is probably the heaviest society in the history of the world." Only smoking kills more people than obesity, according to Harvard endocrinologist Joan Manson, M.D.[12]

With our surroundings so strikingly treacherous, how are we to stay the shape and vigor of youth course? If the majority of restaurants carry no entreés comporting with your low calorie-to-weight-ratio needs, what are you to do? When 60% of the American population is overweight, how are you to stem society's thrusting you toward fatdom? When we are part of a society where the idea of walking three miles to work and then back home again is absurd, how do you fight back?

There is an answer. Despite our dangerous circumstances, we have no choice but to recognize the body's purpose. If the 21st century has wrought conditions contrary to the body's intended use, our defenses must be all the more clever. Consider how telling the effect of modern medicine combined with a life mode corresponding with the body's natural design would be. The marriage of a proper body-design behavior allied with today's wondrous advances in medicine create an opportunity never before existent in the history of man. Living through your 80s and beyond isn't conjecture, a hope or a dream but rather reality, provided you grasp it with full intent. Why, the results would be remarkable. You can be part of this miracle. If you give your body a break by operating it in accordance with its aim of high action and calorie-frugal food combined with modern medicine, you add vitality-filled years to your life.

STAYING THE COURSE: THE 4 KEYS

1 YOU STAY INTERESTED
2 YOU BUILD SKILLS
3 YOU CONTROL CALORIES
4 YOU EXERCISE

The National Weight Control Registry tracks people who have kept at least 30 pounds off for a minimum of one year. The Registry's researchers point out that successful weight losers appear to devote decisive psychological energy to staying thin, "sometimes to the point of seeming obsessive or neurotic—or at least a little loopy."[13]

This is a rather unflattering characterization but you do sometimes have to put up with others' uncomplimentary view of your "overdedication." They likely don't appreciate the dangers. Yes, dangers. The 21st century environment murders you: slow-kill foods, sedentary lifestyle and the incorrect belief that modern medicine can "cure about anything." If being dedicated in the face of the occasional smirk results in an extra 10 or 20 years quality life for you, so be it.

You are the leader of a national trend. Over the next ten years the baby boomer majority will shift toward your lifestyle. You are ahead of the game.

As you know only too well, the art of reduced weight is preserving it. You may decide that one of the best weight maintenance techniques is making personal well-being your avocation, a pastime of enjoyment. What is more important, after all, than cultivating your personal well-being? It concentrates attention on one of your life's most important aspects—a flourishing physique.

1 STAY INTERESTED

We can't help but harbor the hope that our motivation to seek and maintain a flourishing physique will sustain itself through time. But alas, that is not to be. All endeavors suffer incentive deterioration. One of the most powerful flourishing physique skill-building objectives is learning motivation maintenance. Two techniques that work are necessary narcissism and *Sustaining Forces*™.

NECESSARY NARCISSISM

In Greek mythology, the god Narcissus fell in love with his own reflection which he saw in a pool of water. He pined away, eventually changing to the flower bearing his name. For our purposes, Narcissus got a bad rap. "Don't let the 'egocentricity bias/optimism' be snuffed out in you. It's a hell of a lot more productive than humility," says Harvey Mackay in his book *Swim with the Sharks without Being Eaten Alive*.[14]

Many of us have been taught, unfortunately, that self-love is selfish. Puritanical lingerings remain. However, there is an element of self-value obligatory to your long-term shape and vigor of youth success. Necessary narcissism is a form of body appreciation altogether salubrious to your well-being. It creates the internal horsepower necessary to smash through reality's infinite temptations.

Your body has changed and still is changing. Your past pear shape with its bloated middle and thickened thighs is turning upside down. The breadth of your physique will continue to broaden at the shoulders as the waist narrows and thighs slim. Definition will continue to be enhanced as muscle develops and becomes exposed as layers of fat have been and continue to be stripped away. Even round, puffy faces return to the shape of their youth.

If you learn to love your body, behaviors detrimental to it become abhorrent.

This is precisely the mental mode you want to achieve. Narcissism facilitates this state of mind. You want sufficient necessary narcissism to where unbeneficial behaviors (not exercising) and flawed reasoning (you deserve fatty desserts) don't accord with your new convictions.

NECESSARY NARCISSISM MIRROR DRILLS

Although the notion of standing in front of a mirror inspecting oneself might sound suspect, it isn't because mirror drills imprint your lean and fit picture into your mind. This imprint, with continued reinforcement, aids you in maintaining the shape and vigor of youth. Rising self-estimation steels you against the world's taste temptations and the seduction of the easy life.

• **FULL STOP:** Study yourself once a week. Take time for consideration. We buzz through life with much doing but little realizing. Take a close look at yourself.

• **IN YOUR KNICKERS:** Stand in front of a full-length mirror in your undies or *au natural* for a good look at yourself. You do this to admire your progress and to congratulate yourself. It affirms your youthful shape and vigor goals and may offer the opportunity for creating new ones. Take time to love your body and yourself. Admire your progress by spending a minimum of 60 seconds in front of the mirror.

• **FLEX:** Yes, flex in front of the mirror. Those weights you have been lifting are sculpting muscle you must take time to appreciate. Don't be so unwise as to pass it off as "no big deal." You are regaining the shape of your youth.

• **ANGLES:** Take a good look at yourself in the mirror from various vantages. Look at yourself from the front and the side. Look hard at what you've accomplished. Some of that cellulite cottage cheese has melted away.

• **BACKSIDE:** If need be, install a second mirror so you can take a good look at your backside. One of the great things about the Muscle Rebuild™ is its bun-raising potential. You've lost a lot of weight back there, have a look. Much more will go before you're done.

• **FEELING:** As you flex and study your body, take a moment to feel your musculature. Yes, go ahead, feel your improved muscle. Notice your biceps are beginning to harden. You will certainly note how much harder your muscles are than six months ago. Fat that hid muscle is now reduced. Your calves feel firmer. Your stomach is more compact.

• **TALK:** Stephen Sinatra, M.D., says that " ... Speaking aloud to yourself while looking into your eyes is a powerful exercise."[15] Go ahead. Brag to yourself.

NECESSARY NARCISSISM KEY ACTIONS

• **ACCEPT COMPLIMENTS** without apology.

• **REAFFIRM VOLUNTARY VOLITION:** I will not be fat! Necessary narcissism facilitates self-affirmation.

• **WEAR CLOTHES THAT SHOW YOUR SHAPE.** For example, don't be embarrassed wearing a bathing suit. In fact, be proud sitting by the hotel's pool. You look better than most your age.

• **EXPLAIN BodyRenewal™.** When asked, "How did you do it?" *don't* respond with, "Oh, it was nothing."

249

- **COMPARE.** Relish the notion that while others go to seed, your strength, health, longevity, vigor and positive attitude burgeon.

- **RECOGNIZE YOUR BODY IS WONDERFUL:** It dances, walks, hikes, 1•1•2™s, loves, runs computers, invents and sings. It flourishes. You even feel comfortable playing sports with those younger than you because your conditioning warrants it.

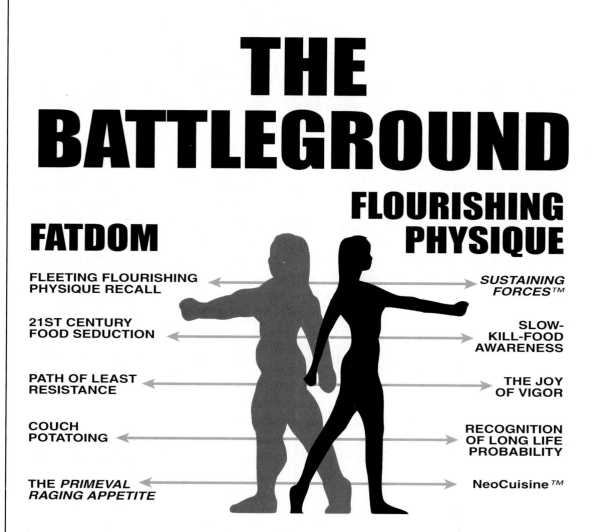

THE BATTLEGROUND

FATDOM

FLOURISHING PHYSIQUE

FLEETING FLOURISHING PHYSIQUE RECALL

21ST CENTURY FOOD SEDUCTION

PATH OF LEAST RESISTANCE

COUCH POTATOING

THE *PRIMEVAL RAGING APPETITE*

SUSTAINING FORCES™

SLOW-KILL-FOOD AWARENESS

THE JOY OF VIGOR

RECOGNITION OF LONG LIFE PROBABILITY

NeoCuisine™

Sustaining Forces™

Sustaining Forces™ are your long-term mental reminders against fatdom.

Bear in mind that experts say we are bombarded with about three million stimuli a day to which we can react.[16] That seems like rather a high number until you consider all the reading, listening and working inputs directed toward you. Think about the number of TV, magazine, newspaper, billboard and radio advertisements we are bombarded with daily. Even walking and driving demand stimulus-response. Concentration is spent on the undertakings of the day. We focus on affairs at hand. With sensory overload, remembering our shape and vigor of youth behaviors and attitudes becomes a challenge.

Some of the following sustaining forces™ suggestions may appear "over the top" but remember we are dealing with psycho-logic, not neocortex rational reason. Circumstances warrant cues (*Sustaining Forces™*) to remind us. For instance, just to remember to review our personalized motivator list, or to glance at your ability-age for a mental boost, is a challenge. So, *Sustaining Forces™* are dramatic and intentionally so. You can't merely hope to sustain, for as Benjamin Franklin observed, "He that lives upon hope will die farting."[17]

YOUR NEW PSYCHOLOGICAL CONTRACT

Your resolve is for a new life. So let's be clear about this. In the end, you must make the mental commitment for a lifetime of lean foods, forgoing the obsolete dining behaviors that made you corpulent. It's a resolution requiring maturity and a little courage.

The foods of fathood may have made us too round but they were fun, all those drippy cheeseburgers, hot fudge sundaes and New York steaks.✶ To say that we are now going to turn our backs on the self-indulgent foods of the past without a sense of loss and a little regret is nonsense. Each day is a challenge to your shape and vigor of youth. It never goes away. It must be managed on an ongoing basis. Each day you must mobilize your internal forces to fend off 21st century foods and ease-

---

✶ Look, both you and I know that occasionally enjoying a greasy cheeseburger does zero harm. The operant word is *occasionally*. A couple of burgers a month (or whatever you choose) expresses the freedom you enjoy in your new flourishing physique life.

251

of-life seductions. If it sounds like a war, it is.

The work involved in staying the course would appear to be somewhat burdensome. But this, in fact, is the key point: Most people don't know the degree of self-reinforcement they require for staying-the-course behavior. Those who understand and accept the self-reinforcement necessary are the most successful.

All conscious behavior is a denouement of the mind. Resolves committed to paper harden them. Your long-term intent is sticking with the shape and vigor of youth resolutions. They deserve memorializing by writing them down. Take the time to draft a shape and vigor of youth contract. Here is a sample.

MY SHAPE AND VIGOR OF YOUTH FOR LIFE

Because I want to look and feel great, age little, fend off sickness and live long:

- I promise myself to read this contract from beginning to end one time a week for the next three months and then monthly thereafter.

- I am going to be active six days a week and in all cases no less than 20 minutes a day, adding more time if I like. I get to define "active" as 1•1•2™, racquetball or whatever I choose that gets me really going.

- I've decided to quit making excuses so often and just get on with what's right. Just do it.

- I will eat NeoCuisine™ six days a week. I've learned that this isn't too hard to do.

- I promise myself to gain no more weight, but if I put on more than five pounds, I promise to execute a 30-day Body Renewal™.

- I'll rewrite this contract at least once a year so I can honestly assess how I'm doing.

- I'm staying slim and fit for ME, not for my husband, kids, friends or employer. This isn't selfish since I am giving more to all those around me because I do my best when I am at my best. All those around me get the best ME when I have the shape and vigor of youth. I deserve it. They deserve it.

A PERSONAL ADVANTAGES LIST

Make it a point to occasionally reread all NeoCuisine™ and Muscle Rebuild™ benefits. Write your own list of benefits. Think about it. You can shop for hours without having to rest every 30 minutes. You may be keeping the fat off to walk with pride on white beaches of St. Thomas. You may be taking special care of yourself so you can see your grandkids grow into successful adulthood. What else?

Counterbalance your perceived "sacrifices" by reacquainting yourself with the good things derived from your life's new mode. Work hard at using Control Psychology™ to dispute the silly fiction of "sacrifice." This negative must be eliminated. Doing so washes your mind of noxious thinking. Don't poison your psyche with ill-conceived fancies.

Post your motivational short list on a 3x5 card. Make copies and "salt" your environment with reminders. Update it at least annually.

THE POST-PICTURE: YOUR ACCOMPLISHMENT

When you've achieved your desired weight, take a picture of yourself. Do this the same way you did at the beginning of BodyRenewal™—in your undies using a full-length mirror. Yes, you see the camera in the picture but this isn't going to be published in *People* magazine.

Your post-picture is effective because in comparing it to the pre-picture, you have dramatic proof of your accomplishment. The pre- and post-pictures represent a visual record of your feat. Don't take your attainment lightly. You worked hard at stripping fat and rebuilding your lost musculature of youth. Enjoy it. Give yourself a much-deserved emotional pat on the back.

SUBSCRIPTIONS

You've been reminded to buy three-year subscriptions to at least four magazines. There isn't a better sustaining force™. Each month you get superior reinforcement. You constantly learn new techniques. Little by little, you become an expert. The learning process is lifelong which makes it exciting. It is a journey of high interest because everything you learn contributes to your well-being.

MONTHLY SUSPENSE FILES

Use one file for each month of the year. In each file, put the information you think best remotivates you. Put in your personal advantages list, copies of your before and after pictures, your new psychological contract and other maintenance motivators. These are be placed in monthly suspense files for you to review on a systematic basis. The idea is to have information reappear for you at the time desired. If all this seems like too much work, do keep in mind that undermining forces are constantly at work to unravel the shape and vigor of youth you are attempting to sustain.

Put in:
- Your contract
- Signs you want to repost
- Your win list for additions and reread
- Your gratitude list for additions and reread
- The most helpful magazine articles to reread
- Your personal advantages list for additions and reread
- Recipes you want to try
- Pages from your journal

BENEVOLENT ADVOCATE

As a sustaining force, become a benevolent advocate of the shape and vigor of youth. By teaching someone else your Body-Renewal™ skills, you reinforce and remind yourself of your flourishing physique behaviors.

SIGNS

You already know the power of signs as a focusing device. Use them to reinforce the flourishing physique behaviors and remind you of maintenance motivators. The same sign rules as before apply: 1) Move signs weekly. 2) Use different shapes and colors. 3) Make fresh signs frequently. 4) Short is best.

CLOTHING CUE

Don't ignore the discomfort of tightening clothes. You don't need the hard data of a scale to know when your weight is going up. Buy a pair of classic tight-fitting jeans. When they start feeling too tight is the time to jump back into NeoCuisine,™ wholeheartedly. Or save one piece of old clothing that represents a high point of your shape and vigor of youth. As your clothes become uncomfortable, get yourself immediately back on track with a week of strict NeoCuisine™. The clothing cue is a powerful mnemonic indeed.

YOUR WEEKLY SCHEDULE

Organize a certain time each week when you automatically sit down and review your maintenance motivators for a couple of minutes. Having a set time and place for maintenance motivator review (like reading this month's suspense file), the likelihood of remembering to reread maintenance motivators substantially increases, remind yourself why STAYING THE COURSE is important to you.

REINFORCING FRIENDS

A friend can be an exceptional mnemonic. It may seem like nagging but someone reminding you of your maintenance motivators can be of considerable help. Imagine a friend who is willing to send you three short letters a year reminding you of your shape and vigor of youth benefits. The same can be accomplished with telephone calls, e-mails and faxes. Make a deal where you must respond as to your status. Believe me, you will not want to tell your friend you've regained 20 pounds. This simple reinforcement helps hold you accountable. Preceisely what you want.

2 BUILD SKILL

The Johns Hopkins University special report *Weight Control* says the answer to controlling weight, "lies not in genetic predisposition or differences in metabolism but in the use of coping strategies."[18] Acquiring and using coping strategies is a skill.

SKILL-BUILDING STEPS

Like any competence, the shape and vigor of youth skills must be mastered. The first step of skill building is **self-watching**. Establishing a skill means that you must self-observe. You watch your performance and analyze it. Self-perception encourages correction of deviations from the ideal.

The second step is **learning information** well enough for quick recall and reaction. Knowledge swiftly brought to the conscious can be brought to bear at the time of need.

The third step is **patient practice.** Dr. Harry Bahrick, a psychologist at Ohio Wesleyan University, says, "The most significant factor in long-term retention of knowledge is being exposed to the material over several years."[19] Give yourself time. Mistakes will be made. Perfection's for angels.

The concept of skill-building seems good on paper but we have resistances. Learning to self-watch, knowing which piece of information to recall, and implementing patient practice looks like work. It is. But don't worry. Missteps are intrinsic to skill building. Practice by its nature means that you do it wrong before you do it right. Don't become discouraged. Understand that the behavioral and psychological skill-building principles prescribed in this book require repetition. Frequent rehearsal leads to assimilation, elevated confidence and the fostering of the prescribed behaviors that eventually become a natural part of your life.

In the beginning, change creates information overload. The data can seem overwhelming. Take the advice of former 49er quarterback Steve Young who says that as he got older, "the game ... slowed down." He doesn't mean that he slowed down, the game itself did. He understood football so well, that each play was not a struggle with new information but a repeat of the past. The game was not the tense blur of new quarterbacks but a plan to be executed with finesse arising only from experience.[20]

What this means to you is that your game will "slow down." The data overload unjams and you maneuver with ease. You're initiated; with practice, skill rises. The tension of remembering and executing reduces significantly through time with skill-building.

SKILL-BUILDING PRACTICE

Let's analyze a particular skill, the Miracle 20™. It advises you to wait at least 20 minutes after a meal before deciding whether or not you're really "still hungry." The Miracle 20™ sounds simple and has an intuitive ring of truth to it but is troublesome nonetheless. The first challenge is remembering to do it, especially if it's something you read six months or a year ago. Once the Miracle 20™ is recalled, you execute it so the brain can catch up with the stomach. Ten minutes won't do

and 15 minutes is iffy. It's only through quick recall and patient practice, however faltering, that the Miracle 20™ becomes part of your shape and vigor of youth skills repertoire.

Here is another skill-building exercise. Establishing a clear picture of your shape and vigor of youth win establishes resolve and motivation. The word build is apropos because few people have a clear image of their vision. Developing your goal picture is like actually painting a portrait, one stroke at a time, gradually forming the vision of where you want to go. You must visit your emerging picture again and again to complete it. Building the win picture takes a little time, initiative and contemplation.

Once the win picture is clearly fixed, you find yourself increasingly stimulated to pursue the shape and vigor of youth. The clearer your winning visualization, the more motivation you have.

The rewards of achieving the shape and vigor of youth through the BodyRenewal™, as you know, are generous. Paint your win image to include visual-

izing your new vigor. Add your substantially improved well-being. Paint in your newfound sense of high self-endorsement. Imagine your new shape. Visualize people's positive reaction. See your flourishing physique. But, you aren't engaging in BodyRenewal™ just to get big muscles or a Cosmopolitan figure. You want more: positive attitude, the shape and vigor of youth, much more endurance, a sound whole and a definite sense of conceding nothing (rejecting negativism) and living in the NOW while unfolding your vast potential.

Practice these mental vignettes.

MEETING FRIENDS

See yourself meeting friends and basking in the glow of your accomplishment. Believe me they'll notice and may even comment on how good you look. Who knows, they may ask you to share your secret. Do so because the more you talk about and teach BodyRenewal™, the more your resolve builds.

256

HEARTY SELF-APPROBATION

Create scenes where you congratulate yourself for attaining the shape and vigor of youth. Maybe this happens during a mirror exercise. You look at yourself and recognize that you have accomplished a great deal. You look terrific. It's obvious you own a flourishing physique.

INCREASED ENDURANCE

See yourself zipping up a stadium's stairs at the next football game. You'll reach your seat easily while the rest of your party is huffing a bit. Or maybe you're on a shopping spree and by midafternoon your friends are begging for mercy because you are on the go. Or see yourself flying through your afternoon's work with little of the fatigue that hampered you in the past.

LONGEVITY

Include in your movie of the win a view of yourself at 90, still fully engaged in life, relishing every day. Why not? Most of us have genes to reach at least our late 80s in relatively good health.[21] Eating correctly and the right exercise allied with the miracles of modern medicine may very well make you a centenarian.

ELEMENTAL EFFORT

Yes, there is elemental effort in achieving the shape and vigor of youth but it is neither too much nor overwhelming. So when you build your movie of the win, be sure to include reasonable elemental effort. Elemental effort means that rebuilding your body requires work, but you will find it rational, enjoyable and invigorating.

CULTIVATE THESE SKILLS

•RECOGNIZE WINS

A skill-building challenge is learning to recognize progress. Shape and vigor of youth advances are often made in such a small degree that perceiving them is difficult. Unnoticed headway creates no encouragement, a critical point because any behavior atrophies without reinforcement. Here is a three-step solution.

STOP. Immerse yourself in paying attention. Break through the barrier of everyday distraction to consciousness.

ANALYZE. Take a full 30 seconds to ponder where you were and where you NOW are. Take heart, have hope. You are going forward.

CONGRATULATE. Self-congratulation for small advances is imperative. Your heightened attention creates the reinforcement assuring continued correct behavior. Celebrating achievement is no small matter and small victories are important.

•NO SLOW SUICIDE

Of the key factors relating to successful long-term flourishing physique, correct attitude development and maintenance are the most important because they lead to right eating and exercise. Cultivate a rising indignation towards fat and sloth.

These may seem to be strong words but it's time to take a stand. Unequivocally wage war against fat. No slow suicide. Dying young makes no sense. Clogging veins with fat plaque is abhorrent to you. Your patience with self-destruction is about zero. You are appalled at others' slow self-murder.

•INSTANT REACTION

How can we stay motivated when the weight loss goal has been achieved? Antony Jay in his book *Management & Machiavelli* offers a solution: "Success is a tempting draught, but to drink from it deadens the vital nerve of desire. The nerve of desire must always be kept alive ... (by a) feedback mechanism."[22] Your best feedback mechanisms are:

1 Your weekly weigh-in: if you are up more than two pounds, take action.
2 Your new clothes: if they feel snug, take action.
3 You mirror drill: if you don't like what you see, take action.
4 You are pinching more than an inch.

3 CONTROL CALORIES

Having a sense of control in our lives is an important aspect of happiness. The commonplace belief is that control correlates to power and wealth. This conventional American definition falls short of other cultures' understanding. Rather than the inelegant view of control as power and money, there are more sophisticated ways of achieving dominion. The fact is, you don't have to be a millionaire or run a large company for primacy.

The Japanese gain control in the world of miniature. Consider the delicate art form of bonsai, dwarf trees aesthetically shaped. The bonsai artist has utter mastery over his creations. Likewise, the Japanese take pride in elegant rock gardens which give their creators complete authority over their compositions.

Achieving a flourishing physique is certainly a form of control. Striding, 1•1•2™ and NeoCuisine™ lead to a robust whole and rising self-regard for all your body success. Nothing is quite so rewarding as being whole.

You have all the mental health-enhancing control you want in your life if you approach the inquiry philosophically. The silly American explanation of power meaning money and power over others is easily supplanted by the more refined ethos of: command over self is ultimate control.

EAT THE NeoCuisine™ PYRAMID WAY

Following USDA Guidelines you quickly over-consume. According to USDA recommendations, almost half of your consumption is from calorie-to-weight ratio foods containing over 80 calories an ounce such as bread, cereal, rice and pasta. Eating these foods in the USDA recommended amounts contributes only 15-20 ounces of the approximately 75 ounces of food weight required per day to calm the *primeval raging appetite*. **Eating USDA recommended calorie-dense foods in the volume required to suppress the PRA makes you fat as a pig.**

You are not on a "program," "diet" or "weight-loss regimen." You merely see NeoCuisine™ as a way of life. It is simply how you've chosen to live your life in achieving and retaining the shape and vigor of you. The NeoCuisine™ pyramid emphasizes white proteins (white fish, white meats and beans), whole grains, nonfat dairy, plenty of fruit and an abundance of vegetables. Following the simple NeoCuisine™ plan strips fat and floods your body with disease-fighting flavonoids, flavones and fiber, and the wealth of other healing phytochemicals science is now uncovering—over 500. Here's the formula:

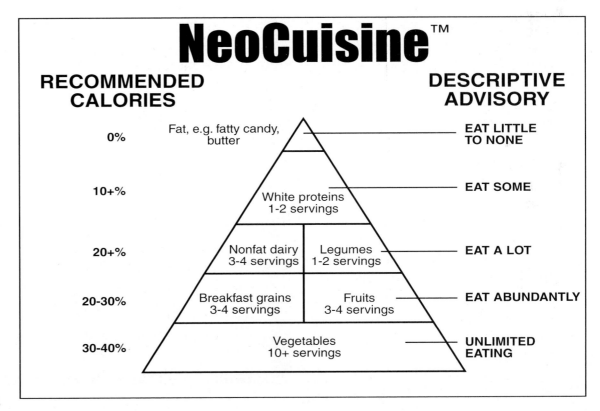

NeoCuisine™

RECOMMENDED CALORIES		DESCRIPTIVE ADVISORY
0%	Fat, e.g. fatty candy, butter	EAT LITTLE TO NONE
10+%	White proteins 1-2 servings	EAT SOME
20+%	Nonfat dairy 3-4 servings / Legumes 1-2 servings	EAT A LOT
20-30%	Breakfast grains 3-4 servings / Fruits 3-4 servings	EAT ABUNDANTLY
30-40%	Vegetables 10+ servings	UNLIMITED EATING

●VEGETABLES: **Unlimited Eating** including salad greens.

●FRUITS AND BREAKFAST GRAINS: These likewise can be consumed in almost unlimited quantities but because they are more cal-dense than vegetables, modest restriction applies: **Eat Abundantly.** Don't, for example, use fruit as your primary diet amplifier at the expense of vegetables because calorie overload results with fat the outcome.

●NONFAT DAIRY AND LEGUMES: Dairy and legumes (beans and lentils) are more cal-dense than vegetables, fruits and whole grains. **Eat a Lot.** Don't, however, center your diet around non-fat dairy and legumes because you will take in too much energy resulting in fat.

●WHITE PROTEINS: **Eat Some.** While still cal-frugal compared to red proteins, white protein calories can add up. Stick to four to eight ounces per day on average. The exception is the HiPro Dream™ which can be consumed abundantly because it's a real hunger stancher with a modest cal-weight ratio of seven calories per ounce.

ENCOURAGEMENT

The Harvard School of Public Health found in a large study that those who don't smoke, exercise and maintain a healthful weight are 82% less likely to have heart disease symptoms.[23]

In studies conducted by the Cooper Institute and the American College of Sports Medicine, a direct correlation between exercise and reduced cancer has been found. Bio-statistician Carolyn Barlow says, "We found that men who were classified as unfit were 80% more likely to die of cancer." It's becoming more apparent as studies unravel the cancer mystery that obesity is a risk factor.[24] Strip fat, live long.

A NeoCuisine™ DAY OF EATING

Here is what a day of fine NeoCuisine™ dining might look like. Start with a steaming bowl of hot cereal, more than you can eat. Go ahead. Fill up. Have a one-quart, rich, thick, satisfying NeoCuisine™ HiPro Dream™ for lunch (Appendix B). Protein gives you an afternoon lift as studies show.[25] Devour an aromatic pear in the late afternoon. Have a salad with a balsamic vinegar dressing and teriyaki fresh halibut dinner with frenched green beans and a NeoCuisine™-style baked potato soaked with beef stock and seasoned with salt, pepper, garlic powder and scallions. Finish the day with No-Fat/Sugar Raspberry Cheesecake.

Through all this, bear in mind that you are not on an "eternal diet." This is the wrong mind set. A "diet" doesn't exist. Your new life pattern simply means intelligently selecting foods, concentrating on fruits, vegetables, whole grains and white proteins. There aren't even any "bad foods" (well, yes: saturated and trans-fats). It's just that if you eat a lot of fat, sugar and refined flour (the perfect cinnamon roll), you overeat because calorie-dense foods sum to prodigious calorie quantities for satiety. An ounce of a cinnamon roll is 150 calories whereas an apple is only 20 calories an ounce.[26] Ounce for ounce you get seven times the quantity with an apple or grapefruit or pear or orange or no-fat/sugar yogurt, etc., etc., etc.

Here are the stats:

FOOD GROUP	NeoCuisine™ Recommended	Servings	Calories	Weight
Fat Serving	0	0	0	0
White protein (e.g. fish)	1	1	300	6 oz
Breakfast grains (e.g. oats)	3 to 4	3	350	24 oz
Nonfat dairy (e.g. yogurt)	3 to 4	2	200	16 oz
Fruit (e.g. pears, apples)	4 to 6	3	240	24 oz
Vegetables (variety)	10 to 15	10	450	32 oz

1540 CALS ÷ 102 OZ

15 CALS/OUNCE

If you are consistently Muscle Rebuilding™ (striding, 1•1•2™, etc.) and eating NeoCuisine™-style there is nothing wrong with occasionally enjoying moderated 21st century fare. This means that about once a week you can take a day off from BodyRenewal™ provided you do not binge. Keep an eye on it and there will be no weight gain. If you enjoy red meat, for example, stick with the lean cuts like eye of the round and what is called denuded tenderloin. If you want to sauté, be sure you use only canola or olive oil, the preferred fats. If you hanker for the typically rich 21st century salad, make a lovely vinaigrette using balsamic vinegar and extra virgin olive oil. If your tastes run toward something special, add nuts to your salad, which are being found to be a fountain of health. Add wonderful king crab. With a little finesse you can enjoy almost any food occasionally without plumping up.

COUNTING IS CONTROL

It is virtually impossible to achieve and maintain the shape and vigor of youth without counting calories. This doesn't have to be the anal-retentive "overwhelming" task one might imagine. Memorizing the Quick Cal Count Card makes calorie accounting entirely doable. In fact, you are becoming so proficient that shortly you will be able to track calories through the day mentally without the aid of pen and paper. You will be able to look at a meal and quickly assess its calorie value without giving it a second thought.

It's axiomatic. If you don't want to gain back pounds you've lost, you can't go back to your old way of eating. The point is so obvious it hardly bears repetition. Yet, most "dieters" quickly return to old habits. That's because they look at a "diet" as having an end point rather than seeing themselves entering a new life mode. The statistics are depressing.

According to the National Institutes of Health, a staggering 99% of all dieters put all lost weight back on within five years of completing a "diet program."[27] *Prevention* magazine says that the number of people in diet programs who lose weight for the long-term (at least seven years) are only 1 in 250.[28] Dr. Judith Wurtman of M.I.T. observes that about 70% of all Weight Watchers members are repeat dieters.[29] Even the famed "Mediterranean Diet" of the Seven Country study that focused mostly on the isle of Crete is in trouble. The research, which began in 1960, was updated, finding that blood pressure, body weight and body fat have increased substantially due to the Cretans abandoning their traditional lifestyle of physical labor and healthful foods.

There are statistical studies proving long-term, permanent weight loss is entirely possible. The National Weight Loss Registry is the largest study ever conducted on long-term weight loss. Participants keep at least 30 pounds off for a minimum of five years. Almost half report it's easier to maintain weight than take it off.[30]

THE CRUX IS NOT GOING BACK TO PAST EATING HABITS.

4 YOU KNOW EXERCISE IS VITAL

We fret. We stew. We obsess. We worry about getting old. We give it too much mind, considering that age is not necessarily a happiness determinant. Our oft-time shallow culture has an inanely limited aging definition: If you are past 40 you are old. A few wrinkles and a spot of gray puts you at our pop culture's far end of the age scale. Those of us who enjoy the ample benefits of age past 40 grasp the absurdity of this.

The correct definition of aging lies in the dominion of action rather than how he or she looks. The best definition of aging must be behavioral because what a person can do accurately determines true age.

WHAT MATTERS MOST IS WHAT A PERSON CAN DO. YOUR ACTION-ABILITY IS THE REAL BIOLOGICAL CLOCK.

What profit is there in being alive but unable to act? Don't running, jumping, climbing, trotting, skiing, surfing, gardening, walking, hiking and swimming and all else embody the range of behaviors we love? If we can play, learn, work, relish life, discover and enjoy our flourishing physique what's the purpose of coupling our mood to a number? The preservation—nay, the enhancement—of our abilities must be foremost in our minds.

The more we can go and do the better, because it is freedom's essence. The ability to do as we please, go where we want and execute as we wish defines the degree of control we have over our lives. Take away freedom and control is lost which inexorably diminishes life's quality. What you can do in large measure determines how you feel and how you feel is ultimate reality. Betty Friedan in her

263

book *The Fountain of Age* says that "A great many gerontologists have come to the conclusion that helplessness—being unable to control or affect one's own life—is the key to physical and psychological deterioration and decline."[31] When you strip fat, increase musculature, add endurance, magnify vigor, dispute silly fictions and feed your body the foods of its design, marvelous psychic boons boost morale.

The vulgarity of a number ruling your life is unacceptable. This is the time of life seasoned with a wealth of personal experience that can now be accompanied by a youthful ability-age. The added advantage of tempered emotions puts you at the height of your powers.

The reason why ability-age is so important is that it is so encouraging. When you can perform a level 10 or 15 years younger—it motivates you to continue. Study after study confirms our potential to regain our abilities. The media regu-larly features 90-year-olds riding horses, 85-year-old marathoners, 70-year-olds waterskiing bare-foot and boxing champs in their 40s. The list goes on and on. And you know your potential ability-recapture because you have already done much of it. You have no control over chro-nological age, but you do have ample command over your abil-ity-age. Your abilities can be elevated to levels sure to please you.

Yes, age brings cosmetic changes but they are meaning-less compared to abilities. We want to DO. Others' cosmetic perceptions of you are entirely secondary to you maintaining and enhancing a full range of behavioral capabilities. How old are you when you lift weights like a kid, walk for miles, work hard all day when you choose, take up new interests and feel like a million bucks? Alex Leif, M.D., of the Harvard Medical School points out, "Regular daily physical activity has been a way of life for virtually every person who has reached the age of 100 in sound condition."[32]

ASSESSING YOUR ABILITY-AGE

Score well on these and you're fit for the world. They measure strength, equilibrium and flexibility, the foremost age-ability measures. If you don't like your results, stay with Muscle Rebuild™. Your scores are sure to improve.

MUSCLE STRENGTH AND ENDURANCE

This test developed by the President's Council on Physical Fitness and Sports assesses mus-cular strength and endurance. You know the exercise well and will likely score better than your chronological age would indicate according to the chart.

NUMBER OF PUSH-UPS

Average Age	Push-up Number
25	36+
35	26-35
45	21-25
55	16-20
65	10-15

[33]

WOMEN: Assume knees-on-the-floor position. Keep shoulders back and buttocks straight; hands directly under shoulders; knees bent so you rest on them. Bend elbows until your chest just touches the floor and back up. Without pausing do as many as you can.

MEN: Same procedure, but with legs straight. Lower yourself bringing your chest to about 3" to 4" from the floor and up again. No pausing.

FLEXIBILITY

This simple test gauges overall flexibility. Tape a yardstick to the floor. After warming up by marching in place three to four minutes, do 30 seconds TCT of T-Reach, page 70. Then sit on the floor with your legs straight in front of you, feet 10" to 12" apart. Position yourself so the yardstick's 1" mark is toward you and its 15" mark is even with your heels. Then place one hand on top of the other (middle fingers should align) and reach as far forward as possible with-

out bouncing or jerking. Do the test three times and record the farthest point you touched along the yardstick. Find your measurement in the chart below to see if you're more or less flexible than the average.

Average Age	Inch-Mark	[34]
25	15"	
35	14"	
45	13"	
55	12"	
65	11"	

DYNAMIC BALANCE™

On the average, a 100% decline occurs in Dynamic Balance™ from age 20 to age 80. Most young people can hold a one-legged eyes-closed stand for 30 seconds or more whereas few untrained persons past 65 can hold the pose longer than a few seconds.

You know the drill well but just in case, here are the instructions. Perform the test either barefoot or wearing an ordinary low-heeled shoe. Stand on a hard surface (not on a rug) with

both feet together, close your eyes, and lift the foot of your dominant leg (right foot if right handed) about six inches off the floor. Bend the knee of the other leg at about a 45° angle. Don't move your floor foot. Just stand on it with your eyes closed. Moving your arms and the lifted leg are okay. How many seconds can you stand this way before you have to open your eyes or move your foot to avoid falling over? Do the test three times and take an average.

Average Age	Seconds	[35]
25	25-35+	
35	16-24	
45	10-15	
55	5-9	
65	4 or less	

CALCULATING YOUR *ABILITY-AGE*

Add all three scores together and divide by three. This is the "birthday" you should be celebrating every year, not the one appearing on your birth certificate. Because you have done some Body Renewing, you will predictably find your biological age lower than your birth certificate birthday. Stick with BodyRenewal™ and your ability-age will continue to fall.

Exercise is vital to your life. Researchers at the University of Chicago found 30 minutes vigorous activity (e.g. striding) to be the minimum required for weight maintenance.[36] Weight expert James Rippe, M.D., says "Unless you are willing to increase the amount of physical activity in your life, you will never achieve lifelong weight management."[37] You must come to regard regular exercise as invaluable to your well-being as eating and sleeping. You must come to see striding, 1•1•2™, Macro Deflexing™ and Dynamic Balance™ as permanent parts of your life. They can't be considered an option.

According to a U.S. Surgeon General's report there are four characteristics making exercise enjoyable lifelong:[38]

●YOU EXERCISE AT A GRATIFYING LEVEL: It is far better to exercise less vigorously but enjoy it than to work overly hard and therefore soon quit. For example, striding is fine. You don't have to run sprints, hike stadium stairs or bike 50 miles. Try choosing a sport you do a few times a week in lieu of striding. Consider swimming, biking, rollerblading or whatever strikes your fancy.

●YOU FEEL LIKE YOU CAN READILY BUILD SKILL IN YOUR EXERCISE: Choose an exercise that you sense you can learn. This is why striding works so well whereas taking up tennis at 50 may not be self-image satisfying. Playing tennis well requires a lot of practice. If you have the time, go for it.

●DAILY INSTANT EXERCISE IS ACCESSIBLE: Choosing an exercise whose site is 45 minutes from your house will soon dampen your enthusiasm. Going to a gym might be inspirational but investing an hour and a half round trip travel time may put a pall on your incentive. Keep your chosen exercise accessible. A simple home gym is ideal.

●KEEP IT CHEAP: Electing to snow ski two or three days a week as an exercise strategy may prove cost-prohibitive when you factor in the gear, gas, tickets and high-priced ski resort food. A primary positive of the Muscle Rebuild™ (1•1•2™, striding, Macro Deflexing™ and Dynamic Balance™) is it costs little. Anyone can afford it.[39]

NO "MAGIC BULLET"

Imagine that science comes up with a cheap "safe" daily pill that allows you to eat as much as you want. What would this mean to you?

Let's do some accounting. You would still want to restrict red meat to avoid the clogging effects of saturated fat. Fatty dairy products like butter, cheese and ice cream would largely be off your eating list for the same reason. And you would assiduously avoid cakes, pastries and doughnuts because of their dangerous trans-fats. You would limit smoked, fried, barbecued and grilled meats because of their carcinogenic danger. Crusty meats contain heterocyclic amines and polycyclic aromatic hydrocarbons, cancer culprits according to Dr. Steven E. Goldfinger of the Harvard Medical School.[40] On the other hand you would still want to eat plenty of vegetables, fruits and whole grains for their phytochemicals and antioxidants.

Exercise would continue to be imperative because our bodies ARE muscle. You stride to lower your blood pressure, strengthen your heart and for sheer enjoyment. You 1•1•2™ to enhance muscle for power, endurance and sports fun. You deflex for full mobility. You Dynamic Balance™ for maximum equilibrium and agility. No pill can do this.

So how much would a "magic bullet" really help? Not at all.

YOUR PLACE IN THE WORLD

As you come to enjoy quicker thinking, increased creativity, reduced anxiety allied with amplified optimism, more strength and higher energy, plus extended longevity and newfound enhanced self-appreciation, you then rightfully see your total being as better. These qualities make you a positive force in the world with the potential of making a greater contribution.

Think of the good you can do. Starting with the obvious, you may perhaps help someone strip a little fat and learn to eat better. Because you have increased energy, you may want to do some fundraising for charity. Your work productivity rises. Your overall action capacity increases.

And last, a life of pleasure pursuit is no pleasure at all. You understand that the persistent pursuit of pleasure yields one of life's supreme ironies: Gratification decline and substantial harm. You know this, of course, but occasional review keeps things clear. Drugs and alcohol lead to addiction, sickness and the loss of personal freedom. A life of leisure leaves our bodies weak and emaciated. Unbridled eating makes us fat and diseased. Indiscriminate sex brings risk of horrendous afflictions and diminished personal relationships. Unremitting entertainment withers creativity and generativity— the essence of life's gratification. It's an implausible paradox: discipline marshals happiness obtained no other way. A disease-free life coupled with reasonable self-control creates ultimate freedom. You have the stamina to do what you want. Your mind is alert. Senses are sharp. All the good things of life are there for you.

STAYING THE COURSE

1 It is normal to **VEER OFF COURSE.** You simply have to **STEER BACK** without guilt and self-recrimination.

2 The **PINCH-AN-INCH** test is probably best. See page 244.

3 Your maintenance calorie intake probably lies between **13 TO 15 TIMES YOUR BODY WEIGHT.**

4 Work at staying interested by developing **NECESSARY NARCISSISM.** Set up **SUSTAINING FORCES**™, best of which are the suspense files, periodical subscriptions and reinforcing friends.

5 **SKILL-BUILD** to:
- Recognize wins
- Instant reaction
- Miracle 20™

6 **EAT NeoCuisine**™ with unlimited vegetables, abundant breakfast grains and fruits, plenty of non-fat dairy and legumes with some white proteins to assure adequate protein intake. Avoid red meats, fats and refined grains such as bread and pasta.

7 You realize **COUNTING IS CONTROL.** Maintain a mental ToteCard every day.

8 You know **EXERCISE IS VITAL.**

9 From now on you will only have **ABILITY-AGE PARTIES.**

10 You believe there are **NO "MAGIC BULLETS"** because musculature demands action to realize a flourishing physique.

[1] "Strategies for Successful Change," *Johns Hopkins Medical Letter; Health After Fifty*, vol. 8, no. 5, July 1996, pages 1-2, BB106.

[2] *The Johns Hopkins White Paper: Weight Control* 1998, Simeon Margolis, M.D., Ph.D. and Lawrence J. Cheskin, M.D., The Johns Hopkins Medical Institutions, Baltimore, Maryland, 1998, MedLetter Associates, Inc., New York, New York, page 26, BB389.

[3] National Center for Health Statistics via Associated Press; "New Health Guidelines Carry Some Weight," Lauran Neergaard, *Seattle Post-Intelligencer*, June 5, 1998, page A3, BB445C.

[4] "How's Your Weight?" *Nutrition Action Health Letter*, vol. 24, no. 10, December 1997, page 11, BB445E.

[5] *Mayo Clinic Medical Essay,* Mayo Foundation for Education and Research, Rochester, Minnesota, 1994, page 4, BB445D.

[6] *Fat Free, Flavor Full*, Gabe Mirkin, M.D., Little, Brown & Company, New York, New York, 1995, page 31, BB388.

[7] *Strong Women Stay Slim,* Miriam E. Nelson, Ph. D., with Sarah Wernick, Ph.D., Bannon Books, New York, New York, 1998, page 4, BB431.

[8] "Master the Slender Life," *Prevention Magazine,* June 1997, page 115, BB447.

[9] *Biomarkers,* William Evans, Ph.D., and Irwin H. Rosenberg, M.D., with Jacqueline Thompson, Fireside (Simon & Schuster), New York, New York, 1991, page 191, BB75.

[10] *Classics of Organizational Behavior,* Walter E. Natemeyer, editor, Moore Publishing Company, Oak Park, Illinois, 1978, page 40, TWF40, BB394.

[11]"From Eating to Pets, Statistical Abstract Has Facts on U.S. Life," Randolph Schmid, Associated Press, *Seattle Post-Intelligencer,* December 5, 1997, page A30, BB345.

[12]"Weight After 50," Michael Fumento, *Modern Maturity,* vol. 41W, no. 3, May-June 1998, page 35, BB401.

[13]*Ibid.,* page 38, BB401.

[14]*Swim with the Sharks Without Being Eaten Alive*, Harvey Mackay, Ivy Books (Valentine), 1988, page 267

[15]"Be Your Own Best Friend," *Total Health,* vol. 20, no. 1, January/ February 1998, page 34, BB472.

[16]"Men and Machines," Dr. Robert H. Guest, California American University, vol. 4, no. 38, July 1979, page 12.

[17]*Fart Proudly*, Carl Japikse, Enthea Press, Canal Winchester, Ohio, 1990, page 60, #121.

[18]"Weight Control," Simeon Margolis, M.D., Ph.D., and Lawrence J. Cheskin, M.D., The *Johns Hopkins White Papers*, The Johns Hopkins Medical Institutions, Baltimore, Maryland, 1997, page 39, BB471.

[19]"Long Term Knowledge," *Time* Magazine, January 7, 1991, page B3, BBA257.

[20]KCPQ, Fox Network, Channel 13, November 1, 1998, 49ers versus Green Bay Packers, 2 PM; "Old Geezers Pump Life Into Pro Game," Norman Chad, *Seattle Post-Intelligencer*, October 23, 1998, E5, BB437.

[21]"Vital Signs," *Seattle Times*, June 27, 1999, page 24, BB476.

[22]*Management & Machiavelli,* Antony Jay, page 28, #11.

[23]Harvard School of Public Health study, *Healthline*, July, 2000, vol. 20, no. 7, page 1, BB500.

[24]"Moving Vigorously Away from Heart Disease—and Cancer," Karl Krucoff, *The Washington Post*, in *the Seattle Times*, July 1, 2000, Page M3, BB501.

[25]*The Anti Diet Book*, Jack L. Groppel, Ph.D., Sport Science, Inc., Orlando, Florida, 1997, pages 64-65, BB395.

[26]Svenhard's® cinnamon roll, 2 oz. total weight, 290 calories, 150 calories from fat, Oakland, California, August 1999, BB475.

[27]*The Serotonin Solution,* Judith J. Wurtman, Ph.D., and Susan Suffes, Fawcett Columbine, New York, New York, 1996, page 3, BB121.

[28]"Big Gains in Weight Loss," *Prevention*'s Fight Fat 1997, Mark Bricklin and Gale Maleskey, Rodale Press, Emmaus, Pennsylvania, 1997, page 222, BB210.

[29]Wurtman, op. cit., page 50, BB121.

[30]*National Weight Loss Registry.*

[31]*The Fountain of Age*, Betty Friedan, Simon & Schuster, New York, New York, 1993, page 261, #123.

[32]"Exercise: The Fountain of Youth," *The Anti-Aging and Longevity Newsletter*, in *Total Health* Magazine, vol. 18, no. 6, page 51, BB441.

[33]"Test Your Fitness," *Corporate Fitness Programs, Inc.*, June 1987, page 3, BB348; "Three Fitness Tests," Joe Kita, *Men's Health*, October, 1996, page 110, BB347.

[34]Kita, op. cit., BB347.

[35]*The 120 Year Diet*, Roy L. Walford, M.D., Simon & Schuster, New York, New York, 1986, page 45, BB166.

[36]"Exercise Prescription for Maintaining Weight Loss," *The New England Journal of Medicine Health News*, October 7, 1997, vol. 3, no. 13, page 6, BB367.

[37]*Fit Over Forty*, James M. Rippe, M.D., William Morrow Co., New York, New York, 1996, page 239, BB283.

[38]*Exercise: A Guide From the National Institute on Aging*, Bethesda, Maryland, 1998, page 23, BB448.

[39]Ibid., BB448.

[40]"By the Way, Doctor …," *Harvard Health Letter,* vol. 24, no. 5, March 1999, page 7, BB477.

THE POWERHOUSE APPLE

Eat just one fresh apple and you get more antioxidant than you'd get from 1,500 mg of vitamin C. A Recent article in *Nature* "confirms that eating fresh fruits and vegetables is the best way to reap antioxidant benefits."[1] Your best bet is to follow the NeoCuisine™ food pyramid.

---

[1]"Remedies," *The Johns Hopkins Medical Letter Health After 50, vol. 12, no. 11, January 2001, page 8, BB523.*

NeoCuisine™ COOKBOOK

NeoCuisine™ is based on four critical principles:

- Amplifiers
- Osmazome Principle™
- Flavor force
- Sweet-sharp counterpoint

You already know a lot about amplifiers. You have been cooking NeoCuisine™ some time now. Calorie-frugal recipes with amplifiers results in 20 calories or less per ounce. This is the all-star amplifier list. Using these amplifiers as the base for a recipe makes it calorie-frugal, exactly what you want.

- All fruits, especially:
  - apples
  - peaches
  - grapefruits
  - kiwi
  - berries
- Whole grains, especially:
  - all oats
  - polenta (corn grits/meal)
  - bulgar wheat

- All green vegetables:
  - broccoli
  - beans
  - etc.

- potato
- squash
- mushrooms
- cauliflower
- no-fat cottage cheese
- no-fat yogurt
- silken low-fat tofu

Amplifiers make an excellent side dish when eating a more calorie concentrated food such as eye of the round steak. The caloric density of the steak (at 50 calories an ounce) can be offset by the inclusion of tasty amplifiers which average the meal to 20 calories an ounce or less. For example, microwaved fresh frozen green beans seasoned with Molly McButter® and "I Can't Believe It's Not Butter,®" ground pepper and a dash of powdered garlic go well. NeoCuisine™ flavored polentas are always a delicious side dish. A baked potato saturated with beef stock topped with scallion, "I Can't Believe It's Not Butter®", a dash of garlic and a grind of fresh pepper is delicious. Salads (BIG) augmented with no-fat cheese or chopped fruit or whole beans and tossed with a no-fat salad dressing (there are many now coming to market) is an excellent amplifier.

Now you are well familiar with the Osmazome Principle™. Using meat stocks and bases provide vertical flavor depth for all NeoCuisine™ recipes. Remember to buy only the highest quality meat bases, those that list meat or meat essence among the first three ingredients. Remember that meat bases replace all salt in NeoCuisine™ recipes. Hint: If you are in a real bind, replace meat bases with soy sauce. Although you will not achieve precisely the same effect, soy sauce in a recipe mimics meat flavor, hence its inclusion in most Asian recipes. Then again, why substitute when you can have real meat flavor with a quality meat base?

A flavor force is achieved with NeoCuisine's™ liberal use of herbs, spices and chilies. Of necessity, the seasoning recommendations given in the recipes are conservative. You are encouraged, therefore, to add more in accordance with your taste preferences. Entreés should be snappy, particularly given that taste perception wanes as we age. This is easily compensated by adding more seasoning. You can't go wrong by replacing black pepper with chilies of all kinds. Of course you know about jalapeños but there are many beyond that for your experimentation. Certainly go to an Asian market and buy several

of its many seasoning pastes and sauces. These keep refrigerated through perpetuity and add bursting flavor for your NeoCuisine™ recipes. Ask a clerk to help you. Remember, herbs, spices and sauces have few, if any, calories. Their addition just makes things taste better.

One of the essential aspects of NeoCuisine™ is its assiduous attention to sweet-sharp counterpoint. The best-tasting food always allows in some way (no matter how subtle) for this all-important principle. Physiology of the pallet demands that it be sweet-sharp satisfied. This is why you will almost invariably find an acid (sharp) and a sweetener in all NeoCuisine™ recipes. A good example is the Ham 'n Clam Chowder. Without the lemon and aspartame, it comes off as flat. If you buy a no-cal salad dressing, you find the addition of aspartame takes off the vinegar edge and smooths the flavor profile. The vast majority of foods can be markedly improved by the addition of acid and sweetener. Think of sweet-sharp counterpoint in exactly the same way you use salt and pepper.

With the exception of celebration days, most of your current books are obsolete. Take heart. With adjustment, many of your favorite recipes can be converted to 20 calories an ounce or less. Follow these steps:

1 Replace red proteins with white.

2 Replace salt with meat bases.

3 Always use stock instead of water. "Sauté" with stocks.

4 Sauté dry. It works beautifully if you use a good non-stick pan. Add stock if you wish.

5 Have the amplifier of choice as a side to reduce the overall calorie to weight ratio.

6 Remove all fat ingredients, e.g. butter, margarine, fatted cheese, etc. Replace with nonfat products, e.g. nonfat cheese (or simply leave out).

7 Apply the flavor force and sweet-sharp counter-point principles.

272

NeoCuisine™

BAKERS

BLACK BEAN CHILI BAKER

BLACK BEANS ARE THE MOST FLAVORSOME OF THE LEGUMES.
THE BLACK BEAN CHILI BAKER
PROVES THE POINT.

CALORIES: 542
NET WEIGHT: 25 OUNCES
PREP TIME: 5 MINUTES
COOK TIME: 13 MINUTES
CALORIE-TO-WEIGHT RATIO: 21 CALORIES PER OUNCE

- Half Taos Chili recipe (see page 296)
- 1/2 to 1 cup beef broth, fat skimmed
- Hot baked potato(es) totaling 16 ounces

- 1/4 cup fat-free cheddar, shredded
- 2 Tablespoons onions, chopped

Microwaving: Wash potato(es), put in a microwavable container, e.g. lidded glass, and microwave for 8 to 10 minutes, turning once. Conventional oven: Wash potato(es) and bake in oven at 400° for about 45 minutes. Check with fork.

Heat Taos Chili. Pour beef broth over fork-mashed potatoes. Potatoes should be saturated. Add chili. Garnish with cheddar and onion.

CHILI VERDE FRIJOLES NEGRO POTATA

MILD GREEN ANAHEIM (CALIFORNIA) CHILIES ADD INTEREST TO THIS BLACK BEAN-STUFFED POTATO. MORE
CHILI POWDER INCREASES THE FLAVOR INTENSITY IF YOU WISH.

CALORIES: 496
NET WEIGHT: 27 OUNCES
PREP TIME: 15 MINUTES
COOK TIME: 25 MINUTES
CALORIE-TO-WEIGHT RATIO: 18 CALORIES PER OUNCE

- Cold baked potato(es) totaling 16 ounces
- 1/2 cup mild, canned chopped green chilies
- 1/4 teaspoon garlic powder
- 1/2 to 1 teaspoon chili powder (be brave)
- 1 teaspoon quality chicken base
- 1/2 teaspoon dried commercial Italian herb seasoning

- 1/4 cup chicken broth, fat skimmed
- 1/2 cup black beans, drained
- 1/2 cup fresh salsa (mild, medium or hot to taste; find in deli case)
- 2 slices no-fat Swiss cheese singles

Microwaving: Microwave in the morning. Wash potato(es), put in a microwavable container, e.g. lidded glass, and microwave for 8 to 10 minutes, turning once. Let sit in the microwave until you're ready to use in the evening. Conventional oven: For potato skins that give more toothsome, crispy gratification, bake conventionally. In the morning, wash potato(es) and bake in oven at 500° for 10 to 15 minutes. Turn off and let potato(es) sit in the oven until ready to use in the evening.

Cut potato(es) in half. Scoop out the meat and mash. Reserve shells.

Add green chilies, garlic powder, chili powder, chicken base, Italian herb seasoning and chicken broth to mashed potato meat and mix.

Add black beans and mix gently.

Fill potato shells with mixture and top each half with Swiss cheese and salsa. Place on nonstick cookie sheet and bake at 400° for 15 minutes.

FESTIVAL SPUD

THIS ENTREÉ'S NAME DERIVES FROM ITS COLORFUL APPEARANCE
AND THAT IT PUFFS SLIGHTLY DURING BAKING, MIMICKING A SOUFFLÉ. IMPORTED REGGIANO
PARMESAN MAKES THIS RECIPE PARTICULARLY TASTY.

CALORIES: 484
NET WEIGHT: 26.5 OUNCES
PREP TIME: 15 MINUTES
COOK TIME: 25 MINUTES
CALORIE-TO-WEIGHT RATIO: 19 CALORIES PER OUNCE

- Cold baked potatoes totaling 16 ounces
- 2 cups frozen vegetables of choice, thawed and chopped
- 1 Tablespoon prepared roasted red bell pepper, diced
- 12 teaspoons quality chicken base
- 1/4 cup quality grated Parmesan cheese, e.g. Reggiano
- 1/4 teaspoon garlic powder
- 1/2 cup chicken broth, fat skimmed

Microwaving: Microwave in the morning. Wash potato(es), put in a microwavable container, e.g. lidded glass, and microwave for 8 to 10 minutes, turning once. Let sit in the microwave until you're ready to use in the evening. Conventional oven: For potato skins that give more toothsome, crispy gratification, bake conventionally. In the morning, wash potato(es) and bake in oven at 500° for 10 to 15 minutes. Turn off and let potato(es) sit in the oven until ready to use in the evening.

Cut potato(es) in half. Scoop out the meat and mash. Reserve shells. Mix all ingredients except potato shells. Add pepper (1/8 teaspoon) to taste.

Fill potato shells with mixture, place on nonstick cookie sheet and bake at 400° for 20 minutes or until browned lightly.

FRENCH ONION AU GRATIN

WITHOUT A SCINTILLA OF FAT, THIS MARVELOUS RECIPE USES
CARAMEL-ONION MASTERPIECE.

CALORIES: 518
NET WEIGHT: 27 OUNCES
PREP TIME: 25 MINUTES
COOK TIME: 20 MINUTES
CALORIE-TO-WEIGHT RATIO: 18.5 CALORIES PER OUNCE

- Cold baked potato(es) totaling 16 ounces
- 1 cup fresh mushrooms, sliced
- 8 ounces zucchini, shredded
- 1 recipe Caramel-Onion Masterpiece (see page 345)
- 1 teaspoon quality beef base
- 2 Tablespoons prepared roasted red bell peppers, chopped
- 1/4 cup nonfat sour cream

Microwaving: Microwave in the morning. Wash potato(es), put in a microwavable container, e.g. lidded glass, and microwave for 8 to 10 minutes, turning once. Let sit in the microwave until you're ready to use in the evening. Conventional oven: For potato skins that give more toothsome, crispy gratification, bake conventionally. In the morning, wash potato(es) and bake in oven at 500° for 10 to 15 minutes. Turn off and let potato(es) sit in the oven until ready to use in the evening.

Cut potato(es) in half. Scoop out the meat and mash. Reserve shells.

Microwave mushrooms and zucchini in a microwavable container, e.g. lidded glass, for 2 to 3 minutes. Drain the excess liquid. Mix Caramel-Onion Masterpiece, mushrooms, zucchini, beef base and red bell peppers.

Add mixture to potato(es). Fill potato shells with mixture. Place on nonstick cookie sheet and bake at 400° for 15 to 20 minutes. Top with sour cream.

JERK BBQ SPUDS

CARIBBEAN COOKS INVENTED JERKING. THE NAME DERIVES FROM THE LUSTY USE OF HEADY SPICES AND PARTICULAR COOKING TECHNIQUE. USING OPEN FLAME, THE CALYPSO COOK JERKS FOOD FROM THE FIRE AT ITS PRECISE MOMENT OF PERFECTION. OUR COOKERY IS CONVENTIONAL BUT THE FLAVORS ARE REAL. ADD RED CHILI PEPPER FLAKES TO THE BBQ SAUCE IF YOU LIKE HEAT.

CALORIES: 594
NET WEIGHT: 28 OUNCES
PREP TIME: 10 MINUTES
COOK TIME: 7 MINUTES
CALORIE-TO-WEIGHT RATIO: 21 CALORIES PER OUNCE

- 4 ounces chicken breast, boned and skinned, cut into 1/4" ribbons
- 1 Tablespoon soy sauce
- 1 Teaspoon ground allspice
- 1/4 teaspoon garlic powder and black pepper

- Hot baked potato(es) totaling 16 ounces
- 1/3 to 1/2 cup chicken broth, fat skimmed
- 1/2 cup BBQ sauce (see page 344)
- Lemon Yogurt Fruit Slaw (see page 350)

Microwaving: Wash potato(es), put in a microwavable container, e.g. lidded glass, and microwave for 8 to 10 minutes, turning once. Conventional oven: Wash potato(es) and bake in oven at 400° for about 45 minutes. Check with fork.

Combine chicken, soy sauce, allspice garlic powder and pepper (1/8 teaspoon) to taste in a Ziplock® bag and refrigerate.

Discard marinade. Reserve chicken. In a small nonstick skillet brown chicken over high heat. Remove chicken. Add 1/3 to 1/2 cup chicken broth to deglaze pan.

Fork mashed potato(es) to fill the plate. Pour chicken broth over. Potato(es) should be saturated. Top with chicken and BBQ sauce. Serve lemon slaw on the side. Enjoy the rest of the yogurt later in the evening or the next day.

MODENA PATATA

FIND A QUALITY ITALIAN-STYLE FROZEN VEGETABLE MIX TYPICALLY INCLUDING SWEET RED BELL PEPPERS, MUSHROOMS AND ZUCCHINI. YOU'LL BE SURPRISED HOW WELL THIS PAIRS WITH A POTATO AMPLIFIER. THE MODENA PATATA STOOD OUT IN OUR FLAVOR TESTS.

CALORIES: 580
NET WEIGHT: 27 OUNCES
PREP TIME: 20 MINUTES
COOK TIME: 25 MINUTES
CALORIE-TO-WEIGHT RATIO: 21 CALORIES PER OUNCE

- Cold baked potato(es) totaling 16 ounces
- 1/4 cup onions, chopped
- 1 teaspoon quality chicken base
- 1 teaspoon dried basil
- 1/4 teaspoon garlic powder
- 1/4 cup quality grated Parmesan cheese, e.g. Reggiano

- 10 to 11 ounces frozen Italian mixed vegetables, thawed and diced
- 1 teaspoon fresh lemon juice
- 1/3 to 1/2 cup chicken broth, fat skimmed
- 1 heaping Tablespoon nonfat sour cream

Microwaving: Microwave in the morning. Wash potato(es), put in a microwavable container, e.g. lidded glass, and microwave for 8 to 10 minutes, turning once. Let stand in microwave until you're to use it in the evening. Conventional oven: For potato skins that give more toothsome, crispy gratification, bake conventionally. In the morning, wash potato(es) and bake in oven at 500° for 10 to 15 minutes. Turn off and let potato(es) sit in the oven until ready to use in the evening.

Cut potato(es) in half. Scoop out the meat and mash. Reserve shells. Meanwhile, microwave onions until soft, about 1 to 1-1/2 minutes.

Add onions, chicken base, basil, garlic powder and Parmesan to mashed potato meat and mix. Add pepper (1/8 teaspoon) to taste, then add vegetables and lemon juice. Add chicken broth. Careful—too little and mixture will be dry.

Fill potato shells with mixture, place on nonstick cookie sheet and bake at 400° for 15 minutes. Top each potato half with sour cream.

PALERMO POTATO

THIS IS AN EXCELLENT EXAMPLE OF THE OSMAZOME PRINCIPLE™ DELIVERING DEEP VERTICAL FLAVOR TO AN ALL-VEGETABLE ENTREÉ. THE SICILIAN GUSTO IS HERE.

CALORIES: 513
NET WEIGHT: 25 OUNCES
PREP TIME: 20 MINUTES
COOK TIME: 25 MINUTES
CALORIE-TO-WEIGHT RATIO: 20 CALORIES PER OUNCE

- Cold baked potatoes totaling 16 ounces
- 1/4 cup zucchini, diced
- 1/4 cup red bell pepper, diced
- 1/2 cup onions, diced
- 1 cup fresh mushrooms, sliced
- 1/2 teaspoon dried commercial Italian herb seasoning
- 1 teaspoon quality chicken base
- 1/4 cup quality grated Parmesan, e.g. Reggiano
- 2 Tablespoons black olives, sliced
- 1/4 to 1/3 cup chicken broth, fat skimmed
- 1/4 cup NeoCuisine™ Red (see page 347)

Microwaving: Microwave in the morning. Wash potato(es), put in a microwavable container, e.g. lidded glass, and microwave for 8 to 10 minutes, turning once. Let sit in the microwave until you're ready to use in the evening. Conventional oven: For potato skins that give more toothsome, crispy gratification, bake conventionally. In the morning, wash potato(es) and bake in oven at 500° for 10 to 15 minutes. Turn off and let potato(es) sit in the oven until ready to use in the evening.

Cut potato(es) in half. Scoop out the meat and mash. Reserve shells.

Microwave zucchini, red bell pepper, onion, mushrooms and Italian herb seasoning for 2 minutes. Add chicken base, Parmesan and olives to vegetables, mix and add to mashed potatoes. Add chicken broth. Careful—too little and mixture will be dry. Put mashed potato/vegetable mixture into shell. Top each potato with NeoCuisine™ Red.

Place on nonstick cookie sheet and bake at 400° for 15 minutes.

SALSA BEEF PATATA

POTATOES ARE INDIGENOUS TO THE AMERICAS AND APROPOS TO MEXICAN COOKERY. WE'VE ADDED THE CLASSIC PEASANT FLAVORS OF SONORA FOR A HEARTY, FILLING DISH.

CALORIES: 527
NET WEIGHT: 25 OUNCES
PREP TIME: 15 MINUTES
COOK TIME: 20 MINUTES
CALORIE-TO-WEIGHT RATIO: 21 CALORIES PER OUNCE

- Cold baked potato(es) totaling 16 ounces
- 3/4 cup onion, chopped
- 1/4 teaspoon garlic powder
- 1 teaspoon chili powder
- 1 teaspoon quality beef base
- 1/3 cup beef broth, fat skimmed
- 1/2 cup drained pinto beans
- 1/2 cup fresh salsa (mild, medium or hot to taste; find in deli section)
- 2 slices no-fat American cheese singles

Microwaving: Microwave in the morning. Wash potato(es), put in a microwavable container, e.g. lidded glass, and microwave for 8 to 10 minutes, turning once. Let sit in the microwave until you're ready to use in the evening. Con ventional oven: For potato skins that give more toothsome, crispy gratification, bake conventionally. In the morning, wash potato(es) and bake in oven at 500° for 10 to 15 minutes. Turn off and let potatoes sit in the oven until ready to use in the evening.

Cut potatoes in half. Scoop out the meat and mash. Reserve shells. Microwave onions until soft, about 1-1/2 minutes. Add onions, garlic powder, chili powder, beef base and beef broth to mashed potato. Mix. Add beans. Mix gently.

Fill potato shells with mixture and top each half with salsa then American cheese. Place on nonstick cookie sheet and bake at 400° for 15 minutes.

CELEBRATION DINNERS

BOILED BOSTON LOBSTER
with MUSHROOM PILAF and BROCCOLI ALA SUISSE

THIS MEAL REQUIRES A FEW MORE STEPS BUT IT'S
A CELEBRATORY SUNDAY DINNER SO TAKE YOUR TIME.

CALORIES: 508
NET WEIGHT: 25 OUNCES
PREP TIME:15 MINUTES
COOK TIME:12 MINUTES
CALORIE-TO-WEIGHT RATIO: 20 CALORIES PER OUNCE

LOBSTER

- 2-1/2 to 3 pounds live lobster or 10 to 12 ounces of lobster tails. Approximately 20% of a lobster is edible meat.
- 1 Tablespoon salt
- 1/2 teaspoon pepper
- 1 bay leaf
- 2 Tablespoons sugar
- 1 lemon

MUSHROOM PILAF

- 2 cups fresh mushrooms, sliced
- 1/4 cup chicken broth, fat skimmed
- 1 Tablespoon red wine vinegar
- 1/2 cup instant rice, uncooked
- 1/2 cup (+) chicken stock, fat skimmed
- 1 Tablespoon Miracle Chop (see page 346)

BROCCOLI

- 8 ounces fresh broccoli, cut in spears
- 1/4 lemon wedge
- "I Can't Believe It's Not Butter"® spray
- 1 Tablespoon quality grated Parmesan, e.g. Reggiano

For Live Lobster:

Fill a large pot with enough water to cover lobster. Add salt, pepper, bay leaf and sugar. Cut one lemon in half, squeeze the juice into the pot and toss in the two halves. Bring to a rapid boil. Plunge the lobster head first into the boiling water. Cover, return to boiling, reduce heat and simmer 12 to 15 minutes.

For Lobster Tails:

Drizzle juice of half a lemon over tail(s). Season with 1/4 teaspoon salt and 1/8 teaspoon pepper. Bake in oven at 400° for 10 to 15 minutes until done (white and firm).

> While cooking lobster, gather remaining ingredients and prepare the rice and then the broccoli.

Mushroom Pilaf:

Put mushrooms, chicken stock and red wine vinegar in a nonstick skillet. Cook covered over medium heat until all liquid is absorbed, about 6 to 8 minutes. Meanwhile, cook rice according to package directions using chicken stock for liquid. Do not add salt or butter. Combine rice, mushrooms and Miracle Chop

Broccoli ala Swisse:

Six minutes before lobster is done, prepare broccoli.
Microwave broccoli for 5 minutes in a microwavable container, e.g. lidded glass. Drizzle with lemon to taste. Spray 10 to 12 times with "I Can't Believe It's Not Butter"® spray. Salt and pepper to taste. Top with Parmesan cheese.

To remove meat from whole lobster (this will be fun):

Separate the tail from the body by simply twisting it off. Hold the tail, flat side up, extended lengthwise in both hands and squeeze between thumbs and fingers until bottom, flat shell cracks.

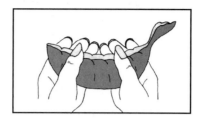

Turn lobster tail 90° and, using thumbs and fingers, pull skeleton apart in an outward motion. The skeleton will split.

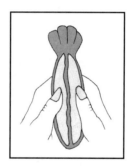

Twist claws off. Discard body. Crack the claws with a hammer, meat mallet or the handle of a heavy knife. Small cracks are okay as shell comes apart without much difficulty. (Double bag shells to prevent odor until trash pickup.)

The fun of lobster is the mess.
Cover up. Lobster squirts.

CELEBRATION BURGER
w/JO-JO FRIES and SLAW

THIS CELEBRATION DINNER INCLUDES A DOWNRIGHT SCRUMPTIOUS THICK (4") BURGER, A BIG STACK OF FRIES WITH PLENTY OF KETCHUP AND A GENEROUS PORTION OF SLAW. IT'S A GREAT CELEBRATION. A SIMILAR McDONALD'S® MEAL HAS TWICE THE CALORIES, TEN TIMES THE FAT AND 40% LESS QUANTITY BY WEIGHT.

CALORIES: 575
NET WEIGHT: 28 OUNCES
PREP TIME: 20 to 25 MINUTES
COOK TIME: 5 to 7 MINUTES
CALORIE-TO-WEIGHT RATIO: 20 CALORIES PER OUNCE

- 4 ounces 1% fat very lean ground turkey breast
- 2 ounces (1/2 cup) fresh mushrooms, finely chopped
- 1 teaspoon quality beef base
- 1 Tablespoon fat-free mayonnaise
- 1 recipe Sugar-Free Ketchup (see page 343)
- 1 teaspoon yellow mustard
- 2 Tablespoons dill pickle, finely chopped
- 1 packet aspartame

- 1 hamburger bun ("light" or reduced calorie if you can find it)
- Lettuce
- 1 tomato slice
- 1 red onion slice
- 1 recipe Fruit Slaw (see page 350)
- 1 recipe Roasted Flavor Fries (see page 354) Use option 1.

Mix turkey, mushrooms and beef base and form into a patty to fit the bun. Salt (1/4 teaspoon) and pepper (1/8 teaspoon) to taste. Cook patty in a nonstick skillet over medium-high heat until browned and cooked through, about 5 to 7 minutes.

Meanwhile, make hamburger sauce by combining mayonnaise, 1 Tablespoon Sugar-Free Ketchup, mustard, dill pickle and aspartame.

Toast the bun in the skillet and spread sauce on the toasted bun. Add the turkey patty, lettuce, tomato and red onion. Plate slaw and serve with Roasted Flavor Fries. Use the remaining ketchup for dipping.

MUSHROOM BORDELAISE FILET MIGNON w/GARLIC POTATO CAKE AND VEGETABLE DU CHEF (YOU)

THIS CELEBRATION DINNER TAKES SOME FIDDLING BUT THE RESULTS ARE WELL WORTH THE EFFORT. TAKE YOUR TIME AND ENJOY THE PROCESS.

CALORIES: 525
NET WEIGHT: 41 OUNCES
PREP TIME / COOK TIME: 30 to 35 MINUTES
CALORIE-TO-WEIGHT RATIO: 20 CALORIES PER OUNCE

- One 14.5-ounce can beef broth, fat skimmed
- 1/4 cup red wine [FYI: All the alcohol boils out.]
- 2 cups fresh mushrooms, sliced
- 6 ounces hash browns, shredded, fat-free
- 5 ounces filet mignon, fat trimmed
- 1/2 Tablespoon Miracle Chop (see page 345)
- 1 teaspoon red wine vinegar

- 1/4 teaspoon dried thyme
- 1/4 teaspoon garlic powder
- 1 teaspoon cornstarch mixed with 1 teaspoon water
- 10 to 16 ounces fresh asparagus or vegetable of choice
- 1 medium tomato, sliced
- 1/2 teaspoon balsamic vinegar
- 1/4 teaspoon Miracle Chop (see page 346)

In a small saucepan combine beef broth, red wine and mushrooms. Bring to a boil and cook over high heat until fluid reduces by 90%. Reduction takes 20 to 25 minutes so don't stand over it. Meanwhile, microwave hash browns in a microwavable container, e.g. lidded glass, 6 to 7 minutes until softened. While microwaving hash browns, preheat oven to 150°.

Cook steak in a small nonstick skillet over highest heat until dark crust forms on both sides. It will smoke but that's okay. Remove filet one degree before desired doneness (if you want medium rare, remove at rare). Test for doneness by making small slits in meat with a knife. Keep steak warm in oven while preparing the rest of the meal. Steak will cook slightly while in the oven. Reserve skillet for potato patty.

Combine 1/2 Tablespoon Miracle Chop, red wine vinegar and pepper (1/8 teaspoon) to taste. Mix and add hash browns. Form into one 3" to 4" patty. In the same skillet used for the filet, cook potato patty over medium-high heat until browned and crusty on both sides. Keep an eye on the mushroom sauce.

Stir mushroom sauce occasionally during the last 5 minutes. Add thyme, garlic powder, pepper (1/8 teaspoon) to taste and the cornstarch and water mix at the last two minutes of cooking. When sauce is done set aside.

Meanwhile, trim asparagus; cut off ends, leaving about 5 to 6 inches. If fresh asparagus is not available use frozen string beans (frozen asparagus is stringy and of poor flavor). Microwave asparagus or the beans in a microwavable container, e.g. lidded glass, for 6 to 8 minutes. Spray (even though it doesn't need it) with "I Can't Believe It's Not Butter."®

On a serving plate, place filet on potato patty. Place asparagus alongside. Top the filet with the mushroom sauce. Put sliced tomatoes on the plate and sprinkle with balsamic vinegar then top with 1/4 teaspoon Miracle Chop. Serve.

PAELLA CAMERONES

NOT EXACTLY A CLASSICAL PAELLA BUT RATHER A HUGE, DELICIOUS BOWL OF HEARTY
AND THICK SHRIMP RAGU. A REAL TREAT PERFUMED WITH SAFFRON.

CALORIES: 541
NET WEIGHT: 41 OUNCES
PREP TIME: 35 MINUTES
COOK TIME: 30 MINUTES
CALORIE-TO-WEIGHT RATIO: 13 CALORIES PER OUNCE

- 10 large uncooked shrimp
- 1 medium zucchini, shredded
- 1 stalk celery cut into 1/4" thick pieces
- 1/2 cup green bell pepper, chopped
- Saffron to taste (start with a pinch)
- One 14.5-ounce can Mexican recipe stewed tomatoes, undrained
- 1/4 cup uncooked instant rice

- 1 teaspoon chili powder
- 1 teaspoon anchovie paste
- 1/2 cup frozen corn
- 1/2 teaspoon salt
- 2 Tablespoons sliced olives
- 1 packet aspartame

In a medium saucepan, combine shrimp with 2 cups water. Bring to a boil and cook 4 minutes. Remove shrimp, reserving liquid. Shell and devein shrimp. Return shells to cooking liquid and boil uncovered until reduced by half, 10 to 15 minutes.

Meanwhile, microwave zucchini, celery and green pepper in a microwavable container, e.g. lidded glass, for 3 minutes.

Remove shells from cooking liquid. Add zucchini, saffron, celery green peppers, stewed tomatoes, rice, chili powder, anchovie paste, corn and salt. Cook on medium heat 3 to 5 minutes.

Add olives, shrimp and aspartame. Serve.

PAGO PAGO PINEAPPLE PORK

SOUTH SEAS-INSPIRED, THIS MELANGE OF FLAVORS IS AN EMINENT CELEBRATORY DINNER. THE SOUTH SEA ISLANDS ARE A WORLD CROSSROADS MAKING ITS COOKERY OUTSTANDING WORLD FLAVOR FUSION.

CALORIES: 568
NET WEIGHT: 29 OUNCES
PREP TIME: 15 MINUTES
COOK TIME: 20 MINUTES
CALORIE-TO-WEIGHT RATIO: 20 CALORIES PER OUNCE

- 8 ounces pork tenderloin, trimmed of fat
- 5 ounces whole baby carrots
- 12 ounces fresh broccoli, cut into spears
- 1/4 cup water chestnuts, drained
- 1 teaspoon red bell pepper, chopped
- 1/2 can (8-ounce can) crushed pineapple packed in its own juice, squeezed of liquid
- 1 Tablespoon scallions, green parts only, chopped
- Pinch red pepper flakes or a dash red pepper sauce
- 2 Tablespoons rice vinegar
- 1 packet aspartame
- 1/2 teaspoon sesame seeds
- 1 recipe Teriyaki Dressing (see page 307)✶

Rub pork liberally (don't be stingy) with salt, pepper and garlic powder. Sear pork in a nonstick skillet over high heat. Reduce heat to medium-low and continue cooking 15 to 20 minutes or until cooked medium-well.✶✶

Meanwhile microwave carrots and broccoli in a microwavable container, e.g. lidded glass, for 8 to 10 minutes. Add water chestnuts the last minute microwaving.

Microwave red bell pepper in a microwavable container, e.g. lidded glass, for 30 seconds. Combine bell pepper, pineapple, scallions, red pepper flakes, vinegar, aspartame and 2 pinches of salt. Microwave 15 to 30 seconds until warm.

Slice tenderloin in 1/4" slices. Arrange in an overlapping circle. Place pineapple salsa in center. Add vegetables to plate and sprinkle with sesame seeds. Pour Teriyaki Dressing over pork and vegetables. Serve.

✶You may wish to thicken the Teriyaki Dressing. If you do, reserve aspartame. Mix 1 Tablespoon cold dressing and 1 teaspoon cornstarch. Reserve. Bring dressing to boil. Add cornstarch/teriyaki mix. Stir. Turn off the heat. Let stand a couple minutes. Then add aspartame.
✶✶Medium-well with a trace of pink brings pork to an internal temperature of about 150°+, the U.S. Federal standard.

PRIMAVERA ALFREDO

AT LESS THAN 1/2 THE CALORIES OF THE FATTY ORIGINAL, THIS DELICIOUS DISH IS A PRAISEWORTHY SUBSTITUTE.

CALORIES: 541
NET WEIGHT: 29 OUNCES
PREP TIME: 20 MINUTES
COOK TIME: 20 MINUTES
CALORIE-TO-WEIGHT RATIO: 20 CALORIES PER OUNCE

- 2 ounces uncooked whole wheat spaghetti
- One 16-ounce bag frozen stir-fry or mixed vegetables of choice(not to exceed 150 calories)
- 2 cups fresh mushrooms, sliced
- 3 dry (no oil) sun-dried tomato halves
- 1 teaspoon balsamic vinegar

- 1/2 cup (4 ounces) fat-free cream cheese
- 1/4 cup nonfat milk
- 1/2 teaspoon garlic powder
- 2 teaspoons quality chicken base
- Scant 1/4 teaspoon pepper

Cook spaghetti according to package directions.

Microwave vegetables 6 to 10 minutes in a microwavable container, e.g. lidded glass, turning once. For the last 3 minutes of microwaving: Add mushrooms and sun-dried tomatoes mixed with balsamic vinegar and 1 Tablespoon water in a separate lidded glass container. Microwave both containers.

Make Alfredo sauce by combining cream cheese and milk in a small saucepan over low heat until cream cheese is soft. Add garlic powder, chicken base and pepper. Whisk until smooth. Chop sun-dried tomatoes.

Combine spaghetti, vegetables and sauce. Toss. Squeeze lemon over the top for added zing.

PUYALLUP FAIR BURGER AND FRISCO FRIES

IN THE NORTHWEST, THE MOST RENOWNED HAMBURGER OF ALL IS FEATURED AT THE FAMOUS PUYALLUP FAIR. SLATHERED WITH BRAISED ONIONS, OUR VERSION HAS FEW CALORIES BUT TASTES BETTER THAN THE ORIGINAL.

CALORIES: 624
NET WEIGHT: 28 OUNCES
PREP TIME: 30 MINUTES
COOK TIME: 10 MINUTES
CALORIE-TO-WEIGHT RATIO: 16 CALORIES PER OUNCE

- 4 ounces 1% very lean ground turkey breast
- 1 hamburger bun ("light" or reduced-calorie if you can find it)
- 1/4 cup rice vinegar (plain)
- 1/4 teaspoon salt
- 1/2 packet aspartame
- 1/2 teaspoon dried commercial Italian herb seasoning
- 1/8 teaspoon garlic powder

- 6 ounces prepared salad greens
- 1 recipe Sugar-Free Ketchup (see page 343)
- 1 teaspoon mustard
- 1 recipe Caramel Onion Masterpiece (see page 345)
- 1 recipe Roasted Flavored Fries (see page 354 use Frisco Fry Style, option 1, omit Parmesan)

Form turkey into a patty to fit the bun. Cook patty in a nonstick skillet over medium-high heat until browned and cooked through, about 5 to 7 minutes. Toast the bun in the skillet.

Meanwhile, combine rice vinegar, salt, aspartame, Italian herb seasoning, garlic powder and a pinch of pepper. Toss lettuce with dressing.

Spread one half of the bun with ketchup and mustard. Add turkey patty then Caramel Onion Masterpiece. Top with bun. Serve with fries and side salad. Use remaining ketchup for fry dipping.

Serve burger with fries and salad.

SHRIMP OR CRAB LOUIE

THE SUGAR/FAT-FREE NeoCuisine™ THOUSAND ISLAND DRESSING MIMICS ITS FATTY SIBLING SO WELL, YOU'LL LIKELY NOT NOTICE ANY DIFFERENCE. BUT THE NeoCuisine™ VERSION HAS ONLY 15% THE CALORIES. WOW.

CALORIES: 483
NET WEIGHT: 36 OUNCES
PREP TIME: 25 MINUTES
CALORIE-TO-WEIGHT RATIO: 13 CALORIES PER OUNCE

- One 12- to 16-ounce prepared salad greens, chopped to a maximum of 1" x 1" by you
- 1 NeoCuisine™ recipe Thousand Island Dressing (see page 306)
- 6 ounces fresh frozen crab or shrimp meat (cooked chicken breast julienned can be substituted)

- 1 medium tomato, cut into 4 wedge
- 2 hard-boiled eggs, whites only, quartered
- 2 Tablespoons olives, sliced
- 8 canned/fresh cooked and chilled asparagus (3 ounces)

Put lettuce on a serving plate. Place dressing over top of lettuce. Arrange crab, tomatoes, eggs and olives. Top with asparagus spears. Serve with 1/4 lemon wedge.

TENDERLOIN WITH CARLENZOLI STEAKS, DEMI-GLAZED EGGPLANT TOURNEDOS and TEPIDINDA

WHO SAYS YOU CAN'T HAVE OPULENT DINING WHILE FAT-STRIPPING? HERE IS A SUPERB PRESENTATION OF MOUTH WATERING TENDERLOIN STEAK MARRIED WITH THE DEEP, RICH FLAVOR OF CARLENZOLI PORTABELLO MUSHROOM STEAKS AND EGGPLANT TOURNEDOS. COMPLETING THE MEAL IS A DELIGHTFUL BUTTERNUT SQUASH TEPIDINDA. IT'S HARD TO IMAGINE ENJOYING A LOVELY DINNER LIKE THIS, GUILT-FREE.

CALORIES: 515
NET WEIGHT: 36 OUNCES
PREP TIME: 20 MINUTES
COOK TIME: 30 MINUTES
CALORIE-TO-WEIGHT RATIO: 18 CALORIES PER OUNCE

- 1 recipe Carlenzoli Steaks and Eggplant Tournados (see page 351)
- 1-1/4 to 1-1/2 pounds gross weight (1 pound butternut squash or 2 cups after cooking), cut in half lengthwise
- 1/2 teaspoon quality chicken base
- 1/8 teaspoon dried thyme
- Pinch to taste nutmeg
- 1/8 to 1/4 cup chicken broth, fat skimmed
- 5 ounces filet mignon (buy 6 to 7 ounces. Trim fat for net 5 oz.)

Start Carlenzoli steaks and Eggplant Tournedos.

Cover squash halves for the tepidinda with plastic wrap and microwave 10 to 15 minutes. Keep working on Carlenzoli steaks and eggplant tournedos while squash is microwaving.

Tepidinda assembly: When squash is cooked, remove seeds. Scoop out meat and measure 2 brimming cups. Mash. Add chicken base, thyme, nutmeg and pepper (1/8 teaspoon) to taste. Add chicken stock as necessary to smooth.

Sprinkle filet with salt, pepper and garlic powder. Put filet in nonstick skillet. Cook slowly, 5 to 10 minutes per side, to desired doneness.

Serve filet atop mushrooms. Top squash and filet with reduced glaze. Plate eggplant and top with tomato and Miracle Chop relish.

WINE-GARLIC SCAMPI SAUTÉ

THE TADICH GRILL IN SAN FRANCISCO SERVES ITS VERSION AT TWICE THE CALORIES. THE TRUTH BE TOLD, THIS NeoCuisine™ RENDITION HAS AN ENTIRELY RESPECTABLE FLAVOR PROFILE SO CLOSE TO THE CLASSIC SAUTÉ YOU DON'T MISS A THING.

CALORIES: 550
NET WEIGHT: 28 OUNCES
PREP TIME: 20 MINUTES
COOK TIME: 30 MINUTES
CALORIE-TO-WEIGHT RATIO: 13 CALORIES PER OUNCE

- 13 ounces medium to large raw unpeeled shrimp (9 ounces peeled)
- 1/4 teaspoon garlic powder
- 1/4 teaspoon dried thyme
- 1/2 cup chicken broth, fat skimmed
- 1/2 cup instant rice, uncooked
- 10 to 12 ounces frozen petite whole greens
- 1/2 cup drinking quality white wine [FYI: All the alcohol boils out.]
- 1 Tablespoon red bell pepper, chopped
- 1 Tablespoon scallions, green parts only, chopped
- "I Can't Believe It's Not Butter"®
- 2 sprays olive oil (aerosol can)

Remove shells from shrimp. Devein and butterfly (use a knife to split down the outside curve 1/2 to 3/4 of the way through the shrimp). Remove black line (vein). Season with salt (1/4 teaspoon) and pepper (1/8 teaspoon) to taste. Sprinkle with the garlic powder and thyme.

Bring chicken broth to a boil. Stir in rice, cover, remove from heat and let sit 5+ minutes or until liquid is absorbed. Microwave green beans in a microwavable container, e.g. lidded glass, for 5 to 7 minutes. Drain.

Meanwhile, in a nonstick skillet, bring wine to a full boil. Reduce by 50% to 75% (this takes 5 to 10 minutes). Add shrimp and cook over medium heat until shrimp turns pink and flesh is white, 1 to 2 minutes. Meanwhile, add red bell pepper and scallions to rice.

Plate shrimp, rice and green beans. Season green beans with salt, pepper and "I Can't Believe It's Not Butter"® spray. Spray shrimp with olive oil.

CHILIS

A GOOD BOWL OF RED

SIMPLE TO MAKE AND DANDY FLAVOR. EGGPLANT ADDS, SURPRISINGLY, TO THE CHILI FLAVOR. YOU'LL LIKE THIS BOWL OF RED.

CALORIES: 650
NET WEIGHT: 33.5 OUNCES
PREP TIME: 20 MINUTES
COOK TIME: 30 MINUTES
CALORIE-TO-WEIGHT RATIO: 19 CALORIES PER OUNCE

- 1/2 onion, chopped
- 1 clove garlic, minced
- 1/2 green bell pepper, chopped
- One 14.5-ounce can diced tomatoes, undrained, chopped

- 1 teaspoon quality beef base
- 1/2 teaspoon chili powder
- 1/2 medium eggplant, unpeeled, cut into 1/2" cubes
- One 15.5-ounce can kidney beans, undrained

Combine all ingredients in a pot. Bring to a boil and simmer for 25 to 30 minutes or until the eggplant is soft. Serve.

ANYLOAF AND LENTIL CHILI

A GOOD USE FOR LEFTOVER MEATLOAF, A NICE VARIANT FOR THIS CHILI. IF YOU'RE UNFAMILIAR WITH LENTILS, THIS IS A LIKABLE INTRODUCTION. YOU WILL ENJOY THEM. GUARANTEED.

CALORIES: 532
NET WEIGHT: 32 OUNCES
PREP TIME: 5 to 10 MINUTES
COOK TIME: 30 MINUTES
CALORIE-TO-WEIGHT RATIO: 17 CALORIES PER OUNCE

- 1/2 cup (4 ounces) lentils
- 1 medium carrot, diced
- 1/4 cup red bell pepper, diced
- 14.5-ounce can chicken broth, fat skimmed
- 1 Tablespoon tomato paste

- 1/2 cup frozen corn
- 1/4 teaspoon cumin
- 1/8 teaspoon pepper
- 1 serving (1/2 loaf) leftover NeoCuisine™ meatloaf
- 1/2 cup frozen peas, defrosted

Combine lentils, carrot, red bell pepper and chicken broth in a saucepan. Cover and cook over medium heat for 25 minutes, stirring occasionally. Add tomato paste, corn, cumin, pepper and meatloaf and cook for 5 minutes.

Meanwhile, slice off meatloaf and dry fry in a nonstick skillet. It browns nicely. Plate. Plate chili over top of meatloaf and garnish with peas. Serve.

BBQ TURKEY AND PINTOS WITH LEMON SLAW

ONE OF THE SPICIEST NeoCuisine™ ENTREÉS—AS YOU DICTATE. MAKE THE BBQ SAUCE HOT WITH TABASCO® OR RED CHILI FLAKES. REMEMBER THAT HOT AND SPICY ARE GENUINE HUNGER SQUELCHERS.

CALORIES: 541
NET WEIGHT: 22 OUNCES
PREP TIME: 10 MINUTES
COOK TIME: 3 MINUTES
CALORIE-TO-WEIGHT RATIO: 24 CALORIES PER OUNCE

- One 15.5-ounce can pinto beans (or beans of choice), drained
- 4 ounces sliced fat-free smoked turkey, e.g. Louis Rich®

- 1/2 recipe BBQ Sauce (see page 344)
- 1 recipe yogurt Fruit Slaw (see page 350) using lemon yogurt

Microwave beans on a serving plate for 2 minutes. Add sliced turkey and BBQ Sauce and microwave 1 minute. Garnish with cilantro if desired. Serve with Fruit Slaw on the side.

LONE STAR BAKED BEANS

BAKED BEANS DONE RIGHT WITH NICE, SMOKY CANADIAN BACON. THE SURPRISE INGREDIENT IS THE ADDITION OF TART, GREEN APPLE LIKE GRANNY SMITH. ADD MORE ARDOR BY MIXING IN FRESH, CHOPPED JALAPEÑOS.

CALORIES: 604
NET WEIGHT: 34.5 OUNCES
PREP TIME: 25 MINUTES
CALORIE-TO-WEIGHT RATIO: 17 CALORIES PER OUNCE

- 1/2 red bell pepper, diced
- 1/2 green bell pepper, diced
- 1/4 onion, diced
- One 15-ounce can white beans, including liquid
- One 14.5-ounce can diced tomato, drained
- 2 ounces Canadian bacon, diced

- 1 teaspoon quality beef base
- 1 teaspoon Worcestershire sauce
- 1/4 teaspoon dry mustard
- 1 tart green apple, such as Granny Smith or pippin, peeled and diced
- 1 recipe Sugar-Free Ketchup (see page 343)

Microwave bell peppers and onions in a microwavable container, e.g. lidded glass, for 3 to 4 minutes.

Meanwhile, combine the rest of the ingredients in a saucepan. Add peppers and onions and cook uncovered over medium heat for 15 to 20 minutes.

TAOS CHILI

YOU CAN GO TO A CHILI COOK-OFF WITH THIS RECIPE. THICK AND RICH, YOU CAN MAKE IT GUSTO MUY BY ADDING MORE CHILI POWDER.

CALORIES: 512 W/OUT CHEESE,
552 W/CHEESE
NET WEIGHT: 24 OUNCES
COOK TIME: 25 MINUTES
PREP TIME: 20 to 25 MINUTES
CALORIE-TO-WEIGHT RATIO: 14 CALORIES PER OUNCE

- 1 cup zucchini, shredded
- 2 cups carrots, unpeeled and shredded
- 1/2 cup onions, chopped
- 2 teaspoons quality beef base
- 2 teaspoons chili powder
- 2 teaspoons cumin

- One 14.5-ounce can black beans, undrained
- One 14.5-ounce can diced tomatoes, drained
- 1/2 packet aspartame
- Garnishes: 1/4 cup chopped onions, 2 Tablespoons chopped scallions, green parts only, and 1/4 cup Kraft® fat-free shredded cheddar cheese (optional)

In a large glass bowl, combine zucchini, carrots, onions, beef base, chili powder and cumin. Cover with a plate and microwave for 10 minutes.

Stir in beans and tomatoes, transfer to a pot and cook on stove over medium heat for 15 minutes.

Remove from heat, add aspartame. Garnish with chopped onions and scallions and, if desired, shredded cheese.

CHOWDERS

APPLE TARRAGON CHICKEN CHOWDER

IF YOU KNOW FLAVOR COMBINATIONS, THIS JUST SOUNDS RIGHT, DOESN'T IT? SINCE TARRAGON IS SUCH AN INTERESTING FLAVOR, START LIGHT BECAUSE A LITTLE GOES A LONG WAY. ADD MORE AS YOUR PREFERENCE DICTATES.

CALORIES: 547
NET WEIGHT: 34 OUNCES
PREP TIME: 20 MINUTES
COOK TIME: 10 to 15 MINUTES
CALORIE-TO-WEIGHT RATIO: 16 CALORIES PER OUNCE

- 4 ounces chicken breast, boned, skinned and diced
- 1/2 medium carrot, unpeeled, shredded
- 1 large stalk celery, diced small
- 1/2 cup onion, chopped
- 1 red apple, unpeeled, diced small
- 1 cup skim milk
- 12-13 ounces extra-firm ultra-low fat tofu
- 2 teaspoons quality chicken base
- 1/2 teaspoon garlic powder
- Generous pinch dried tarragon leaves
- Pinch dried rosemary leaves, crumbled
- 1 Tablespoon prepared roasted red bell pepper, chopped

Microwave chicken, carrot, celery, onion and apple in a microwavable container, e.g. lidded glass, about 8 to 10 minutes.

Meanwhile combine milk, tofu, chicken base, garlic powder, tarragon, rosemary and 1/8 teaspoon pepper in blender and purée until blended and smooth, about 15 to 30 seconds. Put in saucepan. Add chicken and roasted red bell pepper. Bring to a simmer. Add vegetables. Cook 1 to 2 minutes. Serve.

ASPARAGUS CREAM SHRIMP BISQUE

A NICE, LIGHT FANCY DINNER WITH MANY OF THE INGREDIENTS YOU LOVE: ASPARAGUS, REGGIANO PARMESAN, SHRIMP AND ENOUGH GARLIC.

CALORIES: 537
NET WEIGHT: 35 OUNCES
PREP TIME: 10 MINUTES
CALORIE-TO-WEIGHT RATIO: 11 CALORIES PER OUNCE

- 4 ounces potatoes, 1" to 2" dice
- 10 ounces frozen asparagus, thawed and drained
- One 8- to 10-ounce can/jar clam juice
- 1 teaspoon quality chicken base
- 1/8 teaspoon pepper
- 1/2 teaspoon commercial Italian herb seasoning
- 1/4 teaspoon garlic powder

- 2 Tablespoons quality grated Parmesan, e.g. Reggiano
- 1 cup nonfat cottage cheese
- 6 ounces cooked shrimp (use small but not inferior quality salad or "popcorn" shrimp)
- 1/2 packet aspartame
- 1 teaspoon Worcestershire

Microwave in separate microwavable containers, e.g. lidded glass: potatoes for 4 minutes; asparagus for 3 minutes. Cut tips off asparagus and reserve.

Add all ingredients except asparagus tips, shrimp, aspartame and Worcestershire to blender and pureé for 1 minute until smooth. Pour into a serving bowl.

Add shrimp, asparagus tips and microwave for 3 minutes. Add aspartame and serve.

BUTTERNUT CHICKEN BISQUE

I DON'T LIKE SQUASH—AT LEAST THAT'S WHAT MY TAPES AS AN EIGHT-YEAR-OLD TOLD ME. TIME FOR AN UPDATE. SQUASH, DONE RIGHT AS THIS RECIPE DOES, IS DELECTABLE.

CALORIES: 519
NET WEIGHT: 40 OUNCES
PREP TIME: 20 MINUTES
CALORIE-TO-WEIGHT RATIO: 13 CALORIES PER OUNCE

- 1 pound butternut squash, raw, peeled and cubed
- 4 ounces chicken breast, boned and skinned
- 10 ounces frozen cauliflower, thawed and roughly chopped
- One 14.5-ounce can chicken broth, fat skimmed
- 1 teaspoon quality chicken base

- 1/2 teaspoon curry powder
- 1/4 teaspoon garlic powder
- 1/2 cup frozen peas, thawed
- 2 teaspoons fresh lemon juice

Microwave in microwavable container, e.g. lidded glass: squash for 5 minutes. Add chicken and cauliflower. Microwave 2 more minutes.

Combine broth, chicken base, curry powder and garlic powder in a blender. Add squash and pureé 1 minute until smooth. Put in a serving bowl. Microwave if too cool for serving.

Dice chicken and add it to soup along with cauliflower, peas, lemon juice and pepper (1/8 teaspoon) to taste. Serve.

COUNTRY CHICKEN BROCCOLI TUCKER

THICK AND TASTY SOUP THAT'S EASY TO MAKE. WHO SAID A CREAM SOUP HAS TO BE HIGH CAL?

CALORIES: 488
NET WEIGHT: 33 OUNCES
PREP TIME: 15 MINUTES
COOK TIME: 13 MINUTES
CALORIE-TO-WEIGHT RATIO: 14 CALORIES PER OUNCE

- 4 ounces potatoes, diced 1" to 2"
- 8 to 10 ounces fresh or frozen broccoli, thawed
- 3 ounces chicken breast, boned and skinned, diced 1/4" to 1/2"
- 2 cups fresh mushrooms, sliced
- One 14.5-ounce can chicken broth, fat skimmed

- 1 teaspoon quality chicken base
- 1/2 teaspoon commercial Italian herb seasoning
- 1 teaspoon Miracle Chop (see page 346)
- 2 Tablespoons Parmesan cheese, e.g. Reggiano
- 1/2 cup fat-free sour cream

In a microwavable container, e.g. lidded glass, microwave potatoes and broccoli for 5 to 8 minutes or until cooked. In a microwavable container, e.g. lidded glass, microwave chicken breast and mushrooms for 4 to 5 minutes.

While microwaving above, put chicken broth, chicken base, Italian herb seasoning, Miracle Chop, Parmesan cheese and pepper (1/8 teaspoon) to taste in a blender, then add cooked potatoes and broccoli. Blend until smooth, a minimum of 1 minute. Pour into a serving bowl.

Add chicken and mushrooms to soup. Microwave for 3 minutes. Add sour cream and serve.

FRESH TOMATO SCAMPI GAZPACHO

MADE WITH FRESH TOMATO PUREÉ, THIS GAZPACHO HAS RINGING CLEAR FLAVOR. THERE IS A FAIR AMOUNT OF CHOPPING AND DICING BUT THE RESULTS ARE WORTH THE EXTRA TIME. LOTS OF SHRIMP. PLENTY TO EAT. DELICIOUS AND REFRESHING.

CALORIES: 450
NET WEIGHT: 40 OUNCES
PREP TIME: 20 MINUTES
CALORIE-TO-WEIGHT RATIO: 11 CALORIES PER OUNCE

- 3 large or 5 to 6 medium tomatoes
- 1/2 large cucumber, peeled and diced small
- 1/2 green pepper, diced small
- 1/2 large onion, diced small
- 1 teaspoon dried cilantro
- 2 Tablespoons chopped black olives

- 1/2 teaspoon garlic powder
- 1/4 cup fresh lemon juice
- 1/2 teaspoon salt
- 8 ounces shrimp, cooked
- 1 teaspoon anchovie paste
- 1/2 packet aspartame

Grate the tomatoes: Begin by cutting a thin slice off the bottom of the tomato. Place a flat or four-sided grater over a bowl and grate the cut end of the tomato against the course side. Discard the skin.

Add the rest of the ingredients and pepper (1/8 teaspoon) to taste to the tomato. Refrigerate 1 hour. Serve.

HAM N' CLAM CHOWDER

IT'S HARD TO IMAGINE THAT A GOOD-TASTING CHOWDER CAN BE PART OF A DIET, BUT THIS IS AN ESPE-CIALLY GOOD ONE. HERE'S WHERE YOU PUT YOUR QUALITY CLAM BASE TO EXCELLENT USE.

CALORIES: 585
NET WEIGHT: 36 OUNCES
PREP TIME: 15 to 20 MINUTES
COOK TIME: 5 to 8 MINUTES
CALORIE-TO-WEIGHT RATIO: 16 CALORIES PER OUNCE

- 8 ounces potatoes, peeled, diced 1/2"
- 1/2 cup celery, diced small
- 1/2 cup onion, chopped
- 1 cup skim milk
- 12-13 ounces extra-firm ultra-low-fat tofu
- 2 teaspoons quality clam base
- 1/4 teaspoon thyme

- 1/4 teaspoon garlic powder
- 2 Tablespoons prepared roasted red bell peppers, fine diced
- 1 ounce Canadian bacon, fine diced
- Two 6.5-ounce cans minced clams, drained
- 2 teaspoons fresh lemon juice
- Sprinkle (1/4 packet) aspartame

Microwave potatoes, celery and onion in a microwavable container, e.g. lidded glass, 8 to 10 minutes.

Meanwhile, combine milk, tofu, clam base, thyme, garlic powder and 1/8 teaspoon pepper in blender and pureé until well blended and smooth, about 1 minute. Put in saucepan. Add red bell pepper, Canadian bacon, clams and lemon juice. Bring to a simmer. Add microwaved vegetables. Cook 1 to 2 minutes. Add aspartame. Serve.

PUMPKIN CURRIED CREAM CHOWDER

EXCEPTIONALLY QUICK, TASTY AND SATISFYING.

CALORIES: 440
NET WEIGHT: 48 OUNCES
PREP TIME: 5 MINUTES
COOK TIME: 12 to 16 MINUTES
CALORIE-TO-WEIGHT RATIO: 9 CALORIES PER OUNCE

- 1/2 pound fresh mushrooms, sliced
- 1/2 cup onions, chopped
- 1 Tablespoon curry powder
- 1 can (15 ounces) pumpkin
- 1 can (14.5 ounces) chicken broth, fat skimmed

- 1/8 teaspoon nutmeg
- 1 teaspoon quality chicken base
- 1 cup fat-free evaporated milk
- 1 Tablespoon fresh lemon juice
- 1 packet aspartame

Combine mushrooms, onions and curry powder in a microwavable container, e.g. lidded glass, and microwave 8 to 10 minutes.

Meanwhile, combine pumpkin, chicken broth, nutmeg and chicken base. Add mushroom/onion mix, Add evaporated milk, lemon juice and aspartame Microwave until hot, 4 to 6 minutes. Serve.

RED SNAPPER CIOPPINO

YOU'LL THINK YOU'RE AT FISHERMAN'S WHARF IN SAN FRANCISCO.
IF YOU'RE INCLINED, ADD A PINCH OF SAFFRON OR MORE.

CALORIES: 522
NET WEIGHT: 32 OUNCES
PREP TIME: 20 MINUTES
COOK TIME: 20 MINUTES
CALORIE-TO-WEIGHT RATIO: 16 CALORIES PER OUNCE

- 1 can clam juice (8 to 12 ounces)
- 1/2 medium onion, chopped
- 6 ounces potatoes, 1/2" to 1" dice
- 1 stalk celery, cut in 1" chunks
- 1/2 cup Chardonnay wine [FYI: All the alcohol boils out.]
- 1 cup NeoCuisine™ Red (see page 347)

- 1 zucchini, cut in 1/2" coins
- 1 teaspoon anchovie paste
- 8 ounces red snapper (or other white fish), cut in 1/2" to 1" chunks
- 1 heaping teaspoon dried parsley flakes
- 1/2 teaspoon lemon zest

In medium saucepan combine clam juice, onion, potato, celery and wine. Bring to full boil and cook uncovered for 10 to 15 minutes.

Reduce heat and add NeoCuisine™ Red, zucchini and anchovie paste. Add salt (1/4 teaspoon) and pepper (1/8 teaspoon) to taste. Add fish, parsley and lemon zest. Simmer 2 to 4 minutes or until fish flakes.

Remove from heat, add parsley and lemon zest. Serve.

SHRIMP AND CRAB CHOWDER

HOW COULD THIS NOT BE GOOD?

CALORIES: 606
NET WEIGHT: 33 OUNCES
PREP TIME: 15 to 20 MINUTES
COOK TIME: 7 to 10 MINUTES
CALORIE-TO-WEIGHT RATIO: 18 CALORIES PER OUNCE

- 8 ounces potatoes, diced 1/2"
- 1/2 cup onions, chopped
- 1/2 cup fat-free milk
- 12-13 ounces extra-firm ultra-low-fat tofu
- 1 teaspoon quality lobster or clam base
- 1/4 teaspoon garlic powder
- 1/4 teaspoon dried thyme

- 1/4 cup frozen peas
- 1/4 cup frozen corn
- 4 ounces medium cooked shrimp
- 4 ounces crab meat
- 2 Tablespoons white drinking quality wine [FYI: All the alcohol boils out.]
- 2 teaspoons lemon juice

Microwave potatoes and onions in a microwavable container, e.g. lidded glass, for 5 to 7 minutes.

Meanwhile, combine milk, tofu, lobster base, garlic powder, thyme and 1/8 teaspoon pepper in blender and pureé until well blended and smooth—about 30 to 45 seconds. Put in a a saucepan.

Add peas, corn, shrimp, crab, white wine and lemon juice. Bring to a simmer. Add microwaved vegetables and cook 1 to 2 minutes. Serve.

ZUPPA BOLOGNAISE

THIS IS REMINISCENT OF AN EXCELLENT MINESTRONE BUT WITHOUT THE OVERCOOKED, MUSHY PASTA. SO THICK, YOU ALMOST NEED A FORK.

CALORIES: 553
NET WEIGHT: 37 OUNCES
PREP TIME: 15 MINUTES
COOK TIME: 15 to 20 MINUTES
CALORIE-TO-WEIGHT RATIO: 15 CALORIES PER OUNCE

- 8 ounces potatoes, diced large
- 3 large or 4 medium (9 to 10 ounces) carrots, cut in coins
- One 14.5-ounce can beef broth, fat skimmed
- 2 teaspoons quality beef base
- 1/4 teaspoon dried oregano

- 1/2 can (6-ounce can) tomato paste
- 2 cups mushrooms, sliced
- 1/2 cup canned white beans, undrained
- 1 Tablespoon Miracle Chop (see page 346)
- 2 Tablespoons quality grated Parmesan cheese, e.g. Reggiano

Microwave potatoes and carrots in a microwavable container, e.g. lidded glass, for 8 to 10 minutes. Meanwhile, combine the beef broth, beef base, oregano, pepper (1/8 teaspoon) to taste and tomato paste in a blender.

When potatoes and carrots are cooked, add half of them to the blender with other ingredients and blend until smooth, about 1 minute.

Microwave mushrooms in a microwavable container, e.g. lidded glass, for 2 minutes. Drain. Pour blended ingredients into a serving bowl, add the remainder of potatoes, carrots, beans and mushrooms. Microwave for 3 minutes, stir in Miracle Chop and top with Parmesan. Serve with lemon wedge.

DRESSINGS

CAESAR DRESSING

THIS SALAD DRESSING HAS 25% FEWER CALORIES THAN STORE-BOUGHT FAT-FREE
CAESAR AND IN OUR OPINION IT TASTES MUCH MORE CAESAR. DO NOT CUT THE ANCHOVIE QUANTITY. YOU
NEVER TASTE IT.

CALORIES: 146
NET WEIGHT: 6 OUNCES
PREP TIME: 5 MINUTES
YIELD: 3/4 CUP
CALORIE-TO-WEIGHT RATIO: 24 CALORIES PER OUNCE

- 1/2 cup fat-free, sugar-free plain yogurt
- 1 Tablespoon anchovie paste (or 2 anchovie fillets, mashed) depending on preference
- 1 Tablespoon fresh lemon juice
- 1 Tablespoon Dijon mustard

- 1/2 teaspoon garlic powder
- 2 Tablespoons quality grated Parmesan, e.g. Reggiano
- 1/8 teaspoon black pepper
- 1/2 packet aspartame

Combine ingredients. Can be made ahead.

GILROY DRESSING

CALORIES: 66
YIELD: 1/2 CUP
PREP TIME: 5 MINUTES

- 2 Tablespoons Miracle Chop (see page 346)
- 1/2 cup fresh lemon juice
- 1 packet aspartame

- 1/2 teaspoon walnut extract
- 1 teaspoon quality chicken base

Combine ingredients and whisk until well-mixed.

INSTANT ITALIAN ZERO CALORIE DRESSING

CALORIES: 0
NET WEIGHT: 2 OUNCES
PREP TIME: 5 MINUTES
YIELD: 1/4 CUP
CALORIE-TO-WEIGHT RATIO: 0 CALORIES PER OUNCE
SHELF LIFE: 3 DAYS

- 1/4 cup rice vinegar (plain)
- 1/4 teaspoon salt
- Pinch of pepper

- 1/2 packet aspartame
- 1/2 teaspoon commercial Italian herb seasoning
- 1/8 teaspoon garlic powder

Combine ingredients.

NeoCuisine™ THOUSAND ISLAND DRESSING

CALORIES: 124
NET WEIGHT: 8 OUNCES
PREP TIME: 10 MINUTES
YIELD: 1 CUP
CALORIE-TO-WEIGHT RATIO: 14 CALORIES PER OUNCE

NeoCuisine™: 8 CALORIES PER TABLESPOON
CONVENTIONAL: 50 TO 60 CALORIES PER TABLESPOON

- 1/2 cup fat-free mayonnaise
- 1/4 cup Sugar-Free Ketchup (see page 343)
- 1/2 dill pickle, finely chopped
- 1 Tablespoon onion, minced
- 1 teaspoon Miracle Chop (see page 346)
- 1 Tablespoon distilled vinegar
- 1 Tablespoon prepared roasted red bell peppers, minced
- 1 packet aspartame
- 2 to 5 dashes Tabasco® sauce

Combine all ingredients.

NeoCuisine™ VINAIGRETTE

CALORIES: 10
NET WEIGHT: 4 OUNCES
PREP TIME: 5 MINUTES
YIELD: 1/2 CUP
CALORIE-TO-WEIGHT RATIO: 2.5 CALORIES PER OUNCE
SHELF LIFE: 3 DAYS

- 1/4 cup fat-free No-calorie vinaigrette
- 1/4 cup red wine vinegar
- 1/2 teaspoon salt
- 1/4 teaspoon pepper
- 1/4 teaspoon garlic powder
- 1 packet aspartame

Combine ingredients. Can be made a day ahead.

TERIYAKI DRESSING

CALORIES: 79
NET WEIGHT: 4 OUNCES
PREP TIME: 5 MINUTES
YIELD: SHY 1/2 CUP
CALORIE-TO-WEIGHT RATIO: 20 CALORIES PER OUNCE

- 1/4 cup low-sodium soy sauce
- 2 Tablespoons white wine vinegar
- Pinch red pepper flakes
- 1/2 teaspoon garlic powder
- 1 teaspoon dark sesame oil
- 3 packets (or 1 teaspoon) aspartame
- 1 teaspoon sesame seeds

Combine ingredients.

EGGS

CRAB AND ARTICHOKE FRITTATA

THIS LIKABLE DISH HAS A PLEASING COMPLEXITY OF FLAVORS AND NO FANCY EGG-PAN WORK REQUIRED BECAUSE THIS FRITTATA IS BAKED. THE LIST OF INGREDIENTS IS LONGER THAN USUAL BUT GOES TO-GETHER QUICKLY.

CALORIES: 551
NET WEIGHT: 29.5 OUNCES
PREP TIME: 20 MINUTES
COOK TIME: 30 MINUTES
CALORIE-TO-WEIGHT RATIO: 19 CALORIES PER OUNCE

- 4 ounces fresh frozen crab, thawed★
- 1 cup zucchini, chopped (1/2" maximum)
- 1 cup canned artichoke hearts (not marinated), rinsed, chopped (1/2" maximum)
- 1 cup fresh mushrooms, sliced
- 1/4 cup onions, chopped (1/2" maximum)
- Three 4-ounce (1-1/2 cups) containers fat-free egg substitute, e.g. EggBeaters®
- 3 Tablespoons quality grated Parmesan, e.g. Reggiano
- 1 teaspoon quality chicken base or lobster base
- 1/2 teaspoon anchovie paste
- 1/4 cup nonfat sour cream
- 1 Tablespoon Miracle Chop (see page 346)

★ If crab is unavailable, substitute fresh frozen shrimp, lobster or langostino. DO NOT use canned seafood.

Combine crab, zucchini, artichoke hearts, mushrooms, onions, fat-free egg substitute, Parmesan cheese, chicken base and anchovie paste. Add pepper (1/8 teaspoon) to taste.

Spray an 8" x 8" pan (or comparable size, e.g. 6" x 10") with nonstick vegetable spray and add omelet mixture. Bake at 400° for 30 minutes. Frittata is done when sides are firm but center is still soft.

Combine sour cream, Miracle Chop and salt and pepper to taste. Microwave for 30 seconds. Plate omelet and top with sour cream mixture.

MARIA DeLOURDES CHILI RELLENOS

MY FIRST RESTAURANT WAS MEXICAN AND MARIA DeLOURDES MECEDO-OROSCO WAS MY MEXICAN FOOD TUTOR IN THE FINE ART OF SONORAN COOKERY. THIS DISH IS ABOUT 1/3 THE CALORIES OF THE TRADI-TIONAL FRIED VERSION FOR A GREAT CALORIE-TO-WEIGHT RATIO OF 15 CALORIES PER OUNCE.

CALORIES: 525
NET WEIGHT: 36 OUNCES
PREP TIME: 10 MINUTES
COOK TIME: 35 MINUTES
CALORIE-TO-WEIGHT RATIO: 15 CALORIES PER OUNCE

- Three 4-ounce (1-1/2 cups) containers fat-free egg substitute, e.g. EggBeaters®
- 1 cup onion, chopped
- 1 cup mild green chilies, e.g. Ortega® brand, diced (one 7-ounce can or two 4-ounce cans)
- 1 cup tomatoes, diced
- 1/2 cup nonfat cheddar cheese, shredded, e.g. Kraft®
- 1/2 Tablespoon chili powder
- 1/2 teaspoon garlic powder
- 1 teaspoon quality beef base
- 1 cup salsa

Combine all ingredients except salsa.

Spray an 8" x 8" pan (or comparable size, e.g. 6" x 10") with nonstick vegetable spray and add mixture. Bake at 400° for 35 minutes. Rellenos are done when the sides are firm but the center is still soft.

Garnish with salsa.

THE POGETTI SAN FRANCISCO FRITTATA

A FINES HERBES OMELET INSPIRED BY SAN FRANCISCO MASTER CHEF JOHN POGETTI
WHO PUT ON HIS RESTAURANT MENUS "IF YOU DON'T SEE IT ON MY MENU, ASK FOR IT AND I'LL COOK IT."

CALORIES: 574
NET WEIGHT: 35 OUNCES
PREP TIME: 10 MINUTES
COOK TIME: 35 MINUTES
CALORIE-TO-WEIGHT RATIO: 16 CALORIES PER OUNCE

- 1 cup zucchini, chopped (1/2" maximum)
- 1 cup onions, chopped (1/2" maximum)
- 1 cup fresh mushrooms, sliced
- 1 cup chopped canned tomato, drained
- Three 4-ounce (1-1/2 cups) containers fat-free egg substitute, e.g. EggBeaters®
- 1/4 cup quality grated Parmesan cheese, e.g. Reggiano
- 1 teaspoon dried Italian herb seasoning
- 2 teaspoons quality chicken base
- 1 cup fat-free (lite) pasta (marinara) sauce

Combine all ingredients except pasta sauce.

Spray an 8" x 8" pan (or comparable size, e.g. 6" x 10") with nonstick vegetable spray and add frittata mixture. Bake at 400° for 35 minutes. Frittata is done when the sides are firm but the center is still soft.

Heat the pasta sauce and serve over frittata, garnishing with a teaspoon of parsley flakes.

SHRIMP QUICHE

A HIGH-PROTEIN, TASTY QUICHE. QUICHE IS ANOTHER SCARE WORD BUT, YES, MEN EAT IT. ENJOY THIS LARGE SERVING, SURE TO QUIET YOUR PRIMEVAL RAGING APPETITE.

CALORIES: 604
NET WEIGHT: 32 OUNCES
PREP TIME: 15 to 20 MINUTES
COOK TIME: 40 to 45 MINUTES
CALORIE-TO-WEIGHT RATIO: 18.8 CALORIES PER OUNCE

- 2 cups fresh mushrooms, sliced
- 10-ounce package frozen chopped spinach, thawed and lightly squeezed (should be "juicy")
- 1 cup bay shrimp
- 1/4 cup quality grated Parmesan cheese, e.g. Reggiano
- Three 4-ounce (1-1/2 cups) containers fat-free egg substitute, e.g. EggBeaters®

- 1 cup tomato, diced
- 1 teaspoon lemon zest
- 1 generous teaspoon quality lobster base (refer to page 138 for ordering information)or 1/2 teaspoon salt
- 1/4 teaspoon pepper

Combine all ingredients. Spray pie tin with nonstick vegetable spray and add quiche mixture. Bake at 350° for 40 to 45 minutes.

LASAGNES

LASAGNE BEIJING

HERE'S WORLD FUSION COOKING AT ITS BEST. IT'S ITALIAN IN FLAVOR ALL THE WAY BUT COULDN'T BE ENJOYED WITHOUT THE MANDARIN CHINESE INVENTION OF TOFU. LOW-CALORIE TOFU REPLACES CALORIE-DENSE FATTY RICOTTA AND YOU CAN'T TELL THE DIFFERENCE.

CALORIES: 598
NET WEIGHT: 32 OUNCES
PREP TIME: 30 MINUTES
COOK TIME: 45 MINUTES
CALORIE-TO-WEIGHT RATIO: 18.6 CALORIES PER OUNCE

- 12-13 ounces extra-firm ultra-low fat tofu, drained and finely hand crumbled
- 1 teaspoon quality chicken base
- One 10-ounce package chopped spinach, thawed/drained/squeezed
- 1/4 cup scallions, finely sliced
- 1/4 teaspoon garlic powder
- 1/4 teaspoon garlic powder
- 2 recipes NeoCuisine™ Red (see page 347)
- 1/2 cup Kraft fat-free shredded cheddar cheese
- 2 sheets Ronzoni oven-ready lasagne noodles✶
- 2 Tablespoons quality grated Parmesan e.g. Reggiano

Place crumbled tofu and chicken base in medium bowl and microwave for 2 minutes. Stir in chopped spinach, scallions and garlic powder. Mix well.

Place 1/2 cup NeoCuisine™ Red in bottom of 9" loaf pan. Cover with 1/2 tofu/spinach. Top with half of cheddar cheese. Add one lasagne sheet, then the remainder of the tofu/spinach mix and cheddar cheese. Top with 2nd lasagne sheet then the rest of the NeoCuisine™ Red. Top with the Parmesan cheese.

Cover with foil and cook at 350° for 30 minutes. Remove foil and bake 15 minutes. Let set 10 to 15 minutes. Serve.

✶These have been pre-cooked which means you don't have to. Regular lasagna noodles that need to be cooked work as well, but add time.

LASAGNE FIRENZE

A MARVELOUS CHARACTERISTIC OF GOOD LASAGNA IS IT BAKES TO A MELDING OF FLAVORS FOR AN INTEGRATED WHOLE. THIS DISH TASTES UNLIKE ITS INDIVIDUAL INGREDIENTS. MORNING: THAW SPINACH.

MAKES TWO SERVINGS

CALORIES: 594
NET WEIGHT: 32 OUNCES
PREP TIME: 30 MINUTES
COOK TIME: 50 MINUTES
CALORIE-TO-WEIGHT RATIO: 18.5 CALORIES PER OUNCE

- 1 Tablespoon red wine vinegar
- 2 recipes NeoCuisine™ Red (see page 347)
- 4 medium zucchini, cut in 1/4" or less lengthwise slices
- Two 10- to 12-ounce packages frozen chopped spinach, thawed and lightly squeezed
- 2 cups fat-free ricotta cheese (or fat-free cottage cheese)
- 2 teaspoons quality chicken base
- 2 Tablespoons Miracle Chop (see page 346)
- 6 sheets Ronzoni oven-ready lasagne noodles**
- 2 Tablespoons quality grated Parmesan cheese, e.g. Reggiano

Add red wine vinegar to NeoCuisine™ Red.

Salt and pepper zucchini. Microwave in a microwavable container, e.g. lidded glass, for 8 minutes or until cooked, drain. Meanwhile, lightly squeeze spinach of excess water.

Combine spinach, ricotta cheese, chicken base and Miracle Chop.

Spray two 8" x 3" loaf pans with nonstick vegetable spray. Layer each pan equally in the following order:

1st	zucchini		5th	1/2 spinach ricotta mix
2nd	1 lasagne noodle		6th	1 lasagne noodle
3rd	1/2 spinach ricotta mix		7th	NeoCuisine™ Red
4th	1 lasagne noodle		Top	Reggiano Parmesan cheese

Cover one pan with aluminum foil and bake at 350° for 45 minutes. Freeze the second pan.

**These have been pre-cooked which means you don't have to. Regular lasagna noodles that need to be cooked work as well, but add time.

ROASTED VEGETABLE and TURKEY BREAST LASAGNE

IF YOU HAVE AN ITALIAN GRANDMA, EVEN SHE'LL LIKE THIS.

SERVES TWO

CALORIES: 482
NET WEIGHT: 32 OUNCES
PREP TIME: 30 MINUTES
COOK TIME: 45 MINUTES
CALORIE-TO-WEIGHT RATIO: 15 CALORIES PER OUNCE

- 4 medium zucchini, cut lengthwise in 1/2" slices
- 1 large eggplant, cut in 1/2" slices
- 4 ounces 1% fat very lean ground turkey
- 2 Tablespoons Miracle Chop (see page 346)
- 4 recipes NeoCuisine™ Red (see page 347)
- 2 Tablespoons red wine vinegar
- 1 cup fat-free ricotta cheese (or fat-free cottage cheese)
- 6 sheets Ronzoni oven-ready lasagne noodles*
- 2 Tablespoons quality grated Parmesan cheese, e.g. Reggiano

Broil zucchini and eggplant 3 to 5 minutes each side, or until lightly browned (watch carefully so they don't burn), turning once. Meanwhile, combine ground turkey and Miracle Chop. Combine NeoCuisine™ Red and red wine vinegar.

Spray two 8" square pans with Pam®. In each pan, layer half the ingredients in the following order:

1st	zucchini		5th	eggplant slices
2nd	1/2 cup NeoCuisine™ Red mix		6th	turkey
3rd	lasagna noodles		7th	1/2 cup NeoCuisine™ Red mix
4th	ricotta cheese		8th	1 Tablespoon Parmesan

Cover with foil and bake one lasagna at 350° for 45 minutes. Freeze one lasagna for later use.

**These have been pre-cooked which means you don't have to. Regular lasagna noodles that need to be cooked work as well, but add time.

SONORA STRATA

REPLETE WITH PICO DE GALLO, SONORA STRATA HAS THE PIZZAZ OF YOUR FAVORITE MEXICAN COMBO PLATE BUT WITH LESS THAN HALF THE CALORIES. THIS RECIPE MAKES TWO DINNERS.

CALORIES: 605
NET WEIGHT: 36 OUNCES
PREP TIME: 30 MINUTES
COOK TIME: 45 MINUTES
CALORIE-TO-WEIGHT RATIO: 17 CALORIES PER OUNCE

- 4 medium zucchini, 1/2" thick lengthwise slices
- 2 NeoCuisine™ Red recipes (see page 347) using beef base instead of chicken base
- 1 teaspoon chili powder (more if you like)
- 1 teaspoon cumin (more if you like)
- 30 to 40 (2 ounces) baked no-fat tortilla chips
- Two 6- to 8-ounce cans mild whole green chilies, drained
- 1-1/2 cups canned pinto beans, drained
- 1 cup Kraft® fat-free shredded cheddar cheese
- 1-1/2 cups fresh salsa (found in dairy case)

Microwave zucchini for 6 to 8 minutes, drain. Meanwhile, combine NeoCuisine™ Red, chili powder and cumin.

Spray two 8" square or comparable size (e.g. 6" x 10") pans with nonstick vegetable spray. Layer both pans in the following order, dividing ingredients equally between the two pans: tortilla chips, whole green chilies, pinto beans, cheese and zucchini. Cover both with foil. Bake one at 350° for 45 minutes. Freeze the other.

Meanwhile, bring salsa to room temperature. If you prefer more cilantro flavor, add 1 teaspoon dried cilantro to salsa. Split salsa, freezing one. Split NeoCuisine™ Red in half, freezing one. Microwave remaining NeoCuisine™ Red until hot, about 1 minute.

When strata is cooked, turn upside down onto a serving plate. Spoon NeoCuisine™ Red Sauce over the top of strata. Top with salsa.

NeoCuisine™ MEATLOAVES

ALL AMERICAN MEATLOAF

MAKES 2 MEATLOAF SERVINGS.

MEATLOAF, POTATOES AND KETCHUP ON A DIET? YOU CAN HAVE IT THE NeoCuisine™ WAY AT 1/3 THE CALORIES OF THE OLD FATTY ORIGINAL.

CALORIES PER SERVING: 482
NET WEIGHT PER SERVING: 36 OUNCES
PREP TIME: 15 to 20 MINUTES
COOK TIME: 45 MINUTES
CALORIE-TO-WEIGHT RATIO: 18 CALORIES PER OUNCE
(CALORIE COUNT INCLUDES BUTTON MUSHROOM GRAVY OR SUGAR-FREE KETCHUP)

- 3/4 pound (12 ounces) 1% fat very lean ground turkey
- 1 Tablespoon quality beef base
- 1 teaspoon garlic powder
- 1 teaspoon pepper
- 1 teaspoon red wine vinegar
- 1/2 cup onion, finely diced

- 18-20 ounces extra-firm, ultra-low-fat tofu (1-1/2 packages)
- 1 recipe Garlic Mashed Potatoes (see page 352)
- 1 recipe Button Mushroom Thyme Gravy: 39 calories (see page 345)
  OR
  1 recipe Sugar-Free Ketchup: 60 calories (see page 343)

Combine first six ingredients. Set aside.

Crumble tofu into blender and pureé until smooth, about 30 to 45 seconds. You will need to stop blender and stir twice or more. Add to meatloaf mix and stir well to incorporate all ingredients. Pour into 8" x 3" loaf pan. Bake at 350° for 45 minutes.

Make Garlic Mashed Potatoes and Button Mushroom Thyme Gravy.

Pour off excess juice (this is not fat) after loaf is baked. Divide loaf in half and save half for later use. Slice second half and top with Button Mushroom Gravy or Sugar-Free Ketchup. Serve mashed potatoes on the side.

NeoCuisine™ meatloaves are white proteins and are naturally light in color. Brown them if you wish with this heated dip: 1/2 cup hot broth (the same base flavor as used in the loaf) and 1 Tablespoon Kitchen Bouquet®.

¡CARAMBA! CON MOLÉ

MAKES 2 MEATLOAF SERVINGS.

THIS MEXICAN MEATLOAF (REMINISCENT OF TAMALE) IS SOMEWHAT COMPLEX BUT THE ¡SABOR! THE MOLÉ SAUCE IS QUITE GOOD AND SHOULD NOT BE SKIPPED. SINCE IT'S MILD, ADD MORE OF THOSE INGREDIENTS SUGGESTED FOR ENHANCED FLAVOR

CALORIES PER SERVING: 584
NET WEIGHT PER SERVING: 32 OUNCES
PREP TIME: 20 to 25 MINUTES
COOK TIME: 45 MINUTES

CALORIE-TO-WEIGHT RATIO: 18 CALORIES PER OUNCE
(CALORIE COUNT INCLUDES CHILI MASA AND MOLÉ.

- 3/4 pound (12 ounces) 1% fat very lean ground turkey
- 1 Tablespoon quality beef base
- 1 teaspoon garlic powder
- 1 teaspoon pepper
- 1 Tablespoon chili powder
- 1 teaspoon cumin
- 1 teaspoon red wine vinegar
- 1/2 cup onion, finely diced
- 4 to 6 ounces canned diced green chilies, drained
- 18-20 ounces (1-1/2 packages) extra-firm, ultra-low-fat tofu
- 1 recipe Molé (see page 346)

CHILI MASA
- 1-1/2 cups chicken broth, fat skimmed
- 1/4 cup polenta
- 1/4 cup Kraft® fat-free shredded cheddar cheese
- Rounded 1/4 teaspoon red pepper flakes

Combine first 9 ingredients. Set aside.

Crumble tofu into blender and pureé until smooth, about 30 to 45 seconds. You will need to stop blender and stir twice or more. Add to meatloaf mix and stir well to incorporate all ingredients.

Pour into 8" x 3" loaf pan. Bake at 350° for 45 minutes.

In a medium saucepan bring chicken broth to a boil. Stir in polenta with a wire whisk. Return to a full boil, cover, reduce heat to medium-low and cook until thickened, about 3 to 5 minutes. Remove lid and cook over low heat 20 to 25 minutes, stirring occasionally. Stir in cheddar and red pepper flakes.

Pour off excess juice (this is not fat) after loaf is baked. Divide loaf in half and reserve remainder for later use. Slice and top with Molé. Serve with Chili Masa on the side.

NeoCuisine™ meatloaves are white proteins and are naturally light in color. Brown them if you wish with this heated dip: 1/2 cup hot broth (the same base flavor as used in the loaf) and 1 Tablespoon Kitchen Bouquet®.

--- **LEFTOVERS** ---

Meatloaf has a long refrigerator life, at least one week. Reheat as an entreé. Make the Anyloaf Sandwich, page 147. Try an Anyloaf and Lentil Chili, page 294. Cut slabs and fry as the meat in a burger, a side for breakfast or as an addition to an egg scramble for a high protein breakfast. Crumble for a polenta pizza topping. Use your imagination.

317

FENNEL SAUSAGE

MAKES 2 MEATLOAF SERVINGS.

REMINISCENT OF ITALIAN FENNEL SAUSAGE WITH 1/3 THE CALORIES. OUR NeoCuisine™ VERSION HAS AUTHENTIC FLAVOR. EVEN THE LOOK IS SIMILAR AS A PORK AND VEAL FENNEL SAUSAGE LOOK-ALIKE. DRIZZLE RED SAUCE OVER TOP AND ADD A SIDE OF POLENTA TARAGNA FOR A DANDY CALABRIA STYLE DINNER.

CALORIES: 572
NET WEIGHT: 30 OUNCES
PREP TIME: 15 to 20 MINUTES
COOK TIME: 45 MINUTES
CALORIE-TO-WEIGHT RATIO: 20 CALORIES PER OUNCE
(CALORIE COUNT INCLUDES POLENTA TARAGNA NeoCuisine™ RED)

- 3/4 pound (12 ounces) 1% fat very lean ground turkey
- 1 Tablespoon quality beef base
- 1 teaspoon garlic powder
- 1/4 teaspoon red pepper flakes
- 3/4 teaspoon fennel seeds, chopped
- 3/4 teaspoon dried oregano
- 1 Teaspoon red wine vinegar
- 1/2 cup onion, finely diced
- 1 teaspoon pepper
- 18-20 ounces (1-1/2 packages) extra-firm, ultra-low-fat tofu
- 1 recipe NeoCuisine™ Red (see page 347)

POLENTA TARAGNA
- One 14-ounce can or 1-1/2 cups chicken broth, fat skimmed
- 1/4 cup polenta
- 1/4 cup Kraft® fat-free shredded cheddar cheese
- Pinch red pepper flakes

Combine first 9 ingredients. Set aside. Crumble tofu into blender and pureé until smooth, about 30 to 45 seconds. You will need to stop blender and stir twice or more. Add to meatloaf mix and stir well to incorporate all ingredients. Pour into 8" x 3" loaf pan. Bake at 350° for 45 minutes.

In a medium saucepan bring chicken broth to a boil. Stir in polenta with a whisk. Return to a full boil, cover, reduce heat to medium-low and cook until thickened, about 5 minutes. Remove lid and cook over low heat 20 to 25 minutes, stirring occasionally. Stir in cheddar and red pepper flakes when removed from stove.

Pour off excess juice (this is not fat) after loaf is baked. Divide in half and save half for later use. Slice second half and top with sauce. Serve with Polenta Taragna on the side.

318

MADRAS MEATLOAF

MAKES 2 MEATLOAF SERVINGS.

A DIFFERENT WAY TO ENJOY CURRY. THE CHUTNEY NeoCuisine™
STYLE IS ESSENTIAL.

CALORIES: 485
NET WEIGHT: 24 OUNCES
PREP TIME: 15 to 20 MINUTES
COOK TIME: 45 MINUTES
CALORIE-TO-WEIGHT RATIO: 20 CALORIES PER OUNCE

- 3/4 pound (12 ounces) 1% fat very lean ground turkey
- 1 Tablespoon quality chicken base
- 1 teaspoon garlic powder
- 1 teaspoon pepper
- 1/2 teaspoon curry powder (more for flavor)
- 1 teaspoon distilled vinegar
- 1/2 cup onion, finely diced
- 18-20 ounces (1-1/2 packages) extra-firm, ultra-low-fat tofu
- 1 recipe plum or apricot chutney (see page 344)

CURRIED ALOO
- 8 ounce baked potato
- 1/4 cup+ chicken broth, fat skimmed
- 1/4 cup fat-free plain yogurt
- 1/4 teaspoon curry powder (more for flavor)
- 1/2 teaspoon quality chicken base

Combine first 7 ingredients. Set aside.

Crumble tofu into blender and pureé until smooth, about 30 to 45 seconds. You will need to stop blender and stir twice or more. Add to meatloaf mix and stir well to incorporate all ingredients. Pour into 8" x 3" loaf pan. Bake at 350° for 45 minutes.

CURRIED ALOO: Blossom baked potato. Pour chicken broth over potato. Combine rest of ingredients and top potato.

Pour off excess juice (this is not fat) after loaf is baked. Divide loaf in half and save half for later use. Slice second half and top with chutney of choice.

SOUTHERN SMOTHERED CHICKEN LOAF
with REDEYE GRAVY and HOME FRIES

MAKES 2 MEATLOAF SERVINGS.

REDEYE GRAVY IS ALLEGED TO HAVE COME ABOUT WHEN GENERAL ANDY JACKSON WON THE BATTLE OF NEW ORLEANS. THE MORNING AFTER HIS VICTORY HE ORDERED HIS HUNGOVER COOK, WHO'D CELEBRATED ALL NIGHT, TO MAKE "A MESS O' BISCUITS AND GRAVY AS RED AS YOUR EYES."

CALORIES PER SERVING: 512
NET WEIGHT PER SERVING: 30 OUNCES
PREP TIME: 15 to 20 MINUTES
COOK TIME: 45 MINUTES
CALORIE-TO-WEIGHT RATIO: 17 CALORIES PER OUNCE
(CALORIE COUNT INCLUDES REDEYE GRAVY AND HOME FRIES.)

- 3/4 pound (12 ounces) 1% fat very lean ground turkey
- 1 Tablespoon quality chicken base
- 1 teaspoon garlic powder
- 1 teaspoon pepper
- 1 teaspoon red wine vinegar
- 1/2 cup onion, finely diced
- 1 teaspoon Bacobits®
- 18-20 ounces (1-1/2 packages) extra-firm, ultra-low-fat tofu
- 1 recipe Roasted Flavor Fries (see page 354)

REDEYE GRAVY
- 1 cup chicken broth, skimmed of fat
- 1 Tablespoon quality chicken base
- 1 Tablespoon flour
- 1 teaspoon paprika
- 1/4 teaspoon dried thyme
- Pepper to taste

Combine first 7 ingredients. Set aside. Crumble tofu into blender and pureé until smooth, about 30 to 45 seconds. You will need to stop blender and stir twice or more. Add to meatloaf mix and stir well to incorporate all ingredients.

Pour into 8" x 3" loaf pan. Bake at 350° for 45 minutes.

Prepare Flavor Fries of choice. Combine Redeye Gravy ingredients. Bring to a boil. Set aside.

Pour off excess juice (this is not fat) after loaf is baked. Divide loaf in half and save half for later use, up to a week. Slice second half and top with gravy.

BBQ BEEF LOAF

MAKES 2 MEATLOAF SERVINGS.

HERE IS A GRAND BBQ SUBSTITUTE WITHOUT THE FAT OR CANCER DANGER. IT TASTES GREAT WHICH IS IMPORTANT BECAUSE A STEADY DIET OF BBQ IS OFF LIMITS. IT'S TOO FATTY AND CARRIES CARCINOGENS IN THE FORM OF POLYCYCLIC AMINES, THE BROWN CRUST OF LONG-ROASTED MEATS. YOU'LL HARDLY MISS THOSE BABY BACK RIBS, SERIOUSLY.

CALORIES PER SERVING: 570
NET WEIGHT PER SERVING: 30 OUNCES
PREP TIME: 15 to 20 MINUTES
COOK TIME: 45 MINUTES
CALORIE-TO-WEIGHT RATIO: 20 CALORIES PER OUNCE
(CALORIE COUNT INCLUDES BBQ SAUCE AND ROASTED FLAVOR FRIES.)

- 3/4 pound (12 ounces) 1% fat very lean ground turkey
- 1 Tablespoon quality beef base
- 1 teaspoon garlic powder
- 1 teaspoon pepper
- 1 teaspoon red wine vinegar
- 1/2 cup onion, finely diced
- 1 teaspoon Bacobits®
- 18-20 ounces (1-1/2 packages) extra-firm, ultra-low-fat tofu
- 1 recipe Oven Roasted Beef Fries (see page 354)

NeoCuisine™ BBQ SAUCE
- 1 recipe Sugar-Free Ketchup (see page 343)
- 1/4 teaspoon liquid smoke
- 1/2 teaspoon chili powder
- 1/4 teaspoon dry mustard
- 1/2 teaspoon quality beef base

Combine first 7 ingredients. Set aside.

Crumble tofu into blender and pureé until smooth, about 30 to 45 seconds. You will need to stop blender and stir twice or more. Add to meatloaf mix and stir well to incorporate all ingredients. Pour into 8" x 3" loaf pan. Bake at 350° for 45 minutes.

Make Oven Roasted Beef Fries. Make BBQ Sauce by combining all ingredients.

Pour off excess juice (this is not fat) after loaf is baked. Divide loaf in half and save half for later use. Slice second half and top with BBQ Sauce. Serve with Roasted Flavor Fries.

NeoCuisine™ meatloaves are white proteins and are naturally light in color. Brown them if you wish with this heated dip: 1/2 cup hot broth (the same base flavor as used in the loaf) and 1 Tablespoon Kitchen Bouquet®.

NeoCuisine™ PIZZAS

BACON PINEAPPLE POLENTA PIZZA

PIZZA IS PRETTY MUCH A NO-NO FOR ANY DIET. YET, WITH SOME DOING, THE NeoCuisine™ RESEARCHERS EVOLVED POLENTA USING THE OSMAZOME PRINCIPLE™ THAT PRODUCES A CREDIBLE PIZZA. JUST THINK OF IT AS A SOFT, THICK CRUST PIZZA, RICH IN FLAVOR BECAUSE OF THE CHICKEN STOCK. THIS PIZZA WILL REMIND YOU OF ITS STEP-BROTHER FROM THE LOCAL PIZZA PARLOUR. ENJOY THE EXPERIENCE WITHOUT CLOGGING YOUR ARTERIES.

CALORIES: 555
NET WEIGHT: 30 OUNCES
PREP TIME: 15 MINUTES
COOK TIME: 30 + 30 MINUTES
CALORIE-TO-WEIGHT RATIO: 18.5 CALORIES PER OUNCE

- 3 cups chicken broth, fat skimmed
- 1/2 cup polenta
- 1/2 cup NeoCuisine™ Red (see page 347)
- 1/2 cup Kraft® fat-free shredded cheddar cheese
- 1/8 teaspoon red pepper flakes
- 1/2 cup crushed pineapple (in own juice), squeezed and drained
- 2 ounces fat-free Canadian bacon, diced small

In a medium saucepan bring chicken broth to a boil. Stir in polenta with a wire whisk. Return to full boil, cover, reduce heat to medium-low and cook until thickened, about 3 to 5 minutes. Remove lid and continue to cook over low heat 20 to 25 minutes, stirring occasionally.

Pour into ungreased deep dish pie plate and refrigerate 1 to 2 hours or overnight.

Put NeoCuisine™ Red on top of polenta and spread to edges. Top with cheese. Add red pepper flakes to pineapple and put on pizza. Add Canadian bacon. Bake at 350° for 1/2 hour.

322

LOMBARDY POLENTA PIZZA

HAMBURGERS ASIDE, PIZZA IS AMERICA'S FAVORITE FOOD. PIZZA IS ALSO THE PROTOTYPICAL 21ST CEN-
TURY FAT FOOD BECAUSE IT IS LOADED WITH SATURATED FAT AND HAS A CALORIE DENSITY WELL OVER 80
CALORIES AN OUNCE ... OUT OF REACH OF THE ROBUST-WHOLE MINDED. HOWEVER, AFTER TWO YEARS OF
SEARCHING AND EXPERIMENTATION HERE IS NeoCuisine's™ PIZZA SOLUTION. ENJOY. IT'S
SURPRISINGLY TASTY.

CALORIES: 474
NET WEIGHT: 33 OUNCES
PREP TIME: 15 to 20 MINUTES
COOK TIME: 30 + 30 MINUTES
CALORIE-TO-WEIGHT RATIO: 14 CALORIES PER OUNCE

- 3 cups chicken broth, fat skimmed
- 1/2 cup polenta
- 1/2 cup NeoCuisine™ Red (see page 347)
- 1/2 cup Kraft® fat-free shredded cheddar cheese

- 1/4 cup onions, chopped
- 1/2 cup fresh mushrooms, sliced
- 2 Tablespoons sliced black olives (Kalamata if possible)
- 1 Tablespoon capers (optional)

In a medium saucepan bring chicken broth to a boil. Stir in polenta with a wire whisk. Return to full boil, cover, reduce
heat to medium-low and cook until thickened, about 3 to 5 minutes. Remove lid and continue to cook over low heat 20
to 25 minutes, stirring occasionally.

Pour into ungreased deep dish pie plate and refrigerate 1 to 2 hours or overnight.

Put NeoCuisine™ Red on top of polenta and spread to edges. Top with cheese. Add onions, mushrooms, olives and
capers. Bake at 350° for 1/2 hour.

PEPPERONI PIZZA

IMAGINE AFTER HAVING STRIPPED TEN POUNDS OF FAT WITH ANOTHER TEN TO GO THAT YOU CAN ENJOY A NICE, GOOEY PEPPERONI PIZZA. THIS NeoCuisine™ MASTERPIECE INDULGES YOU WITH JUST ABOUT ALL THE FLAVOR YOU GET FROM A DOMINO'S® GUT BOMB BUT WITH 1/3 THE CALORIES.

CALORIES: 469
NET WEIGHT: 33 OUNCES
PREP TIME: 15 to 20 MINUTES
COOK TIME: 30 + 30 MINUTES
CALORIE-TO-WEIGHT RATIO: 14 CALORIES PER OUNCE

- 3 cups chicken broth, fat skimmed
- 1/2 cup polenta
- 1/2 cup NeoCuisine™ Red (see page 347)
- 1/2 cup Kraft® fat-free shredded cheddar cheese
- 1/4 cup onions, chopped
- 1/2 cup sliced mushrooms
- 1/3 green bell pepper, diced small
- 9 slices reduced-fat pepperoni, diced small

In a medium saucepan bring chicken broth to a boil. Stir in polenta with a wire whisk. Return to full boil, cover, reduce heat to medium-low and cook until thickened, about 3 to 5 minutes. Remove lid and continue to cook over low heat 20 to 25 minutes, stirring occasionally.

Pour into ungreased deep dish pie plate and refrigerate 1 to 2 hours or overnight.

Put NeoCuisine™ Red on top of polenta and spread to edges. Top with cheese. Add onion, mushrooms, green bell pepper and pepperoni. Bake at 350° for 1/2 hour.

SALADS

CHICKEN CAESAR SALAD

THIS SALAD IS A FOOLER. IF YOU DIDN'T KNOW BETTER, YOU'D THINK YOU WERE AT YOUR FAVORITE RESTAURANT.

324

CALORIES: 451
NET WEIGHT: 24 OUNCES
PREP TIME: 15 MINUTES
CALORIE-TO-WEIGHT RATIO: 19 CALORIES PER OUNCE

- 4 ounces chicken breast, boned and skinned
- One 14- to 18-ounce package cut Romaine salad
- 1 recipe Caesar Salad Dressing (see page 305)

- 4 sprays olive oil: 2 seconds total
- 1 Tablespoon quality grated Parmesan, e.g. Reggiano

Cook chicken in a nonstick skillet over medium-high heat until well browned and cooked through, about 3 to 5 minutes. Remove. Cool. Cut into 1/4" julienne strips.

Toss Romaine with Caesar Dressing and chicken. Spray with olive oil. Top with parmesan.

CHOPPED SALAD CUCINA

THE GARBANZOS AND BASIL DO TASTE TRICKS. GREAT CALORIE-TO-WEIGHT RATIO AND SPLENDID FLAVOR.

CALORIES: 459
NET WEIGHT: 36 OUNCES
PREP TIME: 15 to 20 MINUTES
CALORIE-TO-WEIGHT RATIO: 12 CALORIES PER OUNCE

- 1 recipe NeoCuisine™ Vinaigrette (see page 307)
- 2 teaspoons dried basil, rubbed between fingers to release flavors
- 1/4 cup scallions, chopped, green parts only
- 2 ounces chicken breast, boned and skinned
- 1 cup garbanzo beans, drained

- 1/2 to whole head iceberg lettuce (depending on its size and your PRA), chopped
- 1 small tomato, finely chopped
- 1/4 cup quality grated Parmesan cheese, e.g. Reggiano

Combine dressing, basil and scallions.

Brown chicken in nonstick skillet over high heat. Reduce heat and cook until done, about 1 to 2-1/2 minutes. Cool and chop into 1/4" dice.

Mash 2/3 of the cup of garbanzo beans and rough chop the remaining 1/3 cup.

Combine dressing mix with lettuce, chicken, tomato, beans and Parmesan cheese. Toss and serve.

DELICIOUS WALNUT BOSC SALAD

HERE IS A SALAD THAT INCORPORATES MANY NeoCuisine™ FLAVOR FORCE PRINCIPLES: WALNUT EXTRACT INSTEAD OF HIGH-CALORIE NUTS, INTENSE SURFACE OILS INSTEAD OF HUGE CALORIE QUANTITIES IN THE DRESSING AND THE OSMAZOME PRINCIPLE™ OF AN EXCELLENT CHICKEN BASE.

CALORIES: 500
NET WEIGHT: 27 OUNCES
PREP TIME: 10 to 15 MINUTES
CALORIE-TO-WEIGHT RATIO: 18.5 CALORIES PER OUNCE

- 2 ounces chicken, boned and skinned
- One 10- to 12-ounce package lettuce mix, European mix preferred
- 1 red (Delicious preferred), sliced
- 1 pear (Bosc preferred), sliced

- 2 Tablespoons quality grated Parmesan cheese, e.g. Reggiano, or 1/2 ounce shaved from brick of Parmesan cheese
- 4 sprays walnut oil: 2 seconds total

In nonstick skillet, cook chicken on high heat to brown, 1 to 2 minutes per side. Slice into strips. Cool. Combine chicken, lettuce, apple, pear and Parmesan. Add dressing and toss well. Spray with walnut oil.

DILLED TUNA TOMATOES

THE PERFECT SUMMER DINNER. THIS LIGHT REPAST HAS NICE FLAVOR FORCE FROM THE SURPRISE INGREDIENT SOY SAUCE. THIS DISH IS ALSO PROTEIN-PACKED OWING TO THE TUNA AND TOFU AND HAS AN EXCELLENT CALORIE-TO-WEIGHT RATIO.

CALORIES: 434
NET WEIGHT: 37 OUNCES
PREP TIME: 20 MINUTES
CALORIE-TO-WEIGHT RATIO: 12 CALORIES PER OUNCE

- 12-13 ounces extra-firm ultra-low-fat tofu, diced
- 1 Tablespoon fresh lemon juice
- 6-ounce can tuna, water-packed, drained
- 1/2 cup celery, diced
- 1-1/2 Tablespoons onion, chopped
- 2 Tablespoons scallions, green part only, chopped
- 1/2 cup nonfat mayonnaise
- 1/4 teaspoon garlic powder
- 2 teaspoons soy sauce
- 1/4 teaspoon dill
- 1 packet aspartame
- 2 medium tomatoes

Fork mix all ingredients except tomatoes. Add salt (1/4 teaspoon) and pepper (1/8 teaspoon) to taste. Prepare the day before for best flavor.

Make 8 cuts into each tomato from top to 3/4 the way down. Pull wedges out from center. Put tuna salad in center of each tomato. Serve.

HI PROTEIN CHICKEN SALAD WITH FRUIT

IF YOU'RE PROTEIN-SHORT YOUR DAY'S REQUIREMENT, THIS ENTREÉ SUPPLIES A WHOPPING
50 GRAMS PROTEIN.

CALORIES: 538
NET WEIGHT: 38 OUNCES
PREP TIME: 20 to 25 MINUTES
CALORIE-TO-WEIGHT RATIO: 13.5 CALORIES PER OUNCE

- 3 ounce chicken breast, boned and skinned
- 12-13 ounces extra-firm ultra-low-fat tofu, 1/2" dice
- 1/3 cup celery, chopped
- 1/4 cup scallions, chopped
- 3/4 cup fat-free mayonnaise
- 2 Tablespoons apple cider vinegar
- 1/2 teaspoon hot pepper sauce

- Scant 1 teaspoon Mrs. Dash Seasonings®
- 1 teaspoon quality chicken base
- 1/2 packet aspartame
- 1/4 medium cantaloupe, diced
- 1/2 red apple, unpeeled, diced small
- 1/4 cup raisins

Microwave chicken in a microwavable container, e.g. lidded glass, for 2 minutes, cool and dice. Fork mix all ingredients except cantaloupe, apple and raisins. Refrigerate overnight to allow flavors to meld. Add cantaloupe, apple and raisins. Serve.

KUSHI YAKI CHICKEN SALAD

FRENCH-INSPIRED WILTED LETTUCE, JAPANESE-BASED SAUCE AND ITALIAN NOODLES COMBINE FOR A TASTY WORLD FUSION SALAD.

CALORIES: 498
NET WEIGHT: 24 OUNCES
PREP TIME: 5 MINUTES
COOK TIME: 10 MINUTES
CALORIE-TO-WEIGHT RATIO: 21 CALORIES PER OUNCE

- 3 ounces chicken breast, boned and skinned.
- 1 recipe Teriyaki Dressing (see page 307)
- 1 cup cooked whole wheat spaghetti

- One 12- to 16-ounce package mixed salad greens
- 1/4 cup red bell pepper, diced
- 1/2 cup scallions, tops included, chopped

Brown chicken breast in nonstick skillet over high heat. Lower heat and cook until done, about 1 to 2 minutes. Remove.

Add dressing to skillet, warming it and scraping up any chicken bits. Slice the chicken into 1/4" strips and return to skillet with the spaghetti. Reheat.

Remove from heat and pour over lettuce. Add red bell pepper and scallions. Toss. Serve.

SALADE NICOISSE IRENE

NAMED FOR ITS CREATOR, A MARVELOUS COOK AND FRIEND, IRENE MULROY. THE FUN IS IN EATING IN-GREDIENTS ALONE AND TOGETHER. TRY WRAPPING THE SHRIMP IN THE BELL PEPPER, MIX TOMATO AND POTATO. TRY MUSHROOMS AND ZUCCHINI.

CALORIES: 500
NET WEIGHT: 33 OUNCES
PREP TIME: 30 MINUTES
COOK TIME: 7 MINUTES
CALORIE-TO-WEIGHT RATIO: 15.5 CALORIES PER OUNCE

- 8 ounces red potatoes, unpeeled, large dice
- 2 recipes NeoCuisine™ Vinaigrette (see page 307)
- 1 cup small whole fresh mushrooms
- 1 large or 2 small zucchini, 1/4" lengthwise slices
- 4 cherry tomatoes, halved
- One 14.5-ounce can plain (unmarinated) whole artichoke hearts, drained and rinsed, halved

- 8 black olives, large
- 1/2 cup prepared roasted red bell peppers
- 4 ounces medium to large shrimp, precooked
- 2 Tablespoons Miracle Chop (see page 346)
- 4 sprays olive oil: 2 seconds total from aerosol can

Microwave potatoes in a microwavable container, e.g. lidded glass, for 3 to 4 minutes or until cooked.

Microwave mushrooms and zucchini about 2-1/2 to 3 minutes or until cooked.

Combine all ingredients except Miracle Chop and olive oil in dressing and marinate in refrigerator 4 hours or more. Assemble, spray olive oil, and sprinkle Miracle Chop.

SALAMI CHOP CHOP

FOR FULL EFFECT, MAKE THE DRESSING IN THE MORNING ADDING THE BASIL AT THAT TIME. THIS ALLOWS FLAVOR EXTRACTION. AND BE SURE TO THOROUGHLY CHOP THE ICEBERG LETTUCE TO ABOUT THE SIZE OF A QUARTER. TASTE PERCEPTION AND MOUTH FEEL CHANGE SIGNIFICANTLY WHEN THESE INSTRUCTIONS ARE FOLLOWED.

CALORIES: 499
NET WEIGHT: 26 OUNCES
PREP TIME: 15 to 20 MINUTES
CALORIE-TO-WEIGHT RATIO: 19 CALORIES PER OUNCE

- 1 recipe NeoCuisine™ Vinaigrette (see page 307)*
- 2 teaspoons dried basil, rubbed between fingers to release flavors
- 1 cup garbanzo beans, drained
- 1/2 cup scallions, green and white parts, chopped

- 7 to 8 slices light salami, diced (allow up to 50 calories)
- 1/2 to 3/4 head iceberg lettuce, chopped (4 to 6 cups)
- 1 tomato, diced
- 1/4 cup quality grated Parmesan cheese, e.g. Reggiano

Combine dressing and basil.

Rough mash garbanzo beans and combine with dressing.

Toss all ingredients. Serve.

*A nice change-up is switching red wine vinegar to balsamic in the recipe.

SALSA CON POLLO ENSALADA

A SOUTHWEST SALAD WITH PLENTY OF CILANTRO. NOTE THE USE OF FRIJOLES AS A DRESSING FLAVOR BOOSTER.

CALORIES: 555
NET WEIGHT: 32 OUNCES
PREP TIME: 20 MINUTES
CALORIE-TO-WEIGHT RATIO: 19 CALORIES PER OUNCE

- 4 ounces chicken breast, boned and skinned and cut into 1/4" strips
- 1 cup (8 ounces) prepared (jarred or canned) medium salsa
- 1 packet aspartame
- 1 teaspoon quality chicken base
- 1/2 cup fat-free refried beans
- 1/2 cup canned or frozen corn

- 1 teaspoon dried cilantro
- One 10- to 14-ounce package American lettuce mix, chopped
- 1/2 ounce nonfat baked tortilla chips, lightly crushed (approximately 10 chips)
- 1/4 cup scallions, green parts only

In a nonstick skillet, cook the chicken strips over medium-high heat 3 to 4 minutes or until done.

Combine salsa, aspartame, chicken base, refried beans, corn and cilantro. Mix to blend. Add chicken.

Pour over lettuce, add tortilla chips and scallions. Toss well. Serve

SHRIMP CHOP SALAD

REMINISCENT OF A SHRIMP CAESAR BUT WITH THE ADDED COMPLEXITY OF BASIL AND RED KIDNEY BEANS.
IT SOUNDS UNUSUAL BUT THE RESULT IS DELICIOUS.

CALORIES: 549
NET WEIGHT: 33 OUNCES
PREP TIME: 15 to 20 MINUTES
CALORIE-TO-WEIGHT RATIO: 17 CALORIES PER OUNCE

- 1 recipe NeoCuisine™ Vinaigrette (see page 307)
- 2 teaspoons dried basil, rubbed between fingers to release flavors
- 1/2 teaspoon anchovie paste
- 6 ounces medium to large shrimp, cooked and shelled
- 1/2 to 3/4 head iceberg lettuce, chopped (4 to 6 cups)
- 1 cup canned red kidney beans, drained, rough chopped
- 1 small tomato, diced
- 1/4 cup quality grated Parmesan cheese, e.g. Reggiano

Combine dressing, basil and anchovie paste. Add shrimp and marinate for 30 minutes or more, up to 8 hours.

Combine all ingredients. Toss. Serve.

SZECHUAN SHRIMP WARM SALAD

A SNAPPY DRESSING ACCENTUATES THIS INTERESTING SALAD WHICH
INCLUDES NOODLES AND SHRIMP FLAVORED WITH CHINESE FIVE-SPICE.

CALORIES: 525
NET WEIGHT: 30 OUNCES
PREP TIME: 15 MINUTES
COOK TIME: 15 MINUTES
CALORIE-TO-WEIGHT RATIO: 18 CALORIES PER OUNCE

- 1 recipe Szechuan Dressing. Add more red pepper to taste.
- 4 ounces medium or large cooked shrimp*
- 1 cup of cooked spaghetti (1/3 cup dry) cooked in 1 cup clam juice,** drained
- One 12- to 16-ounce package of American salad mix, chopped
- 1/4 cup red bell pepper, diced
- 1/2 cup scallions, tops included, chopped

SZECHUAN DRESSING
- 1/4 cup soy sauce
- 2 Tablespoons white wine vinegar
- 1 teaspoon dark sesame oil
- 1 teaspoon sesame seeds
- 3 packets aspartame
- 1/2 teaspoon garlic powder
- Scant 1/4 teaspoon ginger
- 1/4 teaspoon red pepper flakes or to taste
- 1/8 teaspoon Chinese five-spice or 1 pinch each anise and cinnamon (Combine ingredients.)

Heat Szechuan Dressing in a small nonstick skillet to first sign of boil.

Add shrimp and cooked spaghetti; return to boil. Remove from heat and pour over lettuce, red bell pepper and scallions.

Toss and serve.

*Scallops, lobster or crab can be substituted.
**Buy or make with clam base.

TEX-MEX TABBOULEH

A DANDY UNUSUAL DISH WELL WORTH TRYING. DON'T LET THE ATYPICAL INGREDIENT
BLEND SCARE YOU OFF.

CALORIES: 485
NET WEIGHT: 31 OUNCES
PREP TIME: 15 MINUTES
COOK TIME: 15 MINUTES
CALORIE-TO-WEIGHT RATIO: 15 CALORIES PER OUNCE

- 1/2 cup bulgar
- 2 cups beef broth, fat skimmed
- 1 teaspoon quality beef base
- 1/2 red bell pepper, diced
- 1 small zucchini, diced
- 1/4 teaspoon garlic powder
- 2 teaspoons chili powder
- Juice of 1/4 lemon
- 2 Tablespoons fat-free Italian salad dressing
- 6 dry (no oil) sun-dried tomato halves
- 1/2 cup black beans, drained
- 3 scallions, green and white parts, chopped

Combine bulgar, beef broth, beef base, red bell pepper, zucchini, garlic powder and chili powder in a saucepan and bring to a boil. Cover. Reduce heat and simmer 15 minutes.

Put bulgar mixture in a serving bowl. Add lemon juice, Italian dressing and sun-dried tomatoes. Gently fold in black beans. Refrigerate 2 to 3 hours or overnight.

Add scallions. Serve at room temperature (recommended) or chilled on top of a bed of lettuce tossed with a little no-calorie Italian dressing.

WALDORF CHICKEN SALAD

THIS CLASSIC IS FAT-STRIPPED AND FLAVOR-ENHANCED USING THE OSMAZOME PRINCIPLE™.
WALNUT EXTRACT IN LIEU OF HIGH-CALORIE NUTS ADDS NUANCE. SIMPLE. DELICIOUS.

CALORIES: 557
NET WEIGHT: 35 OUNCES
PREP TIME: 20 MINUTES
CALORIE-TO-WEIGHT RATIO: 16 CALORIES PER OUNCE

- 4 ounces chicken breast, boned and skinned
- 1 tart green apple, unpeeled and diced
- 1 Red Delicious apple, unpeeled and diced
- 1/2 stalk celery, minced
- 1/4 cup fat-free mayonnaise
- 1/2 cup sugar-free, fat-free plain yogurt
- 1/2 teaspoon country Dijon mustard (pommard, i.e. with seeds)
- 20 red grapes, halved
- 1 teaspoon quality chicken base
- 1/2 teaspoon black walnut extract
- 1/2 head lettuce, thinly sliced

Microwave chicken in a microwavable container, e.g. lidded glass, for 2-1/2 minutes or until cooked.

Meanwhile, combine rest of ingredients except lettuce. Mix.

Dice chicken and add it to the apple mix. Add pepper (1/8 teaspoon) to taste.

Place lettuce on a serving plate. Top with chicken apple mix.

WARM BACON SALAD

A HUGE SALAD, ENOUGH TO SATISFY THE MOST DEMANDING PRIMEVAL RAGING APPETITE.
TASTY AND PIQUANT, THIS HEARTY SALAD SATES WITH PUNCHY FLAVOR.

CALORIES: 450
NET WEIGHT: 33 OUNCES
PREP TIME: 15 MINUTES
CALORIE-TO-WEIGHT RATIO: 14 CALORIES PER OUNCE

- 16 ounces fat-free Canadian bacon, cut in julienne strips
- 1/2 onion, diced
- 3/4 cup rice vinegar
- 1/2 cup red kidney beans, drained
- 2 Tablespoons red bell pepper, diced small
- 1/4 teaspoon garlic powder
- 3 packets aspartame
- 16 ounces Romaine lettuce, chopped

Combine bacon, onion, vinegar, beans, red bell pepper, garlic powder, salt (a generous 1/4 teaspoon) and pepper (1/8 teaspoon). Microwave to a boil, 4 to 6 minutes, stirring once. Remove from microwave and add aspartame.

Put chopped Romaine in a large warm bowl or plate. Pour dressing over Romaine. Serve.

WARM BLACK BEAN CILANTRO SALAD

THE CONCEPT OF USING A MEAT BASE IN A SALAD MAY STRIKE YOU AS CURIOUS BUT THE TASTE OUTCOME
TELLS THE STORY. HERE IS THE OSMAZOME PRINCIPLE™ AT WORK, MAKING FLAVOR THAT WON'T QUIT.
YOU'LL NOT NOTICE THAT THIS
IS FAT-STRIPPED WITH 1/3 THE CALORIES OF YOUR FAVORITE TACQUERIA TACO SALAD.

CALORIES: 490
NET WEIGHT: 35 OUNCES
PREP TIME: 15 MINUTES
COOK TIME: 4 to 5 MINUTES
CALORIE-TO-WEIGHT RATIO: 14 CALORIES PER OUNCE

- 1-1/2 cups canned black beans, including liquid (stir before measuring)
- 2 teaspoons chili powder
- 2 teaspoons red wine vinegar
- 1 teaspoon dried cilantro, rubbed lightly between fingers to release flavor
- 1 teaspoon quality beef base
- 1/4 cup frozen corn, thawed

- 1 packet aspartame
- 12- to 16-ounce package of American salad mix rough chopped
- 1/2 cup red onion, chopped
- 1 ounce (about 20) fat-free baked tortilla chips crushed
- 1/2 cup tomato, diced
- 1/4 lemon wedge

Combine black beans, chili powder, red wine vinegar, cilantro, beef base, corn and aspartame. Mix and microwave until hot but not boiling, about 4 to 5 minutes.

Add hot dressing mix to salad mix, onion and chips. Toss. Add tomato to top or side. See photo.

(The scallion mariachis are strickly optional.) Squeeze lemon over salad (important for flavor) and serve.

WARM TACO SALAD

THE TACO SALAD, BELIEVE IT OR NOT, WAS INVENTED IN SEATTLE IN THE EARLY 70S. NOW IT HAS, LITER-ALLY, WORLDWIDE POPULARITY. THE TRADITIONAL VERSION IS WELL OVER 1,000 CALORIES. THIS ONE IS 1/2 THAT AMOUNT BUT, IN OUR HUMBLE OPINION, JUST AS GOOD. TRY IT AND SEE.

CALORIES: 540
NET WEIGHT: 34 OUNCES
PREP TIME: 15 MINUTES
COOK TIME: 4 to 5 MINUTES
CALORIE-TO-WEIGHT RATIO: 16 CALORIES PER OUNCE

- 1-1/2 cups canned white beans, including liquid (stir before measuring)
- 2 teaspoons chili powder
- 2 teaspoons red wine vinegar
- 1 teaspoon dried cilantro, rubbed between fingers to release flavor
- 1 teaspoon quality chicken base
- 1/4 cup sliced olives
- 1 packet aspartame
- 12- to 16-ounce package of American salad mix
- 1/2 cup red onion, chopped
- 1 ounce (about 20) fat-free tortilla chips, lightly crushed
- 1/2 cup tomato, diced
- 1/4 lemon wedge

Combine white beans, chili powder, red wine vinegar, cilantro, chicken base, olives and aspartame. Mix and microwave until hot but not boiling, about 4 to 5 minutes.

Add salad mix, onion and chips, and toss. Top with tomato.

Squeeze lemon over salad (important for flavor) and serve.

WOLFGANG PUCK SALAD

INSPIRED BY THE FAMOUS WOLFGANG PUCK CAFÉS, THIS SALAD IS ONE OF THEIR BEST SELLERS. WE'VE DEFATTED IT BUT LEFT IN ALL THE FLAVOR.

CALORIES: 364
NET WEIGHT: 30 OUNCES
PREP TIME: 20 to 25 MINUTES
CALORIE-TO-WEIGHT RATIO: 12 CALORIES PER OUNCE

- 1-1/2 cup tomato, chopped fine 3/8"
- 1/4 cup carrot, chopped fine 3/8"
- 1/2 cup red onion, chopped fine 3/8"
- 1/4 cup green beans, frozen, thawed, chopped 3/8"
- 1/2 cup yellow corn, frozen, thawed
- 1/2 cup frozen peas
- 1/4 cup celery, chopped fine 3/8"
- 1/2 cup canned artichoke bottoms, chopped fine 3/8"
- 1/2 cup canned black beans, drained
- 2 Tablespoons balsamic vinegar
- 4 ounces red leaf lettuce, whole leaves

Combine first nine ingredients. Toss with balsamic vinegar (splurge on a high quality), salt (1/2 teaspoon) and pepper (1/8 teaspoon) to taste. Arrange lettuce around the plate. Spoon salad mix in center. Serve.

WORLD FUSION APPLE CHICKEN SALAD

WITH CANTONESE INFLUENCE (SOY AND GINGER), SWISS FLAVOR (FRUIT YOGURT) AND MEXICAN SABOR (RED CHILI FLAKES), THIS TEMPTING SALAD IS A GOOD EXAMPLE OF WORLD FUSION COOKERY. IT HAS A NOTABLE CALORIE-TO-WEIGHT RATIO OF A MERE 11 CALORIES PER OUNCE.

CALORIES: 448
NET WEIGHT: 40 OUNCES
PREP TIME: 20 MINUTES
CALORIE-TO-WEIGHT RATIO: 11 CALORIES PER OUNCE

- 4 ounces chicken breast, boned and skinned, cut into 1/4" to 1/2" dice
- 1/4 cup soy sauce
- 1/2 teaspoon ginger
- 2 recipes of Fruit Slaw using lemon yogurt (see page 350)

- 1 red skinned apple, cubed
- 1/8 teaspoon red pepper flakes (more if you want)
- 1 heaping Tablespoon dried cranberries, chopped
- 1 Tablespoon scallions, green parts only, chopped

Combine chicken, soy sauce and ginger in a plastic bag. Marinate 30 to 60 minutes. Remove chicken from marinade and brown in a nonstick skillet over high heat until done, about 2 to 3 minutes.

Add apple and red pepper flakes to fruit slaw and put on serving plate.

Top slaw with chopped warm chicken, cranberries and scallions. Serve.

SANDWICHES

CANADIAN BACON GRINDER AND SOUP

LET'S BE HONEST, NOTHING WILL EVER TAKE THE PLACE OF A HOT PASTRAMI SANDWICH FROM ZABAR'S DELI IN NEW YORK CITY. BUT HERE'S A DELI GRINDER WITH GREAT FLAVOR, ALMOST NO FAT AND TERRIFIC CHEW VALUE PLUS NO GUILT.

CALORIES: 514
NET WEIGHT: SANDWICH 10 OUNCES; SOUP 20 OUNCES;
TOTAL: 30 OUNCES
PREP TIME: 20 MINUTES
CALORIE-TO-WEIGHT RATIO: 17 CALORIES PER OUNCE

- Two 1/2" round slices eggplant, unpeeled
- 1/4 teaspoon garlic powder
- 1 teaspoon per slice balsamic vinegar
- 1/4 cup mustard
- 1/2 packet aspartame
- 1 French or hoagie roll (6" to 7" x 2-1/2" to 3")

- 1/4 cup prepared roasted red bell pepper
- 1 ounce (3 thin slices) red onion
- 2 ounces fat-free Canadian bacon, shaved
- 1 can Campbell's® condensed "Healthy Request" soup of choice✶

Sprinkle eggplant with salt, pepper, garlic powder and balsamic vinegar. Microwave, uncovered, for 3 to 4 minutes.

Combine mustard and aspartame. Slice roll in half lengthwise. Spread both cut sides with mustard.

Add red bell pepper, red onion, eggplant and Canadian bacon. Serve with heated soup.

✶ Calories not to exceed 200 calories. Calculate calories by taking the number of servings and multiplying by the number of calories per serving. If salt is not a problem, add 1/2 teaspoon beef or chicken base.

CARAMELIZED ONION
BBQ TURKEY OPENFACE

GOOD SAUCE AND CARAMELIZED ONION ARE BBQ NATURALS. HERE YOU HAVE THE SOULMATES IN A GREAT OPEN-FACED TURKEY SANDWICH.

CALORIES: 540
NET WEIGHT: 35 OUNCES
PREP TIME: 20 MINUTES
CALORIE-TO-WEIGHT RATIO: 14 CALORIES PER OUNCE

- 2 slices light bread (e.g. Wonder® Light)
- 1/2 cup canned, fat-free refried beans
- 4 ounces prepared fat-free turkey breast, shaved
- 1/2 recipe Caramel Onion Masterpiece (see page 345)
- 1 recipe BBQ Sauce (see page 344)

- 2 Tablespoons red onion, chopped (use more or less depending on your taste)
- 2 Tablespoons green bell pepper, chopped
- recipe Fruit Slaw (use strawberry yogurt; see page 350)

Put bread slices in a single layer on microwavable serving plate. Cover each slice with the refried beans, spreading edge to edge so bread will not get soggy.

Put shaved turkey on top of beans. Spread with Caramel-Onion Masterpiece. Cover with BBQ Sauce. Mix red onion and green bell pepper. Top sandwich with the mix.

Microwave 3 to 5 minutes until hot all the way through. Serve with Fruit Slaw on the side.

DIJONNAISE CHICKEN PANINI

A PAN-GRILLED CHICKEN SANDWICH STUFFED WITH BALSAMIC-SEASONED EGGPLANT SLICES AND ZESTY RED ONION. THE MIX OF NO-FAT MAYO, HORSERADISH AND DIJON SETS PIQUANT NUANCES.

CALORIES: 500
NET WEIGHT: 21 OUNCES
PREP TIME: 25 MINUTES
COOK TIME: 20 MINUTES
CALORIE-TO-WEIGHT RATIO: 19 CALORIES PER OUNCE

- 2 ounces chicken breast, boned and skinned
- 1/4 teaspoon garlic powder
- 1/4 teaspoon commercial Italian herb seasoning
- Two 1/2" round slices eggplant, peeled
- 2 teaspoons balsamic vinegar
- 1 recipe Dijonnaise (see page 347)

- 2 slices brown light bread (e.g. Wonder® Light)
- 1/4 cup prepared roasted red bell pepper
- 2 slices red onion, 1/8 to 1/4" thick
- 1 slice fat-free Swiss cheese single
- 1 recipe Cottage Cheese Kiwi-Pineapple Salad (see page 348)

Place chicken breast between two pieces of plastic wrap. Pound gently to flatten to 1/2" thick (use bottom of small sauce pan or wooden mallet). Rub chicken with garlic powder, Italian herb seasoning, salt (1/8 to 1/4 teaspoon) to taste and a pinch of pepper.

Cook in a nonstick skillet over high heat 3 to 4 minutes or until bottom is well-browned and crusty. Turn once and cook 1 minute more. Don't overcook. Cool and slice into thin strips.

While chicken is cooling, sprinkle eggplant with balsamic vinegar and microwave in a microwavable container, e.g. lidded glass, until cooked, about 2 minutes.

Layer in this order, spreading a little dijonnaise on each layer: Wheat bread, eggplant, red bell pepper, onion, chicken strips, swiss cheese, wheat bread. This makes a juicy sandwich.

Place sandwich in nonstick skillet. Cover and cook over medium-low heat, turning once, until heated through and cheese is melted, about 3 to 5 minutes per side. Serve with Cottage Cheese Kiwi-Pineapple Salad.

EGGLESS EGG SALAD PITA

WITH A CALORIE-TO-WEIGHT RATIO OF ONLY 13 CALORIES PER OUNCE, YOU'LL BE PLEASED WITH HOW GOOD IT TASTES. SUBSTITUTING TOFU FOR EGGS COMES SURPRISINGLY CLOSE IN FLAVOR TO THE REAL THING WITH VIRTUALLY ZERO SATURATED FAT.

CALORIES: 390
NET WEIGHT: 30 OUNCES
PREP TIME: 20 to 25 MINUTES
CALORIE-TO-WEIGHT RATIO: 13 CALORIES PER OUNCE

- 12-13 ounces extra-firm ultra-low-fat tofu
- 1 teaspoon apple cider vinegar
- 2-1/2 teaspoons prepared yellow mustard
- 1/2 teaspoon turmeric
- 2 Tablespoons celery, diced
- 3 Tablespoons onion, chopped
- 1 Tablespoon fresh parsley, chopped

- 1 medium dill pickle, chopped
- 1/2 packet aspartame
- 1/2 cup fat-free mayonnaise
- 1/8 teaspoon cayenne pepper
- 1 pita bread
- 2 lettuce leaves
- 1 medium tomato, sliced

Fork crumble tofu into medium mixing bowl. Add vinegar, mustard, turmeric and a generous 1/4 teaspoon of salt. Add celery, onion, parsley, dill pickle, aspartame, mayonnaise and cayenne pepper. Mix thoroughly. Refrigerate at least 30 minutes to allow flavors to meld.

Cut pita bread in half. Put lettuce and tomato in each pocket and fill each with half the Eggless Egg Salad mix. You may have extra Eggless Egg Salad—use the rest to stuff a medium tomato. The tomato adds an extra 26 calories.

FRENCH COUNTRYSIDE SANDWICH

HERE IS A NICE SECOND USE FOR COLD MEATLOAF. IF YOU WISH, THE ADDITION OF TARRAGON OR HERBS DE PROVENCE LENDS MORE AUTHENTICITY.

CALORIES: 449
NET WEIGHT: 31.5 OUNCES
PREP TIME: 10 MINUTES
CALORIE-TO-WEIGHT RATIO: 14 CALORIES PER OUNCE

- 2 Tablespoons fat-free mayonnaise
- 1 Tablespoon country style Dijon mustard
- 1 packet aspartame
- 2 slices light French bread (e.g. Wonder® Light)
- 1 slice red onion

- 1/4 recipe cooked meatloaf of choice, sliced
- 1 medium tomato, sliced
- 1 to 2 leaves of lettuce
- 1 recipe side salad of choice

Combine fat-free mayonnaise, Dijon mustard and aspartame. Spread on both slices of bread. Place onion first then meatloaf and tomato, sprinkled with salt and pepper to taste, lettuce and the second slice of bread.

Cut sandwich in half and serve with side salad of choice.

This sandwich also tastes great with the meatloaf heated.

OPEN FACED BBQ PORK

HEADY AND RICH WITH PLENTY OF ZING. YOU BBQ LOVERS WILL LOVE THIS AND ALL WITHOUT THE GUILT OF YOUR FAVORITE BBQ JOINT.

CALORIES: 525
NET WEIGHT: 32 OUNCES
PREP TIME: 20 MINUTES
COOK TIME: 3 MINUTES
CALORIE-TO-WEIGHT RATIO: 16 CALORIES PER OUNCE

341

- 2 slices light bread (e.g. Wonder® Light)
- 1/2 cup fat-free refried beans
- 4 ounces fat-free Canadian bacon, shaved
- 1 cup BBQ Sauce (see page 344)

- 1/4 to 1/2 cup red onion, chopped (use more or less depending on your taste)
- 3 to 4 slices tomato, 1/2" to 3/8" thick
- 1/2 cup iceberg lettuce, shredded
- 1 recipe Fruit Slaw
  (use strawberry yogurt; see page 350)

Put bread slices in a single layer on microwavable serving plate. Cover each slice with the refried beans, spreading edge to edge so bread will not get soggy.

Put shaved Canadian bacon on top of beans and cover with 3/4 cup BBQ Sauce. Top with all but 1 Tablespoon of onions then tomatoes. Microwave 3 minutes or until hot all the way through.

Add lettuce. Top with 1/4 cup warmed BBQ Sauce remaining and onions. Serve with Fruit Slaw on the side.

RED PEPPER CANADIAN BACON GRILLED GRINDER

SHAVED CANADIAN BACON ACCENTED WITH ROASTED RED PEPPERS AND BUTTERNUT SQUASH SLICES THEN GRILLED WITH CHEESE. TASTY.

CALORIES: 521
NET WEIGHT: 31.5 OUNCES
PREP TIME: 15 to 20 MINUTES
COOK TIME: 6 to 10 MINUTES
CALORIE-TO-WEIGHT RATIO: 17 CALORIES PER OUNCE

- 3 to 4 slices (4 to 6 ounces total with skin) butternut squash
- 2 Tablespoons fat-free Ranch salad dressing
- 2 slices light bread (e.g. Wonder® Light)
- 1/4 cup prepared roasted red bell pepper

- 2 slices red onion
- 2 ounces fat-free Canadian Bacon, shredded
- 1 slice fat-free cheddar cheese single
- White Bean Salad (see page 349)

Microwave butternut squash (with skin on) 5 to 6 minutes. Remove skin and slice.

Layer in order, drizzling a little Ranch dressing on bread and on top of each layer: white bread, red bell pepper, red onion, butternut squash, Canadian bacon, cheddar, white bread.

Place sandwich in a nonstick skillet, cover and cook over medium-low heat, turning once, until heated through and cheese is melted, about 3 to 5 minutes per side.

Serve with White Bean Salad.

SAUCES

SUGAR-FREE KETCHUP

NeoCuisine™ KETCHUP HAS LESS THAN HALF THE CALORIES (6 PER TABLESPOON) OF HEINZ® BEST (15 PER TABLESPOON). SLATHER YOUR FLAVOR FRIES, DOUSE YOUR NeoCuisine™ MEATLOAVES, SMOTHER YOUR MORNING EGGBEATERS® SCRAMBLE.

CALORIES: 36
PREP TIME: 3 MINUTES
YIELD: 1/2 CUP (4 OUNCES)
CALORIE-TO-WEIGHT RATIO: 9 CALORIES PER OUNCE

- 1/2 can (6-ounce can) tomato paste (3 ounces)
- 1/4 cup water
- 2 Tablespoons distilled vinegar
- 1/4 rounded teaspoon onion powder
- 1/4 teaspoon garlic powder
- 3 packets aspartame
- 1/2 teaspoon salt
- 1/8 teaspoon pepper

Combine all ingredients. Keeps up to 4 days in the refrigerator.

BBQ SAUCE

HERE'S A BBQ SAUCE AT 1/4 THE CALORIES AND IT TASTES GOOD TOO. USE IT FOR NeoCuisine™ BURGERS, NeoCuisine™ MEATLOAVES AND MIX WITH CARAMEL-ONION MASTERPIECE (SEE BELOW) FOR THE ULTIMATE BBQ SAUCE.

CALORIES: 80; 7 CALS PER TABLESPOON
NET WEIGHT: 6 OUNCES; YIELD: 2/3 CUP
PREP TIME: 5 MINUTES
CALORIE-TO-WEIGHT RATIO: 13 CALORIES PER OUNCE

- 1 recipe Sugar-Free Ketchup (see page 343)
- 1/4 teaspoon Liquid Smoke
- 1/2 teaspoon chili powder
- 1/4 teaspoon dry mustard
- 1/2 teaspoon quality beef base

Combine all ingredients. Use as a finishing sauce after entreé is cooked.

APRICOT PLUM CHUTNEY

CALORIES: 31
YIELD: 3 TABLESPOONS

- 1/8 cup all-fruit apricot jam
- 1 Tablespoon fresh lemon juice
- 1 teaspoon raisins, chopped
- 1/8 teaspoon ground ginger
- 1/8 teaspoon salt
- 2 packets aspartame

Combine ingredients.

This has a strong flavor—a little goes a long way.

344

BUTTON MUSHROOM THYME GRAVY

CALORIES: 39
NET WEIGHT: 5 OUNCES
PREP TIME: 3 to 5 MINUTES
COOK TIME: 6 MINUTES
CALORIE-TO-WEIGHT RATIO: 8 CALORIES PER OUNCE

- 1/2 cup beef broth, fat skimmed
- 1 Tablespoon flour
- 1/4 teaspoon garlic powder
- 1/8 teaspoon dried thyme
- 1/4 teaspoon quality beef base
- 1/4 cup fresh mushrooms, chopped

Mix 1 Tablespoon beef broth and the flour with a wire whisk and set aside. In a small saucepan bring remainder of broth to a boil. Reduce heat to medium, remix flour/stock and whisk in. Add garlic powder, thyme, beef base and mushrooms. Simmer 5 minutes.

CARAMEL-ONION MASTERPIECE

GOOD COOKERY IS NOT NECESSARILY COMPLEX. NOTE THAT INCOMPARABLE SAN FRANCISCO SOURDOUGH BREAD IS ONLY FLOUR, WATER AND SALT. CARAMEL-ONION MASTERPIECE HAS ONLY TWO INGREDIENTS BUT RESULTS IN A GUSTATORIAL TOUR DE FORCE. SWEET, RICH AND FULL OF INTENSE FLAVOR, IT HAS NO FAT AND FEW CALORIES AT 15 PER OUNCE. CARAMEL-ONION MASTERPIECE IS MADE AHEAD AS AN ON-CALL RECIPE AUGMENT, LASTING UP TO THREE WEEKS IN THE REFRIGERATOR.

CALORIES: 80
NET WEIGHT: 6 OUNCES
PREP TIME: 5 MINUTES
CALORIE-TO-WEIGHT RATIO: 13 CALORIES PER OUNCE

- 2 medium onions, peeled (12 to 16 ounces net peeled weight)
- 2 cups beef broth, fat skimmed

Cut onions into small wedges. Combine ingredients. Microwave for 25 to 30 minutes (or boil uncovered on the stove top) until all the liquid is gone.

The end result is brown, soft onion of high sweet flavor. It's a culinary masterpiece that's good on anything but dessert.

MIRACLE CHOP

CALORIES: 0
YIELD: 1/3 CUP
PREP TIME: 5 - 10 MINUTES

- 1/3 cup packed fresh parsley
- 1 large or 2 small cloves of garlic
- 1/8 teaspoon salt

Finely chop parsley and garlic. Add salt. Mix. Refrigerate tightly covered. Lasts one week plus.

MOLÉ

THIS SAUCE, THE PRIDE OF MEXICO, HAS BEEN DEFATTED WITHOUT FLAVOR DESTRUCTION. THERE ARE AS MANY MOLÉ RECIPES AS THERE ARE MEXICAN COOKS. OFTEN THESE FLAVOR-BLOCKBUSTER SAUCES ARE HANDED DOWN FROM GENERATION TO GENERATION. THIS ONE'S GOOD BUT SIMPLE. TRY ADDING DRIED FRUIT PUREÉD IN BEEF STOCK.

CALORIES: 44
NET WEIGHT: 5 OUNCES
PREP TIME: 5 MINUTES
COOK TIME: 5 MINUTES
CALORIE-TO-WEIGHT RATIO:

- 1/2 cup beef broth, fat skimmed
- 1 Tablespoon flour
- 1/2 teaspoon chili powder (more for flavor)
- 1/2 teaspoon cumin (more for flavor)
- 1/2 teaspoon quality beef base
- 2 Tablespoons NeoCuisine™ Red (see page 347)
- 1/2 teaspoon cocoa (more for flavor)
- 1/2 packet aspartame

Mix 1 Tablespoon beef broth and the flour and set aside. In a small saucepan, bring remainder of broth to a boil. Reduce heat to medium. Remix flour/stock and whisk in. Add chili powder, cumin, beef base, tomato sauce and cocoa; simmer 5 minutes. Add aspartame.

346

NeoCuisine™ RED

THIS SAUCE IS FLAVOR FORCE LOADED AND THEREFORE RECOMMENDED.

- 1/2 cup fat-free (lite) pasta (marinara) sauce
- 1 teaspoon oregano
- 1 teaspoon quality chicken base
- 1/4 teaspoon garlic powder
- 1/8 teaspoon pepper
- 1/2 packet aspartame

Combine ingredients.

SANDWICH DIJONNAISE

CALORIES: 105
NET WEIGHT: 4 OUNCES
PREP TIME: 5 MINUTES
YIELD: 1/2 CUP
CALORIE-TO-WEIGHT RATIO: 26 CALORIES PER OUNCE

- 1/4 cup fat-free mayonnaise
- 1/4 cup Country Dijon mustard
- 1/2 teaspoon prepared horseradish

Combine ingredients.

SIDES - COLD

CLASSIC SIDE SALAD

CALORIES: 57
NET WEIGHT: 11 OUNCES
PREP TIME: 10 MINUTES
CALORIE-TO-WEIGHT RATIO: 5 CALORIES PER OUNCE

- 6 ounces prepared salad greens
- 1/4 cup tomato, chopped
- 1/4 cup cucumber, chopped
- 1 Tablespoon red onion, chopped
- 1 recipe Instant Italian Zero Calorie Dressing (see page 306)

Combine all ingredients. Toss.

COTTAGE CHEESE KIWI-PINEAPPLE SALAD

CALORIES: 130
NET WEIGHT: 10 OUNCES
PREP TIME: 10 MINUTES
CALORIE-TO-WEIGHT RATIO: 13 CALORIES PER OUNCE

- 1/2 cup fat-free cottage cheese
- 1/4 cup canned pineapple, in its own juice, drained, diced
- 1 kiwi, peeled and diced
- 1 teaspoon dried cranberries, chopped
- 1/2 packet aspartame
- Lettuce leaf

Combine all ingredients. Serve on lettuce leaf. Add a dash of salt and pepper to taste.

348

COTTAGE CHEESE AND TOMATO SALAD

CALORIES: 110
NET WEIGHT: 9.5 OUNCES
PREP TIME: 5 to 7 MINUTES
CALORIE-TO-WEIGHT RATIO: 11.5 CALORIES PER OUNCE

- 1 dry (no oil) sun-dried tomato half
- 1/2 cup fat-free cottage cheese
- 1/2 Tablespoon scallions, green part only, chopped
- A pinch each of garlic powder and pepper
- 1/2 medium tomato, sliced
- 1 Tablespoon no fat NeoCuisine™ Vinaigrette dressing (see page 307)
- 1/4 teaspoon dried basil

Put sun-dried tomato in 1 Tablespoon of water and microwave for 10 seconds. Drain and finely chop. Combine chopped sun-dried tomato with cottage cheese, scallions, garlic powder and pepper.

Put tomato slices on a plate. Drizzle with vinaigrette and sprinkle with dried basil. Top with cottage cheese mix. Serve. (This is best if made 1 to 3 hours ahead of time so the flavors can marry.)

WHITE BEAN SALAD

CALORIES: 242
NET WEIGHT: 20.5 OUNCES
PREP TIME: 15 MINUTES
CALORIE-TO-WEIGHT RATIO: 12 CALORIES PER OUNCE

- 1 recipe no fat NeoCuisine™ Vinaigrette (see page 307)
- 1/2 can (15-ounce can) of white beans with liquid
- One 10-ounce prepackaged salad greens, your choice
- 2 Tablespoons quality grated Parmesan cheese, e.g. Reggiano

Combine dressing and beans; mix.

Add to salad greens and toss. Sprinkle with Parmesan and serve.

YOGURT FRUIT SLAW

CALORIES: 58
NET WEIGHT: 8.5 OUNCES
PREP TIME: 3 MINUTES
CALORIE-TO-WEIGHT RATIO: 13 CALORIES PER OUNCE

- 4 ounces packaged shredded cabbage (coleslaw)
- 2 ounces (1/4 cup) sugar-free, fat-free yogurt (best flavors are lemon, orange, strawberry and peach)
- 1/4 teaspoon salt

- 1 Tablespoon unseasoned rice vinegar
- 1/4 teaspoon Dijon mustard
- Pinch of pepper
- 1 packet aspartame

Combine all ingredients.

SIDES - HOT

BASIL PARMESAN POLENTA

CALORIES: 170
NET WEIGHT: 8 OUNCES
PREP TIME: 5 MINUTES
COOK TIME: 25 MINUTES
CALORIE-TO-WEIGHT RATIO: 21 CALORIES PER OUNCE

- One 14-ounce can or 1-1/2 cups chicken broth, fat skimmed
- 1/4 cup polenta

- 1/2 teaspoon dried basil
- 1 Tablespoon quality grated Parmesan cheese, e.g. Reggiano

In a medium saucepan bring chicken broth to a boil. Stir in polenta with a wire whisk. Return to a full boil, cover, reduce heat to medium low and cook until thickened, about 3 to 5 minutes. Remove lid and cook over low heat 20 to 25 minutes, stirring occasionally. Stir in basil and Parmesan.✳ Pour into 6-3/4" x 3-1/2" loaf pan and refrigerate 1/2

✳May be served immediately as savory soft polenta or cooled, sliced and fried.

350

hour (may do night before) until firm.

Cut polenta in 1/2" slices. Spray a nonstick skillet with a nonstick spray. Cook slices over low heat until warmed through and crust is formed on both sides, about 5 minutes.

CARLENZOLI STEAKS AND BEEF GLAZED EGGPLANT TOURNEDOS

CALORIES: 65
NET WEIGHT: 10 OUNCES
PREP TIME: 5 MINUTES
COOK TIME: 20 to 30 MINUTES
CALORIE-TO-WEIGHT RATIO: 6.5 CALORIES PER OUNCE

- 1 large (or 2 medium if necessary) portabello mushrooms* or 6 to 7 extra large button mushrooms
- One 14.5-ounce can beef broth, fat skimmed
- 1 Tablespoon red wine vinegar
- 1/4 teaspoon garlic powder

- 1/4 teaspoon dried thyme
- Two or three 1" thick eggplant rounds
- 1/2 recipe of Miracle Chop (see page 346)
- 1/4 cup tomato, diced

Wash mushroom(s) and cut stem off even with the mushroom base.

In a large nonstick frying pan put beef broth, red wine vinegar, garlic powder and thyme. Pepper (1/8 teaspoon) to taste. Add eggplant and mushroom, stem side up. Bring to a boil. Cook until liquid is reduced 70% to 80%, about 10 to 15 minutes. Turn vegetables and continue to cook. (You may need to reduce heat to control reduction.) Remove vegetables to a plate.

Scrape (deglaze) pan to get all the bits. Add a dash of red wine vinegar if needed. Add more beef stock for more sauce. Thicken with cornstarch if desired. Reserve.

Combine Miracle Chop and tomatoes and arrange over top of eggplant.

*Portabello mushrooms are highly recommended. The Carlenzoli family enjoyed them in place of meat, hence the name. You'll like the texture and flavor.

351

CLASSIC BAKED POTATO

CALORIES: 147
NET WEIGHT: 11 OUNCES
PREP TIME: 5 MINUTES
CALORIE-TO-WEIGHT RATIO: 13 CALORIES PER OUNCE

- One 8-ounce potato
- 1/4 cup or more beef broth, fat skimmed
- 10 sprays "I Can't Believe It's Not Butter"® and 1 teaspoon Molly McButter®
- 1 Tablespoon fat-free sour cream
- 1 heaping Tablespoon scallions, green part only, chopped
- 1 teaspoon Bacobits® (optional)

Microwaving: Wash potato(es), put in a microwavable container, e.g. lidded glass, and microwave for 8 to 10 minutes, turning once. Conventional oven: Wash potato(es) and bake in oven at 400° for about 45 minutes. Check with fork.

Blossom potato. Top with beef broth and "I Can't Believe It's Not Butter"® and Molly McButter®. Add salt (1/4 teaspoon) and pepper (1/8 teaspoon) to taste. You may also add an optional sprinkle of garlic powder. Top with sour cream, scallions and Bacobits®.

GARLIC MASHED POTATOES

CALORIES: 120
NET WEIGHT: 8 OUNCES
PREP TIME: 5 MINUTES
COOK TIME: 4 to 6 MINUTES
CALORIE-TO-WEIGHT RATIO: 15 CALORIES PER OUNCE

- 8 ounces potatoes, peeled and diced
- 1/4 cup skim milk
- 1/4 teaspoon garlic powder

Microwave potatoes in a microwavable container, e.g. lidded glass, 4 to 6 minutes.

Mash potatoes with skim milk. Add garlic powder, salt (1/4 teaspoon) and pepper (scant 1/8 teaspoon) to taste.

I CAN'T BELIEVE IT'S BROCCOLI

BROCCOLI IS A "DIET" VEGETABLE THAT SOUNDS AWFUL READ FROM THE WRITTEN PAGE.
HERE'S A RECIPE THAT WILL CHANGE YOUR MIND. YOU'LL BE SURPRISED.

CALORIES: 95 to 120
NET WEIGHT: 12 to 16 OUNCES
PREP TIME: 10 MINUTES
COOK TIME: 7 MINUTES
CALORIE-TO-WEIGHT RATIO: 7.5 CALORIES PER OUNCE

- 12 to 16 ounces broccoli
- No-fat butter spray ("I Can't Believe It's Not Butter"® is best)
- Molly McButter® to taste
- Lemon for squeezing
- Pepper grinder
- 1 Tablespoon quality grated Parmesan cheese, e.g. Reggiano

Microwave broccoli dry (no water) in a microwavable container, e.g. lidded glass, for 3 to 7 minutes. Check doneness by squeezing flowerettes. When they're soft, they're ready.

Spray 4 to 6 times with no-fat butter flavor spray. Add Molly McButter® to taste.

Squeeze a bit of lemon, not too much. Salt and grind pepper to taste. Garnish with the ground fresh Parmesan.

POLENTA TARAGNA (CHEESE POLENTA)

CALORIES: 185
NET WEIGHT: 9 OUNCES
PREP TIME: 5 MINUTES
COOK TIME: 25 MINUTES
CALORIE-TO-WEIGHT RATIO: 20 CALORIES PER OUNCE

- One 14-ounce can or 1-1/2 cups chicken broth, fat skimmed
- 1/4 cup polenta
- 1/4 cup Kraft® fat-free shredded cheddar cheese
- Pinch red pepper flakes

In a medium saucepan bring chicken broth to a boil. Stir in polenta with a wire whisk. Return to a full boil, cover, reduce heat to medium-low and cook until thickened, about 3 to 5 minutes. Remove lid and cook over low heat 20 to 25 minutes, stirring occasionally. Stir in cheddar and a pinch of pepper.✶ Pour into 6-3/4" x 3-1/2" loaf pan and refrigerate 1/2 hour (may do night before) until firm.

Cut polenta in 1/2" slices. Spray a nonstick skillet with a nonstick spray. Cook slices over low heat until warmed through and crust is formed on both sides, about 5 minutes.

✶May be served immediately as savory soft polenta or cooled, sliced and fried.

ROASTED FLAVOR FRIES

THESE RECIPES USE MEAT BASES RUBBED DIRECTLY ONTO THE POTATO. DEFINITELY NOT KIDS' FRIES.

CALORIES: 185
NET WEIGHT: 9 OUNCES
PREP TIME: 5 MINUTES
COOK TIME: 25 MINUTES
CALORIE-TO-WEIGHT RATIO: 20 CALORIES PER OUNCE

1 OVEN-ROASTED BEEF FRIES
- 12 ounce baking potato
- 1 teaspoon quality beef base (You will need to add a drop or two of water to make spreading easier.)
- 1/2 teaspoon dried thyme
- 1/4 teaspoon garlic powder
- 1 Tablespoon quality grated Parmesan cheese, e.g. Reggiano (add 20 calories to total)

2 CHILI FRIES
- 12 ounce baking potato
- 1 teaspoon quality chicken base (You may need to add a drop or two of water to make spreading easier.)
- 1/2 teaspoon chili powder

3 OVEN-ROASTED PARMESAN FRIES
- 12 ounce baking potato
- 1 teaspoon quality chicken base (You may need to add a drop or two of water to make spreading easier.)
- 1/4 teaspoon garlic powder
- 1 Tablespoon quality grated Parmesan cheese, e.g. Reggiano (add 20 calories to total)

Microwaving: Microwave in the morning. Wash potato(es), put in a microwavable container, e.g. lidded glass, and microwave for 8 to 10 minutes, turning once. Let sit in the microwave until you're ready to use in the evening. Conventional oven: For potato skins that give more toothsome, crispy gratification, bake conventionally. In the morning, wash potato(es) and bake in oven at 500° for 10 to 15 minutes. Turn off and let potatoes sit in the oven until ready to use in the evening.

Cut into 8 thick wedges and rub surface with base mix. For Frisco Fry style: Prepare the same as roasted Flavor Fries but cut potatoes into 1/4" to 1/2" rounds/coins.

Combine base with seasoning options listed above. If called for, sprinkle with Parmesan cheese. Bake at 500° for 12 to 15 minutes or until browned.

STEWS

BASIL CHICKEN STEW

THIS SICILIAN PEASANT STEW IS QUICK-FIXED USING AN ITALIAN SALAD SEASONING PACKET AND PLENTY OF BASIL. FLAVORS INTENSIFY WITH A HIGH-HEAT REDUCTION OF CHICKEN STOCK.

CALORIES: 553
NET WEIGHT: 30 OUNCES
PREP TIME: 15 MINUTES
COOK TIME: 27 MINUTES
CALORIE-TO-WEIGHT RATIO: 18 CALORIES PER OUNCE

- 2 ounces of chicken breast, boned and skinned, rough chopped into 1/4" pieces
- One 14.5-ounce can chicken broth, fat skimmed
- 12 ounces of raw peeled potatoes, diced
- 8 ounces of carrots, sliced, or ready to eat baby carrots
- 10 dry (no oil) sun-dried tomato halves, cut in half

- 1 cup (5 ounces) of chopped onions
- 1/2 package Good Seasons Italian® salad dressing mix
- 1 teaspoon dried basil
- 1 teaspoon quality chicken base
- Juice of 1/4 lemon

In a large nonstick skillet over high heat, brown chicken and remove. To same pan add chicken broth, potatoes, carrots, sun-dried tomatoes and onion. Bring to a boil and cook uncovered 15 to 20 minutes until reduced by 1/3 to 1/2. (For thicker sauce, use a fork or spoon to mash some potato against the inside of the pan.)

Add chicken, Good Seasons® dressing mix, basil and chicken base. Cook 2 minutes. Add lemon juice and pepper (1/8 teaspoon) to taste. Serve.

BOEUF BOURGUIGNONNE

AS TASTY AS THE CLASSIC FRENCH PRESENTATION IN HALF THE TIME WITH 1/3 THE CALORIES AND FAT.

CALORIES: 595
NET WEIGHT: 28 OUNCES
PREP TIME: 20 MINUTES
COOK TIME: 30 MINUTES
CALORIE-TO-WEIGHT RATIO: 21 CALORIES PER OUN

- 4 ounces top round, rough chopped in 1/4" pieces
- One 14.5-ounce can beef broth, fat skimmed
- 1 teaspoon quality beef base
- 1 cup drinking quality red wine [FYI: All the alcohol boils out.]
- 8 ounces potatoes, 1" dice

- 2 cups whole baby carrots
- 2 cups small whole mushrooms
- 1/2 teaspoon dried thyme
- 1/2 cup fat-free (lite) pasta (marinara) sauce
- 1/4 cup frozen peas

In a large nonstick skillet brown meat. Add beef broth, beef base, red wine, potatoes, carrots, mushrooms and thyme. Bring to a full boil and cook uncovered for 20 to 25 minutes, or until about 1/2 cup of liquid remains.

Reduce heat and add pasta sauce and pepper (1/8 teaspoon) to taste. Cook 3 to 4 minutes. Add peas. Serve.

BUDDHIST VEGETABLE CURRY

DON'T LET THE WORDS CURRY OR VEGETABLE SCARE YOU. THIS IS A
DELICIOUS DISH.

CALORIES: 475
NET WEIGHT: 32 OUNCES
PREP TIME: 15 MINUTES
COOK TIME: 12 to 17 MINUTES
CALORIE-TO-WEIGHT RATIO: 15 CALORIES PER OUNCE

- One 14.5-ounce can chicken broth, fat skimmed
- 12 teaspoons quality chicken base
- 16 ounces of potatoes, diced
- 1/2 cup onions, diced
- 1 Tablespoon sliced scallions, green part only
- 1 teaspoon curry powder (Spice Islands® is excellent)
- 8 ounces frozen cauliflower
- 2 ounces frozen peas
- Juice of 1/4 lemon
- 12 canned (unsweetened) Mandarin orange sections

In a medium saucepan combine chicken broth, chicken base, potatoes and onions. Bring to a full boil and cook uncovered 10 to 15 minutes or until potatoes are done. Meanwhile, slice scallions.

Add curry powder and cauliflower. Cook 2 minutes. Add peas. Remove from heat and add lemon juice. Put on serving plate and garnish with Mandarin orange sections and scallions.

CABO SAN LUCAS BOWL

IF YOU ENJOY LIVELY ENTREÉS, THIS MEXICAN FISH MEDLEY HAS PLENTY OF ACTION.

357

CALORIES: 581
NET WEIGHT: 38 OUNCES
PREP TIME: 15 MINUTES
COOK TIME: 11 MINUTES
CALORIE-TO-WEIGHT RATIO: 15 CALORIES PER OUNCE

- 1 medium zucchini, shredded
- 1 stalk celery, cut into 1/4" thick slices
- 1/2 cup green bell pepper, diced
- 8 to 10 ounces clam juice
- One 14.5-ounce can Mexican recipe stewed tomatoes, undrained
- 1 cup black beans, drained

- 1 teaspoon chili powder
- 1 teaspoon anchovie paste (All you anchovie phobes relax. The anchovie taste disappears.)
- 1/2 cup frozen corn
- 1 packet aspartame
- 6 ounces filet of sole or other white fish, cut into 1" pieces

Microwave zucchini, celery and green pepper in a microwavable container, e.g. lidded glass, for 3 minutes.

In a serving bowl, combine all ingredients. Cover with plastic wrap and microwave 5 minutes. Stir once gently. Don't break fish. Cook an additional 3 minutes. Salt (1/4 teaspoon) to taste. Serve.

CACCIATORE CON POLENTA

CACCIATORE SERVED WITH POLENTA IN PLACE OF PASTA, A NICE TOUCH INDEED. WHEREAS PASTA IS JUST BOILED WHEAT, POLENTA IS PREPARED WITH STOCK FOR MUCH MORE FLAVORFUL RESULTS.

CALORIES: 587
NET WEIGHT: 31 OUNCES
PREP TIME: 20 MINUTES
COOK TIME: 20 to 25 MINUTES
CALORIE-TO-WEIGHT RATIO: 19 CALORIES PER OUNCE

- 2 cups of chicken broth, skimmed of fat
- 1/3 cup polenta
- 4 ounces chicken breast, boned and skinned
- 1/2 cup fat-free (lite) pasta (marinara) sauce

- 1 cup sliced fresh mushrooms
- 1/4 cup onion, chopped
- 1/2 cup whole baby carrots—smallest size
- 10 to 12 ounces frozen petite green beans

In a medium saucepan bring chicken broth to a boil. Stir in polenta with a wire whisk. Return to full boil, cover, reduce heat to medium-low and cook until thickened, about 3 to 5 minutes. Remove lid and continue to cook over low heat 20 to 25 minutes, stirring occasionally. Polenta should be very thick.

Meanwhile, cut chicken breasts into 1/2" - 3/4" cubes. Sprinkle with salt, pepper and garlic powder. Cook in a non-stick skillet over medium-high until browned on all sides. Add pasta sauce and 1/4 cup of water and stir to deglaze pan. Simmer for 5 minutes.

Microwave mushrooms, onions and carrots in a microwavable container, e.g. lidded glass, for 3 minutes. Add to pasta sauce and cook for 1 to 2 minutes.

Microwave green beans in a microwavable container, e.g. lidded glass, for 6 minutes. Put on a serving plate. Add salt and pepper to taste and 3 to 4 sprays of "I Can't Believe It's Not Butter."® Place polenta on serving plate, top with pasta sauce and serve with a quarter lemon.

CATFISH JAMBALAYA

JAMBALAYA IS FUN. USE ANY WHITE FISH. FOR RICHER FISH FLAVOR, SUBSTITUTE CLAM BASE FOR CHICKEN BASE.

CALORIES: 585
NET WEIGHT: 37 OUNCES
PREP TIME: 15 MINUTES
COOK TIME: 20 MINUTES
CALORIE-TO-WEIGHT RATIO: 16 CALORIES PER OUNCE

- 16 to 20 ounces clam juice
- 1 teaspoon quality chicken base
- 10 ounces peeled potatoes, diced
- 1 cup (5 ounces) onions, chopped
- 1/2 cup red kidney beans (canned), drained
- 1 cup canned okra, drained

- 1/4 cup each red and green bell peppers, diced
- 4 ounces catfish (or any white fish), cut into 1/2" to 3/4" chunks
- 1 ounce Canadian bacon, diced
- 1 teaspoon Cajun Creole seasoning
- 1/2 cup fat-free (lite) pasta (marinara) sauce

In medium saucepan combine clam juice, chicken base, potatoes and onions. Bring to a boil and cook uncovered 15 minutes until reduced by half.

Add kidney beans, okra, bell peppers, fish, Canadian bacon and Cajun Creole seasoning. Add salt (1/4 teaspoon) and

359

pepper (1/8 teaspoon) to taste. Reduce heat to simmer and cook 2 to 3 minutes or until fish flakes.

Serve in bowl and top with marinara. Serve with 1/4 lemon squeezed to taste.

CHARDONNAY POULET ETUVÉE

THE "WHITE" VERSION OF CLASSIC BOEUF BOURGUIGNONNE FOR A MORE
DELICATE FLAVOR.

CALORIES: 630
NET WEIGHT: 36 OUNCES
PREP TIME: 20 MINUTES
COOK TIME: 30 MINUTES
CALORIE-TO-WEIGHT RATIO: 17 CALORIES PER OUNCE

- 4 ounces chicken breast, boned, skinned and rough chopped in 1/4" pieces
- One 14.5-ounce can chicken broth, fat skimmed
- 1 teaspoon quality chicken base
- 1 cup drinking quality Chardonnay wine
  [FYI: All the alcohol boils out]
- 8 ounces potatoes, 1" dice

- 2 cups whole baby carrots
- 2 cups small whole mushrooms
- 1/2 teaspoon commercial Italian herb seasoning
- 1/2 cup fat-free (lite) pasta (marinara) sauce
- 1/4 cup (1 ounce) frozen peas
- 12 Tablespoons quality grated Parmesan cheese, e.g. Reggiano

In a large nonstick skillet brown chicken. Remove.

To skillet add chicken broth, chicken base, Chardonnay, potatoes, carrots, mushrooms and Italian seasoning. Bring to a full boil and cook uncovered for 20 to 25 minutes, or until about 1/2 cup of liquid remains.

Reduce heat and add pasta sauce, chicken and pepper (1/8 teaspoon) to taste. Cook 3 to 4 minutes. Add peas. Garnish with Parmesan. Serve.

CHICKEN MARENGO NOUVEAU

THE ORIGINAL CHICKEN MARENGO WAS CREATED FOR NAPOLEON BY HIS PERSONAL CHEF AFTER THE BATTLE OF MARENGO. THE NeoCuisine™ VERSION IS JUST AS TASTY AT 1/2 THE CALORIES.

CALORIES: 537
NET WEIGHT: 34 OUNCES
PREP TIME: 20 MINUTES
COOK TIME: 25 MINUTES
CALORIE-TO-WEIGHT RATIO: 15.7 CALORIES PER OUNCE

- 1-1/2 cups low-sodium chicken broth, fat skimmed
- 1/3 cup of orzo pasta
- 1/2 medium onion, cut in wedges
- 1 medium zucchini, cubed
- 1 cup halved small fresh mushrooms
- 1/2 can (14.5-ounce can) redi-cut diced tomatoes, drained
- 1/2 can (6-ounce can) tomato paste
- 1 (scant) cup low-sodium chicken broth, fat skimmed
- 3 strips of orange rind
- 1/2 teaspoon of dried commercial Italian herb seasoning
- 1 bay leaf
- 1/4 teaspoon garlic powder
- 4 ounces extra-firm ultra-low-fat tofu, cut in 1/2" cubes
- 1/2 packet aspartame
- 1/2 teaspoon dried basil

Bring 1 1/2 cups of chicken broth to a boil. Add orzo pasta and cook over medium heat until broth is absorbed and pasta is cooked, about 15 minutes.

Spray large saucepan with cooking spray. Add onion, zucchini and mushrooms. Sauté 5 minutes. Add tomatoes, tomato paste, one cup of chicken broth, orange rind, Italian seasoning, bay leaf and garlic powder. Bring to a boil, reduce heat, and add tofu.

Simmer covered until vegetables are tender; 10 to 15 minutes. Add aspartame, salt (1/4 teaspoon) and pepper (1/8 teaspoon) to taste. Discard bay leaf and orange rind. Add basil to orzo. Serve vegetables alongside orzo pasta.

COUNTRY UKRAINE STEW

CALORIES: 567
NET WEIGHT: 31 OUNCES
PREP TIME: 20 MINUTES
COOK TIME: 30 MINUTES

- 1/2 cup whole baby carrots (smallest size) or split larger size
- 1 medium onion, chopped
- 1 cup beef broth, skimmed of fat
- 1/4 cup uncooked bulgar
- 1/4 cup prepared roasted red bell peppers, cut in 1" pieces
- 4 ounces small red potatoes, unpeeled and quartered

- 2 cups halved fresh mushrooms
- 1 teaspoon quality beef base
- 1/4 teaspoon garlic powder
- 3/4 teaspoon dried thyme
- 1/4 teaspoon pepper
- 5 ounces eye of round, trimmed of fat

Combine all ingredients except eye of round in pot or large frying pan and bring to a boil. Reduce heat, cover and simmer until vegetables are tender and stew is thickened, about 30 minutes.

Meanwhile, preheat small nonstick skillet over high heat 2 to 3 minutes or until very hot. Rub eye of round with pepper and garlic salt to taste. Cook meat over high heat until both sides are well-browned and crusty. Cook to desired doneness. Remove and slice in 1/8" strips. Serve atop stew. Serve with quarter lemon wedge.

FLORENTINE SALMAGUNDI

A FILLING, QUICK VEGETABLE STEW WITH CHARACTER BELYING ITS NO-MEAT
HUMBLE ORIGINS.

CALORIES: 500
NET WEIGHT: 33 OUNCES
PREP TIME: 15 MINUTES
COOK TIME: 25 MINUTES
CALORIE-TO-WEIGHT RATIO: 15 CALORIES PER OUNCE

- 12 ounces potatoes, diced
- 8 ounces carrots, sliced
- 10 dry (no oil) sun-dried tomato halves, cut in half
- 1 cup (5 ounces) of onions, chopped
- 1 cup small whole mushrooms
- One 4.5-ounce can chicken broth, fat skimmed
- 1/4 cup frozen peas
- Juice of 1/4 lemon
- 1/2 package Good Seasons® Italian salad dressing mix

In a medium saucepan combine potatoes, carrots, sun-dried tomatoes, onions, mushrooms and chicken broth. Bring to a full boil and cook uncovered 15 to 20 minutes until reduced 1/3 to 1/2. (For a thicker sauce, use a fork or spoon to mash some potato against the inside of the pan.)

Add peas, lemon juice and Good Seasons®. Stir. Serve with 1/4 lemon wedge squeezed to taste.

FUSION STEW

BEAUTIFUL HARD WINTER CRACKED WHEAT—BULGAR—MAKES THIS RUSSIAN-ITALIAN FUSION HEARTY AND FILLING. THE USE OF QUALITY BALSAMIC IN THE AMALGAM SETS OFF THE STEW'S FLAVOR.

CALORIES: 557
NET WEIGHT: 38 OUNCES
PREP TIME: 5 MINUTES
CALORIE-TO-WEIGHT RATIO: 15 CALORIES PER OUNCE

- One and a half 14.5-ounce cans chicken broth, fat skimmed
- 1/2 teaspoon quality chicken base
- 1/3 cup uncooked bulgar
- 1/2 can (14.5-ounce can) redi-cut Italian recipe tomatoes, undrained
- 2 teaspoons balsamic vinegar
- 1 medium zucchini, halved lengthwise, thinly sliced
- 4 ounces frozen corn
- 1/2 can (15-ounce can) white beans, drained and rinsed
- 1 scant teaspoon commercial Italian herb seasoning
- 1 teaspoon Miracle Chop (see page 346)

In a heavy medium saucepan over medium-high heat, bring broth and chicken base to a boil. Stir in bulgar, tomatoes, balsamic vinegar and pepper (1/8 teaspoon) to taste. Return to boil, reduce heat to medium-low, cover and cook for 15 minutes.

Add zucchini, corn, beans, Italian herb seasoning and Miracle Chop. Cover and return to boil, then reduce heat to medium-low and cook 3 to 4 minutes or until bulgar and zucchini are tender.

GREEK LENTIL HOTCHPOT

LENTILS ARE UNDERUTILIZED BY AMERICANS. ONE WONDERS WHY GIVEN THEIR QUICK COOKING QUALITIES, HIGH NUTRITIONAL VALUE AND FLAVOR ADAPTABILITY. HERE'S A GOOD EXAMPLE OF LENTILS' VERSATILITY.

CALORIES: 430
NET WEIGHT: 34 OUNCES
PREP TIME: 20 MINUTES
COOK TIME: 36 to 37 MINUTES
CALORIE-TO-WEIGHT RATIO: 12.6 CALORIES PER OUNCE

- 1/2 cup onion, chopped
- 1/2 cup green bell pepper, chopped
- 1 cup peeled potatoes, 1" dice
- 1/2 cup lentils, washed and sorted
- 1/2 can (14.5-ounce can) redi-cut diced tomatoes; drain reserving fluid
- 1 teaspoon quality beef base
- 1-1/2 cups beef broth, fat skimmed

- 1/2 medium zucchini, sliced
- 4 ounces frozen petite green beans
- 1 teaspoon dried oregano
- 1/2 teaspoon dried mint
- 1/4 teaspoon ground coriander
- 1/4 teaspoon ground allspice
- 1/2 packet aspartame
- 1 teaspoon fresh lemon juice

In a large saucepan combine onion, green bell pepper, potatoes, lentils, juice of the diced tomatoes, beef base and beef stock. Bring to a boil. Reduce heat and simmer covered until lentils are tender, about 25 to 30 minutes.

Add zucchini, green beans, oregano, mint, coriander and allspice; simmer uncovered until vegetables are tender and stew is thickened, about 10 minutes. Add the drained tomatoes, aspartame and lemon juice. Add salt (1/4 teaspoon) and pepper (1/8 teaspoon) to taste. Cook 1 to 2 minutes. Serve.

MARSEILLES FISH STEW

HERE IS A SHORTCUT BOUILLABAISSE USING GOOD SEASONS® SALAD DRESSING MIX.

Calories: 530
Net weight: 31 ounces
Prep time: 15 minutes
Cook time: 28 minutes
Calorie-to-weight ratio: 17 calories per ounce

- 10 to 12 ounces potatoes, diced
- 7 to 8 ounces carrots, sliced or ready-to-eat baby carrots
- 10 dry (no oil) sun-dried tomato halves, cut in half
- 1 cup (5 ounces) onions, chopped
- Two 8- to 10-ounce cans/jars of clam juice: 16 to 20 ounces total

- 1/2 package Good Seasons® Italian salad dressing mix
- 1/2 teaspoon dried thyme
- 4 ounces red snapper, cut into 1/2" to 1" chunks
- Juice of 1 lemon

In a medium saucepan combine potatoes, carrots, sun-dried tomatoes, onions and clam juice. Bring to a full boil and cook uncovered 15 to 20 minutes until reduced by 1/3 to 1/2. (For a thicker sauce, use a fork or spoon to mash some potato against the inside of the pan.)

Add Good Seasons® dressing mix, thyme and snapper. Add salt (1/4 teaspoon) and pepper (1/8 teaspoon) to taste and cook 3 minutes or until fish begins to flake. Add lemon juice to stew. Serve.

MEZZ

SOUTHERN MEDITERRANEAN (THINK MOROCCO) FLAVOR BURSTS ON THE PALATE.
TRY THIS FOR DIFFERENT TASTE TONIGHT.

CALORIES: 548
NET WEIGHT: 36 OUNCES
PREP TIME: 10 to 15 MINUTES
COOK TIME: 40 MINUTES
CALORIE-TO-WEIGHT RATIO: 15 CALORIES PER OUNCE

- 1/2 cup uncooked cracked wheat bulgar
- 1-1/2 14.5-ounce cans beef broth, fat skimmed
- 2 medium carrots, peeled, leave whole
- 1 medium turnip, unpeeled, quartered
- 1 cup small red potatoes, unpeeled, quartered
- 2 cups whole small mushrooms
- 1/2 teaspoon cinnamon

- 1/4 teaspoon red pepper flakes
- 1 teaspoon ginger
- 1/4 teaspoon allspice
- 1/2 Tablespoon quality beef base
- 2 Tablespoons fresh parsley, chopped
- 1 packet aspartame

In large skillet combine all ingredients except parsley and aspartame. Bring to a boil. Reduce heat, cover and simmer 35 to 40 minutes. Add parsley and aspartame. Essential: Serve with 1/4 lemon wedge.

PHO

(PRONOUNCED FAW)

THIS IS THE FAMOUS NATIONAL DISH OF VIETNAM. RATHER THAN HAVE YOU RUN ALL OVER TOWN FOR PURPLE-TIPPED BASIL AND MUNG BEAN SPROUTS, THE RECIPE HAS BEEN ALTERED FOR INGREDIENTS READILY AT HAND ... WITH NO LOSS OF FLAVOR.

CALORIES: 521
NET WEIGHT: 33 OUNCES
PREP TIME: 20 MINUTES
COOK TIME: 20 MINUTES
CALORIE-TO-WEIGHT RATIO: 16 CALORIES PER OUNCE

- Two 14.5-ounce cans beef broth, fat skimmed
- 1 teaspoon quality beef base
- 1/8 teaspoon red pepper flakes
- 4 ounces uncooked whole wheat spaghetti
- 1 Tablespoon Hoisin sauce
- 2 teaspoons dried cilantro

- 2 rounded teaspoons dried basil
- 1 Tablespoon fresh lemon juice
- 1/2 cup scallions, chopped, white and green parts
- 1/2 packet aspartame
- 3 cups iceberg lettuce, shredded (or mung bean sprouts)

Combine beef broth, beef base, red pepper flakes and spaghetti in a medium sauce pan. Boil until spaghetti is done.

Add Hoisin sauce, cilantro, basil, lemon juice, scallions and aspartame. Return to a boil and remove from heat.

Put lettuce in a large serving bowl. Pour spaghetti and broth over lettuce. Mix and serve. Eat immediately with chop sticks and soup spoon.

366

ROSEMARY CHICKEN STROGANOFF

THIS HEART-SAVING RENDITION OF THE OLD AND HEAVY BEEF STROGANOFF VERSION IS NONETHELESS PALATE-REWARDING.

CALORIES: 563
NET WEIGHT: 30 OUNCES
PREP TIME: 15 MINUTES
COOK TIME: 5 MINUTES
CALORIE-TO-WEIGHT RATIO: 19 CALORIES PER OUNCE

- Hot baked potatoes totaling 16 ounces
- 2 ounces chicken breast, boned and skinned, cut into 1/4" ribbons
- 3 cups fresh mushrooms, sliced
- 1/4 cup red bell pepper, diced
- 1/4 teaspoon dried rosemary
- 2/3 cup nonfat plain yogurt
- 1/4 cup scallions, finely chopped, green parts only
- 2 teaspoons quality chicken base
- 1/2 packet aspartame
- 1/3 cup chicken broth, fat skimmed

Microwaving: Wash potato(es), put in a microwavable container, e.g. lidded glass, and microwave for 8 to 10 minutes, turning once. Conventional oven: Wash potato(s) and bake in oven at 400° for about 45 minutes. Check with fork.

In a medium nonstick skillet, brown chicken, mushrooms, red pepper and rosemary over high heat about 2 minutes or until any liquid is absorbed. Add yogurt, scallions, chicken base, aspartame and pepper (1/8 teaspoon) or to taste and cook until hot.

Pour chicken broth over fork-mashed potatoes. Potatoes should be well saturated. Add more broth if necessary. Top with chicken mixture.

SAUSAGE STEW

THIS RECIPE USES ONE OF THE EXCELLENT FAT-FREE SAUSAGES NOW AVAILABLE. THE BUTTERBALL® BRAND ADDS A NICE SMOKY FLAVOR.

CALORIES: 565
NET WEIGHT: 31 OUNCES
PREP TIME: 15 MINUTES
COOK TIME: 18 TO 23 MINUTES
CALORIE-TO-WEIGHT RATIO: 18 CALORIES PER OUNCE

- 12 ounces potatoes, diced
- 8 ounces carrots, sliced or ready-to-eat baby carrots
- 10 dry (no oil) sun-dried tomato halves, cut in half
- 1 cup (5 ounces) onions, chopped
- One 14.5-ounce can chicken broth, fat skimmed

- 4 ounces fat-free sausage (e.g. Butterball® turkey), sliced on diagonal
- 1/2 package Good Seasons® Italian salad dressing mix
- Juice of 1/4 lemon

In a medium saucepan combine potatoes, carrots, sun-dried tomatoes, onions and chicken broth. Bring to a full boil and cook uncovered 15 to 20 minutes until broth is reduced by 1/3 to 1/2. (For a thicker sauce, use a fork or spoon to mash a few potatoes against the inside of the pan). Add sausage and Good Seasons® dressing mix. Cook 2 to 3 minutes. Add lemon juice. Serve.

SHEPHERD'S PIE

THIS IS A NO-FAT VERSION OF THE CLASSIC. IT TAKES A LITTLE EXTRA TIME TO PREPARE, BUT THE RESULTS SPEAK FOR THEMSELVES.

CALORIES: 569
NET WEIGHT: 36 OUNCES
PREP TIME: 25 MINUTES
COOK TIME: 15 MINUTES
CALORIE-TO-WEIGHT RATIO: 16 CALORIES PER OUNCE

- One 14.5-ounce can beef broth, fat skimmed
- 6 ounces small baby carrots
- 2 teaspoons quality beef base
- Scant 1/2 teaspoon dried thyme
- 1/2 teaspoon garlic powder
- 1/4 cup tomato paste

- 2 cups sliced mushrooms
- 1 scallion (chop green and white parts separately)
- 1 medium zucchini
- 16 ounces peeled potatoes, diced large
- 1/4 cup peas
- 2 Tablespoons fat-free cream cheese

In a medium saucepan, combine 3/4 of the can of beef broth (reserve the rest for the crust), carrots, beef base, thyme, garlic powder, tomato paste, mushrooms, white part of scallion, zucchini and pepper (1/4 teaspoon) to taste. Bring to a full boil and cook until liquid is reduced by 1/3 to 1/2, 10 to 15 minutes.

Meanwhile, microwave potatoes in a microwavable container, e.g. lidded glass, 6 to 8 minutes until cooked through. Add half of the potatoes and the peas plus the saucepan ingredients to an oven-proof casserole.

Mash remaining potatoes, adding cream cheese and the green part of the scallion. Add 1 to 2 Tablespoons of the beef broth to smooth the mixture. Put mashed potatoes on waxed paper and form into a shape to cover the entire top of the casserole. Invert spud crust onto top of casserole.

Put under broiler 1 to 2 minutes or until potato crust is browned. Serve.

SOUTHWEST SMOKED PORK AND SQUASH STEW

CALORIES: 492
NET WEIGHT: 38 OUNCES
PREP TIME: 20 MINUTES
COOK TIME: 13 MINUTES

- 1-1/4 to 1-1/2 pounds raw butternut squash, split half lengthwise
- 1/4 cup prepared roasted red bell pepper
- One 14.5-ounce can chicken broth, fat skimmed
- 1 teaspoon quality beef base
- 1 teaspoon chili powder✶
- 4 ounces fat-free Canadian bacon, diced
- 1/4 teaspoon dried cilantro✶✶
- 1/2 cup canned black beans, drained
- 1/2 cup frozen corn, thawed and drained
- 1 lemon wedge

In a microwavable container, e.g. lidded glass, microwave squash for 8 to 10 minutes. Remove seeds. Scrape meat into blender.

Combine red bell pepper, chicken broth, beef base and chili powder in blender with squash. Pureé 1 minute until smooth. Pour pureé into a serving bowl.

Brown Canadian bacon and cilantro over medium-high heat. Add beans to Canadian bacon. Stir until heated. Add beans, bacon and corn to pureé. (Or hold out and heat separately as garnish.) Microwave 3 minutes. Serve with lemon wedge.

✶ Add another teaspoon if you like it hotter and more flavorful.
✶✶ Cilantro is a somewhat aquired taste. If you are unsure start with 1/8 teaspoon.

STROGANOFF RAGOUT

THIS IS A HUGE, FILLING DINNER OF FINE FLAVOR. THE CABBAGE IS BEEF-INFUSED, MAKING IT ESPECIALLY TASTY.

CALORIES: 554
NET WEIGHT: 37 OUNCES
PREP TIME: 15 MINUTES
COOK TIME: 20 MINUTES
CALORIE-TO-WEIGHT RATIO: 15 CALORIES PER OUNCE

- 2 ounces top round, sliced into 1/4" ribbons
- 12 ounces (5 to 6 cups) packaged shredded cabbage (cole slaw mix)
- 6 to 7 ounces whole baby carrots
- 8 ounces potatoes, diced
- 8 ounces small whole mushrooms
- One 14.5-ounce can beef broth, fat skimmed

- 2 teaspoons quality beef base
- 1/2 teaspoon dried thyme
- 1/2 teaspoon garlic powder
- 1/2 packet aspartame
- 1/4 cup nonfat sour cream

In large nonstick skillet brown top round on high heat. Add shredded cabbage, carrots, potatoes, mushrooms, beef broth, beef base, thyme and garlic powder. Bring to full boil and cook uncovered for 10 minutes.

Reduce heat, cover and simmer for 10 minutes more or until cabbage is cooked. Add pepper (1/8 teaspoon) to taste and aspartame. Meanwhile warm sour cream in microwave for 30 seconds.

Plate ragout. Drizzle with sour cream. Garnish with parsley.

SWEET APPLE KRAUT with BACON and SAUSAGE

USER-FRIENDLY MILD KRAUT WITH APPLE, RAISINS, BACON AND NO-FAT TURKEY SAUSAGE.

CALORIES: 491
NET WEIGHT: 32 OUNCES
PREP TIME: 5 MINUTES
COOK TIME: 20 MINUTES
CALORIE-TO-WEIGHT RATIO: 15 CALORIES PER OUNCE

- 3 cups sauerkraut, rinsed well and squeezed
- 1 red apple, skin on, diced
- 1 cup beef broth, fat skimmed
- 1 Tablespoon raisins
- 1 large link (7 ounces) fat-free smoked turkey sausage (200 to 250 calories) cut into 1/2" coins
- 1/2 teaspoon dried thyme
- 1/4 teaspoon caraway seeds
- 2 ounces Canadian bacon, julienned

Combine all ingredients in a saucepan and bring to a boil. Reduce heat, cover and simmer for 5 minutes. Optional: Leave sausage whole and boil.

WARM CHICKEN TABBOULEH

TABBOULEH IS TYPICALLY SERVED COLD AS A SALAD BUT IN WORLD FLAVOR
FUSION FASHION, IT'S SERVED HOT FOR A SAPID NEW EXPERIENCE.

CALORIES: 553
NET WEIGHT: 32 OUNCES
PREP TIME: 25 MINUTES
COOK TIME: 20 MINUTES
CALORIE-TO-WEIGHT RATIO: 17 CALORIES PER OUNCE

- 1/2 cup bulgar wheat
- 1 cup chicken broth, fat skimmed
- 1 teaspoon quality chicken base
- 2 cups zucchini, cut in 1/4" coins
- 1 cup fresh mushrooms, sliced
- 3 ounces chicken breast, boned and skinned
- 2 Tablespoons Miracle Chop (see page 346)
- 2 scallions, finely minced, white and green parts
- 1/2 teaspoon dried mint leaves
- 1 medium tomato, diced
- 1/2 cup prepared roasted red bell peppers, chopped
- 1/2 packet aspartame

Combine bulgar, chicken stock, chicken base, zucchini and mushrooms in a medium saucepan. Bring to a boil and cook uncovered over medium heat for 15 minutes or until almost all liquid is absorbed.

Meanwhile quickly brown chicken breast in a nonstick skillet over high heat until cooked. Cut into strips.

Combine all ingredients except chicken. Add pepper (1/8 teaspoon) to taste. Put on a serving dish and top with chicken strips. Important: Finish with a squeeze of 1/4 to 1/2 lemon.

STIR-FRIES

CHILI'D CHICKEN STIR-FRY

NOTED FOR ITS FIERY HOT FOOD, SZECHUANESE COOKERY DIDN'T GET CHILI PEPPERS UNTIL THE 16TH CENTURY. PORTUGUESE TRADERS BROUGHT THE NEW WORLD CHILIES TO THEIR MACAU COLONY AND FROM THERE, CHILI'S POPULARITY SPREAD LIKE WILDFIRE, SO TO SPEAK. THE CULINARY ARTS OF THE WORLD WERE LITERALLY TURNED UPSIDE DOWN FROM THE SPREAD OF NEW WORLD FOODS. MAKE THIS AS HOT AS YOU LIKE WITH ADDITIONAL RED CHILI PEPPER FLAKES.

CALORIES: 550
NET WEIGHT: 28 OUNCES
PREP TIME: 10 MINUTES
COOK TIME: 5 MINUTES
CALORIE-TO-WEIGHT RATIO: 20 CALORIES PER OUNCE

- 1 cup instant rice
- 1 cup low-sodium chicken broth, skimmed of fat
- 2 ounces chicken breast, boned and skinned, cut in 1/4" ribbons
- 16 ounces stir-fry vegetables, thawed and drained of excess water✶
- 1/4 cup soy sauce
- 1 Tablespoon white wine vinegar

- 1/8 teaspoon crushed red pepper flakes
- 1/2 teaspoon garlic powder
- 1 teaspoon dark sesame oil
- 1 teaspoon quality chicken base
- 2 packets aspartame

Prepare rice according to box directions (do not use salt or butter) using chicken broth for the liquid. While rice sits, prepare the chicken and vegetables. In a large skillet, brown the chicken over high heat. Add soy sauce, white wine vinegar, red pepper flakes, garlic powder, sesame oil and chicken base. Deglaze pan.

Add drained vegetables and aspartame and stir until heated, but do not cook.

Put on one side of serving plate with rice alongside and serve.

✶Do not buy a vegetable mix that comes with its own sauce. Note that stir-fry vegetables only need to be heated. Generally, no extended cooking is required. You want crispiness.

CHINESE-FRIED CHICKEN NOODLES

CLASSICAL INGREDIENTS INCLUDING THE REQUISITE GINGER TO MAKE YOU BELIEVE YOU ORDERED IN CHINESE. BUT, NeoCuisine™ STIR-FRIES REDUCE CALORIES BY ALMOST 1/2.

CALORIES: 582
NET WEIGHT: 30 OUNCES
PREP TIME: 5 to 10 MINUTES
COOK TIME: 5 MINUTES
CALORIE-TO-WEIGHT RATIO: 19 CALORIES PER OUNCE

- 1 cup cooked whole wheat spaghetti
- 2 ounces chicken breast, boned and skinned, cut in 1/4" ribbons
- 16 ounces stir-fry vegetables, thawed and drained of excess water✶
- 1/4 cup low-sodium soy sauce
- 1 Tablespoon white wine vinegar
- 1/2 teaspoon lemon zest
- 1/8 teaspoon crushed red pepper flakes✶✶

- 1/2 teaspoon garlic powder
- 1/2 teaspoon ginger
- 1 teaspoon quality chicken base
- 8 to 10 ounces (4 to 5 cups) shredded cole slaw cabbage
- 2 packets aspartame

Prepare spaghetti according to package directions. While spaghetti is cooking, prepare chicken and vegetables.

In a large nonstick skillet or wok, brown chicken over high heat. Add soy sauce, white wine vinegar, red pepper flakes, garlic powder, ginger, chicken base and cole slaw. Deglaze pan and cook for 3 minutes.

Add drained vegetables, lemon zest, spaghetti and aspartame. Reheat and serve immediately.

✶Do not buy a vegetable mix that comes with its own sauce. Note that stir-fry vegetables only need to be heated. Generally, no extended cooking is required. You want crispiness.

✶✶Use less for less kick

SHRIMP WOK

ROCKEFELLER UNIVERSITY IN NYC DISCOVERED SHRIMP IS GREAT FOR THE HEART. ALTHOUGH HIGH IN CHOLESTEROL, SHRIMP CONTAINS LOW SATURATED FAT, THE REAL CULPRIT IN BLOOD CHOLESTEROL ELEVATION. SHRIMP IS ALSO RICH IN OMEGA 3s WHICH PLAY A BENEFICIAL ROLE IN PREVENTING HEART DISEASE.[1]

CALORIES: 495
NET WEIGHT: 28 OUNCES
PREP TIME: 5 MINUTES
COOK TIME: 5 MINUTES
CALORIE-TO-WEIGHT RATIO: 18 CALORIES PER OUNCE

- 1 cup instant rice
- 1 cup clam juice
- 1/4 cup low-sodium soy sauce
- 1 Tablespoon white wine vinegar
- 1/8 teaspoon crushed red pepper flakes
- 1/2 teaspoon garlic powder

- 1 teaspoon dark sesame oil
- 1 teaspoon quality chicken base
- 2 packets aspartame
- 2 ounces large shrimp, cooked (not little popcorn shrimp
- 16 ounces frozen stir-fry vegetables, thawed and drained of excess water✶

Prepare rice according to box directions (do not use salt or butter) using clam juice for liquid. Meanwhile, prepare rest of dish.

In a large skillet or wok, add soy sauce, white wine vinegar, red pepper flakes, garlic powder, sesame oil and chicken base. Bring to a boil. Reduce heat and add aspartame, shrimp and drained vegetables. Stir until heated, but do not cook. Put on one side of serving plate with rice alongside or as shown in picture. Serve.

✶Do not buy a vegetable mix that comes with its own sauce. Note that stir-fry
vegetables only need to be heated. Generally, no extended cooking is required. You want crispiness.

SZECHUAN BEEF AND VEGETABLE STIR-FRY

CLASSIC STIR-FRY WITH NO FAT OR SUGAR AND OPULENT FLAVOR.

CALORIES: 515
NET WEIGHT: 27 OUNCES
PREP TIME: 10 MINUTES
COOK TIME: 5 MINUTES
CALORIE-TO-WEIGHT RATIO: 19 CALORIES PER OUNCE

- 1 cup instant rice
- 1 cup beef broth, fat skimmed
- 2 ounces top round cut in 1/4" ribbons
- 16 ounces stir-fry vegetables, thawed and drained of excess water
- 1/4 cup low-sodium soy sauce
- 1 Tablespoon white wine vinegar
- 1/4 teaspoon crushed red pepper flakes
- 1/2 teaspoon garlic powder
- 1 teaspoon dark sesame oil
- 1 teaspoon quality beef base
- 2 packets aspartame

Prepare rice according to box directions (do not use salt or butter) using beef broth for the liquid. While rice sits, prepare the beef and vegetables.

In a large skillet or wok, brown the beef over high heat. Add soy sauce, white wine vinegar, red pepper flakes, garlic powder, sesame oil and beef base. Deglaze pan.

Add drained vegetables and aspartame. Stir until thoroughly heated, but do not cook.

Put on one side of serving plate with rice alongside and serve.

VEGETABLE BOATS

ACORN WHITE BEAN CHILI

A QUICK RECIPE WITH AN UNUSUAL PRESENTATION. EATING FOOD OUT OF A NATURAL FOOD CONTAINER ADDS A BIT OF HUMOR TO THE DINNER HOUR. ENJOY THE FRIVOLITY.

CALORIES: 541
NET WEIGHT: 41 OUNCES
PREP TIME: 35 MINUTES
COOK TIME: 30 MINUTES
CALORIE-TO-WEIGHT RATIO: 13 CALORIES PER OUNCE

- 4 ounces red potatoes with skin on, diced
- 1/2 medium carrot, grated
- 1/2 stalk celery, chopped
- 1/2 14.5-ounce can white beans, undrained
- 1 teaspoon red wine vinegar
- 1 teaspoon cumin powder

- 1 teaspoon chili powder
- 1/2 teaspoon dried cilantro
- 1/8 cup chicken broth, fat skimmed
- 1/2 Tablespoon quality chicken base
- 1/4 packet aspartame
- One 1-1/2 pound acorn squash

Combine potatoes, carrot and celery in a microwavable container, e.g. lidded glass, and microwave for 7 to 10 minutes until well-cooked.

Put in a bowl and add white beans, red wine vinegar, cumin powder, chili powder, cilantro, chicken broth and chicken base. Cover with a plate and microwave until hot, about 3 minutes. remove and add aspartame.

Cut squash in half and remove seeds. Slice a small piece off each bottom so squash sits evenly. Cover with plastic wrap and microwave for 8 minutes, turning once.

Fill center with chili. Serve with a lemon wedge (you will want it).

BLACK BEAN CHILI IN EGGPLANT

Although eggplant may not be everyone's favorite vegetable, this dish will surprise you. Neutral in flavor, eggplant picks up the redolent native Sonoran spices of cominos and chilies. Eat the skin too, you'll be surprised how much
you enjoy it.

Calories: 341
Net weight: 23 ounces
Prep time: 5 minutes
Cook time: 13 minutes
Calorie-to-weight ratio: 15 calories per ounce

- 1 pound eggplant
- One 14.5-ounce can black beans, drained
- One 14.5-ounce can redi-cut Italian tomatoes, drained
- 1 Tablespoon quality beef base
- 1 Tablespoon chili powder
  (add more or less as personal tastes dictate)

- 1 Tablespoon cumin powder
- 1 packet aspartame
- 1/4 cup Kraft® fat-free shredded cheddar cheese
- 2 Tablespoons onions, chopped

376

Cut eggplant in half, cover each half with plastic wrap and microwave for 8 minutes (or until done), turning once.

While eggplant cooks: Combine black beans, tomatoes, beef base, chili powder and cumin. Bring to a boil. Remove. Add aspartame.

Spread eggplant meat in shell to form a well. Fill with half the chili mixture. Garnish with cheddar and onion.

THE BEST GIFT

Of all of life's great joys—the love of a child, the job of your dreams, a marriage filled with love—one of the most profound is giving yourself a new body. The gift of a new body is one of the most prized because it is the physical presence of who you are. Pride in your body, the health of your body, the strength of your body, the endurance of your body dictate to a large measure your happiness and self-appreciation. It's not something to be taken lightly.

We all love new things. Buy a new watch and the excitement lasts for maybe a week? A new car six months? A new house a year? How about the gift of something the excitement of which lasts your entire lifetime? Your new body is a gift to yourself you will appreciate every day. First of all, you feel immensely better physically. No matter what the activity, you notice you do it with noticeably more vigor. You surprise yourself with your strength, endurance and improved sense of balance and grace. Around the house you lift with greater ease. When you shop you charge full ahead. Whatever your sport, you perform it faster and better. Yard work seems easier and goes apace. In all, you will be considerably more fit.

[1]"Keep Shrimp on the Team," *U.C. Berkeley Wellness Letter,* vol. 13, no. 6, March 1997, pages 1-2, BB251.

NeoCuisine™ DESSERTS

NeoCuisine™ desserts range in calorie-to-weight ratios of 15 to 25 calories per ounce. These calorie to weight ratios are in marked contrast to conventional desserts which typically have 80 to 150 calories per ounce. Accordingly, you can have marvelous dainties for the day's greatest period of temptation—the dreaded 7 to Bed day-part.

NeoCuisine™ desserts range from Anyberry pies to three cheesecake varieties to custards, brown Betseys and puddings. The approaches are innovative with, for example, pie crusts being made with low-fat bread crumbs versus the typical high fat pastry dough.

All recipes use aspartame which requires some explanation. You may be slightly surprised when you read a recipe calling for, say, 25 packages of aspartame. But as you know, despite the occasional aspartame yellow-press over the Internet, it is thoroughly well-researched and entirely safe according to the Mayo Clinic.

The United States Centers for Disease Control has investigated hundreds of aspartame complaints and concluded it does not cause health problems. This coincides with the FDA and American Medical Association findings.[1]

The amount of aspartame you consume in a dessert is actually less than the amount contained in a diet soda. Be aware not to confuse Sweet 'n' Low® with aspartame. Sweet 'n' Low® is saccharin and does not have the correct flavor profile for NeoCuisine™ desserts.

Technical considerations aside, you will be more than pleased with NeoCuisine™ desserts based on their quantity, flavor and appeal. For what amounts to typically just 25% of the calories found in the original, NeoCuisine™ desserts are just short of amazing. Try them all. You won't be disappointed.

One of the certain surprises of many NeoCuisine™ desserts is their protein content. If you haven't quite achieved the recommended 1/2 gram protein per pound of body weight goal, NeoCuisine™ desserts can help make up the shortfall. See all the cheesecakes, Flan with Maple Sauce and Anyberry Frappe (which contains a whopping 24 grams protein).

ANYBERRY FRAPPE

HERE IS A DESSERT SHAKE THAT HAS IT ALL. LOW CALORIE-TO-WEIGHT RATIO, MARVELOUS KEEPING QUALITIES (IT CAN BE KEPT IN YOUR REFRIGERATOR FOR A COUPLE OF DAYS) FINE SATIETY QUALITIES AND A HUGE DOSE OF PROTEIN—24 GRAMS! MORE THAN THAT, IT TASTES GREAT.

CALORIES: APPROXIMATELY 280 OR LESS (DEPENDING ON BERRY)
YIELD: 1 QUART SERVING
PREP TIME: 5 MINUTES
CALORIE-TO-WEIGHT RATIO: 9 CALORIES PER OUNCE
PROTEIN PER QUART: 24 GRAMS ←LOOK AT THIS!

- 12-13 ounces extra-firm ultra-low fat tofu
- 1 pint of favorite berry
- 10 packets aspartame, or to taste
- Pinch of salt (optional)
- 1 teaspoon vanilla
- 1 cup+ ice cubes

In blender combine all ingredients except ice. Blend until smooth, about 1 minute. Add ice and blend another minute.

Make in the morning and take to work—it keeps well in the refrigerator. It will get a little thicker but will not separate and the flavor remains unchanged.

APPLE BROWN BETSEY

HERE IS A NO-FAT, NO-SUGAR, FIRST-RATE, OLD-FASHIONED APPLE BREAD PUDDING, EVERY BIT AS GOOD AS ITS HIGH-FAT AND CALORIE COUSINS AT 1/3 THE CALORIES.

CALORIES: 205 PER SERVING
YIELD: 2 SERVINGS
PREP TIME: 15 MINUTES
CALORIE-TO-WEIGHT RATIO: 23 CALORIES PER OUNCE

- 2 medium green apples, pared, cored and cut into 8 wedges each
- 1 Tablespoon fresh lemon juice
- 1/4 teaspoon nutmeg
- 1 teaspoon cinnamon
- 2 slices light bread (such as Wonder® Bread Light)

- 5 packets aspartame
- 1/2 cup EggBeaters®
- 1/2 cup nonfat milk
- 5 packets aspartame
- 1/2 cup 70% reduced calorie maple syrup
- 12 packets aspartame
- 1 teaspoon vanilla

Combine apples, lemon juice, nutmeg and cinnamon in a microwavable container, e.g. lidded glass. Microwave 5 minutes or until apples are soft.

Choose an oven proof square dish to fit bread slices snugly (7 to 8 inches each side). Lay one slice in the bottom of the dish. Add apple mix. Sprinkle with 5 packets aspartame. Top with second slice of bread and press lightly.

Combine EggBeaters®, milk and 5 packets aspartame. Pour over the top. Bake uncovered at 400° for 30 to 35 minutes.

Combine syrup, 12 packets aspartame and vanilla. Microwave 1 minute. Pour over cooked Betsey. Garnish with chopped dried cranberries or raisins.

BAVARIAN CREAM

AN ALL-PURPOSE SAUCE GOOD ON ABOUT ANYTHING SWEET.

CALORIES: 280
YIELD: 2-1/2 CUPS
PREP TIME: 6 MINUTES
CALORIE-TO-WEIGHT RATIO: 15 CALORIES PER OUNCE

- 1 package fat-free, sugar-free instant vanilla pudding
- 2 cups nonfat milk
- 1 teaspoon vanilla
- 1/4 teaspoon almond extract
- 1/8 teaspoon salt
- Pinch nutmeg
- 25 packets aspartame

Make pudding following the package directions using nonfat milk. Add the rest of the ingredients. Mix.

BAVARIAN CREAM WITH ANYBERRIES

ALTHOUGH BAVARIAN CREAM IS FAT-FREE, IT MIMICS REAL CREAM.

CALORIES: 186
YIELD: 1 SERVING
PREP TIME: 7 MINUTES
CALORIE-TO-WEIGHT RATIO: 13 CALORIES PER OUNCE

- 1 cup any berries, sliced
- 2 packets aspartame
- 1 cup Bavarian Cream (see page 380)

Mix berries with aspartame. Serve with Bavarian Cream.

BERRY SAUCE

MADE WITH EITHER FRESH OR FROZEN BERRIES THIS SAUCE CAN BE USED WITH CHEESECAKE, ANGEL FOOD CAKE, ATOP FAT-FREE/SUGAR-FREE FROZEN YOGURT, AND MANY OTHER USES YOUR CREATIVE MIND DEVISES. THE PUREÉING RELEASES FLAVORS .

CALORIES: 100
YIELD: 1 CUP
PREP TIME: 2 MINUTES
CALORIE-TO-WEIGHT RATIO: 12 CALORIES PER OUNCE

- 1-1/2 cups individual quick frozen (IQF) thawed or fresh berries (such as raspberries, strawberries, blackberries and Marion berries)
- 20 packets aspartame

Combine berries and aspartame in a blender and pureé 10 to 15 seconds.

FAT-FREE, SUGAR-FREE ANYBERRY CHEESECAKE

THIS ONE IS MY CHEESECAKE PERSONAL FAVORITE. THE BERRY SAUCE THICKENS ON ITS OWN BECAUSE OF THE FRUIT'S NATURAL PECTIN. YOU'LL LIKE THIS NeoCuisine™ DESSERT. AS AN ADDED BONUS, EACH CHEESECAKE IS RICH IN PROTEIN WHICH HELPS YOU FILL YOUR DAY'S PROTEIN REQUIREMENT. EACH SLICE OF NeoCuisine™ CHEESECAKE HAS 7-1/2 GRAMS PROTEIN.

CALORIES: 94 PER SERVING
YIELD: 8 SERVINGS
PREP TIME: 20 MINUTES
CALORIE-TO-WEIGHT RATIO: 24 CALORIES PER OUNCE
PROTEIN: 7.5 GRAMS PER SLICE

- 12 ounces fat-free block cream cheese (not in tub)
- 1 cup nonfat milk
- 1 Tablespoon vanilla
- 1 package Knox® unflavored gelatin
- 1 Tablespoon fresh lemon juice
- 1 teaspoon lemon zest
- 48 packets aspartame
- 1 recipe Crumb Crust (see page 383)
- 1 recipe Berry Sauce (see page 381)

Remove cream cheese from foil wrap. Microwave for 1 to 2 minutes or until soft.

Heat milk and vanilla until hot. Remove from heat, add gelatin and stir until dissolved.

Add cream cheese to milk and whisk until smooth. Add lemon juice, lemon zest and aspartame. Gently pour into pie plate and chill until set, about one hour.

Pour Berry Sauce over top. Chill for several hours. Best served at room temperature.

CLASSIC N.Y. CHEESECAKE

IF YOU LIKE YOUR CHEESECAKE AU NATURAL, THEN THE CLASSIC NEW YORK STYLE IS FOR YOU. FLAVORED WITH LEMON JUICE AND ZEST, IT HAS A NICE, FRESH, CLEAN FLAVOR. A FINISH OF VANILLA SOUR CREAM TOPPING COMPLETES THE PRESENTATION. A SLICE OF THIS AT 9 PM MAKES YOU THINK THAT YOU CAN HARDLY BE STRIPPING FAT WHILE ENJOYING A TASTY TREAT.

CALORIES: 100 PER SERVING
YIELD: 8 SERVINGS
PREP TIME: 20 MINUTES
CALORIE-TO-WEIGHT RATIO: 25 CALORIES PER OUNCE
PROTEIN: 7.5 GRAMS PER SLICE

- 12 ounces fat-free block cream cheese (not in tub)
- 1 cup nonfat milk
- 1 Tablespoon vanilla
- 1 package Knox® unflavored gelatin
- 1 Tablespoon fresh lemon juice
- 1 teaspoon lemon zest
- 48 packets aspartame
- 1 recipe Crumb Crust (see below)
- 1/2 cup nonfat sour cream
- 1 teaspoon vanilla
- 4 packets aspartame

Remove cream cheese from foil wrap. Microwave for 1 to 2 minutes or until soft.

Heat milk and 1 Tablespoon vanilla to hot. Remove from heat, add gelatin and stir until dissolved.

Add cream cheese, lemon juice, lemon zest and 48 packets aspartame to milk and whisk until smooth. Pour into pie plate and chill until set, about one hour.

Combine sour cream, 1 teaspoon vanilla and 4 packets aspartame. Pour over cheescake and refrigerate. Best served at room temperature.

CRUMB CRUST

THIS ULTRA-LOW-FAT CRUST HAS 75% FEWER CALORIES THAN REGULAR CRUST AND
IS A BREEZE TO MAKE.

Calories: 200
Prep time: 2 minutes

- 1/2 cup plain bread crumbs
- 4 packets aspartame
- 1 Tablespoon water
- 1 teaspoon vanilla
- 1 teaspoon "I Can't Believe It's Not Butter"®

Combine bread crumbs and aspartame in a pie plate. Add water, vanilla and "I Can't Believe It's Not Butter."® Mix using fingers to break up lumps. Crumbs stick together slightly but should not be doughy. Even out crust on bottom only of pie plate using your hand. Press firmly.

DOUBLE DUTCH CHOCOLATE PUDDING

MASS-MARKETED FLAVOR PROFILES (ALL NATIONAL BRANDS) MAKE THEIR PRODUCTS FOR THE LITTLE OLD LADIES IN LARAMIE AND THE BABIES IN BOISE. YOU WANT FLAVOR FORCE. HERE IT IS.

CALORIES: 180 PER SERVING
YIELD: 2 ONE-CUP + SERVINGS
PREP TIME: 5 MINUTES
CALORIE-TO-WEIGHT RATIO: 20 CALORIES PER OUNCE

- 1 package fat-free, sugar-free instant chocolate pudding
- 2 cups nonfat milk
- 2 Tablespoons Dutch cocoa✶
- 25 packets aspartame
- 1/8 teaspoon salt
- 1 teaspoon vanilla
- 1 Tablespoon chocolate extract

Make chocolate pudding according to the package directions using nonfat milk. Add the rest of the ingredients. Mix. Chill.

✶ It is not an affectation using genuine imported Dutch cocoa (e.g. Droestes®). The flavor is different and better.

FLAN WITH MAPLE SAUCE

DON'T DISMISS THIS RECIPE FOR ITS FEW INGREDIENTS. IT'S EXQUISITE AND PROTEIN-PACKED. THIS RECIPE MAKES TWO SERVINGS AT ONLY 102 CALORIES EACH.

CALORIES: 102 PER SERVING
YIELD: TWO 5-1/2 OUNCE SERVINGS
PREP TIME: 2 MINUTES
CALORIE-TO-WEIGHT RATIO: 19 CALORIES PER OUNCE
PROTEIN: 7 GRAMS PER SERVING

- 1 cup nonfat milk
- 1/4 cup fat-free egg substitute, e.g. Eggbeaters®
- 5 packets aspartame

384

- 1 teaspoon vanilla
- 1/4 cup 70% reduced-calorie maple syrup
- 4 packets aspartame

In a medium bowl, whisk together milk, EggBeaters®, aspartame and vanilla. Pour into 1 or 2 large custard cups.

Put the cup(s) into a larger pan, pour in hot water to within 2 inches of the top of the pan and bake 35 to 40 minutes at 325° or until the center is set.

Mix aspartame with reduced calorie maple syrup.

Let flan set for 1 hour before serving. Pour syrup over the top.

NEW ORLEANS RICE PUDDING

REMINISCENT OF TAPIOCA AT HALF THE CALORIES.

CALORIES: 235
YIELD: 1 LARGE SERVING
PREP TIME: 10 MINUTES
CALORIE-TO-WEIGHT RATIO: 22 CALORIES PER OUNCE

INGREDIENTS
- 1/2 cup cooked instant rice
- 1 cup Bavarian Cream (see page 380)

Prepare rice according to package directions (do not use salt or butter). Combine rice with Bavarian Cream. Chill.

PUMPKIN CHEESECAKE

IF YOU'VE NEVER HAD PUMPKIN CHEESECAKE, THIS WON'T DISAPPOINT. IF YOU ARE A PUMPKIN CHEESE-CAKE AFFICIONADO, THEN YOU'LL ENJOY THIS VERSION AT ABOUT 1/3 THE CALORIES. IT HAS PLENTY OF PUMPKIN PIE SPICE FOR AUTHENTIC HOMEMADE FLAVOR.

CALORIES: 97 PER SERVING
YIELD: 8 SERVINGS
PREP TIME: 20 to 25 MINUTES
CALORIE-TO-WEIGHT RATIO: 24 CALORIES PER OUNCE
PROTEIN: 7.5 GRAMS PER SLICE

- 12 ounces nonfat block cream cheese (not in tub)
- 1 cup nonfat milk
- 1 Tablespoon vanilla
- 1 package Knox® unflavored gelatin
- 1 cup canned pumpkin
- 2 teaspoons pumpkin pie spice
- 50 packets aspartame
- 1 Crumb Crust (see page 383)
- 1/2 cup nonfat sour cream
- 1 teaspoon vanilla
- 4 packets aspartame

Remove cream cheese from its foil wrap. Microwave 1 to 2 minutes or until soft.

Meanwhile heat milk and 1 Tablespoon vanilla until hot. Remove milk from heat, add gelatin and stir until dissolved.

Add cream cheese to milk and whisk until smooth. Then add pumpkin, pumpkin pie spice and 50 packets aspartame. Pour into prepared pie plate and chill until set, about one hour.

Combine sour cream, 1 teaspoon vanilla and 4 packets aspartame. Pour over cheesecake and refrigerate. Best served at room temperature.

RASPBERRY PIE

OWING TO THEIR FRAGILITY, RASPBERRIES REQUIRE NO COOKING. RASPBERRY JELLO IS USED TO SET THE PIE, ADDING FLAVOR. A QUARTER OF THIS PIE IS A MERE 150 CALORIES. YOU'LL FIND OUT WHY THE FRENCH LOVE THEIR *FRAMBROISE*.

CALORIES: 150 PER SERVING
YIELD: 4 SERVINGS
PREP TIME: 10 MINUTES
CALORIE-TO-WEIGHT RATIO: 2 CALORIES PER OUNCE

- 1 small package sugar-free raspberry Jell-O®
- 1/2 cup boiling water
- 1 recipe Crumb Crust (see page 383)
- 20 packets aspartame
- Juice of 1 lemon
- 24 to 36 ounces of individual quick-frozen (IQF) whole raspberries; defrosted, undrained

Mix Jell-O® with 1/2 cup of boiling water. Stir constantly until dissolved. Set aside.

Make Crumb Crust.

Again, stir Jell-O® thoroughly. Add aspartame and lemon juice. Stir. Add raspberries. Stir gently. Fill pie plate with mixture. Refrigerate until set or overnight.

RICOTTA FRUIT PARFAIT

**VERY CONTINENTAL, THIS RECIPE USES FAT-FREE RICOTTA CHEESE
AND BERRIES OF YOUR CHOICE.**

- CALORIES: 200
- YIELD: 1 SERVING
- PREP TIME: 5 MINUTES
- CALORIE-TO-WEIGHT RATIO: 15 CALORIES PER OUNCE

INGREDIENTS
- 8 ounces fat-free ricotta cheese
- 10 packets aspartame
- 1/2 Tablespoon fresh lemon juice
- Zest of one lemon
- 1/2 cup berries of choice; frozen (thawed) or fresh

Combine ricotta, aspartame, lemon juice and a pinch of salt. Mix with electric mixer until smooth, about 1 minute. Stir in lemon zest.

In a glass dessert bowl or wine glass put 1/2 cup of cheese mixture. Add 1/4 cup of fruit. Top with remaining cheese mixture then rest of fruit.

[1]"Low-Calorie Sweeteners," *Mayo Clinic Health Letter,* August 1999, page 7, BB480.

1,000,000-YEAR INSTINCT

Through the millennia of man's evolution, the human body taught itself to demand quick action when hungry. Hunger meant serious hunting and food gathering. After all, it took only a few foodless days before the body became weak with starvation and death the inevitable end. So the body forcefully fights starvation. Overwhelming hunger messages spurred our ancestral hunters to seek food. Unfortunately we live with the same biology as our forebears of 50,000 years ago. Hunger drives us to eat. No wonder hunger management challenges us. When the body's hungry, it wants action *now*.

NC HI PRO NO-FAT/SUGAR DREAM™

This is the perfect lunch because it's protein-rich, thus stimulating catecholamine neurotransmitter increase.[1] Sometimes these kinds of things sound like so much hocus-pocus but many studies conclude that protein really does help wake us up. You'll notice and appreciate the afternoon boost.

Using whey protein recommended in the recipe offers the highest natural source of immune-boosting immunoglobulins. This is one of the primary reasons why pediatricians recommend breastfeeding since mother's milk is rich in infection-suppressing immunoglobulins.[2]

Done right, the NC HiPro Dream™ is a match for anything mixed at Baskin Robbins. Seriously. The name comes, justifiably, from the amalgam's opulence. Note the recipe calls for whey protein powder mix. There are numerous protein powders but this shake requires the use of whey as its protein source versus soybean extractives. Soy protein powder doesn't give you the same delicious results as a whey protein powder. Buy vanilla flavor as a neutral base for all added flavorings.

A couple of other things. The recipe's recommended unsweetened psyllium powder adds soluble fiber to the shake which is great for constitutional regularity, slowing digestion for maximized fullness perception, lowering cholesterol and enhanced Dream smoothness and thickness. The amount of aspartame called for may seem high but the recipe is correct. Also, make sure you buy unsugared whey protein powder. Keep an eye out for the words fructose, corn syrup and other sugar variants. These simply add unwanted calories. It's important to blend the shake the full three minutes+ indicated in the recipe. Short of that consistency suffers. There is some skill in learning to blend HiPro's. By your third one, you'll have it down.

And last, as with all things, you get what you pay for. Buying a cheap whey protein powder gives you cheap flavor. Buy a good one for your enjoyment's sake. The cost per serving as a meal replacement is less than half what you'd pay for a restaurant meal.

NO BANANAS

Forget the bananas. Most "smoothies" call for them to thicken the shake but they just add calories and little flavor. Whey protein powders blend to delicious creaminess provided you spin for two minutes or more.

INGREDIENTS	200 Calories ±30g protein	300 Calories ±45g protein
● Whey-based protein powder	200-calorie portion	300-calorie portion
● Aspartame	10 to 15 packets	15 to 20 packets
● Unflavored psyllium powder (Optional)	1 teaspoon	1 teaspoon
● Flavorings	See ✦	See ✦
● Water and ice	2 cups ice with	3 cups ice with
● Pinch of salt (Optional)	sufficient water to cover	sufficient water to cover

PROCEDURE

Put the ice cubes in first. Add water until ice is covered. With practice, you add the amount of water and ice for the shake consistency you want. Less water and ice make a thicker, creamier Dream. The more ice you add makes the Dream colder, but add too much and it won't blend. Practice sets you aright. Follow the water and ice with the protein powder on top. Next add psyllium powder and salt (both optional). Last, add your desired flavoring and aspartame. Experiment with how much flavoring and sweetness you like. More is usually better.

See✦. Start the blender in short bursts so the fluid doesn't shoot out. Blend the shake for a minimum of a full three minutes.

FOR LUNCH: Simple. Put the whipped HiPro Dream™ in a container. Rewhip or shake vigorously for lunch. The Dream can be refrigerated for days. It separates but miraculously reblends to creamy smoothness.

✦FLAVORINGS

CHOCOLATE: An especially rich, triple-chocolate shake is a chocolate flavored protein powder with one or two Tablespoons chocolate extract or a Tablespoon of cocoa powder and a teaspoon of instant coffee.

FRUIT: All berries make superb Dreams. One to two cups work well. Account for calorie increase: 75 calories per cup. For mild fruits like apples, nectarines and peaches, add a squeeze of lemon for more flavor. If using fruit, psyllium usually isn't needed because fruit is rich in fiber.

EXTRACTS: Try vanilla (1 Tablespoon), butterscotch (1 teaspoon), rum (1 teaspoon), almond (1 teaspoon) and strawberry extracts (2 Tablespoons). Extracts vary widely in strength so you have to experiment. Use sugar-free Kool-Aid® as a flavoring: 1/2 small package. Strawberry, raspberry and lime are especially good.

IMAGINATION: Once you're adept at NC Dreams, flavor approaches are limited only to your imagination. Try instant coffee, maple flavoring, butter powder, etc. The "etc." is up to you.

[1]"A Day in the Life of a Brain Longevity Seeker," Dharma Singha Khalsa, M.D., *Total Health*, vol. 20, no. 2, pages 52-54, BB398.
[2]"Whey to Health," Sid Shastri, CCN, *Total Health*, vol. 20, no. 2, pages 45-50, BB399.

SUGGESTED PUBLICATIONS

OVERALL HEALTH

These magazines deal with vital issues of health, nutrition and exercise. They read easily, are topical and meticulously document their sources.

- *Bottom Line/HEALTH*
  PO Box 51236
  Boulder, Colorado   80323-1236
  1-800-289-0409

- *Health*
  Box 56876
  Boulder, Colorado   80323-6876
  1-800-640-7743

- *Prevention*
  Box 7585
  Red Oak, Iowa   51591-2585
  1-800-666-1920

RUNNING AND WALKING

Subscribe to one of these two magazines for insights into aerobic exercise including inline skating, cycling, hiking and so on. Be sure to subscribe to one of these. Both are first rate.

- *Walking*
  Box 420557
  Palm Coast, Florida   32142-8937
  1-800-829-5585

- *Runner's World*
  Box 7307
  Red Oak, Iowa   51591-0307
  1-800-666-2828
  E-mail: runnerswdm@aol.com
  Internet: http://www.runnersworld.com

CULINARY

These magazines provide fresh ideas monthly for experimentation. Apply NeoCuisine™ principles to the recipes, cutting fat and increasing quantity. Don't be afraid to experiment. This is how you learn and increase your youthful look and vigor repertoire.

- *Cooking Light*
  Box 830656
  Birmingham, Alabama   35282-9086
  1-800-336-0125

GENDER

You may be surprised to learn that there are more health and fitness magazines published for women than men and they are all quite good. Some of the men's magazines tend to be somewhat "muscle-oriented" but the information is accurate and helpful.

MEN'S

- *Men's Health*
  Box 7595
  Red Oak, Iowa 51591-2595
  1-800-666-2303

- *Muscle and Fitness*
  Box 37208
  Boone, Iowa 50037-2208
  1-800-340-8954

WOMEN'S

- *Fit*
  Box 483
  Mount Morris, Illinois   61054-7706
  1-800-877-5366

- *Fitness*
  Box 5309
  Harlan, Iowa 51593-2809
  1-800-888-1181

- *Men's Fitness*
  Box 37211
  Boone, Iowa 50037-2211
  1-800-340-8958

- *Self*
  Box 51988
  Boulder, Colorado 80323-1988
  1-800-274-6111

- *Shape*
  Box 37207
  Boone, Iowa 50037-2207
  1-800-340-8958

HEALTH LETTERS

The idea of receiving a health letter from a university probably doesn't prompt much enthusiasm but you will be surprised at the topics covered and the information you will garner. These publications are layperson-oriented and you always know that you are getting highly credible advice. Subscribe to at least one; you will find it most informative.

- *UC Berkeley Wellness Letter*
  PO Box 42018
  Palm Coast, Florida 32142
  1-800-829-9177
  E-mail: www.wellnessletter.com

- *Mayo Clinic Health Letter*
  Box 53889
  Boulder, Colorado 80322-3889
  1-800-333-9037

- *Harvard Health Letter*
  PO Box 420300
  Palm Coast, Florida 32142-0300
  1-800-829-9045

- *Johns Hopkins Medical Letter Health After 50*
  Box 420325
  Palm Coast, Florida 32142
  1-800-829-0422

- *Tufts University Diet and Nutrition Letter*
  PO Box 57857
  Boulder, Colorado 80322-7857
  1-800-274-7581

- *The Mirkin Report*
  PO Box 10
  Kensington, Maryland 20895
  1-800-686-4754
  E-mail: www.drmirkin.com

PERSONAL SPORTS

After the BodyRenewal™, take up a sport if you don't have one. Add another if you wish. The place to start is subscribing to a magazine and reading.

- *Bicycling Magazine*
  PO Box 7592
  Red Oak, Iowa   51591-2592
  1-800-666-2806

- *Runner's World*
  PO Box 7307
  Red Oak, Iowa   51591-0307
  1-800-666-2828
  E-mail: runnerswdm@aol.com
  Internet: http://www.runnersworld.com

- *Mountain Bike*
  Rodale Press
  Customer Satisfaction Center
  Emmaus, Pennsylvania   18098
  1-800-666-1920

- *Backpacker*
  Rodale Press
  Customer Satisfaction Center
  Emmaus, Pennsylvania   18098
  1-800-666-1920

- *Golf Magazine*
  PO Box 51413
  Boulder, Colorado   80323-1413
  1-800-876-7726

- *Rodale's Fitness Swimmer*
  Rodale Press
  Customer Satisfaction Center
  Emmaus, Pennsylvania   18098
  1-800-666-1920

- *Rodale's Scuba Diving*
  Rodale Press
  Customer Satisfaction Center
  Emmaus, Pennsylvania   18098
  1-800-666-1920

7 TO BED LIST SUMMARY

NO-CAL

- Fluids
- Go to Bed
- Night Walk
- Hunger Wave Riding

SAVORY

- Baby Carrots
- Jerkies
- NeoCuisine™ Leftovers
- Soft Pretzel and Mustard
- A Gallon of Air-Popped Popcorn
- Baked Chips and Salsa
- Low-Fat Soup Cups
- Pickled Anything
- Two No-Fat Dogs
- Zucchini and Sweet Mustard

SWEET/MADE

- Apple Varieties
- Fat-free, Sugar-free Yogurt
- Kiwi
- Orange Orgy—4 peeled=250 cals
- Sugar-Free Popsicles
- Welch's No Sugar Added Fruit Juice Bars
- Breakfast Again
- Hot Old-Fashioned Cinnamon Applesauce and Creme Fraiche
- One Pint Sugar-Free Jell-O
- One Quart HiPro™ Dreams
- Sugar Free, Fat Free Berry Pie
- 4 oz Dried Fruit with 12 oz Water
- Fruit Roll-Ups
- No-fat, no-sugar Frozen Yogurt
- Power Bar®
- Water-Packed Fruits
- NeoCuisine™ Fat-Free, Sugar-Free, No-Cook Cheesecakes
- One Pound Papaya
- Quick Fresh Fruit Sorbets

7,000,000 YEARS ON THE CUSP OF STARVATION

Consider Neolithic man's dreadful life. Half were dead by age 20 and all died by age 40. One can only imagine the disease and distress caused by weather and the threat of predatory animals. But worst of all, Neolithic man suffered from lack of food. There were times of plenty but more often than not, there simply wasn't enough to eat. This had enormous effect on the body's evolution. It became quite cunning constantly contending with inadequate nutruition.[1] As a result, we are plagued by the *Primeval Raging Appetite* which dictates that we naturally tend to overeat.

[1]"Fears That Save Us," Dianne Ackerman, *Parade Magazine*, January 26, 1997, pages 18-19, BB213.

QUICK CAL COUNT POCKET CARD

- VEGETABLE: ***UNLIMITED.***
  - Leaf (e.g. chopped lettuce, cabbage): 0 calories per cup.
  - Regular (e.g. broccoli, carrots): 50 calories per cup.
  - Starch (e.g. potato, peas, winter squash): 100 calories per cup.
- FRUIT: ***EAT ABUNDANTLY.***
  75 calories per whole piece or cup.
- DAIRY: ***EAT A LOT.***
  - 1 cup no-fat/sugar dairy (e.g. yogurt, no-fat milk): 100 calories
  - 1/2 cup no-fat, concentrated dairy (e.g. no-fat cheese, no-fat ice cream): 100 calories.
- BEANS AND LENTILS: ***EAT A LOT.***
  200 calories per cup.
- COOKED WHITE PROTEIN: ***EAT SOME.***
  - Skinless chicken breast, white fish, shrimp, etc.: 50 calories per ounce, 4 ounces cooked equals a deck of cards.
  - All other meats: 100 cals/ounce. ***RESTRICT.***
- BREAD/RICE/PASTA: ***EAT SPARINGLY.***
  - 75 calories per standard bread slice (1 ounce).
  - White rice, white pasta: 200 calories per cup.

- VEGETABLE: ***UNLIMITED.***
  - Leaf (e.g. chopped lettuce, cabbage): 0 calories per cup.
  - Regular (e.g. broccoli, carrots): 50 calories per cup.
  - Starch (e.g. potato, peas, winter squash): 100 calories per cup.
- FRUIT: ***EAT ABUNDANTLY.***
  75 calories per whole piece or cup.
- DAIRY: ***EAT A LOT.***
  - 1 cup no-fat/sugar dairy (e.g. yogurt, no-fat milk): 100 calories
  - 1/2 cup no-fat, concentrated dairy (e.g. no-fat cheese, no-fat ice cream): 100 calories.
- BEANS AND LENTILS: ***EAT A LOT.***
  200 calories per cup.
- COOKED WHITE PROTEIN: ***EAT SOME.***
  - Skinless chicken breast, white fish, shrimp, etc.: 50 calories per ounce, 4 ounces cooked equals a deck of cards.
  - All other meats: 100 cals/ounce: ***RESTRICT.***
- BREAD/RICE/PASTA: ***EAT SPARINGLY.***
  - 75 calories per standard bread slice (1 ounce).
  - White Rice, white pasta: 200 calories per cup.

- VEGETABLE: ***UNLIMITED.***
  - Leaf (e.g. chopped lettuce, cabbage): 0 calories per cup.
  - Regular (e.g. broccoli, carrots): 50 calories per cup.
  - Starch (e.g. potato, peas, winter squash): 100 calories per cup.
- FRUIT: ***EAT ABUNDANTLY.***
  75 calories per whole piece or cup.
- DAIRY: ***EAT A LOT.***
  - 1 cup no-fat/sugar dairy (e.g. yogurt, no-fat milk): 100 calories
  - 1/2 cup no-fat, concentrated dairy (e.g. no-fat cheese, no-fat ice cream): 100 calories.
- BEANS AND LENTILS: ***EAT A LOT.***
  200 calories per cup.
- COOKED WHITE PROTEIN: ***EAT SOME.***
  - Skinless chicken breast, white fish, shrimp, etc.: 50 calories per ounce, 4 ounces cooked equals a deck of cards.
  - All other meats: 100 cals/ounce: ***RESTRICT.***
- BREAD/RICE/PASTA: ***EAT SPARINGLY.***
  - 75 calories per standard bread slice (1 ounce).
  - White Rice, white pasta: 200 calories per cup.

- VEGETABLE: ***UNLIMITED.***
  - Leaf (e.g. chopped lettuce, cabbage): 0 calories per cup.
  - Regular (e.g. broccoli, carrots): 50 calories per cup.
  - Starch (e.g. potato, peas, winter squash): 100 calories per cup.
- FRUIT: ***EAT ABUNDANTLY.***
  75 calories per whole piece or cup.
- DAIRY: ***EAT A LOT.***
  - 1 cup no-fat/sugar dairy (e.g. yogurt, no-fat milk): 100 calories
  - 1/2 cup no-fat, concentrated dairy (e.g. no-fat cheese, no-fat ice cream): 100 calories.
- BEANS AND LENTILS: ***EAT A LOT.***
  200 calories per cup.
- COOKED WHITE PROTEIN: ***EAT SOME.***
  - Skinless chicken breast, white fish, shrimp, etc.: 50 calories per ounce, 4 ounces cooked equals a deck of cards.
  - All other meats: 100 cals/ounce: ***RESTRICT.***
- BREAD/RICE/PASTA: ***EAT SPARINGLY.***
  - 75 calories per standard bread slice (1 ounce).
  - White Rice, white pasta: 200 calories per cup.

FOOD AND EMPIRES

Food not only sustains life but enormously impacts society. In fact, the very beginnings of civilization can be traced to rudimentary irrigation systems which required ditch and canal maintenance management. These gatherings of two or three families developed into villages and then towns, the towns into cities and civilization was born.[1] The development of farming subsequently led to greater leisure time and the opportunity for constructive thinking, formulating plans and setting up the first primitive governments. As our ancestral hunter-gatherers settled into farming, awareness of boundaries and frontiers grew—an awareness that stimulated a sense of social unity and the first notion of countries.[2] From this, empires developed, again fueled by food.

---

[1]*Food in History*, Reay Tannahill, Crown Trade Paperbacks, New York, New York, 1988, pages 31-33, BB103.

[2]Ibid., page 42, BB103.

NO-FEAR AGING

We fear age too much. We fret about what it may do to our bodies. We worry about our minds deteriorating. We think we're starting to "look and feel old." If you share these concerns, you read the wrong books, talk to the wrong people and are sorely misinformed about aging's realities. Here's an example. The pedestrian belief is we lose memory recall as we grow older. Really? How about those fourth graders who leave all those hats and gloves at school mid-winter? Or your teenaged son who doesn't remember anyone's birthday? Scientists now believe memory loss is largely culturally induced. We're supposed to lose our wits as we age. However, mainland Chinese—who revere age—suffer no memory loss as they age, according to the *Johns Hopkins Medical Letter*. Our vacuous, youth-oriented culture (what does a 20-year-old know compared to you?) hoodwinks us into mistakenly believing myths of aging.

The reason we exercise and fat-strip is to deter aging ... a good thing. But it's also to stop the fear of growing older. There has never been a better time in the history of mankind to grow older because we now know so much about it. Today we understand better than at any time that aging doesn't mean getting old. There are advantages that come with the adding years. Some things are forgone, like perfect vision, but consider these advantages had only with time:

1 Things get done more quickly and easily because you know how to do them. You're practiced which is not the case at age 20. In fact, you are probably doing the best work of your life because you've never known more. You even see the world as a friendlier place because you manage it better.

2 The Baltimore Longitudinal Study of Aging verified what you suspected all along: Aging does not affect reasoning ability. In fact, tests show 60-year-olds out-thinking 20-year-olds in problem solving.[1]

3 Psychologist Brian Schwartz rightfully points out, based on numerous studies, that older employees make fewer mistakes, have fewer accidents, lower absenteeism, a stronger work ethic, are more objective and reality-based and are more even-tempered than their younger cohorts.[2]

4 As years advance, Montaigne's observation that "all men bear the whole stamp of the human condition" makes sense. We are not so intimidated by others because we now understand Montaigne.

5 Age balances expectation. Youth expects a painless life which exacerbates its inevitable bumps. Pain understood as normal makes its reality less impacting, a perspective only age grants.

6 Advancing years allow contemplation which Aristotle said "... is admittedly the pleasantest of virtuous activities."[3] It is the time to pursue the intellectual and spiritual talents thus far dormant. Our gifts lay awaiting development.

7 There is a peace that comes with age. Sophocles spoke of age mitigating unbridled and misguided passions, "... perfect riddance of the frantic slavedrivers, the whole horde of them."[4]

8 And finally, after years of indecision, you now have well-formed opinions. You are not in thrall of fads or pushed by popular culture. You know who you are and what's right for you.

We are truly at a new era's edge. Consider that all Neanderthals died by 40, half of them by 20.[5] It got no better by the Middle Ages which had surprisingly similar life spans due primarily to the appalling hygiene of medieval markets and farms. Rats, offal, excrement and insects were nonchalantly taken for granted. Today, with proper nutrition, moderate exercise and modern medicine's disease control, each of us will grow older but can retain our vigor and shape of youth. There are, after all, many to emulate who enjoyed dynamic advanced years.

Sophocles, who lived to be more than 90, wrote *Oedipus Rex* at 75 and *Oedipus et Colonus* at 89. Titian completed his masterpiece, The Battle of LaPonto, at 95; he began work on the most famous paintings in the world, The Descent from the Cross, when he was 97. Benjamin Franklin invented bifocals at 78.[6] At age 67, President Harry Truman regularly put in 15-hour days with upward of 15 to 20 appointments, not infrequently giving a speech at 10 PM.[7] During the Second World War, Winston Churchill was an indefatigable worker at age 68. His typical day, which included a two-hour afternoon nap, started at 7 AM and went on to one or two in the morning with "... energy and stamina [that] were prodigious," according to biographer William Manchester.[8] At 90, Frank Lloyd Wright embarked on his greatest architectural achievement, the Guggenheim Museum of Modern Art in New York City.[9] In fact, Wright's most productive period occurred from age 69 through his death in 1959 at age 91.[10] Past 90, Pablo Casals played the cello as no other man ever did.[11] And of course no list of advanced-years achievements would be complete without Colonel Sanders. At age 66, he founded Kentucky Fried Chicken, which he sold ten years later for today's equivalent of $35 million. We saw him for years thereafter as Kentucky Fried Chicken's TV spokesman. The Colonel's favorite saying was, "A man will rust out quicker'n he'll wear out, and I aim to keep shuffling around enough to keep the rust off."[12] And last, at age 70 actor Paul Newman won his class at the 24 Hours of Daytona car race, coming in third overall against the world's best drivers.[13]

With proper exercise and the right diet, sports careers last far longer than at any other time. It had been thought that after age 30, sports careers ended. That's what we thought, anyway, until Nolan Ryan at age 44 pitched his seventh no-hitter.[14] Or take George Foreman. At age 45, he fought Michael Moorer who was 26 years old and had a record of 35 and 1 with 30 knockouts. The formidable Moorer was a 10-to-1 favorite to put ol' George away. Yet in 2 minutes, 3 seconds of the tenth round, Michael Moorer was knocked out by big, bad George who became the oldest heavyweight champ in history ... just a few months shy of his 46th birthday.

It's never too late to try something new. One hundred-year old S.L. Potter made his first bungie jump from a 210-foot tower, hoping for the title of "The World's Oldest Bungie Jumper." Potter stepped off the platform and plummeted toward the ground. He bounced four times as if on the end of a giant yo-yo. For several seconds, the stooped, 119-pound Potter dangled motionless and the crowd hushed. "Oh my God!" an elderly neighbor said, wondering if Potter had died. But then Potter kicked his feet as if riding a bicycle and waved his bony right arm. The crowd broke out into laughter and heaved sighs of relief. Asked if he had been scared, he looked offended. "Hell, no," he said. "I don't get scared. If I die, I die. I told everybody to bring a shovel and a mop, just in case."[15]

Studies prove that exercise, good diet and proper medical care not only increase one's life but considerably enhance life's quality. Staying lean through exercise and correct diet really does make a difference. Here are the facts.

• Dr. Ronald Klatz, president of the American Society of Anti-Aging Medicine, predicts that 50% of the baby boomers will reach 100.[16] The 50% that do will follow the kind of protocols outlined in this book.

• According to a study done at NASA by Aerobics Research, lean men doing three hours a week of aerobic exercise maintain 93% of their age-30 aerobic capacity at age 70.[17]

• Past 40, Olympians routinely win medals in sailing (strategy and strength), fencing (speed and stamina), shooting (hand and eye coordination) and equestrian (balance and agility).[18]

• Long-term exercisers in their 60s have reaction times equal to or better than inactive 20-year-olds, according to UCLA gerontologist Dr. Roy Walford.[19]

• Researchers at the University of Texas in Austin studied people learning new motor skills, finding healthy 60-year-olds were as coordinated and learned behavioral tasks as quickly as 20-year-olds.[20]

• The *Harvard Health Letter* reported a study in which weight trainers in their 70s have the same muscle mass and power as nonlifters in their 20s.[21] The 50-year difference disappears with strength training. The *University of Texas Lifetime Health Letter* reports people in their 90s triple their power in less than two months of strength training.[22] In a report to the American Heart Association, researchers at Johns Hopkins University School of Medicine stated older people who exercise can increase cardiac output just as younger people do.[23]

ANTI-AGING CORNERSTONES

The cardinal strategy of anti-aging is attitude. Nolan Ryan threw his no-hitter at 44 because he had the will. Frank Lloyd Wright designed the Guggenheim at 90 because he refused to let go of life. It is true youth is a state of mind. My grandfather kept this poem on his desk through the Depression, during which he made himself a millionaire, built the largest home in Washington state in 1933, and put four children through college during the most trying economic times in U.S. history. My recollection is of a man who laughed and joked his way through life. I never saw him angry or unhappy. He believed what you are about to read.

YOUTH

Youth is not a time of life —
it is a state of mind.

Youth means a predomi-
nance of courage over
timidity,
of the appetite of ad-
venture over love of
ease.

There is the potential in
every man's heart for
the love of wonder,
the sweet amazement
at the stars and star-
light, things and
thoughts, the un-
daunted challenge of
events, the unfailing
childlike appetite for
what next, and the joy
of life's game.

You are as young as your
faith, as old as your
doubt; as young as
your self-confidence,
as old as your fear; as
young as your hope, as
old as your despair.

Anonymous

402

At age 70, Grandpa decided to become a master boat builder. He taught himself how to design, bend wood and fit joints. He built dozens of boats for his 16 grandchildren. He died, by the way, at 88 hoeing his sunflower garden.

Here are cornerstone canons that keep us young.

UNFOLDING POTENTIAL OUTRACES AGING

Life mastery philosopher Dr. Deepak Chopra cites research showing that sending the "time is running out" message to your body's cells is the same as programming them to age and die.[24] Growing old is in part emotional debt that increases until the body's coping mechanisms can no longer deal with the stress.[25]

The solution is to grow so gain is greater than loss. You might not play football the way you did in high school or work the parallel bars as you did when you were 13 but on the other hand, the whole world awaits you right now, at this instant. Life's real artists never believe that they have "arrived." The best is always yet to be.

If the body dissipates, there is no pain. When a mind stops growing, there is no ache. We must monitor continued self-growth lest it stop. Psychiatrist Harry Levinson reflects that, "The essence of gratification in living is the continued feeling of being generative."[26] Being generative, becoming, self-actualizing, takes conscious work and effort, truths you've understood all your adult life.

The correct life is continued blossoming. Developing interests requires the commitment and effort you have used throughout your life to achieve your worthwhile goals. Chopra steadfastly maintains that, "Beyond any body of evidence about aging and how to prevent it, the single most important factor is that you make something creative from your existence."[27] It is essential to consciously develop your latent skills. Why not become a master weaver or epicurean NeoCuisine™ chef or poet or ...?

In his 60s, Noel Johnson's doctor told him he had no more than six months to live and a brisk walk could kill him. The news came as no surprise. He'd been overweight and a heavy smoker for 35 years. Characteristic of the indomitable human spirit, Johnson decided to die moving. He started walking, then running, and within two years was setting age-group records in the mile. Between the ages of 70 and 90, he ran more than 20 marathons and in the 1980s he was regularly the oldest man to complete the New York City Marathon. His times at 84 and at age 88 are records. Throughout his 80s, Johnson ran nine miles three times a week then worked out on his stationary bike. He lifted weights on alternate days.

During all this activity he found time to write an autobiography: *A Dud at 70, a Stud at 80*. He died at 96, the doctor missing his departure by 35 years.[28]

Surprisingly, one of life's ironic gifts is boredom because it is the springboard that pushes us into new thoughts and activities, like making the youth connection. Losing weight and getting into shape is one of the most powerful acts of becoming you can undertake. If there was ever a motivator to energize you, it is the gift of a new body.

You may have spent your first economic life as an engineer or carpenter or civil servant. How will you spend your second and possibly third economic lives? Why not? Who says at 75 you can't be a top residential real estate salesman at a local office? Who says you can't sell suits at Nordstrom? Why not be a kindergarten teacher or mentor youths on career choices or teach woodworking skills? What stops you from being a part-time business consultant or stock broker or commodities trader or ??? With BodyRenewal™ you'll likely live to 90. It doesn't make much sense to quit work at 60 or 65.

There is another payback. One of the marvelous compensations of self-actualization—personal development—is it stretches time. Old habits and routines speed time along at an alarming rate. Learning, new situations and unfamiliar environments slow things down. Just remember how long you thought it took to get through high school. The act of becoming enriches your life and stretches it just as God intended.

THE HERE AND NOW ARE MATCHLESS

It's wise for me to learn from my past and prepare for the future. But it is not wise for me to be *in* either. That is how I lose myself. My real home is in this place at this time. The present is for action, for doing, for becoming and for growing. Here is one of life's most noble perceptions.

The present moment is my most precious reality of all time.

Our attitude must be to maximize life in the present, right now, because we have the present only to the degree we possess it. Here we are, conscious, alive and reality awaits.[29]

Enjoy this moment's experience, it may not come again. As philosopher William Carlos Williams said, "The proper response to the world is applause."[30]

Operating in the now means you forgo the guilt and anguish of the uncontrollable. You renounce the self-destroying anxiety of things beyond your power. The now means you manage what is in your control, such as conditioning your body to your self betterment. Making yourself invigorated, heightening your self-appreciation, increasing endurance and the manifold other benefits is the NOW.

Grandma Moses didn't start painting until she was 80 with 25% of her 1,500 paintings completed after she was 100. Michelangelo was 71 when he started the Sistine Chapel.[31]

CONCEDE NOTHING

Exercise philosopher George Sheehan, M.D., said we must concede nothing.[32] Maybe this is the best advice of all. Studies indicate we expect far too little from our aging bodies.[33] Several years ago a friend told me he would never ride a motorcycle because his reflexes were gone. Today he is portly because he conceded to the silly fictions in his head. Norman Cousins' famous aphorism is, "Belief creates biology."

At age 58, Bob Messersmith entered his first masters marathon. Four years later at age 62, he captured the U.S. national 100-mile run record, covering that distance in 20 hours and 35 minutes.[34] Well, so much for "inappropriate high levels of sports activity."

At 121 years old, Jeanne Calment was the world's oldest person. On the event of her birthday, she decided to tell the world her story. Look for her life's exploits CD in record stores. She conceded nothing to age and considered life an adventure.[35]

The vortex of potential unhappiness swirls madly around us. It takes no effort to be sucked into its murky milieu. There is much to mourn in this world. But our task is to unfold our potential, live in the now and concede nothing. What you are doing is realizing these three physio and psychological life-saving principles. Operating in the now and conceding nothing lead you to a preponderance of gains. Harry Truman said, "I've had a few setbacks in my life. But I never gave up. I went right ahead and did what was required of me."[36]

405

[1]"Fear of Forgetting," David Schardt and Stephen Schmidt, *Nutrition Action*, vol. 24, no. 4, May 1997, page 6, BB284.

[2]"The Rise and Fall of Retirement," Stephan M. Pollan and Mark Levine, Worth, December/January 1995, page 74, BB228.

[3]*The Pocket Aristotle,* edited by Justin Kaplan, Washington Square Press [Pocket Books], Division of Simon & Schuster, New York, New York, 1988, page 264.

[4]*Great Dialogues of Plato,* Socrates, *The New American Library* [Mentor], New York, New York, 1987, page 127, BB76.

[5]*Food in History*, Reay Tannahall, Crown Trade Paperbacks, New York, New York, 1988 page 6, BB103.

[6]*The Great Jackass Fallacy,* Harry Levinson, Division of Research, Graduate School of Business Administration, Harvard University, Boston, Massachusetts, 1993, page 48, BB70, #8.

[7]*Truman*, David McCullough, Simon & Schuster, New York, 1992, pages 895-896.

[8]*Winston Churchill ... Alone* 1932-1940, William Manchester, Little, Brown and Co., Boston 1988, page 555, #88.

[9]Seattle Art Museum Exhibit, 1990.

[10]*About Wright*, Edgar Tafel, John Wiley & Sons, Inc, New York, New York, 1993, page XXIV, BB148.

[11]Levinson, op. cit., page 48, BB70, #8.

[12]"Colonel Sanders," *Restaurant Hospitality Magazine*, March 1981, pages 81-82.

[13]*Car and Driver*, January 1996, page 60, BB28; *Men's Fitness*, December 1995, page 39, BB28.

[14]"Nolan Ryan: Awe-Inspiring," *Seattle Times*, Michael Kay, July 24, 1990, page D5, A251.

[15]"News Makers," *Seattle Times*, Thursday, October 14, 1993, page 1.

[16]Speech before the AAM conference, reported in *Total Health*, vol. 19, no. 1, December 1996, BB271.

[17]"Young at 70," *UC Berkeley Wellness Letter*, May 1995, page 3, BB232.

[18]"Aging Athletes Keep on Keeping On," Maria A. Fiatarone, M.D., and Leah R. Garnet, Harvard Health Letter, vol. 22, no. 5, March, 1992, page 4, BB263

[19]*The 120-Year Diet*, Roy L. Walford, M.D., Simon & Schuster, New York, New York, 1986, page 186, BB166.

[20]Waneen W. Spirduso, Ph.D., Professor of Kinetics, University of Texas at Austin. From: "You're Never Too Old to Learn New Tricks," *Men's Confidential*, February 1997, page 11, BB235.

[21]"Aging Athletes Keep on Keeping On," Maria A. Fiatarone, M.D., and Leah R. Garnet, *Harvard Health Letter*, vol. 22, no. 5, March 1997, page 4, BB263.

[22]Senior Citizens Are Pumping Iron," Michael A. Giarrusso, Associated Press, Journal American, August 22, 1995, page B3, BB29.

[23]"The Heart Does Not Wear Out with Age," Ray Johnson, M.D., *Nutritional Health Review*, Haverford, Pennsylvania, #76, 4th quarter, 1996, page 11, BB238.

[24]*Ageless Body, Timeless Mind,* Deepak Chopra, Harmony Books, Division of Crown Publishers, New York, New York, 1993, page 286, #109.

[25]Ibid., page 173, #109.

[26]Levinson, op. cit., page 172, #8.

[27]Chopra, op. cit., page 257, #109.

[28]"A Dud at 70, a Stud at 80," David Fujii, *Men's Fitness*, May 1996, page 122, BB239.

[29]Johnson, op. cit., pages 52 and 67, BB238.

[30]*Personal Best*, George Sheehan, M.D., Rodale Press, Emmaus, Pennsylvania, 1989, page 225, #97.

[31]Speaker's Source Book, Glenn Van Ekeren, Prentice-Hall, New York.

[32]Sheehan, op. cit., page 223.

[33]Chopra, op. cit., page 253, #109.

[34]"Messersmith: This Long Distance Runner Is an Ultra Champion," *Over 50 and Fit*, November 1995, page 1, BB1.

[35]"Don't Even Think About It," *Men's Fitness*, June 1996, page 118, BB82.

[36]McCullough, op. cit., pages 70-71.

Write Your Key *BodyRenewal*™ Thoughts Here

_____

_____

_____

_____

_____

_____

_____

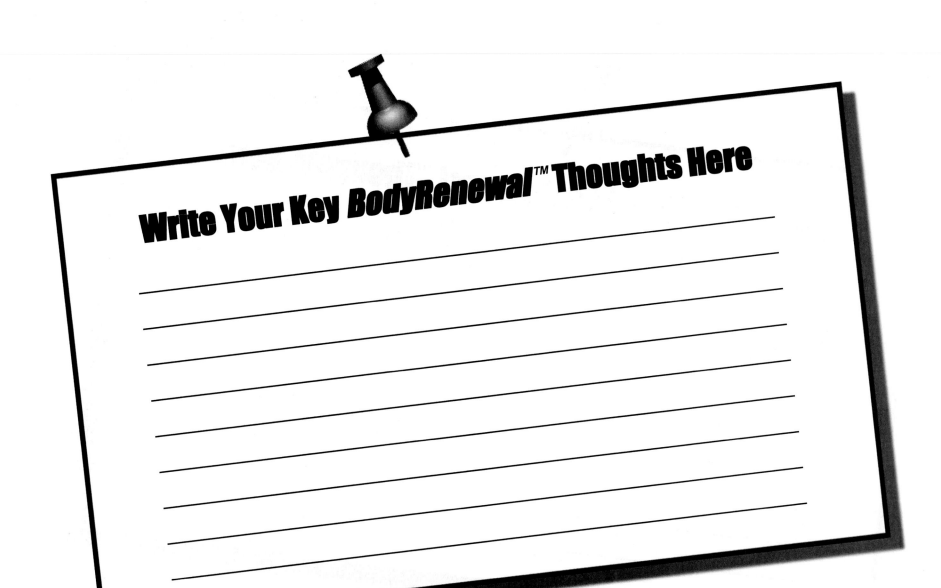

Write Your Key *BodyRenewal*™ Thoughts Here

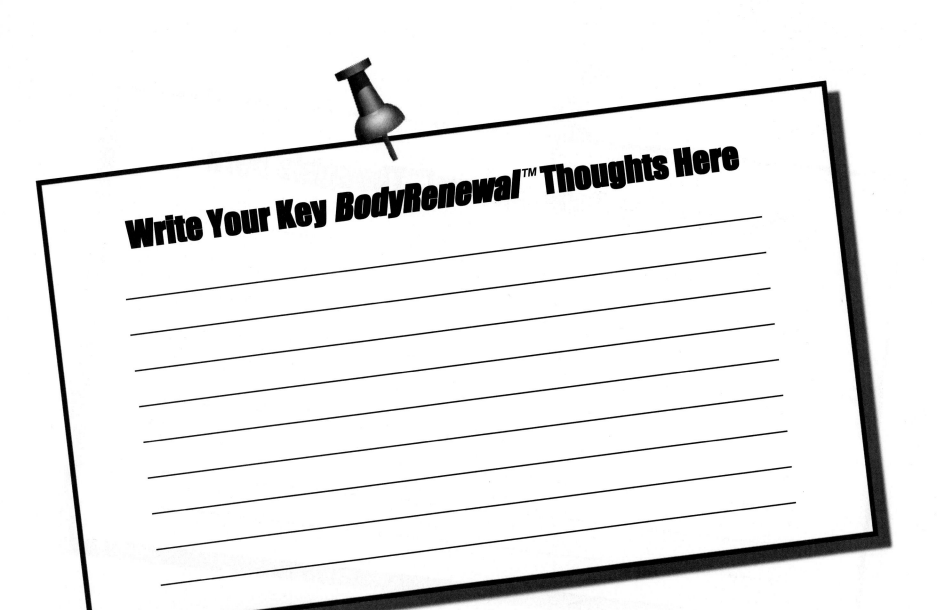

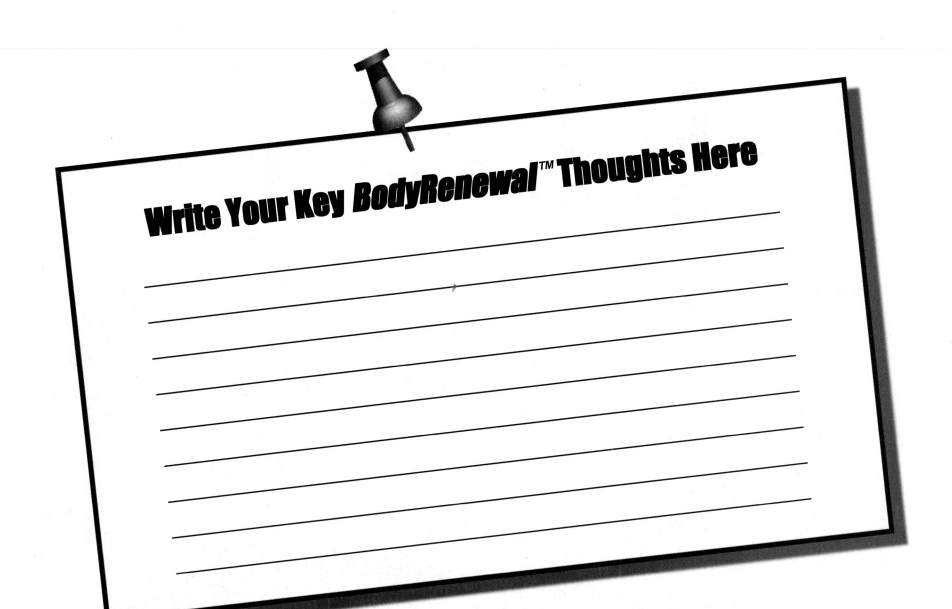

Write Your Key *BodyRenewal*™ Thoughts Here